# RAUTAVAARA'S JOURNEY IN MUSIC

**Figure 1:** Rautavaara (1928-2016) at his piano. Perhaps the best internationally known Finnish composer of his day after Sibelius, he produced a wealth of compositions-- orchestral works, operas, chamber music, solo vocal works and choruses. His topics ranged widely, from shipwreck to old ladies, to unicorns and a bird concerto, from angels to taunting demons. For many years he was a composition teacher, learning and experimenting with twentieth century techniques himself before teaching them. He eventually settled into a combination of serialism for underlying structure and freer melody for expressiveness. His boundless creativity will be long admired.

Photo credit: Ari Korkala/Music Finland

# RAUTAVAARA'S JOURNEY IN MUSIC

Barbara Blanchard Hong

ROWMAN & LITTLEFIELD
*Lanham • Boulder • New York • London*

Published by Rowman & Littlefield
An imprint of The Rowman & Littlefield Publishing Group, Inc.
4501 Forbes Boulevard, Suite 200, Lanham, Maryland 20706
www.rowman.com

86-90 Paul Street, London EC2A 4NE

Copyright © 2022 by The Rowman & Littlefield Publishing Group, Inc.

*All rights reserved.* No part of this book may be reproduced in any form or by any electronic or mechanical means, including information storage and retrieval systems, without written permission from the publisher, except by a reviewer who may quote passages in a review.

British Library Cataloguing in Publication Information Available

### Library of Congress Cataloging-in-Publication Data

Names: Hong, Barbara Blanchard, author.
Title: Rautavaara's journey in music / Barbara Blanchard Hong.
Description: Lanham : Rowman & Littlefield Publishers, 2022. | Includes bibliographical references and index.
Identifiers: LCCN 2022022377 (print) | LCCN 2022022378 (ebook) | ISBN 9781538172339 (cloth) | ISBN 9781538196380 (pbk.) | ISBN 9781538172346 (ebook)
Subjects: LCSH: Rautavaara, Einojuhani, 1928-2016. | Rautavaara, Einojuhani, 1928-2016—Criticism and interpretation. | Music—20th century—History and criticism. | Composers—Finland—Biography.
Classification: LCC ML410.R229 H65 2022 (print) | LCC ML410.R229 (ebook) | DDC 780.92 [B]—dc23/eng/20220510
LC record available at https://lccn.loc.gov/2022022377
LC ebook record available at https://lccn.loc.gov/2022022378

# Table of Contents

| | |
|---|---|
| List of Illustrations | vi |
| Introduction | vii |

**PART ONE: Biography and Works** — 1

| | |
|---|---|
| Chapter One: Becoming a Composer, 1928-53 | 3 |
| Chapter Two: The Study Years in Helsinki, Vienna, and the United States, 1948-57 | 8 |
| Chapter Three: First Serial Works, 1957 | 28 |
| Chapter Four: Serialism, Opera, Third and Fourth Symphonies, 1957-66 | 35 |
| Chapter Five: Neo-Romanticism, 1965-73 | 52 |
| Chapter Six: The Kalevala and Angel Works, 1974-80 | 71 |
| Chapter Seven: Postmodernism, 1981-89 | 80 |
| Chapter Eight: The 1990s | 90 |
| Chapter Nine: After 2000, This Journey Goes On | 107 |

**PART TWO: Works by Genre** — 123

| | |
|---|---|
| Chapter Ten: Operas | 124 |
| Chapter Eleven: Orchestral Works | 136 |
| Chapter Twelve: Concertos | 165 |
| Chapter Thirteen: Solo Vocal Works | 181 |
| Chapter Fourteen: Choral Works | 192 |
| Chapter Fifteen: Solo Keyboard Works | 219 |
| Chapter Sixteen: Chamber Music | 233 |
| Chapter Seventeen: Music for Electronic Tape | 249 |
| Chronology of Works | 250 |
| Bibliography | 265 |
| Index | 271 |

# List of Illustrations

| | |
|---|---|
| Figure 1. Rautavaara (1928-2016) at his piano. | ii |
| Figure 2. Einojuhani Rautavaara, 1950's | x |
| Example One: *Pelimannit* (Fiddlers), No. 1 "Närböläisten braa speli" (The Fiddlers Arrive); No. 3 "Jacob Könni." | 11 |
| Example Two: *Three Sonnets of Shakespeare*, No. 1 "That time of year," No. 3 "Shall I compare Thee to a Summer's Day." | 12 |
| Example Three: *A Requiem in Our Time*, No. 1 "Hymnus." | 14-15 |
| Example Four: *Ikonit* (Icons), No. 1 "Death of the Mother of God," No. 6 "Archangel Michael." | 20 |
| Example Five: Symphony No. 1, first movement, Andante, mm. 1-10. | 22 |
| Example Six: Second Symphony, IV., Presto, mm. 1-4 | 26 |
| Example Seven: *Modificata*, I. Recitatio, mm.1-5 | 31 |
| Example Eight: *Praevariata*, mm.1-10 | 32 |
| Example Nine: *Kaivos* (The Mine), Act One, mm.1-8. | 37 |
| Example Ten: String Quartet No. 2, First movement, Moderato, mm.1-5. | 40 |
| Example Eleven: Third Symphony, First movement, Langsam, breit, ruhig, mm.1-10. | 43–44 |
| Example Twelve: *Arabescata* "Quadratus," mm. 1-9. | 47–48 |
| Example Thirteen: A Cartoonist's View of Contemporary Orchestral Music. | 50 |
| Example Fourteen: *Anadyomene*. | 55 |
| Example Fifteen: Piano Concert No. 1, mm. 1-4. | 56 |
| Example Sixteen: Piano Sonata No. 1, *Christ and the Fishermen*. | 57 |
| Example Seventeen: *Vigilia*, No.2, "Alkpsalmi." | 65–66 |
| Example Eighteen: *Lorca Suite*, No. 4, *Malaguena*. | 68 |
| Example Nineteen: Fifth Symphony, Kalevi Aho's graph of form. | 84 |
| Example Twenty: Sixth Symphony, *Vincentiana*, "The Crows." | 92 |
| Example Twenty-one: Seventh Symphony, *Angel of Light*, Bloomington | 96 |
| Example Twenty-two: *Aleksis Kivi*, "Sydämeni Laulu (Song of My Heart). | 99 |

# Introduction

A concerto for arctic birds and orchestra? A symphony depicting an angel? Pregnant by swallowing a lingonberry? Jesus dancing in a ballet? A terrifying shipwreck for chorus and orchestra? Multiple style changes, at times simultaneous? All are but a small sample of the enormous output and wide ranging topics of the Finnish composer Einojuhani Rautavaara (1928-2016).

Rautavaara, long well known and honored in his own country, began to receive considerable international attention in the 1990s, to the extent that he has been called Finland's most notable musical export after Sibelius. In 1997 his Seventh Symphony *Angel of Light* received a Grammy Award nomination, a Cannes Classical Award, a Gramophone Award, as well as several critics' nominations as record of the year. This set off an international interest in his works, with his violin concerto and operas performed in many places abroad. Commissions soon followed from orchestras and performers, from the Philadelphia Orchestra for his Eighth Symphony *The Journey*, from pianist Vladimir Ashkenazy for a piano concerto, to Hilary Hahn and Anne Akiko Meyers, for works for violin and orchestra. Festivals have been devoted to his works in Minneapolis, Minnesota in 1999, at the Hampstead and Highgate Festival in London in 1999, the Hitzacher Musiktage 1999, in Helsinki, Finland, in 2001, the Luxembourg Festival 2002, and the Aboa Musica Festival in Turku, Finland, 2003.

Despite the fact that Rautavaara's works are receiving recognition, wide performance exposure, extensive recording, and frequent reviews, there remains no definitive source for information of his life and works in English. The only sources of any length are his 1989 autobiography, a cursory biography in the year 2000 by Pekka Hako, a prolific writer on Finnish composers and multi-talented musician, and an exhaustive 2014 study on Rautavaara by Samuli Tiikkaja, all in the Finnish language. Since the facts available in these works and information on his Finnish literary sources for his operas and vocal works are difficult to obtain in English, this book hopes to open all these works to an international audience.

The book's first half combines biography and descriptions of significant works that show his musical style and the changes in his approach through his many years of composition. This chronological overview shows a great variety of changing techniques and styles. They not only change according to the needs of the particular work, but also show the serious consideration of a composer aware of compositional trends and of his own need to study a new style by using it in a new work. In this way he could actually try it as well as become better equipped to teach it to his composition students at the Helsinki Sibelius Academy. A list of these twentieth century techniques would prove lengthy.

The book's second half presents an annotated catalog of works according to genre with a discussion of compositional details and text sources. Information on those works discussed in the main text is given in more detail to serve the reader seeking out a specific work. Of importance in this section is the translation of the Finnish and Swedish titles. In his choice of texts for songs, choral works, and operas, we find a wide range of sources, types, and languages, all pointing to the fact that Rautavaara was a well-read man, deeply moved by poetry and literary images. Often called a mystic, his sacred choral pieces include works for the Orthodox Church, the Catholic Church, Lutheran hymns and psalms, Kalevala mythology from Finland's pagan era, and Hinduism. His operas, nearly all on his own libretti, feature individuals struggling and misunderstood, such as the painter Van Gogh, Alexis Kivi the first author to write in the Finnish language, the Russian monk Rasputin, a strike leader in a mine, and others. His choice of poets include not only Finnish and Swedish writers, but Rilke, T. S. Eliot, Shakespeare, Browning, Lorca, Omar Khayyam, his own poetry, and texts from folksongs.

Even as awareness of Finland as a small country lying between Sweden and Russia is not widespread, her pre-twentieth century music history and composers other than Sibelius remain obscure. Dominated by German performers, teachers, and repertoire during the nineteenth century, the first European trained Finnish musicians began to take the lead at that century's end. From the 1890s on, Sibelius dominated the music of Finland through the first half of the twentieth century, despite the efforts of a second tier of younger composers such as Leevi Madetoja, Toivo Kuula, Selim Palmgren, and Erkki Melartin. A brief time of experimentation in the 1920s by the composers Ernst Pingoud, Aarre Merikanto, and Väinö Raitio met with cool reception by the public. Success in the concert hall required a return to conservative National Romanticism in the 1930s, with programs featuring Sibelius, the works of Uuno Klami and the Lied composer Yrjö Kilpinen. After the disruptions of the World War II years, much that was new began to arrive on Finland's shores from Europe. In the 1950s Finnish composers were exposed to all the European music styles of the first half of the century, compressed into the span of a decade or so. A dizzying sequence of styles confused and divided both the young and the established musicians as well as the audiences—neoclassicism, serialism, electronic music, aleatoric music, and "happenings." At the same time, Sibelius, though he had ceased composing about 1929, received admiring visitors from abroad until his death in 1957. Young composers from the time of the 1950s, including Rautavaara, struggled with the issues of new styles and how best to make composition in Finland as contemporary and respected as that in central Europe.

I am indebted to many: the writings of previous admirers of Rautavaara, Dr. Pekka Hako, musicologist Dr. Anne Sivuoja-Gunaratnam, the exhaustive

## Introduction

Finnish language study by Samuli Tiikkaja; to the irrepressible enthusiasm of my former research colleague Dr. Ruth-Esther Hillila, to the Fulbright Foundation for sponsoring my year in Finland researching pianist composer Selim Palmgren (1878-1951), to his wife Minna Palmgren, to composer and theory teacher Kalervo Tuukkanen, and to the constant encouragement of the members of the "Scandies," a group of Scandinavian enthusiasts in Kalamazoo, Michigan. Most of all, I give thanks to Rautavaara himself for his many stories in his autobiography, his informative program liner notes in his CDs, his journal articles, for the pleasure and awe of many hours of listening to his compositions, and for his gracious interview.

I dedicate this work to Einojuhani Rautavaara, wishing him a lasting immortality through his compositions.

**Figure 2:** Einojuhani Rautavaara, 1950's.

# PART ONE

# BIOGRAPHY AND WORKS

CHAPTER ONE

# BECOMING A COMPOSER, 1928-53

A survey over the almost seven decades of Einojuhani Rautavaara's compositional work amazes with the sheer quantity and variety. He became Finland's best known composer since Sibelius, and was honored with festivals devoted to his works and by a long discography of his recorded works. But it wasn't always so. His early years were full of experiences no one would wish on a child. A lonely youth, he dreamed of a solitary creative life unconcerned with financial cares. Focusing on a possible music career, his early piano teacher exposed him to contemporary music and encouraged his compositions. Fortunately, he began to win awards while in his teenage years and even his first Sibelius Academy efforts were sent off to music festivals by his teachers.

> I didn't think being a child was much fun. And youth didn't seem very enjoyable, either. I always thought that, in old age, I would reach all that I'd ever dreamt about. And that I would live in a tower...somewhere up high, where I could be alone, and do my work. And send my compositions out through the window, and they would float down...[1]

On the ninth of October in 1928, a child was born to opera singer Eino (Jernberg) Rautavaara (1876-1939) and his wife Elsa (Träskelin) Teräskeli (1900-1944), a physician, in Helsinki, Finland.[2] His father was a baritone opera singer best known for his roles as Figaro in *Barber of Seville* and Scarpia in *Tosca*, and roles in *Magic Flute*, *Lohengrin*, and *Cavallieria Rusticana*. Father was also the cantor at Helsinki's Kallio Lutheran church and a teacher at the Church Music school. He was already fifty-two when his son was born, and died at the age of sixty-three, when Einojuhani was only ten.

Rautavaara's father was one of four brothers who came from Ilmajoki in Ostrobothnia, northwest Finland, to study in Helsinki about the turn of the twentieth century. Albin Evald, "Jolli," was a featured tenor in the university singers, the male voice choir Ylioppilaskunnan Laulajat (YL, the University Singers), and became a lawyer and politician, serving as Minister of Justice in the 1930s. Äänis, a bass in the YL, became a constable in Jäläsjärvi. Wäinö,

---

[1] Hilary Finch, "Angel of the North," *BBC Music Magazine* Vol.19 Number 12 (Sept. 2011): 44.
[2] Both parents had Swedish last names which had been changed to their Finnish equivalents, following the patriotic trend about the turn of the twentieth century. "Jernberg" became "Rautavaara," or "Rautawaara," both meaning "Iron Mountain." Even so, one cannot assume Swedish ancestry because of the earlier fashion for changing Finnish surnames to the more elite Swedish versions.

also a singer, became a choir director and organist at Suurkirkko in Helsinki.[3] Eino, a baritone, went on to study in Rome, Berlin, Paris, and Milan. One of the founders of the Finnish Opera in 1911, he had many leading roles for years.[4]

Rautavaara's mother, Elsa, was a doctor with a reception room and office serving poor patients from the Kallio district, on the east side of Helsinki. With her dark hair and dark eyes, she was said by family lore to be descended from an Oulu woman and an anonymous German stranger, probably Jewish. Elsa Katarina Teräskeli came from the town of Oulu, a coastal area of northwest Finland, also in Ostrobothnia. Her father, adopted by the Träskelin family, had a Finnish mother and probably a German Jewish father, perhaps a sailor, who remained unidentified. Elsa and her sister Hilja had been sent to a girl's school. Elsa became a doctor and the sister became a professor of ophthalmology in Turku, in southwest Finland.

Einojuhani's family lived in a second floor apartment around the corner from the Kallio church in Helsinki, over a barber shop. Father and Mother both belonged to the Christian Art Society, whose founder and chairman was the poetess Hilja Haahti, wife of Ilmari Krohn, father's organist at Kallio church and professor of musicology at the University of Helsinki. Mother arranged piano lessons for Einojuhani with his aunt Wenny, the mother of opera singer Aulikki Rautavaara, and later with Greta Carlson and Helvi Leiviskä, a female composer. At age seven or eight he played at giving a composition recital,[5] but was not a particularly dedicated music student. He liked literature more and also art. He was not a distinguished student, either. He had already learned to read before going to school and found schoolwork boring, spending his time daydreaming. Einojuhani enjoyed meeting his father's friends on walks, when his father would introduce him as his latest opus. Father soon moved the family to the Pitkäsilta area of Helsinki. Summers, because he was an urban child, were spent with his family as a summer guest in the country, near a lake, cows, and horseflies. His parents enjoyed this brief return to their childhood environment, while Einojuhani disliked the mattresses of hay, farm chores, biting horses and horseflies, saying he had been hysterically afraid of insects at that age.[6]

From those early years, Rautavaara remembers a group of playmates, sometimes mischievously getting into his mother's things in her clinic. However, at night, a recurring nightmare of an ominous being, big, powerful, gray, and

---

[3] Samuli Tikkaja, Liner notes to *Rautavaara: Complete Works for Male Choir*, Ondine ODE 1125-2D.
[4] Ruth-Esther Hillila and Barbara Blanchard Hong, *Historical Dictionary of the Music and Musicians of Finland* (Westport, Conn.: Greenwood Press, 1997), "Rautavaara, Eino."
[5] Pekka Hako, *Unien lahja* [Gift of Dreams] (Helsinki: Ajatus Kustannus, 2000), 21.
[6] Einojuhani Rautavaara, *Omakuva* [Self-Portrait], Juva, Finland: W. Söderström, 1989, second printing, 1998, passim 7-17.

speechless, continually returned. The being seemed to smother him while he struggled, an exhausting nightly routine which he feared. Another dream of being alone in the world recurred, with safety and the freedom to go wherever he wished, in and out of any doors, a youthful desire to have control over his own world.[7] These dreams were later to find expression in his "Angel" series of works, depicting a struggle with a being similar to the Biblical angel that Jacob wrestled with.

All of this was soon upset by the 1939 Winter War with Russia. Rautavaara's father died in August of 1939, on the eve of the Winter War (between Finland and Russia) which began in November of 1939. Mother was appointed director of a war hospital during the Winter War and, later, during the Continuation War of 1941-44,[8] worked at a front line military hospital caring for the soldiers. Einojuhani stayed with another aunt in Helsinki and then was sent to school in Norway the following spring of 1940, at the age of eleven. Bombing in Norway in early 1944 closed schools there and Einojuhani returned to Helsinki. Mother had suffered a nervous breakdown from overwork and spent some time at an asylum. Not thinking clearly, she sometimes ran away into the woods overnight and was returned by local farmers the next day. For a time, she was well enough to return home to Helsinki with her son and a healthcare attendant. Living in poverty, she sublet rooms in the apartment for some income, bringing bedbugs. Einojuhani sometimes woke up to bloody sheets and moved to the dining table to sleep. With air raid sirens, mother and son fled to an air raid shelter or to the bomb shelter in the basement with their neighbors. The building was eventually hit and burned, forcing them all to leave the cellar. Outside, everything in sight was burning, with dead horses lying on the street. Mother decided to flee to her family in Oulu. With a train so packed with people that Rautavaara vomited from the smell, they traveled overnight north to Oulu, only to find it had also been bombed, with its wooden houses all in ruins, still smoking. Mother couldn't comprehend it all, and, unable to function, was taken to the hospital. She didn't receive her usual doses of morphine, routinely given to military doctors to combat fatigue and stress, and passed away within two weeks, at the age of forty-four. Rautavaara, a fourteen year old boy, was so disoriented by his mother's behavior and sudden death, the bombing of his house, and the chaos around him, that he refused go to the hospital nor to the funeral home. Some ten years later, he was able to mourn her and dedicate his *A Requiem in Our Time* (1953), a brass ensemble work, to her.[9]

---

[7] Hako, passim 18-20.

[8] Given this name because it was again between Russia and Finland, despite the Second World War raging elsewhere.

[9] Rautavaara, *Omakuva*, 25, 28, 30-33 passim.

As an orphan, he was sent again to Norway for the school year of 1944-45. Returning to Finland in the summer, he then was taken in by his unmarried maternal aunt, Hilja Teräskeli. Like Einojuhani's mother, she had been working in military hospitals but in 1945 was appointed to a stable position as professor of ophthalmology in Turku (Åbo in Swedish), the early capital of Finland in the southwest of Finland. Because of the ongoing war and housing shortage, the two lived for some time in a Turku hotel. The stability of the hotel routines was a wonder to the boy, now sixteen, though lacking in companions of his own age. New to his school, and slow in making friends, he spent his free time fascinated by the newly published books by Sulho Ranta, the 1945 publications *Suomen säveltäjiä* (Finnish Composers) and *Sävelten mestareita* (Masters of Composition). Finding the independent creative life described in the books appealing, he arranged to take piano lessons from Astrid Joutsenon, best known as long time accompanist and companion to the concertizing violinist, Kerttu Wanne. Studying with this pianist of international performance experience, he encountered contemporary repertoire, including compositions of Debussy, Ravel, Hindemith, and Respighi. About this time he began to dream of being a composer. He imagined himself owning a tobacco shop, where he would peacefully live and compose in the back.[10] He wrote to his father's friend Arvo Laitinen at the Sibelius Academy about music theory lessons and made arrangements to study with him during the summer vacation time in 1946. Aunt Hilja arranged a summer apartment in Helsinki for the seventeen year old with a cook coming every few days to provide food. Returning to Turku for the fall school year, Rautavaara began to compose songs and piano pieces. Particularly fond of Debussy, some of his earliest efforts at piano composition reflect that atmospheric style and were given French titles. *La prémier neige* won a first prize in the first Suomen teiniliito (Finnish Teen League) competition in 1946, when Einojuhani was seventeen. A song of his, *Hunnuton* (Unveiled), on a text by Aila Meriluoto won the second prize. In 1947 the competition became national, Nuorison kulttuuripäivä kilpailu (Youth Cultural Day competition), and Einojuhani won a second prize with *La premier neige* since no first prize was awarded. In the summer of 1947, Tyra Forssling, a friend of his father's, arranged a summer job in Sweden, caring for the flowers at an estate near Stockholm. In his last year of school at Turku he continued to prepare for college but also composed. As a Christmas present he sent a song, *Ensi lumen aikaan* (At the Time of First Snow, 1947) on a text by Kaarlo Sarkia to a fellow summer student, a girl friend in Helsinki. Long forgotten, it was returned to him by mail anonymously after the turn of the century. Another piano piece, *Kaupungissa sataa* (Snow Falling in the City) from 1948, may well have been influenced by Debussy's "The Snow is Dancing" from the *Children's Corner Suite*.

---

[10] Hako, 24.

## Becoming a Composer

On graduation in 1948, Einojuhani sought permission from his aunt to enroll at the Sibelius Academy in Helsinki, where he intended to again study with theory teacher Arvo Laitenen. Before she would agree to what seemed an impractical profession, she wrote to an authority, choral director Heikki Klemetti,[11] requesting his opinion on her nephew's compositions and future prospects. The young prospective student went to Klemetti's home, which, coincidentally, some forty years later would become his own. Klemetti listened to some of his piano pieces, then gave him a text to set to music in the next half hour. Klemetti's appraisal was moderately positive, but also mentioned to the hopeful student that his relative who drove a truck made twice as much money as Klemetti did, and that if young Rautavaara didn't succeed at composition he could always become a driver.[12] A compromise was evidently reached, for Rautavaara enrolled at the University of Helsinki, and soon after, was simultaneously enrolled at the Sibelius Academy.

---

[11] Heikki Klemetti (1876-1953) was perhaps Finland's leading choral director, also a composer, writer, pedagogue, music critic, historian, with decided opinions on voice production. See Ruth-Esther Hillila and Barbara Blanchard Hong, *Historical Dictionary of the Music and Musicians of Finland* (Westport, Conn.: Greenwood Press, 1997), "Klemetti, Heikki."

[12] Rautavaara, *Omakuva*, 45-46.

CHAPTER TWO

# THE STUDY YEARS IN HELSINKI, VIENNA, AND THE UNITED STATES, 1948-57

Though Finland was not officially involved in World War II, having just finished a separate war with Russia, it was a time of great hardship. It not only involved transit of Russian and German soldiers, bombings, and a scorched earth policy in the north on the Nazi departure. It also made a gap in the transmission of cultural trends and styles from Europe. The resumption of contacts in the 1950s brought exposure to serialism, panserialism, aleatory, electronic music, and the musical anarchy of John Cage's ideas, all nearly simultaneously. Often, awareness of the new trends came only through newspapers and periodicals rather than by performances.[1] In January of 1949 the Contemporary Music Society (Nykymusiikki) was founded in Helsinki, growing from the original sixteen members to seventy-five by the end of the year. The group accepted not only composers, but performers, scholars, critics, and music students. Rautavaara later became its vice president 1958-61 and a member of its board in 1963. Monthly meetings discussed contemporary composers such as Schoenberg, Webern, Bartok, Messiaen, Stravinsky, and Hindemith, and their music was played, either recorded or live. The group became the national representative to the International Society for Contemporary Music (ISCM) over the opposition of the competing Society of Finnish Composers, founded in 1945 as a union of professional composers. A lecture in 1949 on serialism made a great impact on Rautavaara, though as a student, he was obliged to follow the teachings of his professor, Aarre Merikanto, who was strongly opposed to it, as were many established composers and critics of the day.[2] In 1954 Erik Bergman (1911-2006) composed Finland's first significant twelve-tone work, *Kolme fantasia* (Three Fantasias), for clarinet and piano. The same year Nils-Eric Fougstedt (1910-1961) composed *Angoscia: Variations, Chorale, e Fuga*, probably the first Finnish twelve-tone work for orchestra. Twelve-tone music was still a curiosity in Finland, but Bergman had been to study with Wladimir Vogel in Switzerland, bringing back a new skill in twelve-tone music, the style of sprechchor (speaking choir), and

---

[1] Anne Sivuoja-Gunaratnam, *Narrating with Twelve Tones: Einojuhani Rautavaara's First Serial Period (ca. 1957-1965)* (Helsinki: The Finnish Academy of Science and Letters, 1997), 21.
[2] Ibid., 22-24.

recommendations to several Finnish composers to go study with this teacher. On taking this advice, Rautavaara's compositions were to change dramatically.

Rautavaara began studies at the Sibelius Academy in 1948, entering the piano class of Janne Raitio, a pianist, organist, and composer. At that period, Rautavaara, like many new music students, had no interest in music not directly relevant to him. Most of the Classical period music and the biggest part of the Romantic period had no appeal to him. He thought Handel's music was machine-like, Mozart's was uninspiringly flat, Schubert's naïve, Mahler's, just vulgar.[3] His first piano assignments from Raitio were Clementi Sonatinas, which he detested. Other than Schönberg and Stravinsky, all earlier music was unimportant to him. For theory, he had his father's friend, Arvo Laitinen. Laitinen was a Wagner enthusiast who had given all the leitmotifs Finnish names and was such an admirer of German culture that for a long time he could not believe in Nazi atrocities. As a teacher he was incomparable and thorough.[4]

Composition as a field of study was loosely defined at that time. On going with manuscripts of some of his songs to the Sibelius Academy's composition teacher, Selim Palmgren, he was told that his Södergran songs showed some originality and that he should come back again after taking more theory and harmony classes. Rautavaara was quite disappointed, since he admired Palmgren's rich and full harmonies. By that time, of course, Palmgren was in his seventies and, though active in composers' groups, he himself composed in the late Romantic and Impressionist style, with touches of Neoclassicism.[5] Known for his diplomacy, he probably was polite to Rautavaara but had no great interest in young students who wanted immediate success in contemporary styles without bothering to appreciate the past. Prof. Laitenen was an advocate of Finnish musicologist Ilmari Krohn's architectural concepts of music form, which builds hierarchically from a pair of beats to phrases to periods to sections to movements, etc. At that time Rautavaara found this rigid and mechanical. Studies of musical forms under Laitenen seemed to stifle musical expression while harmony and chord studies under Eino Linnala seemed artificial, always requiring a single correct solution. While recognizing the necessity to practice the historical disciplines, he found it all somewhat irksome. But, counterpoint with Sulho Ranta came vividly to life, and the connection between the historical and modern use of counterpoint soon became vital and significant.[6]

---

[3] Rautavaara, *Omakuva*, 39.
[4] Hillila and Hong, "Laitinen, Arvo."
[5] Hillila and Hong, "Palmgren, Selim."
[6] Rautavaara, *Omakuva*, 48-50.

Impatient with his overall course of study and uninterested in anything but contemporary music, such as that by Prokofiev and Shostakovich, Rautavaara produced some compositions on his own. A *Concerto for winds*, completed in 1950, was first performed by the Academy orchestra under Jussi Jalas in Helsinki as a student entry in the Nordic Music Days festival, evidently recommended by his teachers, and was then revised and taken to Stockholm for a performance. Coolly received by both audiences, it was quietly shelved by the composer. About 1952 Rautavaara submitted four choral songs to a Sulasol (Suomen laulajain ja soittajain liito, or The Finnish Amateur Musicians' Association) competition. Texts were used from a collection of folk poetry edited by poet Martti Haavio called *Laulupuu* (Singing Tree). Of these, only one, *Taivahan ilohon* (Joy of Heaven) received recognition, a shared third prize. Along with two others, *Tuo'os metta kielellesi* (Honey on Your Tongue) and *Saunarukous* (Sauna Prayer), they were deposited and lost in the association's archives under the name of Rautavaara's father, Eino Rautavaara. Only *Laulupuu* (Singing Tree) was returned in 1952. Years later, in cleaning out the archives, the works were discovered, returned, and performed under the name of *Suomalainen rukouskirja* (Finnish Prayerbook) in 2013. Another set of choral songs, *Lapsen virret* (Children's Tunes) was sent off to the Muntra Musikanter (Merry Musicians) competition but did not receive any prize.

Other early works, including *Pelimannit* (Fiddlers) (1952), *Kolme symmetristä preludia* (Three Symmetrical Preludes, 1950), and the *String Quartet No. 1* (1952), all completed before any formal study of composition, were more successful.

Of these, the *Pelimannit* suite for piano became well known and recorded. With study of music history at the University of Helsinki, simultaneous with his Academy studies, Rautavaara's eyes were opened to Finnish folk music. He found a group of old fiddle tunes collected and written down by Samuel Rinda-Nickola in the seventeenth century. Seeing new possibilities in these tunes, and having learned about Bartok's collection and reworkings of folk tunes, Rautavaara was inspired to do something similar.[7] He performed the first version of the suite, then titled *From the Notebook of Samuel Rinda-Nickola*, in his piano class, with the encouragement of his teacher Janne Raitio. After revision and publication, the suite then received its first public performance by faculty pianist Kurt Walldén under the name *Pelimannit* at the Sibelius Academy in 1953, and received a positive review by the critics.

Rautavaara's suite for piano, *Pelimannit* (The Fiddlers, 1952), Op. 1, was his first important work. Actual Finnish folk music from the west and northwest of Finland describing fiddlers and country organists of western

---

[7] Pekka Hako, *Unien lahja* [Gift of Dreams] (Helsinki: Ajatus Kustannus, 2000), 36.

**Example One:** *Pelimannit* (Fiddlers) (1952), No. 1 "Narboläisten braa speli" (The Fiddlers Arrive)," No. 2 "Jacob Könni." Seventeenth century Finnish fiddle tunes with both Gregorian modes and tonality, with added clashing seconds; the fiddlers arrive to lead the wedding party to the church. "Jacob Könni," the clockmaker, alternates mechanical ticking with a chorale, later used to express 'Doubt and Creed" in *Requiem in Our Time*. ©Fennica Gehrman Oy, Helsinki. Printed with permission.

Finland was used as the source for new compositions with a dissonant harmonic style, tonal, but with added clashing seconds perhaps influenced by Stravinsky, and both modal and metric alterations. *Pelimannit* consists of six short movements, lasting about eight minutes in all. The third movement, "Jacob Könni," was transcribed for brass ensemble and used in *A Requiem in Our Time* (1953) as "Credo et dubito," perhaps beginning Rautavaara's lifelong practice of unabashedly reusing his own material in later compositions (Example One, *Pelimannit*. [*The Fiddlers Arrive*]).

**Example Two:** *Three Sonnets of Shakespeare* (1951), No. 1 "That time of year," No. 3 "Shall I compare Thee to a summers' day." Superimposed triads and bitonality, of No. 3 later used in his first symphony's finale. ©Fennica Gehrman Oy, Helsinki. Printed with permission.

## The Study Years in Helsinki, Vienna, and the United States, 1947-57

About 1951 a friend, Seppo Nummi, invited Rautavaara to submit some song compositions to his weekly cultural journal *Kuva* (Picture). The journal was inserting scores of short contemporary compositions at that time. Rautavaara had just received the complete works of Shakespeare as a gift and arranged three of the sonnets as songs for voice and piano, trying out a new admiration for bitonality seen in some songs by Benjamin Britten. The songs were performed once in 1951 in Copenhagen at the Young Nordic Music festival, with baritone Matti Lehtinen and Rautavaara at the piano, with glowing reviews. The manuscript of the three songs, *Three Sonnets of Shakespeare*, though published in *Kuva*, thereafter disappeared, and the journal ceased publication. In 1973 Rautavaara reconstructed the songs for publication, not remembering exactly what he composed earlier. This did not bother him, for he claimed he constantly reworked and improved his compositions anyway, always seeing new possibilities.[8] Reworking his own material was to become one of his standard compositional procedures. This characteristic, though a mark of constant creativity, leads to confusion in describing the many interrelationships between his compositions.

In these songs we can clearly see Rautavaara looking for new harmonic sounds. In the first song we see a three part form with superimposed triads, a recitative-like vocal line accompanied by parallel thirds, but with a single note non-tonal bass line. Both melody and accompaniment tend to focus on the pitches of F sharp and C sharp (Example Two, *Three sonnets of Shakespeare*, page 12). The piano part in the second song follows the declamation of the voice with diads, open octaves with the bass note and the third above it, all moving non-tonally, or with superimposed clashing triads. The last song "Shall I compare thee to a summer's day" is lively, and tries out a bit of bitonality, with an established B flat major and a B major countermelody. Its melodic and accompaniment themes were incorporated in the revised First Symphony finale in 1988, adding to that work's neoclassical style.

Rautavaara's first string quartet, *Quartettino* (1952) was also composed at the Sibelius Academy before he had taken any composition classes. Studying Palestrina's counterpoint certainly helped with his fugue in this string quartet. Of interest in this work is the use of a symmetrical or octotonic scale, an eight note scale of alternating whole and half steps, in the melodies of the first two of the three movements. A year later, Rautavaara arranged the first string quartet for string orchestra, adding a double bass, and gave it the title *Suite for String Orchestra*, using the same opus number. Recognized for its quality, it was first performed by the Tampere City Orchestra that year, with Jorma Panula[9] as conductor.

---

[8] Rautavaara, *Omakuva*, 162.

[9] Jorma Panula, b. 1930, is well known as the teacher of many famous conductors. Himself the conductor of various orchestras, including the Helsinki Philharmonic, he taught Esa-Pekka Salonen, Mikko Franck, Sakari Oramo, Jukka-Pekka Saraste, Osmo Vanska, and many others. See Hillila & Hong, *Historical Dirctionary of the Music and Musicians of Finland*, "Panula, Jorma."

**Example Three:** *A Requiem in Our Time.* No. 1 "Hymnus," No. 2 "Credo et Dubito." A 1953 prize winning work for 13-part brass ensemble with percussion, tonal with clashing seconds, materials adapted from earlier works. ©Fennica Gehrman Oy, Helsinki. Printed with permission.

## The Study Years in Helsinki, Vienna, and the United States, 1947-57

Example Three, page 2.

On the death of Selim Palmgren (1878-1951), composer and concert pianist Aarre Merikanto (1893-1958)[10] was appointed composition teacher at the Sibelius Academy. Merikanto was an encouraging teacher, though little concerned with matters of musical form and thematic interrelationships. Under Merikanto's supervision Rautavaara wrote his *A Requiem in Our Time* (1953), Op. 3, dedicated to the memory of his mother. It was written for the scoring required by an American competition for thirteen-part brass choir with percussion. In 1954 the work won the first prize in the Thor Johnson composition competition in Cincinnati, Ohio, and was performed there by the Cincinnati Brass Choir.

Because the March 1954 deadline was fast approaching and Rautavaara was required to report for military service that February, he borrowed and arranged movements from his earlier works. The *Requiem* contains four movements. The opening "Hymnus," came from his *Laulupuu* (1952) choral song. Marked Festivamente, the trumpet section alternates phrases with the French horns. The trumpet melody is followed by a second trumpet with clashing parallel minor seconds, an added major seventh to a triad, in a style like that in *Pelimannit*. The second movement, "Credo et Dubito," comes from the earlier "Jacob Könni" movement in the *Pelimannit* suite for piano, and alternates a rapid repeated note motif with a slower calm chordal section (Example Three, *A Requiem in Our Time*, pages 14-15). A march-like theme in the "Dies Irae" third movement derives from Rautavaara's *Concerto for Winds* (1950), a student work with awkward instrumental registers. Its brass interjections, horn glissandi, and snare drum conjure up the Day of Judgement. The last slow movement of the *Requiem*, "Lachrymoso," came from his song "Ken tuskia ei ikipäivin nähnyt" (Who examines [such a thing] never seen) (1952, text by Socrates). It features a solo baritone horn in such a high register that, according to Rautavaara,[11] the player often unwittingly adds a fearful tremolo.

In 1953 Rautavaara graduated from the University of Helsinki with a Masters degree in musicology. His master's thesis was on the opera *Princess*

---

[10] The son of well-known song composer Oskar Merikanto, he had won composition awards and achieved some success only in the late 1940s after many discouraging years. His now highly esteemed opera *Juha* (1922) was rejected as too orchestral by singer Aino Ackté and the conservative directors of the National Opera. His earlier studies abroad had exposed him to the chromaticism of Reger, the harmonic innovations and colorful orchestrations of Scriabin, Impressionism, Expressionism, polytonality and atonality. In Finland his works in the 1920s were dismissed and ignored. See Hillila & Hong, "Merikanto, Aarre."

[11] Rautavaara, *Omakuva*, 75-76.

*Cecilia* (1934) by Finnish composer Väinö Raitio (1891-1945).[12] His 1957 composition diploma from the Sibelius Academy took a little longer. With Rautavaara's 1953 graduation from the University, important to his aunt, he felt ready to enter the professional music world of Finland. The prize money from his *Requiem* and a scholarship pointed him toward a study trip to Vienna. But first, there was an interruption not especially welcome, the period of compulsory military service, required of all able-bodied Finnish men. He served at the Niinisalo Garrison, northwest of Turku, during most of 1954, leaving as a lieutenant in the reserves.

Rautavaara gave his first composition recital in Raisio, a shipyard town near the city of Turku, May 8, 1954, arranged while he was doing military service nearby. He played his own piano compositions, *Tema con variazione* (1953, later withdrawn), *Adagio and Toccata* (1954, lost), and *Pelimannit* (1952), and also accompanied baritone Hannu Heikkilä in *Two Nocturnes* for voice and piano on Rautavaara's own texts (1951, lost), plus the vocal works *Pyhia päiviä* (Sacred Feasts, 1953), a set of four songs on poetry of K. Lounasheimo from the conservative Laestadian religious group in Lapland, northern Finland, and *Die Sonetten an Orpheus* (1954-55), the first three of what would later become a set of five songs.

Finished with his university degree and military service, Rautavaara was open to new opportunities and found them in two scholarships for study abroad. A few months in Vienna saw the completion of several works and made impressions that later saw fruition in compositions based on the poetry of Rilke and an opera, *Kaivos* (The Mine), influenced by the nearby Hungarian uprising of 1956.

In the early months of 1955 Rautavaara studied briefly in Vienna on a Kordelin grant. He rented a room in a Baroque era building, the Palais Schönberg, which housed foreign music students. The building had a salon still decorated in Baroque style with golden angels and wonderful acoustics. Liking what he saw, he begged for a room there. The only one available was in the attic, not rented because it was difficult to heat. It also had the reputation of a resident ghost, since someone had once been murdered there. On taking the room, the ghost began to walk on the first night, since heating the long cold wooden walls and floors make the wood crack as it expanded.[13] An unusual house full of an assortment of music lovers and musicians of various nationalities, it was conducive to composition, though Rautavaara had not yet

---

[12] Väinö Raitio was a reclusive avant-garde composer of orchestral works and operas of the 1920s and 1930s, influenced by Scriabin and Impressionism, known for shimmering orchestral writing and what he called "color poetry." See Hillila and Hong, "Raitio, Väinö."

[13] Rautavaara, *Omakuva*, 106-108.

made any composition lesson arrangements. The last two of Rautavaara's *Five Sonettes to Orpheus*, Op. 9, on texts by Rainer Maria Rilke were composed there, as well as the *Two Preludes and Fugues* for cello and piano based on letters from the names of composers BEla BArtok and EinAr EnGlunD, a Finnish composer (1916-1999).[14] The *Five Sonettes to Orpheus* were based on texts which dealt not so much with the Greek story of Orpheus and Euridice as with Orpheus as a representation of the art of music, as a transcendent existence that appears and vanishes. The songs are mostly tonal and full of bits of word-painting.

While still in Vienna, Rautavaara got a dramatic telegram from Jussi Jalas, Sibelius's son-in-law and a conductor: "Sibelius has recommended you for a study grant to the United States. Can you leave?" As a ninetieth birthday gift, the Sergei Koussevitsky Foundation gave Sibelius a study grant to award to any Finnish student of his choice. Rautavaara's prize winning *Requiem* and his first string quartet were being played on Finnish radio, where Sibelius, no longer able to attend concerts, had heard them. Returning to Helsinki in the early summer, Rautavaara accompanied two newsmen to Sibelius's home at Ainola during the Sibelius Week Festival, and was able to thank Sibelius personally. Sibelius then was a mythic figure. Though he was considered a national hero he had effectively ceased composition about 1928. A rumored Eighth Symphony had never appeared and may have been burned by Sibelius himself. In the U.S. in 1955, as winner of the Koussevitsky scholarship, Rautavaara was surprised to find that everyone assumed him to be Sibelius's favorite pupil, and probable successor. To Rautavaara, Sibelius was remote, a long retired teacher and composer, and considerably out of date. After the year in America, Rautavaara often accompanied guests to Ainola. Sibelius told anecdotes about himself, which all had already heard, leading some to think he was simply a tired old man. Rautavaara, however, suspected the twinkle in Sibelius's eye meant a bit of irony.[15]

The Koussevitsky scholarship included a summer course at the Tanglewood Music Center, and afterwards study at either Juilliard in New York or at Eastman School in Rochester. Rautavaara's travel to the U.S. was by the MS Stockholm in tourist class, where he passed the time reading Franz Kafka novels, with characters and situations that influenced his later librettos for the operas *Kaivos* (The Mine), *Thomas*, and *Vincent*. At Tanglewood, summer home of the Boston Symphony and site of summer courses, he found the countryside to be a "softer version of Finland, small lakes, ridges, forests."[16] Rautavaara joined a group of five students,

---

[14] Englund, some ten years older than Rautavaara, gained renown with his neoclassical works in the 1950s, withdrew from music life for a decade or so during a twelve-tone era in the 60s in Finland, and later returned to favor. See Hillila and Hong, "Englund, Einar."

[15] Rautavaara, *Omakuva*, 116-118.

[16] Rautavaara, *Omakuva*, 123.

who filled their spare time driving around the countryside in an open convertible, singing, laughing together, in a time of optimism and self-confidence.

He was assigned to composer Roger Sessions. Other composers there that summer were Aaron Copeland, the German Boris Blacher, and Italian Geoffredo Petrassi, as well as Leonard Bernstein. He soon learned, much to his surprise, that the techniques of Schoenberg, Webern, and Berg were considered taboo, from the "enemy" camp. After a few days of settling in, Rautavaara began to compose a piano concerto under the direction of Sessions. It was finished in New York, entered in the Suomen Kultuurirahasto (Finnish Culture Prize) competition in Finland, and won third prize. After that, he withdrew it, being dissatisfied with its form and technique, and also took it out of his composition list. Sessions had criticized its formlessness. Rautavaara claimed that it represented modern music; Session politely objected. Sessions's compositions then were nearly atonal and dissonant. Rautavaara, following the style of his composition teacher Aarre Merikanto, kept to symmetrical structures, added tones to triadic harmonies, octatonic scales, mixed meters, and employed ostinato patterns.[17]

At Juilliard that fall he was required to take an entrance exam to determine what courses and program he could follow. Part of the exam was aural dictation of chords, which Rautavaara had never done at the Sibelius Academy. Despite poor results, he was encouraged and passed on. Vincent Persichetti became his composition teacher and also lecturer in a class called Literature and Materials of Music 3, a music theory class. Persichetti at that time was in the middle of writing his famous textbook, *20th Century Harmony*. Composition lessons with Persichetti were definitely more interesting and productive than with Aarre Merikanto in Helsinki. In Finland the emphasis had been on sections of melody with interesting chord sounds. At Juilliard the emphasis was on the whole conception, its growth and logic. Both Copland and Persichetti insisted that their composition students play their works at the piano, no matter what genre the music was designed for, nor the level of the student's skill, emphasizing a physical connection with the music. Persichetti was a well-rounded musician who played the organ. His comments were short, exact, full of irony, but always friendly and understanding of the student. In 1956 Rautavaara also began a string trio under Persichetti's supervision, but couldn't finish it. Materials from that were reworked in a 1957 orchestral piece, *Modificata*.

The piano suite *Ikonit* (Icons), Op. 6, was begun in Vienna, and completed in Manhattan a year later. Icons came from memories of a trip to Karelia, in southeast Finland, in the summer of 1939 before his father's death and

---

[17] Rautavaara, *Omakuva*, 127.

**Example Four:** *Ikoinit* (Icons), No. 1 "Death of the Mother of God," No. 6 "Archangel Michael." Superimposed triads, bitonality. Archangel Michael battling the Anti-Christ in constant running sixteenths in modality. ©Fennica Gehrman Oy, Helsinki. Printed with permission

before the 1939 Winter War with Russia. They visited Viipuri, Suomussalmen, Sortavala, and then Valamo, a fairytale-like island in Lake Ladoga and home of an Orthodox monastery. Eager to go there, he was reminded of an adventure story about the Karelian monks. Prepared to experience his fantasy, he saw the island emerging out of fog, with many churches, onion dome towers, all of gold shining in the sun, with all the bells beginning to ring just at that time. Inside the churches the vaulted ceilings were high, on the roofs the statues of angels and saints seemed to sing, and black-bearded monks served food at the tables. All these colors and sounds remained in his memory, finding later expression in the piano suite *Ikonit* (Icons) and the choral work *Vigils* of 1971-72.[18] Finding a book in the New York Public Library on icons, he checked it out and found himself already composing "The Death of the Mother of God" on the subway home. Pages of illustrations in the book inspired "Two Saints," and then, "The Black Madonna of Blakernaya." In two weeks the suite was finished. Further refinements were made under Persichetti's guidance. Now, all the technical apparatus of his earlier *Pelimannit* (Fiddlers), *The Symmetrical Preludes*, and the String Quartet—use of quartal harmonies (chords based on superimposed fourths), polyharmonies, changing meters, motoric rhythms, triadic thirds, tritones, massive superimposed triads on top of triads creating impressions of grandeur—all were employed systematically and logically, as required by the new teacher (Example Four *Ikonit* [Icons], p. 21).[19] The work has six movements, alternating slow and fast, titled after Orthodox icon paintings. The first performance of *Ikonit* was at the Juilliard Composer's Forum that summer.

Seeing the manuscript of Rautavaara's piano suite *Icons*, Persichetti recommended that Rautavaara put in some small change of tonality, very near the end of the "Two Village Saints," changing the melody from A minor to A-flat and then returning to A minor. For Rautavaara, this made sense, with the change similar to making a bow of respect before the icon of the saints.

> On seeing the final piece in the set, "The Archangel Fighting the Antichrist," Persichetti asked me to play it again, then finally said that it was the type of virtuoso piece which a composer might play at his aunt's club. On hearing it once more, however, he affirmed its substantial quality, saying "It's probably really a secret club of virtuosi."[20]

The Juilliard Music School proved intellectually stimulating, along with the book stores, its nearness to Broadway, music score shops, coffee shops,

---

[18] Rautavaara, *Omakuva*, 140-41.

[19] Rautavaara, *Omakuva*, 142.

[20] Rautavaara, *Omakuva*, 133-34.

**Example Five**: First Symphony (1956, 1988, 2003), I. Andante. Begun at Juilliard under teacher Persichetti, not yet serial, tonal with clashing seconds, many metric changes. Revised in 1988 from 4 movements into 2, a slow movement added in 2003. ©Fennica Gehrman Oy, Helsinki. Printed with permission.

and students. At that time, Juilliard was still located near Columbia University. Rautavaara had found a place to live across from St. John's Cathedral, an area near to Harlem and full of Puerto Rican immigrants. Some of his new experiences were learning the distinction between the kitchen cockroaches and the Puerto Rican dance, the cucaracha, and dealing with black waterbugs and racial intolerance. These eventually caused him to move to a cleaner place in Greenwich Village.[21] Exploring New York, he often walked in different neighborhoods or took the subway. In the Bronx he came across Orthodox deacons with black beards, churches with recitations in deep bass voices, all of which was later captured in his *Vigils* for the Orthodox Church.[22] Movies and cartoons also made their impressions, remaining in his memory for some later use.

Though the Koussevitsky scholarship was intended for a summer course at Tanglewood and an optional semester at Juilliard, Rautavaara wished to extend this, and succeeded in gaining another summer at the idyllic Tanglewood, in 1956. This time he became a student of Copland, and noted that Copland didn't take the summer course very seriously. Rautavaara's *String Quartet No. 1, Quartettino* (1952) and his *Orpheus Sonnets* (1955) were performed by students.[23]

The first symphony, Op. 5, was begun before the second summer in Tanglewood in 1956, and included concepts derived from all his prior composition teachers—Merikanto, Persichetti, Roger Sessions and Copland. The work took its thematic inspiration from the first of the *Orpheus Sonnets* of 1954-55, "Da stieg ein Baum" (A Tree Arose), probably its ascending melodic line, though this theme was removed in the later revision.[24] Already at Tanglewood the work stalled, for its compositional language and ties to traditional tonality no longer seemed relevant or productive to Rautavaara. However, it was necessary to finish it. It originally had four movements, in a slow-fast-slow-fast sequence, but was revised in 1988 when the scores of his first five symphonies were scheduled for publication. The 1988 version resulted in two contrasting movements with some changes of orchestration. The two slow movements of the original were combined into an extended slow first movement (Example Five, Symphony No. 1, p. 22) and the original fast second movement became the finale, with the first version's finale discarded. Rautavaara discussed this in his autobiography, saying that in returning to an old piece, he often saw new possibilities, new solutions to old problems, and could see the awkwardness of himself as a young composer. Though he felt his ideas and techniques to be constantly evolving and growing, the necessity of publication forced him to settle

---

[21] Rautavaara, *Omakuva*, 144.
[22] Rautavaara, *Omakuva*, 138.
[23] Rautavaara, *Omakuva*, 157-8.
[24] Rautavaara, *Omakuva*, 160.

for some hard decisions on a definitive version of a particular work.[25] In the new finale, themes are borrowed from the third of his *Three Sonnets of Shakespeare*, Op. 14 (1951), (Example 2, page 12) for voice and soprano, "Shall I compare thee to a summer's day," namely the ascending scale accompaniment and the leaping triadic melody.[26] The wholesale revision of the work left the imprint of his younger self mainly in the style and mood, recalling the romantic pathos of Shostakovich in the first movement's Andante and the sarcasm of Prokofiev in the finale.[27]

Although the original symphony was performed in 1957 by the Radio Symphony Orchestra in Helsinki, it was then withdrawn. After the revision and its 1990 Helsinki performance, Rautavaara added a lyrical slow movement in 2002. "Poetico," the new middle movement, was based on his solo song "Die Liebende," the third song in his song cycle, *Die Liebenden*, of 1958.

On meeting a Finn who was conductor of the New York Finnish Men's Chorus, Jussi Himanka, Rautavaara occasionally went along for their concerts, even substituting for the conductor at a rehearsal. Despite his complete lack of experience, all went well, and led to the composition of "Laulaja" (The Singer) for men's chorus, on a text from the Finnish folk epic, Kalevala. This became the first of many works for male chorus, a Europe-wide college tradition. In Helsinki, the most famous male chorus was the Helsinki University Singers (Ylioppilaskunnan Laulajat or YL), which gave the first performance of "Laulaja" in 1956. Notable in this choral song about the singing of a skylark is the constant alliteration of the Kalevala rhymes, the fully tonal harmonies, and the selecting of various words for special treatment, such as the repetitions on "pahasti" (ill or blame), "vihaisen äänen" (angry voice) set for basses, "lapsi" (child) set for a single male soprano, and the ascending crescendo on "nuorisossa nousevassa" (among the rising young people).[28] Kalevala rhyme and chant styles were to play a significant role in three of his later operas. Another male chorus work also dates from the New York period. The *Two Preludes by T. S. Eliot* (1956, revised in 1967) are based on texts depicting the London scene of 100 years earlier, but are also appropriate for New York City. The musical word painting of phrases such as "withered leaves and newspaper scraps," "raising dingy shades," and "smells of stale beer" convey the age-old aspects of city life.

Rautavaara began his seven preludes, *Seitsemän preludia pianolle* (Seven Preludes for Piano), Op. 7, while at Tanglewood but was still struggling with them in the following summer of 1957. Despite his teachers' emphasis on logical growth and overall form, the ideas for these preludes grew spontaneously.

---

[25] Rautavaara, *Omakuva*, 162.
[26] Rautavaara, *Omakuva*, 162.
[27] Kalevi Aho, Liner noters to *Rautavaara: Symphonies 1, 2, & 3*, Ondine ODE 740-2.
[28] Rautavaara, *Omakuva*, 151-2.

Rautavaara described them and their later manifestations as movements in his Second Symphony as "bare, sketchy, aphoristic, unconventional, ascetic, and dissonant but still supported with tonality."[29] The seven miniatures last only eleven minutes. Besides being developed further into far lengthier symphonic movements in his Second Symphony, they were also later transformed into a work for string orchestra, *Finnisch, heute* (Finnish, Today) of 1970.

Returning to Finland in the fall of 1956, Rautavaara completed his composition diploma in a further year at the Sibelius Academy, scheduled his First Symphony for a January 1957 performance, and then began a new symphony in a more dissonant style. Rautavaara's Symphony No. 2, Op. 8 (1957), composed on his return to Finland, was a move in the direction of total chromaticism, a sort of expressionistic antithesis to the First. The performance of the First Symphony in January of 1957 had received mixed reviews, making Rautavaara unsatisfied. Thinking that the critics had pegged him as a conservative, he wanted to write a new symphony that would show his skills in contemporary styles. All the musical material for this four-movement work is derived from the 1957 seven Preludes for Piano. A quick comparison of the lengths of the movements shows that the eleven minutes of preludes have been expanded in length to over twenty-one minutes of symphonic movements. This symphony is not merely "new wine in old wineskins."[30] Rautavaara would be similarly inspired to further develop materials from one work into another through much of his life, perhaps most notably in his Sixth Symphony (1992), "Vincentiana," based on material from his opera *Vincent* (1987).

The four movements of the Second Symphony are not based on thematic development. Though tonal, the work is highly dissonant. In both the melodies and harmonies, minor ninths, perfect fifths, and the tritone prevail. According to Kimmo Korhonen, the work is an intermediate stage between Rautavaara's Neoclassicim and his twelve-tone works of the 1960s.[31] A somber funereal opening movement leads to the extremely fast and rhythmic second movement. The slow third movement is an example of Bartok-like night music. The last movement, Presto, evokes Stravinsky's *Rite of Spring* with its constant change of meter signs (Example Six, Second Symphony, page 26). The work was ready for its first performance in October of 1957.

On Rautavaara's return to Helsinki in the fall of 1956, he had gotten to know his musical Rautawaara cousins better. They belonged to a branch of

---

[29] Rautavaara, *Omakuva*, 174-175.

[30] Rautavaara, *Omakuva*, 173.

[31] Kimmo Korhonen, *Orchestral Music 2* (Jyväskylä, Finland: Finnish Music Information Centre, 1995), 38.

**Example Six:** Second Symphony (1957, 1984), IV. Presto.  Materials derived from his Seven Preludes (1957).  Tonal but very dissonant, many metric changes.  ©Fennica Gehrman Oy, Helsinki.  Printed with permission.

the family that, during the nationalism at the turn of the century, chose to spell the Finnish translation of their original Swedish name, Jernberg, with a "w" rather than a "v." The two were the gifted children of Uncle Wäinö Rautawaara, the organist, and Aunt Wenny Rautawaara. Pentti Rautawaara was the Radio Symphony's first chair cellist. Pentti's sister Aulikki had already been a famous singer when Rautavaara was still a child, and their mother, Aunt Wenny, had been his first piano teacher. In 1956, Aulikki, at age fifty, made a sensational marriage to composer Erik Bergman, Finland's leading twelve-tone modern composer. The pair went off on their honeymoon to Turkey, where Bergman did some research and composing. Though the marriage lasted only two years, a strong connection between Rautavaara and Bergman was established. They had known each other earlier, from membership in the Nykymusiikki (Society of Contemporary Music) established in 1949, which later became the Finnish representative to the ISCM (International Society for Contemporary Music).[32] Bergman was influential in pointing Rautavaara toward an exploration of twelve-tone serialism, pointed him toward a teacher of serialism, in Switzerland, for the summer of 1957.

---

[32] Rautavaara, *Omakuva*, 179.

CHAPTER THREE

# FIRST SERIAL WORKS, 1957

Study at Anscona, Switzerland, and then at Darmstadt in Germany introduced Rautavaara to the techniques of serialism, total serialism, sprechchor, electronic music, and aleatory. With each new work, we can see Rautavaara trying out some new technique, enough to gain those skills, and then moving on, looking for a style that would combine his need for a means of formal construction with expressive freedom.

In the summer of 1957, Rautavaara took Bergman's advice and went to Anscona, Switzerland, to study with Wladimir Vogel (1896-1984). Of Vogel's compositions, he knew about works for sprechchor (speaking choir), unusual instrumentation such as a quartet of flute, clarinet, viola, and cello, or a quartet of saxophones, and his stylistic leaning toward Alban Berg's serialism rather than Schoenberg's or Webern's.[1] In June of 1957, Vogel, and his Finnish students Rautavaara and Eric Bergman attended the first performance of Schoenberg's opera *Moses und Aron* (1930-32) in Zurich, in which all three enthusiasts admired the use of speaking chorus. From the techniques learned from Vogel, Rautavaara wrote his first suite for speaking choir, *Ludus verbalis*, Op. 10b (1957). Rautavaara was to again use Sprechchor technique in his opera *Kaivos* (The Mine) (1957/1963), in a set of choral pieces called *Practisch Deutsch* (1969), and in the 1985 opera *Thomas*.

In *Ludus verbalis*, the text contains only four different categories of German words, each in its own separate movement. The first short movement is titled "Personalia" and the text is "Wer? Er, sie, du und er, jemand, niemand, wer?" The second movement. "Temporalia," uses the German for time words like "When, then," etc. The third is based on Qualitative words like "such, what sort," and the fourth is Quantitative, "A little, more, enough." Pitch is defined on a relative scale of low-medium-high, with some register changes from alternation of female and male voices, but rhythms and dynamics are precisely notated.[2]

Vogel, a Russian Jew who had moved successively from Russia to Berlin to Switzerland for refuge, admired the serialism of Berg, and has had his style

---

[1] Rautavaara, *Omakuva*, 184.

[2] Rautavaara, program notes for *Works for Mixed Chorus*, Ondine CD ODE 851-2.

referred to as "consonant dodecaphony."³ According to Rautavaara, "Vogel was authoritative, very pedantic and dry...but he was the most important teacher for me, taught me a solid composition technique."⁴ Vogel discussed two kinds of 12-tone series, the melodic series, designed to produce consonant melodies and harmonies, and the all-interval row.

A much rarer form of the row was the Quintenreihe (fifth series) and its inversion, the Quartenreihe (fourth series), generated from the prime form, the chromatic scale, and the circle of fifths.⁵ To create a Quintenreihe, a chromatic scale beginning on the same first note of the original row is laid out, above every second note is a fifth higher than the first note, creating an augmented fourth tritone interval. The higher pitch replaces every other normal chromatic note in the chromatic scale, in whatever position it falls in the original row. For example, in a chromatic scale starting on C, the next note is C# and will have a G (the fifth above the previous C) sitting above it. In the original row, the C#, no matter where it occurs in the row, will be replaced by a G. This process of substitution for every other note of the original row continues until all twelve tones are used. This provides a logical means of derivation, and the result is a new row that relates to the original, though more remotely than the usual transpositions, inversions, and retrogrades of a serial row. For Rautavaara it was a means of obtaining a whole new set of sounds while actually keeping the original row.

Fascinated with the almost mystic connection of the two series, the Quintenreihe and the Quartenreihe, Rautavaara used them in his choral piece *Ave Maria*, Op. 10a (1957), commissioned by his friend Erik Bergman for his choral group, Muntra Musikanter (Merry Musicians). Though the row appears in its original, inversion, retrograde and retrograde inversion forms, as well as fourth and fifth series for contrast, *Ave Maria* has otherwise traditional parameters, with mainly polyphonic texture with the four voices in free imitation, giving way to homophonic climaxes, and a clear 4/4 pulse maintained throughout.

With new techniques and inspiration, compositions came forth quickly. Also finished in Ascona was the first movement of *Modificata* (1957), for orchestra. With Vogel's encouragement, *Modificata* was completed from the earlier 1956 string trio begun under Persichetti's supervision. The first movement, "Recitatio," was written as an exercise for Vogel, but in Helsinki, Rautavaara continued the work in two further movements not in serial technique, "Meditatio," and "Affectio."

³ Sivuoja-Gunaratnam, Anne. *Narrating with Twelve-Tones: Einojuhani Rautavaara's First Serial Period (ca. 1957-1965)*. Helsinki: Finnish Academy of Science and Letters, 1997, 29.
⁴ Rautavaara, quoted in Sivuoja-Gunaratnam, 35n.
⁵ For an explanation of how the fifth series and fourth series are derived, see Sivuoja-Gunaratnam, 36.

The first movement's row is palindromic, with its retrograde version keeping the original intervals (C-E flat-B-B flat-G sharp-C sharp-G-D-E-F-A-F sharp). A short melodic figure at the opening, C, E-flat, B, B♭, links all the movements, passing through melodic and rhythmic changes (Example Seven, *Modificata*, page 31) A trill or tremolo motive also appears prominently in the first and second movements. Formal unity is further reinforced by repetition of sections only slightly changed, achieving a large-scale formal unity which Rautavaara had earlier felt was missing in his compositional skills.

*Modificata* was performed by conductor Tauno Hannikainen with the Helsinki City Orchestra, in April of 1958. The first rehearsal brought an embarrassment for the young composer. The solo trumpet beginning was scored for a C trumpet, and the player used the more common B-flat trumpet, producing the line a whole step lower than written. The composer heard something a bit strange but did not wish to appear as a nervous perfectionist. After a while, the trumpeter arose and questioned if the part was really for a B-flat trumpet. On being told that it was for C trumpet, he commented sarcastically that both the conductor and the composer hadn't even noticed. Despite warm praise from his former composition teacher, Aarre Merikanto, the work didn't satisfy Rautavaara, and was never performed again. In 1964 the thematic material was reworked once more and became the basis for a quartet for oboe and strings, Op. 11.[6] Of this quartet's four movements, only the third movement, "Interludio," is new and the remainder are either shortened or exact copies of the *Modificata* movements. This new metamorphosis had as little success as the original.

After Anscona, that summer of 1957, Rautavaara did some sight-seeing in Italy, visiting Milan, Venice, and Florence, and then made a stop at Darmstadt, the center for twelve-tone music study, to attend the International Summer Courses for New Music. In Darmstadt, Rautavaara and Bergman attended lectures on total serialism given by Stockhausen and Luigi Nono. A paper on chance techniques by Pierre Boulez was read, Herbert Eimert and Bruno Maderna presented information on electronic music, and a Webern seminar was arranged by Theodor Adorno, Henri Pousseur, and Hermann Scherchen. Rautavaara concluded that the lectures were interesting, but also dry and technical, dismissing any expression of emotions as old-fashioned.[7]

Although Vogel paid little attention to total or pan serialism, Rautavaara wrote his first such piece in 1957, interrupting work on *Modificata* to begin a new work of total serialism in the late summer. *Praevariata*, for orchestra with

---

[6] Rautavaara, *Omakuva*, 150-1.
[7] Sivuoja-Gunaratnam, 41-42.

## First Serial Works, 1957

**Example Seven:** *Modificata* (1957), I. Recitatio. Written while studying serialism with Wladimir Vogel, this early serial work uses the opening intervals of the row as a melodic motif in the first and second movements. Continuing, the second and third movements were not serial and, dissatisfied, Rautavaara withdrew the work. ©Fennica Gehrman Oy, Helsinki. Printed with permission.

**Example Eight:** *Praevariata* (1957). A work of total serialism, with not only a tone row, but serially derived rhythms, dynamics, orchestration, and form. Note that the first measure has one xylophone with one note, in a nine beat measure, at the dynamic level of pp. The second measure has two notes, adding violins, in a 10 beat measure, increasing the dynamics to p. After a 13 beat measure, the process reverses, completing the first of 11 variations. ©Fennica Gehrman Oy, Helsinki. Printed with permission.

English horn, contrabassoon, and extra percussion, was completed in the fall of 1957. It was constructed from a symmetrical tone row plus a rhythmic row, from serially derived irregular rhythmic figures. The title, representing to Rautavaara all the decisions planned before composition, didn't satisfy Vogel, who thought variation should take place during the composition, not before or "pre."[8] The twelve-tone row is symmetrical in several ways: the first hexachord, C-E-F-G♯-A-C♯, contains two patterns of a major third followed by a minor second, as does the second hexachord, E♭-B-B♭-G-F♯-D. Notable is the use of thirds and seconds, keeping a connection with tonality, which was to be Rautavaara's later method. The work begins and ends with a xylophone solo, with the final solo in retrograde pitches. The measures vary serially in number of beats, beginning in the first measure with 9 sixteenths, then a 10 sixteenths measure, 11, 12, 13, and then in reverse, 12, 11, 10, followed by 9, which begins the pattern anew. Dynamics are symmetrical, too, with the xylophone beginning pp, the work increasing to ff, and returning to pp. The number of notes played by the xylophone in each bar also increases from 1 to 5, and then decreases. Overall, there are eleven variations which reach a climax in the seventh variation, with the greatest expansion of the orchestral instrumentation, followed by fewer instruments, thinner texture, and decreasing dynamic levels (Example Eight, *Praevariata*, page 32).[9]

Sent off in the fall of 1957 to the Finnish jury of the ISCM, *Praevariata* was chosen as the only Finnish representative of new music for the ISCM festival of 1958, and was debuted with the Strasbourg radio symphony under Charles Bruck in June of 1958. It was never played in Helsinki, however. At the Strasbourg ISCM festival first performance of *Praevariata*, a French critic said "At last you Finns have de-Sibeliused yourselves." Rautavaara was very surprised, since, for him, Sibelius was already far in the past, and an isolated figure, musically, who had few followers.[10]

In 1964 *Praevariata* was included in the original Fourth Symphony as its second (and final) movement entitled "Variazioni," and performed under that format in 1965 by the Helsinki City Orchestra under Jorma Panula. A new version of the symphony appeared in 1968, and was performed in 1970 by the Finnish Radio Orchestra under Paavo Berglund. In 1986, he removed this work from his catalog and named another work, *Arabescata*, as his Fourth Symphony. Today *Praevariata* exists only in the original Strasbourg recording and hidden in the second movement, "Variazioni," of the recorded original Fourth Symphony,

---

[8] Rautavaara, *Omakuva*, 195.
[9] Sivuoja-Gunaratnam, 70-77.
[10] Rautavaara, *Omakuva*, 199.

now discarded by the composer.[11] A similar fate happened to a piano work begun at the same time as *Praevariata*. Changing its setting from piano to violin and piano, to string quartet, to string orchestra, its materials became the first movement of the original Fourth Symphony, then was reset as an organ work in *Ta Tou Theou* in 1967.

With these first few works using the serial technique, we can see Rautavaara experimenting with this approach. First came a short choral work, then a larger orchestral work with melodic material that didn't seem to want to stay within the bounds of serialism, and then attempts at total serialism. Not satisfied with these works, he continued to look for a means to combine this structural approach with his own need for expressiveness.

---

[11] Sivuoja-Gunaratnam, 69.

CHAPTER FOUR

# SERIALISM, OPERA, THIRD AND FOURTH SYMPHONIES, 1957-66

Serialism dominated Rautavaara's works of the late 50s and 60s. A quick overview of this period shows him wrestling with dodecaphony and his eventual settling into a compromise with tonality. Entering an opera competition with a twelve-tone opera, *Kaivos* (The Mine), he encountered musical success but political opposition to his subject matter. The 1960 orchestral works such as Cantos I and Cantos II were further products of his *Kaivos* opera materials. With a shift to tonal dodecaphony, his Second String Quartet of 1959 won great praise, as did his Third Symphony of 1961 in homage to Bruckner. Dissatisfaction with his Fourth Symphony led to its replacement by the 1962 *Arabescata* Fourth Symphony, Finland's first total serialist symphony. Marriage in 1959 and a son in 1960 were a source of joy for a time, but soon brought discord. During this period, he taught music theory and composition, and was a music critic for the Helsinki *Ilta-Sanomat* (Evening News) newspaper from 1963 through 1967, and even took on a position as a music school director for a year, 1965-66.

On return to Helsinki in the fall of 1957, Rautavaara decided to enter an opera composition competition. After discussing with a writer a possible libretto, Rautavaara decided that, to make the words and music interwoven, he needed to write the libretto himself. His story revolved around the Hungarian uprising of 1956, and stories heard from Hungarian refugees during his study days in Ascona with Wladimir Vogel. The title *Kaivos* (The Mine), symbolized both the depths of the mine and the depths of humanity. It was his first attempt at writing a drama. Unfortunately, he had no means to support himself while composing such a lengthy work. Aunt Hilja came to the rescue with financial help and the suggestion that he remove himself to her summer lake place at Sääksranta, near the small town of Mäntsälä, perhaps some 20 miles north of Helsinki. She was able to visit him there at Christmastime, but passed away on the 18th of January, 1958. Rautavaara travelled to Helsinki to make the funeral arrangements and then to Oulu for the burial among family graves. Returning to composition, he finished the first act of the opera in the spring. The competition jury made comments such as "hammer and sickle" political content, gave the opera first place, but then reneged under pressure from politicians, and chose to give the prize to another, with *Kaivos* getting an honorable mention. During the Cold War period following World War II and Finland's Continuation War with Russia,

Finland followed a policy of appeasement, later known as "Finlandization," toward Russia, hoping to avoid further conflict with its larger neighbor. Any overt criticism of Russian affairs was avoided in the media, even in the arts. The connection of the opera's subject with the Hungarian uprising was too controversial. Jouko Tolonen, head of the Finnish National Opera, showed some interest in the opera and suggested some revisions to make the work more politically acceptable. The opera was actually scheduled for performance in December of 1960, but was soon quietly replaced. Tolonen left his position in 1960 to teach at the Sibelius Academy. When Tauno Pylkkänen was named artistic director, no more was said about *Kaivos,* despite Pylkkänen's support.[1]

The opera became a television production in April of 1963, making it the first Finnish television opera. Alterations had to be made to allow its performance. The setting was changed to the Spanish Civil War of 1937, the Commissar was changed to a Prefect, the word "sickle" was removed, among others, in order to avoid any connections to Communism.[2] Rautavaara's wife, Mariaheidi Rautavaara, was cast as the young destructive girl, to his dismay, as he had wanted a short, dark, thin girl in the role, rather than a tall blonde. Not getting much joy out of the opera, he turned to other projects.[3] The opera was subsequently withdrawn and material from *Kaivos* later found its way into *Cantos I and II* (1960) and the String Quartet No. 3 (1965), which all are based on the same serial row and its Quintenreihe.[4] In 2010 the opera was presented in a concert version in Tampere, Finland, and recorded. A fully staged version waited until October of 2016, presented in Budapest, Hungary, in commemoration of the 60th anniversary of the Revolution. Performed as a one act opera, it was done in Finnish with English and Hungarian subtitles.

The story of the opera *Kaivos* tells of a group of mine workers caught up in a nation-wide rebellion against the ruling Party. The two main opponents are the Commissar, who not only believes in the Party but in its mission to make the workers' lives better, and Simon, a former rebel leader, urged against his will to become a leader once more and take on that responsibility. Ira, his much younger girlfriend, wants Simon to choose either her or the people and becomes an emotional catalyst for the later tragic events. The miners and their wives flee into the mine. In the climax of the third act, much takes place. The priest gives communion to the hiding miners and their wives, the miners drink to relieve their fear, one of them panics and runs. In the confusion, Ira is shot, an old

---

[1] Rautavaara, *Omakuva*, 211; Sivuoja-Gunaratnam, 88.
[2] Tiikkaja, 212.
[3] Rautavaara, *Omakuva*, 203-7.
[4] Sivuoja-Gunaratnam, 93.

**Example Nine:** *Kaivos* (The Mine) (1957), opening of Act One. A serial opera based on a miners' rebellion during the Hungarian revolution of 1956. Despite the difficult musical style, the political problem was far greater. Out of fear of offending Russia, the scene was changed to Spain, and the original not fully appreciated until a performance during the Hungarian 60th Celebration of its revolution in 2016. ©Fennica Gehrman Oy, Helsinki. Printed with permission.

tunnel falls open and allows the group to escape. The victorious Party soldiers enter and bayonet Simon. The next scene shows the escaping miners emerging into daylight, Simon, with his sacrifice, having provided them time to get away.

In this 3-act opera, the music is in the 12-tone technique but instead of the austerity of *Praevariata* it has an expressiveness and melodic sweep reminiscent of Alban Berg (Example Nine, *Kaivos (The Mine)*, page 37). The chorus uses a spoken choral technique, speaking, shouting, and whispering, often as background to a sung part. Contrasting musical styles, called for by the libretto, are heard in the jazz band playing on the radio in the background of Ira's solo, and tonal music in the communion scene and in the drinking song of the miners.

The libretto of this opera was influenced by the views of French philosopher Jean-Paul Sartre. Rautavaara at one time chuckled at his opera, probably convinced it would never be revived, saying *Kaivos* was a gloomy work of his youth inspired by the 1956 Hungarian uprising, in a difficult musical style, with a lot of dying going on.[5] More recently, with the concert version and recording accomplished, he wrote "*Kaivos* is perhaps the best opera I have ever written, a real thriller whose underlying theme—that a human being defines himself through his choices—is nevertheless universal."[6]

From 1957-59 Rautavaara taught harmony and composition at the Sibelius Academy and also worked as the Helsinki City Orchestra librarian. Some of his earliest students were Paavo Heininen, later a respected teacher and composer himself, and Kay Chydenius, successful at lighter music with radical socialist themes.[7] The director of the Sibelius Academy, Taneli Kuusisto, asked if Rautavaara would be interested in a West German scholarship for the summer of 1958, as there seemed to be difficulty finding suitable candidates. The school was the Cologne Musikhochschule, a conservatory. A composition course was listed with Frank Martin, an unknown to Rautavaara at the time. On arriving in Cologne, Frank Martin had moved, and another teacher, Rudolf Petzold, was assigned.[8]

Rautavaara spent the summer of 1958 studying at the Cologne Music Academy. There he began to compose his second string quartet in a classical twelve-tone style, using the technique as a starting point for his own creation.

---

[5] Rautavaara interview with the author, 2000.

[6] Einojuhani Rautavaara, Foreword to the recording of *Kaivos*, Ondine ODE 11742, Tampere, Finland, 2010.

[7] Rautavaara, *Omakuva*, 196.

[8] Rautavaara, *Omakuva*, 198.

In my second string quartet I wanted to give myself up to true musical expression and my characteristic idiom within the confines of that strict method. The four movements of the quartet present the same motifs in different lights, tempos and moods. "Tonal" harmony was so important as the basis for all my music that I set about seeking a practical way of combining a living harmonic event with a dodecaphonic construction, often marrying organism with discipline. This attempt at synthesis then continued in the third symphony and my opera *Kaivos* (The Mine). And in fact it is still going on.[9]

The Second String Quartet, Op. 12 (1958), acclaimed a masterpiece at its first performance,[10] was chosen for performance at the 1960 Nordic Music Days in Stockholm. Its twelve-tone row consists of four segments, each with a minor third and a second. Its derived Quintenreihe (based on substituting fifths on alternate notes of the original row's chromatic scale) offered contrasting sounds, though derived from the original row, by allowing for four triads. The polyphonic opening movement in moderate tempo is followed by a dance-like scherzo, a melodic slow movement, and a fast finale. The same melodic idea underpins all four movements, and the whole work is rigorously organized. In comparison to the first quartet, it is more melodic, more contrapuntal in nature, and uses serial procedures within a tonal frame (Example Ten, String Quartet No. 2, page 40).

Among his compositions begun at that time in Cologne is the set of lengthy songs called *Die Liebenden* (The Lovers) (1958-59) on four poems of Rainer Maria Rilke. The four song texts alternate the voices of the lovers: 1. Liebes-Lied (Love Song); 2. Der Schauende (Man Looking); 3. Die Liebende (Woman Loving); and 4. Der Tod der Geliebten (Death of the Beloved). The moods vary from the woman's dream-like contemplation of the state of being in love, to the man viewing a storm and feeling caught up in something infinitely bigger than himself, the woman feeling afloat, and the final song where the man rages and then accepts the death of the woman. Noteworthy is the appearance in the second song's text of Rilke's angel, an Old Testament being like that which wrestles with Jacob. Rilke's concept of the angel would prevail in later Rautavaara "angel" works, the overture *Angels and Visitations* (1978), the *Angel of Dusk* double bass concerto (1980), and the *Angel of Light* seventh symphony (1994).

Completion of the songs was delayed by work on Rautavaara's first opera, *Kaivos*. Rautavaara has said that the song set was dedicated in March, 1959, to his future wife, Mariaheidi, whom he married in June and who did the first performance. The work was already underway in Cologne, in the summer of

---

[9] Rautavaara, *String Quintet "Unknown Heavens", String Quartets 1 & 2*, Ondine 909-2, liner notes.
[10] Sivuoja-Gunaratnam, 55.

**Example Ten:** String Quartet No. 2 (1958), I. Moderato. With a serial row that allows for tonality and melodic expressiveness, the opening polyphonic motif unites the four movements. © by Breitkopf & Härtel, Wiesbaden.

1958, at a time when Rautavaara was spending much time with another female singer, also a student at Cologne. Whether either woman was his inspiration, far more important is Rautavaara's lifelong admiration of Rilke's poetry, seen already in his *Orpheus* songs of 1955 and in many of his later vocal and choral works, as well as his series of *Angel* orchestral works.

*Die Liebenden* was composed in a modified twelve tone technique. Rautavaara has described this:

> the tone rows generate a polyphonic texture using what I call interpolation. Against the harmonies thus generated, the solo voice part is 'free' in its musical conception—in other words, it employs those pitches in the harmony that make up an expressive melodic line.[11]

Here Rautavaara has given us the key to what has become his long lasting approach to serialism. The expressive melody moves in a smooth conjunct Romantic style, rather than in widely spaced intervals. Free of the strict rules of serialism, it is allowed to be expressive but still never settles in any tonal center. The orchestral accompaniment is supportive and less austere than the piano version, its angular leaps tempered by the string timbres. Some word-painting is there, in "die Stürme" (the tempests bluster) of the second song, "durchsichtig wie eines Kristalles" (transparent as glass) in the third song. Material from this set of songs was later used in the String Quartet No. 4 (1975), with the second movement based on the third song, and the third movement based on the second song. In 2002 he took the third song, "Die Liebende," arranged it as "Poetico," and added it as a middle slow movement to his First Symphony of 1956.

In 1959 Rautavaara married Mariaheidi Suovanen (1927-2004), a mezzo-soprano singer. The marriage, perhaps begun too hastily, lasted about twenty years. There were three children, a girl from a previous relationship of Mariaheidi's, and two boys, Markojuhani (b. 1960) and Olof (b. 1968), as well as much conflict, unfortunately publicized widely by the news media. Mariaheidi lost their first child in a miscarriage and soon found herself pregnant again, leaving her unable to accept an operatic contract at Bayreuth. Rautavaara had no clue how to be a parent and Mariaheidi, not domestically inclined, continued to concertize and teach. Within a year of their son Markojuhani's 1960 birth, tension was so difficult between the couple that Rautavaara fled in despair to a rented cottage in Norway, in May of 1961. Reclaimed by Mariaheidi's appearance on his doorstep, he dutifully returned home. Soon after Mariaheidi was admitted to a mental institution,[12] where her mother had had her admitted as a teenager for excessive physical abuse.[13] Rautavaara himself took up an ax during an argument in December of 1962. Mariaheidi refused to press charges, claiming she fell down some stairs. The two went home from the emergency room that night

---

[11] Rautavaara, *Song of my Heart, Orchestral Songs*, Ondine 1085-2, liner notes.
[12] Rautavaara, *Omakuva*, 215.
[13] Hako, 111.

and continued on. Rautavaara refers to the time of his first marriage as one of apartments, houses, children, dogs, cars, vacation places, boats, trips, and conflict, 1959-1982, with great pressure for compositions needed to pay the bills.[14]

In 1960 Rautavaara produced two orchestral works, *Canto I*, Op. 16, for string orchestra, and *Canto II*, Op. 17, for full orchestra, four Wagner tubas, celeste, and harp. The name of the composition refers not only to Ezra Pound's near stream of consciousness poetry, but also to vocal expression.[15] *Canto I* is based on material from Acts One and Three of the opera *Kaivos*. *Canto II* comes from the first half of Act Two, reproducing the ABA form of bars 102-149 of the second act. Another work, the Third String Quartet (1965), also draws material from *Kaivos*, from the second half of Act Two.[16]

> "...the series of Cantos, which are all the same twelve-tone series, but which are intended to be performed separately. The basic motivation stems from my opera *The Mine*...I want to emphasize that it is not a question of being a suite from the opera. I just accomplished certain ideas that were born during the composition of *The Mine*."[17]

In 1961 Rautavaara referred to three *Cantos*, the first for string orchestra, the second for strings, brass, and timpani, and the third for a large orchestra. A reorchestration and reversal of the order of two *Cantos* in 1972 has confused the issue of which *Canto* was eliminated. The later works designated as *Third Canto* (1972), *Fourth Canto* (1992), and *Fifth Canto* (*Into the Heart of Light, Canto V* of 2011 for chamber orchestra) are thematically unrelated to the earlier two.

Another work from this style period is his Third Symphony, Op. 20 (1961). Mixing 12-tone serialism with consonant music, the composer calls it "non-atonal dodecaphony." The twelve tone row at its base contains three triads, with fourths, fifths, and thirds allowing tonal references. Orchestration effects parallel those of Bruckner. A specifically Brucknerian touch is the spacious horn motif played against a quiet tremolo in the strings at the very beginning, opening like Bruckner's Fourth Symphony. Other similarities are the characteristic texture, the use of the Wagner tuba, brass tuttis, themes and motives in sequences, and performance marks in German (Example Eleven, Third Symphony, pages 43-44).[18] According to composer and writer Kalevi Aho:

---

[14] Rautavaara, *Omakuva*, 214-215.

[15] Rautavaara, quoted in Sivuoja-Gunaratnam, 190-1.

[16] Sivuoja-Gunaratnam 95.

[17] Rautavaara, as quoted in Sivuoja-Gunaratnam, 97.

[18] Kimmo Korhonen, *Finnish Orchestral Music* (Jyväskylä: Finnish Music Information Centre, 1995), 39.

SERIALISM, OPERA, THIRD, FOURTH SYMPNONIES, 1957-66

**Example Eleven:** Third Symphony (1961), I. Langsam, breit, ruhig. With a tone row that allows for tonality, many features of Bruckner's Fourth Symphony are included. Note the French horn opening in fourths and fifths over string tremolo, flute flutters affirming the D minor tonality, doublings of octaves and thirds. Later traits include brass tuttis, a Wagner tuba, themes in sequences. ©Fennica Gehrman Oy, Helsinki. Printed with permission.

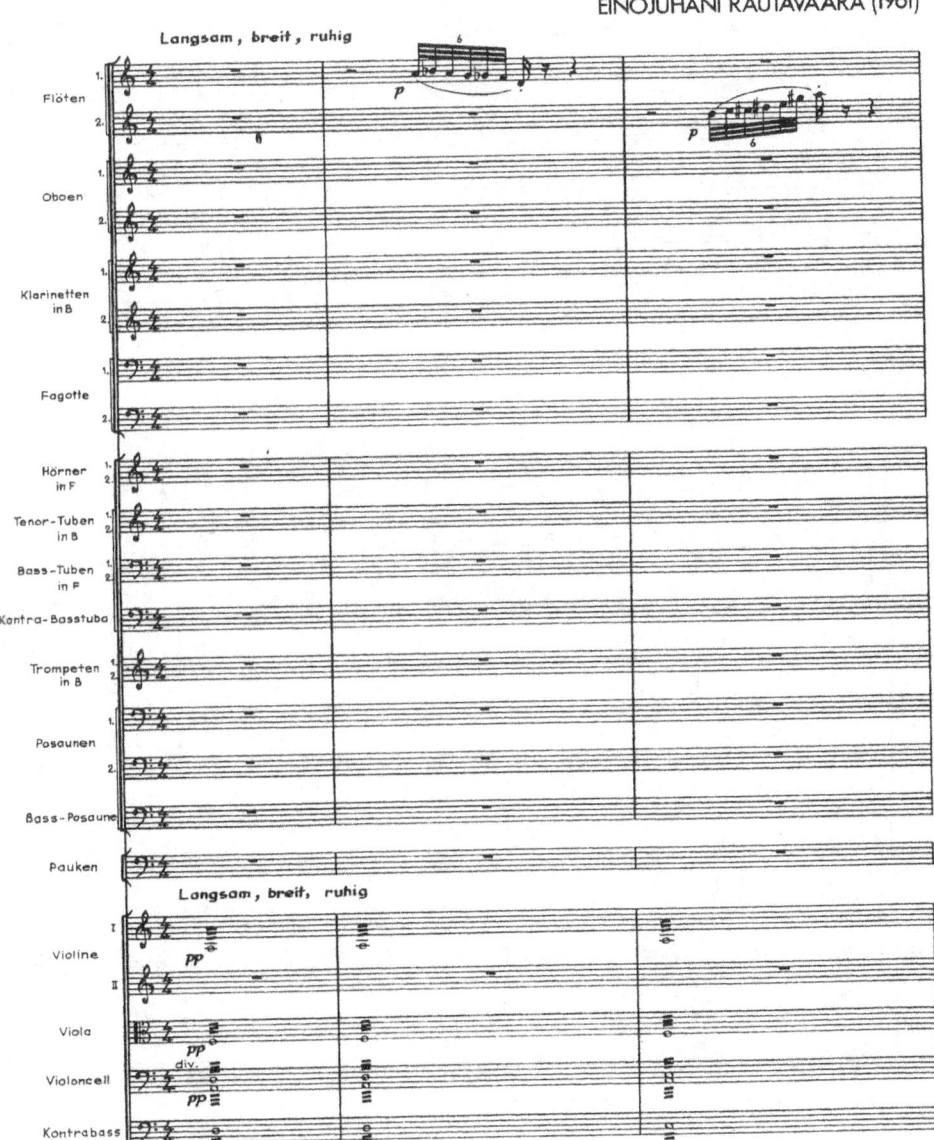

Example Eleven, page 2.

Rautavaara's Third Symphony is unique in Finnish music in its response to Bruckner--in no other Finnish symphony have Bruckner's musical idiom and formal thinking become such a clearly perceptible part of the personality of another composer living at a totally different period. This does not, however, diminish the work's value: it was his most important work to date and his first real symphonic masterpiece. It has four movements and breathes in broad spans. As in Bruckner's late symphonies, the score includes 4 Wagner tubas.[19]

The symphony's first performance took place on April 10, 1962, in the University Great Hall, Helsinki, with the Finnish Radio Symphony Orchestra under conductor Paavo Berglund. As might be expected, the reception of the symphony was conflicting. The modernists felt disappointed at the return of tonal references and to the musical past, including Vogel, Rautavaara's former teacher, who was in Helsinki for another concert. One critic even nicknamed the composer "Antonrichard Rautavaara." Others praised the mix of old and new: "Allowing his own personality to be reflected in a Brucknerian mirror, he composed a symphony about the symphonies of Bruckner."[20] Eventually, the work grew in popularity, and was even performed in 2000 with the Bruckner Fourth on the same program in Linz, Austria, the home city of Anton Bruckner.

In 1960, when Erik Bergman was appointed professor of composition at the Sibelius Academy, international techniques and guest lecturers from Europe were incorporated into the learning environment. In Finland, serialism in the style of Schoenberg and Webern was only used by Erik Bergman. The only composers who extended serialism beyond pitch organization to other parameters were Bergman, Rautavaara, and Paavo Heininen.

With acceptance of musical modernism by the leading musical establishments, the need for the Contemporary Music Society waned and its representation at the ISCM was transferred to the Society of Finnish Composers. In 1962 the Finnish Broadcasting Company (Yleisradio) organized the first annual Contemporary Music Days, and in 1965 founded an ensemble for contemporary music which gave concerts around Finland and made tapes of compositions. Other Finnish orchestras began to program contemporary works, though not without some dissent. Rautavaara had a public dispute with conductor Paavo Berglund over graphic patterns included in the score of *Arabescata* (1962), a total serial orchestral work originally calling for 10 percussionists. As a result, Rautavaara eventually conducted the work himself, February 26, 1963.

---

[19] Kalevi Aho, program notes to *Rautavaara Symphonies 1, 2 & 3*, Ondine ODE 740-2.
[20] Kimmo Korhonen, *Finnish Orchestral Music* (Jyväskylä: Finnish Music Information Centre, 1995), 39.

Rautavaara's Symphony 4 *Arabescata* (1962), Op. 24, was commissioned by the Finnish Broadcasting Company. Rautavaara named it the Fourth Symphony in 1986, some twenty four years after its composition, when he decided to withdraw the original Fourth Symphony (1964), Op. 25. Rautavaara's *Arabescata* was first performed as a three movement pan serial work submitted to the Finnish section of the International Society of Contemporary Music (ISCM), founded 1922. Accepted as the only Finnish representative for 1963, the fourth movement added a few months later did not make the deadline for the Amsterdam performance. By November all four movements were in rehearsal in Helsinki. According to Rautavaara, the name "arabescata" refers to an Italian marble stone with interesting graphic patterning, and also to the verb "arabescare," meaning to ornament with bizarre, interlacing figures, or arabesques, perhaps referring to all the symmetries at both large and small levels in his music.[21]

The *Arabescata* Symphony is the only totally serial symphony to have been composed in Finland. In the first three movements, pitch, rhythm, dynamics, and timbre are controlled by rows, the last movement is aleatoric. The score calls for an orchestra with added saxophone, Wagner tuba, harp, celeste, and piano, plus a full range of unusual sizes of standard reed and brass instruments, and a long list of percussion. The instruments are divided into five groups: the woodwind, brass, strings, percussion, and a fifth group composed of celesta, harp, and piano.

The first movement is dominated by a symmetrical arrangement of the parameters, ABA forms at both the large level and in the smallest levels. The second movement consists of 5 sections, played without a break, each converted into music from a figure drawn on graph paper and included in the score. The five graphic designs determine from their coordinates: instrumentation, pitches and their registers, rhythmic values, density of simultaneous events, and dynamics. The third movement is a faster scherzo, ending as an Andante, half as fast. The last movement, in an aleatoric or chance music arrangement, gives the five instrumental groups their own music fragment in sections numbered one through ten. Each group's music is strictly notated, but may be combined one after another, simultaneously, or overlapping, but each group is required to maintain its own numeric order of entries. When each group has completed its assigned fragment, they all move on to the next section. Commenting on the use of aleatory in the last movement, Rautavaara wrote: "the liberty was no greater than in a furnished room, where you can only change the arrangement of the furniture, but nothing else" (Example Twelve, *Arabescata*, pages 47-48).[22]

---

[21] Sivuoja-Gunaratnam, 207.

[22] Rautavaara, *Omakuva*, 154.

# SERIALISM, OPERA, THIRD, FOURTH SYMPHONIES, 1957-66

**Example Twelve:** Fourth Symphony, *Arabescata* (1962), I. The only totally serial Finnish symphony, controlling pitch, rhythm, duration, dynamics, timbre, density and form. The instruments are in five groups, each entering with a differing level of activity. The second movement with five instructive graphic designs the conductor didn't understand caused a scandal, the third had many metric changes, and the last movement was aleatoric. ©Fennica Gehrman Oy, Helsinki. Printed with permission.

EINOJUHANI RAUTAVAARA (1962)

Example Twelve, page 2.

The first performance in Finland created a scandal discussed in the newspapers. *Arabescata* was scheduled to be conducted by Paavo Berglund, who began rehearsals in November of 1962. Difficulties with the notation and the need for 10 percussion players postponed the debut. Rautavaara made some revisions and an offhand comment to the press about conductors, in general, who were unwilling to study a new notation. With the story picked up by another newspaper, now with the name of the conductor, Berglund replied to the press that he didn't feel the analytical drawings were essential to the musical realization. The graphic patterns, in fact, served as generators for the strict total serialist parameters, and were not necessary for performance, but did aid in helping the coordination of all the players. Two newspapermen added to the controversy. One made jokes about "Pekkajukkawaldemar vaararaita's" composition "Abragadabra." (the made-up name of the composer being a long link of multiple Finnish and German first names plus a play on the last name which implies a dangerous road). Earlier that week, the orchestra members had refused to perform Jan Bark's *Pyknos*, programmed for the Young Nordic Music Festival, claiming that the piece would ruin their instruments. A newspaper cartoonist combined both of these controversies, plus earlier "musical happenings," in a sketch depicting the players sawing a cello, jumping on drums, blowing water bubbles from a tuba, pulling a cat's tail, while the conductor stands on one hand attempting to decipher a geometric drawing. At the side door, a man enters asking the opinion of the players on the planned subway of Helsinki, holding a big map (Example Thirteen, page 50).[23] As a result, Rautavaara was asked to conduct the work himself. He hoped for a few lessons from Jorma Panula, Finland's famous conducting teacher, but ended by studying some textbooks, and hoping for the best. At the first rehearsal the players were mystified and complained they couldn't understand the conductor's beat patterns. With the help of the assistant conductor, everything was smoothed over and the performance came about, with reviews even praising the new conductor. Fortunately, relations between the composer and conductor Berglund were soon repaired.

Regarding integral (pan or total) serialism, Rautavaara later commented that he felt compelled to explore what the expansion of control over all the parameters of music might do for his composition work:

> I had to find out what this integral serialism was about, what it could offer me and was it really the solution toward which my development was logically proceeding…That took place in *Arabescata*.[24]

---

[23] Sivuoja-Gunaratnam, 84-85.
[24] Rautavaara, quoted in Sivuoja-Gunaratnam, 79.

**Example Thirteen:** *A Cartoonist's View of Contemporary Orchestral Music.* A cartoon by Kari Suomalainen, Helsingin Sanomat, 10 February, 1963. Note the odd playing techniques, the conductor standing on his hand trying to read a graph, while someone enters with a map of the proposed subway system to ask advice. ©The Kari Suomalainen Estate. Printed with permission.

In his autobiography, Rautavaara calls the years of 1964-66 a period of emptiness in his compositional life, partly due to marital problems. Mariaheidi insisted on taking the lead female role in the opera *Kaivos* despite his objections and got involved with the fallout with conductor Paavo Berglund over *Arabescata* and the opera. Appearing together in performances, the couple managed to appear loving, but out of the public eye sometimes came to blows.

At this time he released works based on his earlier serial compositions, such as the *Quartet for Oboe and Strings*, Op. 11 (1957/64), based on *Modificata* (1957), the *String Quartet No. 3*, (1965) based on *Kaivos* (1957-58, 60/63), and the original *Fourth Symphony* of 1964, which included *Praevariata* of 1957 as its second movement. An earlier work for piano, *Apotheosis* (1957), was reshaped into *Fantasy for violin and piano* (1960), then rearranged into a violin concerto, a string quartet, a string orchestra, and in 1962 as a work for a full orchestra, named the Fourth Symphony, but never performed. Rautavaara's *Third String Quartet*, Op. 18 (1965), won a first prize in the Camden, England, Composition Competition in 1966. Based on material from the second act of his opera, *Kaivos* (The Mine), it has only a single slow movement. Though he announced work on another pan serialistic work, he soon abandoned it as tedious and unrewarding, with its controlling logic unable to allow for any personal expression. Another work announced in 1964 was an aleatoric symphony, also later abandoned.

In 1964, Rautavaara completed another symphony, titled the Fourth Symphony, in two movements, "Sonata," and "Variazioni." The second movement is based on his earlier 1957 serial work, *Praevariata*, newly orchestrated and with a new inserted variation. In 1965 Rautavaara described his orchestration: "The timbral idea was to divide the orchestra into four 'quartets': four woodwinds, four brass, four percussion...and four groups of strings."[25] Later, the symphony was withdrawn and revised, appearing again in 1969 as "Quarto sinfonia per quattro quartetti." The changes were made to the first movement, which became shorter, had longer melodic lines, and contains temporary tonal centers, evidence of Rautavaara's stylistic shift from serialism to neotonality. When the revised Fourth Symphony was performed in February, 1970, Rautavaara was still not satisfied with it, and eventually discarded it, naming his *Arabescata*, Op. 24 of 1962 as his Fourth Symphony.

In the fall of 1963, Rautavaara began writing concert reviews for the *Ilta Sanomat* (Evening News) newspaper, continuing until the newspaper discontinued reviews in 1967. Rautavaara took a position as the director of the music school in Käpylä, a suburb of Helsinki, in 1965-66, but found the work load enormous. One year was enough to show him that the position was not right for him.

---

[25] Rautavaara, quoted in Sivuoja-Gunaratnam, 104.

CHAPTER FIVE

# NEO-ROMANTICISM, 1967-73

In 1966 Rautavaara began work as a lecturer at the Sibelius Academy, a notch higher than his previous term as instructor of theory, becoming one of the most influential composition teachers of the next generation. From 1971-76 he held the title of Arts Professor, awarded by the Finnish State for a period of five years. This allowed him to take time off from his teaching position, though he took on students in addition in order to pay the rent. A sizable part of his income came from entering, and usually winning, composition competitions, for example, nearly $15,000 in today's values for his opera *Apollo and Marsyas*, about $5,000 for his ballet *Kiuskaukset* (The Temptations), and so on. Working towards the competitions' often simultaneous deadlines caused a considerable amount of stress.

In the late 1960s Rautavaara's work and compositions began to change, some works still serial and atonal, and others free with references to tonality. Some of his best known works date from this period. His 1968 First Cello Concerto with its triadic harmonies and Neo-Romantic style has continued to be an audience favorite. Piano compositions are prominent here: his First Piano Concerto, designed for himself to perform with wide-ranging arpeggios, forearm clusters, and samba-like finale, and the two piano sonatas with religious titles and similar materials. A true post-modern work, *True and False Unicorn*, in 1971 mixes the absurd with the serious, folk idioms, and speech in a wild mix of styles. The next year brought his most famous work, *Cantus Arcticus*, subtitled concerto for birds and orchestra, with one of Rautavaara's earliest use of recorded tape. Already well established as an orchestral composer, Rautavaara then brought out stunning choral works such as the orthodox *Vigils* of 1972 and the 1973 surreal *Lorca Suite* full of imagery and rhythmic intensity, which became internationally much performed and recorded. He ended this period with a unique work, a concerto using four sizes of flutes played by a single performer.

In the 1970s the composer wrote an article in which he spoke of serialism in a very negative way, showing his definite move away from this style into that of the next few years, a new style of neotonality, a new romanticism, and a new organic growth technique:

> He equated Arnold Schoenberg with 'structural police,' Anton Webern with 'structural Gestapo,' and Darmstadt with Buchenwald"... "where

a composer was obliged to undergo masochistic exercises (for instance under a death threat to avoid all pleasing harmonies), to persecute in an authentic, witch-hunting manner the incubus of tonality from the corner of his dodecaphonic bed, and furthermore to get involved with mathematics (of which he understood nothing), to make doctoral dissertations about his own compositions (which nobody understood), and to write 'analyses' and 'explanations' about them. Thereafter the composition itself was unnecessary, and furthermore, a disappointment."[1]

In the 1960s, several moves had taken Rautavaara and his family from one dwelling to another, always bigger, thinking that this might be the cure for the various family stresses, some of them horrific. Despite all the marital unrest and a teenage step-daughter who temporarily ran away from home, the couple remained together and a second son, Olof, was born in 1968. In the beginning of the 1970s, marital problems came to such a point that Rautavaara moved from the family home into a place of his own more agreeable in the Westend area of Helsinki.

For Finland's 50th anniversary of her independence in 1917 from Russia, Rautavaara composed the prize-winning entry in the Independence Cantata Composition with his *Itsenäisyyskantaatti* (Independence Cantata, 1967), Op. 29. The work called for a soloist, a reciter, mixed choir, and orchestra. The soprano soloist for its feted performance in Tampere, Finland, was the composer's wife, Mariaheidi Rautavaara, with a leading operatic baritone Matti Tuloisela, and famed movie and TV actor Veikko Sinisalo as narrator. A large combined orchestra and combined choruses were also assembled for the event. The Finnish texts in the fourteen movements are based on the writings of Paavo Haavikko (1931-2008), one of Finland's most outstanding writers, V. A. Koskenniemi (1885-1962), poet and critic, and from the speeches of historical figures at the time of the independence. The music shows Rautavaara moving toward a kind of free tonality. Besides his expressive thematic material, sprechchor techniques, and limited use of aleatory, there is a new interest in choral clusters or "field" technique.

In 1968 Rautavaara began the first of his twelve concertos for a soloist and orchestra. The *Cello Concerto*, Op. 41 (1968), was composed for Erkki Rautio. At the first rehearsal it was apparent that the orchestra drowned out the soloist at the beginning. Knowing that something needed to be altered, Rautavaara was stumped, until the soloist suggested dropping out the orchestra altogether, giving the soloist that passage. In this way Rautavaara learned the demands

---

[1] Sivuoja-Gunaratnam, 109, quote of Einojuhani Rautavaara, "Aikamme musiikki" (Our Music Today), *Uuden Suomen Uutisraportti* (New Finnish News Report), Vol. 4 (April 11-12, 1970).

of the solo concerto genre, and of the necessity to keep the soloist in the foreground. The first of three movements opens with the solo cello passage introducing the dramatic main theme in double stops, implying tonal areas. An intensely beautiful Largo follows. The third movement is a dance-like Vivace with a cello cadenza, ending with a codetta where the cello and flute exchange segments, dying away. The work has an overall Neo-Romantic style with its homophonic texture with references to tonality.[2]

In the orchestral work *Anadyomene (Adoration of Aphrodite)* (1968) Rautavaara intended to write a serial work using the letters HCE (B natural-C-E), letters used prominently throughout James Joyce's *Finnigan's Wake*. During the course of composition, the music refused to stay confined to the row and became organic, with soft harmonies, usually without tonal connotations. It contains rapid alternation and superimposition of two lines in symmetrical polyphony, and some tonal melodic figures. Rautavaara described how the Joyce work opens with the descriptive sentence "riverrun, past Eve and Adam's, from swerve of shore to bend of bay, brings us by a commodius vicus of recirculation back to Howth Castle and Environs." The music begins with strings quietly flowing, using the serial row, altered to include note repetitions, in original and retrograde, a musical recirculation. Many murmuring layers join together and constantly recycle. The entrance of the bassoons brings a disguised reference to H-C-E, followed a few measures later by trumpets intoning E-B-E, A-D, A-D-A-B-Es, musically representing "Eve and Adam's." In his book, Joyce later writes "Sir Tristram, violer d'amores, fr'over the short sea." This is musically translated by Rautavaara into the opening motifs of Wagner's "Tristan and Isolde," well hidden as a compositional joke.

Despite Rautavaara's original intentions, the music then evolved away from serialism and from literary connection into a freely structured sea portrait reminiscent of the works of Debussy (Example Fourteen, *Anodyomene*, page 55). The subtitle, *The Adoration of Aphrodite*, according to Rautavaara, probably came from his fleeting interest in studying Greek, in order to read Homer's *Odysseus* in its original language.[3] In the Greek legend of Aphrodite, as depicted by the Renaissance Italian painter Botticelli, Aphrodite arose from the sea, arriving on a sea shell.

Though Rautavaara wrote a piano concerto in 1955 during his student years which won a third prize in the Suomen Kultturi (Finnish Culture) composition competition, he later withdrew it. His next piano concerto composed in 1969 became known as Piano Concerto No. 1. Written for himself as soloist, he took

---

[2] Rautavaara, *Omakuva*, 250-1.

[3] Rautavaara, *Omakuva*, 222-225.

**Example Fourteen:** *Anadyomene (Adoration of Aphrodite)* (1968). The concept of flowing waters recirculating and letter pitches for motifs originally came from James Joyce's *Finnegan's Wake,* but then turned into a Debussy-like sea portrait. Layers of strings in a pattern of half steps and thirds, and, later, harp arpeggios and bird calls from flute evoke foaming waves and the arrival of Aphrodite from the sea, conveyed on a shell. ©Fennica Gehrman Oy, Helsinki. Printed with permission.

**Example Fifteen:** Piano Concerto No. 1 (1969), I. Con grandezza. Written for his own abilities as a pianist, the concerto opens with loud tone clusters played with the flat of the right hand along with wide-ranging arppegios as accompaniment. The slow movement has superimposed triads for its hymn-like theme, and the finale's perpetual motion in 3+2+3 has been called "samba-like." ©1972/2000 by Breitkopf & Härtel, Wiesbaden.

it on tour around Finland. The concerto returns to a sweeping Romantic style with wide-ranging arpeggios from top to bottom of the piano's register, as well as expressive melodies. At the same time, however, it includes smashing clusters of dissonances and decidedly unromantic vertical sonorities. The opening movement, Con grandezza, opens with diatonic tone clusters done with the flat of the hand, which, in the recapitulation become forearm clusters. Harmonies consist of triads and polyharmonies (Example Fifteen, Piano Concert No. 1, p. 57). The Andante slow movement intersperses its chorale-like phrases with rippling arpeggios. The strings eventually take over the chorale-like lead, while the piano grows ever more agitated, performing a dissonant cadenza leading to the samba-like finale, Molto Vivace. The 3+2+3 rhythms were termed by critics as Gershwin material.

NEOROMANTICISM 1967-1973

**Example Sixteen:** Piano Sonata No. 1, "Christ and the Fishermen" (1969). I, II, and III. Inspired by a framed picture of Christ calling the fishermen, the work opens with a series of step wise descending ninth chords made of two superimposed fifths. The accompaniment is a series of ascending fifths, establishing a B flat tonality. Though mostly quiet, the movement ends in huge forearm clusters, with a final E flat chord of harmonics remaining after the pedal is released. The faster second movement in a meter of 3+2+3 also ends in a tone cluster with remaining E flat harmonics. The slow finale chorale is created from unrelated triadic chords, recalls the opening movement, and ends on a G minor chord. ©Fennica Gehrman Oy, Helsinki. Printed with permission.

The piano sonata *Christ and the Fishermen* (1969) was inspired by a nineteenth century painting of E. Zimmerman, simply showing the figures against a lake landscape. The print hung on the wall above Rautavaara's piano at his summer villa on the Baltic Sea. "Perhaps the devout atmosphere of the print and the sound of the sea translated into the heavy rhythm of the opening."[4] The three movements of this sonata feature wide spaced intervals of ninths for one hand, rapid arpeggiation, tone clusters using the flat of the hand or the whole forearm, overtone harmonics, unusual meters such as 13/8 in the second movement (actually 3+2+3+2+3), and a free non-tonal use of triads, often superimposed (Piano Sonata No. 1, page 56). One can easily imagine a connected story. The first movement might depict the gentle speaking and calling of Jesus with some following measures of answering quiet awe of the fishermen, ending with the animated commitment of the new disciples. The second movement is dance-like, implying the joy of being with Jesus, and the final movement is a slow chorale, the confession of their faith.

*The Fire Sermon*, sonata no. 2, op. 64 (1969), written the same year as the first piano sonata, is also in three movements. The title comes from a section of T. S. Eliot's *The Wasteland*. "The magic words, *Fire Sermon*, in English, stuck in my mind, repeating themselves like a mantra. There is no conscious link, however, with T. S. Eliot's poem of the same name or Buddha's famous sermon."[5] The themes of the sonata often have modal contours, as do the harmonies, using a scale with alternating major and minor seconds. The writing for the keyboard is very pianistic, with arpeggios, octaves, rapid scales, clusters, echo effects, and harmonics. The first movement opens with sharply rhythmic marcato motifs describing the fire, at times flaring up. The rhythm is established in an 8/8 meter in 3+2+3 pattern, as seen earlier in the first piano sonata's similar pattern in the second movement, though extended there to 3+2+3+2+3. A slower lyrical theme above all the accompanying activity reaches its frenzied climax combined with scale passages in the right hand made up of alternating major and minor seconds. At the end of the movement, a slow chorale theme is proclaimed four times in slow and dramatic chords, beginning low in the bass and repeating each time in a higher octave register.

In the second movement, Andante assai, a calm and simple melody alternates with a gloomy more aggressive theme. It reaches a climax in clusters, and dies away restating the opening melody.

---

[4] Einojuhani Rautavaara, Liner notes to *Einojuhani Rautavaara: Works for Piano*, Naxos CD DDD 8.554292.
[5] Rautavaara, *Omakuva*, 225.

The third movement, Allegro brutale, begins in the bass with a spiky fugato, reiterates the subjects of the first movement, and ends fortissimo with a series of slow chords, with a final D major chord of harmonics remaining from the last big cluster. "The mysticism and devotion of the *First Sonata* have here given way to pessimism, to a repeated and frustrating struggle."[6]

The ballet *Kiusaukset* (The Temptations, 1969), on a libretto by the composer, was composed for a composition contest for a one-act ballet sponsored by the Finnish National Ballet and won first prize. Based on the three temptations of Jesus in the wilderness, the work caused some controversy and criticism before the first performance, all because Jesus danced. One reviewer called it blasphemy. Rautavaara replied in the press that "if this [The Temptations] is offensive, that sacred persons and happenings are depicted in choreography, then for consistency one must ban such representations in theater, art, and in music expression, as the Calvinists have done."[7] Later reviews found the portrayal of Jesus very convincing. The ballet received its first performance in 1973 at the Finnish National Opera. The main characters were that of Jesus and a snake-like Satan, with the corps de ballet fulfilling other varied needs. Rautavaara found this project difficult, sometimes even embarrassing, since it depended on pantomime without any narration.[8] The orchestral music used various ideas from his piano *Etydit* (Etudes) composed the same year.

A second set of pieces for speaking choir was requested by a choral group in 1969. *Praktisch Deutsch* (Practical German) (1969) takes its texts from a German conversational dictionary. Each of the pieces, "The Hotel," "Shopping," "At the Tailor," and "At a party," illustrate samples of sentences useful in these situations but without any story line. The disjunction of isolated sentences and repetitions of words or syllables without any logical purpose create a bizarre atmosphere. Vocal techniques include combining the varied sounds of female voices alternating with male voices, sliding indefinite pitches unconnected to normal intonation patterns versus repetition of the same pitch, and speech reduced to whispers. The effect is somewhat tied to reality in the final piece, "At the party," where one could easily imagine the sound effect of several dozen people speaking at once with isolated snippets of meanings overheard. In listening to this set of pieces, one needs to overcome the urge to find meaning in the connection of sentences and accept the whole as a presentation of sliding intonations, percussive consonants, hissing sibilants, contrasting timbres, and fascinating rhythms.

---

[6] Rautavaara, *Omakuva*, 225.
[7] Tiikkaja, 344.
[8] Rautavaara, *Omakuva*, 246.

The comic opera/musical *Apollo contra Marsyas* (1970) on a libretto by Swedish author Bengt V. Wall, combines different stylistic elements, using jazz for satirical purposes. This three act opera won the first prize in a composition contest of the Finnish National Opera. The first performance was mounted on August 30, 1973, at the Finnish National Opera.

In the ancient Greek story Marsyas played the pipes, an aulos, a single or double piped instrument with an internal double reed similar to a bagpipe. The aulos was loud and harsh, used for martial and athletic events, and often caused the player to have puffed cheeks from the effort to play. Apollo played the more sedate lyre. According to the Greek myth, Marsyas challenged Apollo to a competition, with the winner allowed to do whatever he liked to the loser. For the opera story, there is a prologue with a professor explaining the story in a pedantic style, giving Rautavaara a chance to poke fun at music critics. A side plot includes the myth of Daphne, as Apollo's hanger-on girlfriend who likes the expensive lifestyle. Rautavaara's opera has three acts, the first and last set in antiquity and the second brought into the present day. The first and third acts follow the ancient myth with Marsyas losing and being flayed alive and Daphne fleeing, turning into the wood of river reed. In the second act, Apollo is a pop singer of refined standards and Marsyas the managing director of Mass Production Ltd., a conflict of music styles or music cultures. Business manager Marsyas wins out by the fact that Apollo is killed in an auto accident of rather obvious origin.

Rautavaara described in his autobiography how a teenage classmate who could improvise jazz always gathered a crowd of admirers, while Rautavaara had only his own compositions to offer, nowhere near as enticing to his peers. The contrast and opposition of the two musical styles was not only something he had experienced personally but was the topic for wider discussion in the music world. The same competition in which this opera won also offered prizes for the categories of light music and organ music. For submission to the light music prize, Rautavaara took excerpts from the second act and combined them into a prize-winning suite called *Helsinki Dancing*, later withdrawn. He demonstrated that he could indeed write light music, if necessary. A third submission, not a prize winner, went to the organ category with his *Toccata* in a somewhat Baroque style. Besides these three entries, Rautavaara had several other compositions underway and was on tour with his first piano concerto. That the two separate stories of *Apollo*, with two different outcomes, do not quite add up to a logical whole may have been due to haste to meet deadlines.[9]

In 1970, Rautavaara received a commission for a cantata from a Danish

---

[9] Rautavaara, *Omakuva*, 244.

chamber choir, the Holstebro Musikhøjskolen. The result was a work in twenty movements, *True and False Unicorn,* Op. 58 (1971). The cantata is scored for three reciters, chamber chorus, orchestra, and tape (the first version of 1971 used piano, tape, and string quartet for instruments, and was revised in 2000, omitting the tape). A postmodern work before postmodernism was declared a style, the music includes references to jazz, swing from American musicals, a collage of national anthems from various countries, Sprechstimme, and, in the original version, use of taped music for the interludes.

The text was based on poems by James Broughton (1913-1999), an American poet and filmmaker. A forerunner of the "beat generation," Broughton's poem focuses on the identity of the artist, as others see him and as he views himself. The unicorn subject matter, although described in antiquity, is best known today from the series of seven Renaissance unicorn tapestries, *The Hunt of the Unicorn,* displayed at the Cloisters, a part of the New York Metropolitan Museum. The colorful tapestries depict the progress of the hunt by richly clad nobility, the hounds, the death and reincarnation of the unicorn, and the taming by the maiden. A mythical symbol of purity, the unicorn could do miraculous things, neutralize poisons with its horn, and could only be tamed by a pure maiden. During medieval times the myth was often combined with an incarnation of Jesus and the Virgin Mary. Broughton's poems were titled *A Tapestry of Voices,* representing the views of some of the characters represented in the actual tapestries, as well as the unicorn, symbol of the two sides of an artist, his fame and creativity and his personal, often lonely, vulnerability.

The characters and the mythical animals in the Renaissance tapestry speak one by one about the unicorn, which represents the artist. The "Lion," often the unicorn's companion in heraldry, speaks of the unicorn as an indestructible defender through the singing of the chorus. "Sigmund of Vienna" is a spoken Sprechstimme part and a hunter of the unicorn. "The Empress of Byzantine" is a low-pitched female Sprechstimme role demanding the horn be brought to her. "Queen Victoria" wishes to gain control of the unicorn's behavior with promises of treats; the music has the chorus singing trivial words, "O Pretty Pony, naughty pet," to the tune of God Save the Queen, with interjections of the French, Austrian, and American national anthems. "His Honor the Mayor" speaks in Sprechstimme accusing the unicorn of being a highbrow jackass, with a hee-haw from the horns and threat of jail with a siren. In "Big Black Sambo" the chorus sings of a black man in the American south wanting an exceptional racehorse, with musical quotes of "Swing Low, Sweet Chariot." "The Virgin" sings of fear and of luring the unicorn's head to her lap, and later, having tamed him, sings the unicorn a lullaby. "The Unicorn" sings of his inability to understand himself, his seemingly miraculous place in the world but lack of acceptance, and final reconciliation of his fantasy and reality as one being, all a metaphor for the artist and his art as two distinct aspects of one whole. One has only to think of Picasso, the tormentor of several women in his life as opposed to his art, Wagner's antisemitism and his music, or Gesualdo the Renaissance murderer of his wife and her lover and his magnificent madrigals, to understand this concept. Rautavaara often spoke of his own wonder at the works which came from him as though they were already formed, and how he viewed his own role as like that of a midwife. In 1974 the work won the Prix Italia competition in Florence, Italy. In 1986 Rautavaara reset "The Virgin's Lullaby," No. 19, for a female a cappella choir.

An aleatory work for orchestra, *Säännöllisiä yksikköjaksoja puolisäännöllisessä tilanteessa* (Regular Sets of Elements in a Semiregular Situation, 1971), was also called *Garden of Spaces*. It was inspired by the Finnish architect Reima Pietilä's exhibition, entitled *Tilatarha* (Garden of Spaces, 1971) and also dedicated to the architect. Pietilä's buildings were designed to fit in structurally and visually with their setting in nature, often using locally available granite and types of wood. Rautavaara's musical interpretation of this concept is similar to the last aleatoric movement in his *Arabescata*, Symphony No. 4.

> The work comprises regular (precisely notated) sections played by different groups of instruments (elements) set into motion by the conductor at different times freely chosen during the performance. They may be played consecutively, simultaneously or staggered as they overlap.[10] However, an instrumental group must maintain its own numeric order of entries.[11]

Scored originally for a 17-player orchestra divided into five groups and in 2003 revised for a full orchestra, the work combines Neoromantic sound with variable form. It was first performed and conducted by the composer in 1972 at a concert of his own works in a concert series called "Conducting Composers." Arranged by the Finnish Broadcasting Company (YLE), the other composers involved were Leonid Bashmakov (1923-2016), Usko Meriläinen (1931-2004), Aulis Sallinen (b. 1935), and Jarmo Sermilä (b. 1939). At the time, Rautavaara was aware of his own limited conducting skills, thinking the aleatoric format would be easier for himself to conduct. It has been recorded as "Garden of Spaces" by the Helsinki Philharmonic for Ondine label, which, of course, is only one possible version, using the choices of conductor Leif Segerstam. This is Rautavaara's most important contribution to aleatoric form, his other, to that date being his *Arabescata*, fourth movement, of 1962.

The setting of the Vigils service of the Orthodox church, *Vigilia* (All-

---

[10] Rautavaara, liner notes, Onine: ODE867-2, 1995.

[11] Rautavaara, note on the score of the work.

Night Vigil, 1971-72), was jointly commissioned by the Helsinki Festival and the Orthodox Church of Finland. Seppo Nummi (1932-1981), a music journalist, composer, and long time director of the Helsinki Festival, mentioned to Rautavaara that he wanted three Masses of three different faiths for the next festival. He had already arranged for the Lutheran Mass to be done by Bengt Johansson (1914-1989) and the Catholic Mass by Erik Bergman (1911-2006). On hearing that the Orthodox Mass was still not assigned, Rautavaara volunteered, enthusiastically.[12] The premiere of *All-Night Vigils* took place at divine service in the red brick Uspenski Cathedral in central Helsinki, the Evening Service in 1971 and the Morning Service in 1972. The concert version of 1997 is an independent work later adapted from the original.

The *All-Night Vigil* stems from a childhood visit to the island monastery of Valamo in the middle of Lake Ladoga, in the southeast of Finland, just before the Winter War with Russia in 1939; after that war Valamo no longer belonged to Finland. Rautavaara has described this visit with his family at about age 10 as connected with a story about the monks he had been reading at that time. They approached the island by boat in fog and the colorful domes and towers gradually emerged, as though still in his story. The buildings, the bells, the icons, and the bearded monks all combined into an exotic locale. Some of these impressions went into the composition of his earlier *Icons* for piano, and others into the *All Night Vigil*. Another contributing experience was the Eisenstein 1945 movie *Ivan the Terrible* that Rautavaara saw several times while studying in New York City. The coronation scene with the low bass chanting of the Orthodox priests in the glittering golden church made a deep impression.

In preparing for this composition, Rautavaara familiarized himself with the Finnish Orthodox Church and its music. Separated from the Russian Orthodox Church at the time of Finland's 1917 independence, it uses the Finnish language for its services but keeps the 18$^{th}$ century Russian style of chant, using very simple chordal a cappella settings. The original Byzantine chant brought to Russia with Christian missionaries about the ninth or tenth century had been monophonic, used glissandos, and kept to the Byzantine modes, the Oktoechoes, rather than the Western Gregorian chant modes. In the early 18$^{th}$ century Peter the Great pressured the church to change to western harmonies, under the influence of Italian musicians like Galuppi at his court in the newly constructed St. Petersburg capital city. Later Russian composers in the 19$^{th}$ century like Glinka wanted a switch to Western modes and Romantic chromaticism. Despite the compositions of Tschaikovsky and Rachmaninoff, most services were still sung in the older

---

[12] Tiikkaja, 319.

St. Petersburg style. Rautavaara chose to put aside the old St. Petersburg style to take elements from the Byzantine chant and his own modern compositional vocabulary. Particularly of interest to him were the Oktoechoes modes, with some scale steps smaller than a half step, some larger than a whole step. These offered microtones to add to his musical vocabulary.

His completed Vigils for the feast of John the Baptist set the entire liturgy, suitable for use in the service, with both Vespers and Matins running about three hours. Since the work was too long for the Helsinki festival purpose, only the Vespers was performed in 1971, with the Matins reserved for the feast day in 1972. For practical performance purposes, in 1997 Rautavaara deleted many of the chants, reset portions to lower the soprano parts a whole step, and created about an hour long concert version with 32 sections, taking the best parts of both Vespers and Matins.

The *Vigilia* calls for changes in choral and solo settings. Among the various solos and duets, the basso profundo solos near the opening stand out, evoking the sound world of the deep Russian basses. At one point there is a long sustained low B flat for the basses in the choir. The varied choral techniques include archaic chant, speaking, whispering, clusters, micro intervals, parallel intervals, and glissandi, this last a traditional part of the earliest Orthodox liturgy. A variation structure holds the whole work together, mostly through repetition of the text (Example Seventeen, *Vigilia*, pp. 65-66). The liturgy is that of the Festival of the Beheading of St. John the Baptist, and includes mention of the Virgin, the Mother of God, and a panoply of saints.[13]

*Cantus Arcticus* (1972), a concerto for birds (recorded on tape), and orchestra, was commissioned by the University of Oulu, in Finland's northwest, for its first degree-granting ceremony. Rautavaara felt uninspired by the request for the usual vocal cantata and filled the commission with an "arctic" work for the university so close to the Arctic Circle. The work is in three movements: "The Bog," "Melancholy," and "Swans Migrating." He collected the sounds of marsh birds himself near Oulu, and added swan sounds, sometimes altering the sounds electronically in what he referred to as "creative ornithology."[14] In the second movement the recorded tape slows down the actual bird sounds, lowering their pitch. The third movement, "Swans Migrating," creates the sounds of many swans by overdubbing the recorded tape, multiplying the birdcalls. He then combined the birdsong, aleatory counterpoint from the orchestra imitating with their own crane-like sounds, archaic modal melodies in simple orchestral texture, and mediant triad harmonies, triads moving a third away, rather than in the usual functional harmonic progressions. Many rapid scales accompany simple step-

---

[13] Einojuhani Rautavaara, Liner notes to *Vigilia*, Ondine ODE 910-2 (1998).
[14] Rautavaara, *Omakuva*, 259.

**Example Seventeen**: *Vigilia* (1972), No. 1 Avuksihuutopsalmi (Psalm of Invocation), No. 2 Ehtoohymni (Evening Hymn). The All-Night Vigil for the Orthodox Feast Day of St. John the Baptist displays a wondrous variety of vocal and choral techniques, including microtones from the original Byzantine chant, basso profundo low range, choral glissandos, whispering, clusters built by adding voices. Note the opening polyphony and the choral glissando in the first piece, and in the second, the low B flats for the basses. ©Fennica Gehrman Oy, Helsinki. Printed with permission.

Example Seventeen, page 2

wise melodies, using the octotonic scale, an eight note scale with alternating whole and half steps.

Beginning in the 1970s, the use of electronic instruments and prerecorded taped sounds became one of the latest musical trends. At the time, though, recorded sounds of animals in musical compositions was a rarity. Many earlier works had only invoked the sounds of animals and birds through use of the instruments, such as in Saint-Saëns's 1886 *Carnival of Animals*. Respighi's 1924 *Pines of Rome* requires a brief recording of a nightingale at the end of the third movement. Alan Hovhaness includes recordings of whales in his *And God Created Great Whales* of 1970, but the whales' song and orchestral parts are mostly separate elements, not combined. In the next twenty years, Rautavaara was also intrigued by the possible resource of added recordings to his compositions, producing nearly a dozen works either entirely of electronic sounds or as added extensions to an orchestra. Rautavaara had already used taped electronic instruments in his 1971 *True and False Unicorn*.

Although Rautavaara didn't attend the first performance at the University Hall in Oulu, Finland, afterwards he received a short letter of praise from then Finnish President Urho Kekkonen, an avid outdoorsman and former Olympic skier, who recognized the bird sounds as authentic. In 1983, when Rautavaara was awarded an honorary doctorate in natural sciences from the University of Oulu for giving the northern regions such worldwide recognition, he commented that his school science teacher would have been quite surprised.[15]

The title of *Canto III "A Portrait of the Artist at a Certain Moment"* (1972) for strings makes reference to James Joyce's "A Portrait of the Artist as a Young Man." Rautavaara wanted to suggest an attempt to find a way amid the multitude of styles he had been using to that time. It is a ten minute work in one movement with a growing density and a building crescendo.[16] The work opens with a theme in mirror image between upper strings harmonized in parallel triads and lower strings in a single line opposition to the top most melody. This opening symmetry turns to canonic entrances, grows with a new motive sequentially through ever higher pitches, is interrupted by a rhythmic growling section for the basses, then climbs melodically with the main theme to the end. Although scored for a similar string orchestra and bearing the same title as his Canto I and Canto II, this work bears no musical relationship to the earlier two, which are based on material from his opera, *Kaivos* (The Mine, 1957-58, 1960/1963).

*Elämän kirja* (Book of Life, 1972), for a cappella male chorus, has eleven

---

[15] Rautavaara, *Omakuva*, 262.

[16] Einojuhani Rautavaara, Liner notes to *Complete Works for String Orchestra, Vol. 2*, Ondine CD ODE 836-2 (1993).

**Example Eighteen**: *Lorca Suite* (1973), IV. "Malaguena." Based on poems by Federico Garcia Lorca, the last song for a children's chorus has the sounds of a stamping Spanish dance, but the words tell of Death going in and out of the tavern. ©Fennica Gehrman Oy, Helsinki. Printed with permission

movements and is in five different languages. Dedicated to the University of Helsinki's Ylioppilaskunnan Laulajat male choir, each movement's text comes from a different poet, including Rilke, Rimbaud, Goethe, Dickenson, Whitman, and others. The overall theme is the progression of human life from childhood to old age. Rautavaara undoubtedly identified with all of the texts, from Rilke's "Kindheit," (Childhood), "School is an unending torment," to Rimbaud's "Ma bohème" "I walk, my hands in my tattered pockets," to the one he chose as his own funeral song with text by Dag Hammerskjöld, "Sa var det" (So was it), "I am driven further into an unknown land...I shall arrive where life's bell falls silent, a clear simple tone in the silence."

In 1973 the Tapiola Children's Choir and the Helsinki suburb city of Espoo offered a composition prize. Of the many children's choruses in Finland, the Tapiola group is outstanding, not only for its recordings, international tours, and commissioned contemporary works, but for the fact that the children also study instruments and provide their own chamber orchestra when needed. Rautavaara's first prize entry was the *Lapsimessu* (Children's Mass), based on the Latin mass text. Rather than the usual five movements of the Mass Ordinary, the sequence of the movements includes "Kyrie," "Meditatio super Kyrie" for orchestra, "Gloria," "Meditatio super Gloria" for orchestra, "Agnus Dei," "Meditatio super Agnum" for orchestra, and a concluding "Halleluja" for both chorus and orchestra. The movements alternate the three part a cappella sung text with an instrumental meditation, and the work concludes with the two performing units combined in the "Halleluja" choir accompanied by the orchestra. The three instrumental movements can also be performed as "Three Meditations for Orchestra." The texture of the three vocal parts is often homophonic and tonal, or in a transparently simple polyphony. The lively "Gloria" adds a solo descant above the choir in a middle section.

Of those works written for children's chorus, the *Lorca Suite* (1973), a set of four Spanish-influenced songs for mixed choir or children's choir on texts by Federico Garcia Lorca, is the most widely performed piece of Finnish choral music outside Finland. Rautavaara's comments on these songs stress their imagery and rhythmic power, as well as earthiness and mystery. In "The Rider's Song," the ostinato of the rhythm underlines the image of the solitary horse rider at night with death staring down. "The Scream" tells of a mysterious night scream in the hills, conveyed musically by a vocal glissando. "The Moon Peeps Out" is still and eerie, conveying iciness and isolation through a Phrygian scale. The last song, "Dance from Malaga," has the excitement of a guitar accompanied dance, with the stamping accents, but it is Death who goes in and out of the tavern (Example Eighteen, *Lorca Suite*, p. 68).[17] Written about the same time as the *Lapsimessu* (Children's Mass), which won first prize in the Espoo city composition competition, the *Lorca Suite,* which won only a third prize, became far more well known. Rautavaara was surprised at the international success of this set, saying that he received programs listing it from Japan, Israel, Cuba, Macedonia, and that it had been recorded four or five times by 1985.[18]

*Tuulten tansseja* (Dances of the Winds, 1973), a concerto for flute and orchestra, calls for four different sizes of flutes. At times, a single movement calls for changing from one size to another, a daunting task for a flute player, requiring a quick adaptation of the mouth's embouchere. The work was commissioned by and composed for a specific flautist in mind, the Swedish performer Gunilla von Bahr. The first movement calls for a standard flute and then a bass flute. The orchestra often opposes the flute, alternating angry responses to the opening melodic flights of the flute, and in the second theme area, brings in an important chorale in the low brass as a countermelody to the musings of the flute. The second movement, a scherzo, requires a piccolo, invoking the medieval fair's dancing bear. Its drum and piccolo folk music, a variation on the first movement's chorale theme, then depict a chaotic crowd, a lumbering bear and taunts of "raspberries" from the excited people. The third slow movement asks for an alto flute. Its steady paced theme winds and turns back on itself in a narrow range, at times varying bits of the chorale theme. A four note "fate" motive from the orchestra adds to the melancholy. The finale features the bass flute, brings in elements from previous movements, offers a bass flute cadenza and ends, fading away, with a coda for the standard flute.

---

[17] Einojuhani Rautavaara, Liner notes to *Works for Mixed Chorus,* Ondine CD ODE 851-2.
[18] Rautavaara, *Omakuva*, 261.

CHAPTER SIX

# THE KALEVALA AND ANGEL WORKS, 1974-80

During the mid and late 1970s Rautavaara began a series of three operas on the pagan pre-Christian era of the Kalevala folk epic. An orchestral series came about through a commission for three orchestral works for the Finnish Radio Symphony Orchestra, which Rautavaara planned as an overture, concerto, and a symphony. The last part was completed in 1994 and all became known as his "Angel" works. In between these large-scale works he also found time and energy to produce two other concertos, one for organ, and one for violin. Though all of these works stayed within the same combination of serialism and free tonality, the subjects ranged widely, from the terrifying added taped sounds in *The Abduction of the Sampo* opera to the innocence of the *Marjatta* legend of the virgin birth in a stable-converted sauna, to the nightmarish *Matka* (Journey) song cycle, to the *Angels and Visitations* overture incorporating a human scream. Rautavaara produced in these six years what another composer would be content to have accomplished in a lifetime. By the end of the 1970s, the number of his compositions had grown to such an extent that Rautavaara stopped assigning opus numbers. In addition to all these completed compositions, from 1976 to 1988 Rautavaara was again a professor of composition, succeeding Erik Bergman as Professor.

The 1970s was a period of opera boom in Finland with the spectacular success of Joonas Kokkonen's *Viimeiset Kiusaukset* (The Last Temptations, 1975), premiered at the Finnish National Opera in Helsinki and performed more than three hundred times in Finland and abroad. This opera on the life of an early nineteenth century Pietist lay preacher, Paavo Ruotsalainen, and his reflections on his deathbed attracted busloads of rural people to see this drama about a church-related figure. In doing so, it introduced a whole new audience to opera and a flood of new operas to satisfy them. About the same time composer Aulis Sallinen won a 1972 opera competition at the Savonlinna Opera Festival with his *Ratsumies* (The Horseman, 1974), produced in 1975, his first attempt at an opera, followed soon by *Punainen viiva* (The Red Line, 1978). Both dealt with the subject of rural Finns tragically caught up in historical events beyond their control.

Paavo Ruotsalainen, the main character of Kokkonen's opera, had traveled widely through Finland, trying to bring a more personal relationship with God than was advocated by the conservative Lutheran state church. In doing so, he ignored the needs of his family, even taking the children's last bread on one occasion. On his deathbed, he worries whether he was right or wrong, and if the gates of heaven will be opened for him. The horseman of Sallinen's opera is a slave forced to fight in a war between Russia and Sweden and tells of his relationship with the woman he loves. In Sallinen's next opera, the red line was the mark of an illiterate first time voter in 1907 who could not read nor write his own name, who speculates on using blood from his finger to make an X for lack of pens or ink. The opera ends with another red line, a bear's gash across the neck of the main character. Both operas were freely tonal and melodic. Kokkonen's was organized in scenes, like a number opera but without arias. Both motives and the important hymn of Paavo are woven throughout. Sallinen's opera is near symphonic in its motivic development, with an important orchestral role. Both this opera of Sallinen's and Kokkonen's *Last Temptations* were taken on numerous tours abroad from 1979 to 1983, including to New York's Metropolitan Opera with the original cast, conductor, and production.[1]

Rautavaara also began work on a nationalistic work in 1972, beginning a trilogy of operas based on the Kalevala epic. *Runo 42: Sammon ryöstö* (Poem 42: The Abduction of the Sampo, 1974, rev. 1981), a dramatic work for soloists, male chorus, and prerecorded tape giving a description of Finland around the year 800 A.D., was the first. Next came *Marjatta, matala neiti* (Marjatta, the Lowly Maiden, 1975), on the Kalevala's folk interpretation of the Virgin Mary, for three soloists, children's choir, small ensemble and prominent flute. A decade later came *Thomas* (1985), the first medieval bishop of Finland who led a failed crusade against Novgorod.

In its 1974 version *Runo 42* was a work for soloists, three pianos with one of them "prepared," and percussion. Though it was scheduled to be performed at the Helsinki Festival in 1976, Rautavaara was still not satisfied with it and withdrew it. In 1981 Rautavaara received a commission from the YL (University Singers) male chorus for its 100th anniversary. The opera was greatly revised and retitled *Sammon ryöstö* (The Abduction of the Sampo), changed into a choral opera in one act, for four soloists, male chorus, synthesizer, and recorded tape. Rautavaara had already done some work with tapes and electronic manipulation of sound in his works *True and False Unicorn* (1971) and in *Cantus Arcticus* (1972). In 1981 he also had a student enthusiastic about electronic music, so chose to go to the Finnish Broadcasting experimental studios and work there.

Rautavaara's libretto is based on Runo 42, a tale in the Kalevala. The three Kalevala heroes, Väinämöinen, Lemminkäinen, and Ilmarinen, set out for

---

[1] Pekka Hako, *Finnish Opera* (Helsinki: Finnish Music Information Centre, 2002), 111-107.

Pohjola, the North Farm, to win back the magic mill, the Sampo, stolen by Louhi, the mistress of Pohjola. This magical machine created by Ilmarinen, the smith, can grind out grain, salt, and coins. Arriving at the gruesome North Farm surrounded by pikes displaying severed human heads, the three heroes charm the inhabitants to sleep with song. With the help of a strong bull, they steal the Sampo and flee by sea. Louhi pursues them at first with an armada of ships, but Väinämöinen magically summons up a sandbar to wreck and stop her ships. Louhi then turns herself into an eagle, and smashes their ship with her terrible energy. The Sampo is then lost in the sea.

Rautavaara added both a prologue and epilogue, musing on the parallelisms of the quests of men in both ancient and modern times. "The shards of broken dreams are buried and give birth to dreams once more."[2]

Though the work has four vocal soloists, the three heroes and Louhi, the chorus predominates in a variety of roles, helping both to tell the story and to create atmosphere. The live voices have mostly traditional styles of tonal and modal melody and harmony, with canons, and tone clusters. The tape has spoken narrative with Rautavaara's own electronically altered voice, various sound effects, distorted voices, and whisperings, and is used as an accompaniment. Most striking is the truly terrifying distorted sounds of the sorceress Louhi, a primitivism produced by modern technology.

*Marjatta Matalan Neiti* (Marjatta, the Lowly Maiden, 1975) is a mystery play or opera in one act for children's chorus, four soloists, a small instrumental group with a solo flute, plus narrator. The libretto was written by Rautavaara after the Kalevala tale. Commissioned by the city of Espoo for the Tapiola Children's Choir, it is a 22 minute long work, based on the story of Marjatta in Rune 50 of the Kalevala. In this folk version of the Virgin Mary and the birth of the Christ Child, the miraculous conception takes place by eating a lingonberry, and the birth takes place in an old sauna being used as a stable. The musical materials combine old modal scales evoking the sounds of Finnish folk music or hymns, newly invented scales, aleatoric elements in the flute part, and speaking choir effects, where, for example, the children baa like sheep or hiss, to create the warming breath of the horse at the birthplace. The first performance took place on Sept. 3, 1977, at Tapiola Church, Espoo. Although Rautavaara had promised to conduct the work, he realized after the first rehearsal that a better conductor was needed. That role was taken over by conductor Jussi Tapola. The Tapiola choir performed the work ten times, taking the work on tour through Finland and then abroad. Rautavaara went with them and became the narrator, explaining the Finnish text to the audiences in their native

---

[2] Einojuhani Rautavaara, liner notes to *The Myth of the Sampo*, Ondine ODE 842-2.

language, even going to the extent of reading his narration in a written out phonetic Hungarian.[3] Notable is the fact that the first soprano soloist was Sinikka Koivisto, a twenty-year old, who became Einojuhani's second wife in 1984, at the age of 27.

With the success of Kokkonen's and Sallinen's operas based on rural Finnish topics, plus the two from Rautavaara on Kalevala tales in the 1970s, the next generation of Finnish composers mockingly called these the "fur hat" operas. A younger group of composers formed a coalition to sponsor concerts, seminars, and discussions of contemporary music called Korvat auki (Ears Open) in 1977. The members included Esa-Pekka Salonen, Magnus Lindberg, Eero Hämeenniemi, Kaija Saariaho, Jukka Tiensuu, Tapani Lansiö, Olli Kortekangas, and Jouni Kaipainen, all former students of Paavo Heininen. As postserialists they used an atonal language, complex polyphony, and often a complicated notation. They rejected the rural Finnish opera genre, as well as symphonic traditions, wanting to keep up with international trends. Older Finnish composers were often alienated. Within ten years, the group had all gone their separate ways and had become the new musical establishment. Rautavaara, then 49 and a professor of composition with many successful years as a composer, remained uninvolved.

In 1975, Rautavaara was honored by election to membership in the Royal Swedish Academy of Music. Founded in 1771 by King Gustav III, the Royal Academy promotes the development of music by awarding membership and prizes to leading musicians of the world. Past recipients of honors includes Haydn, the performers Isaac Stern and M. Rostropovich, composers William Walton, Steve Reich, G. Ligeti, Stockhausen, and among other Finns, Joonas Kokkonen, Pacius (actually a German working in Finland in the 19th century), and Selim Palmgren.

The following year, *En dramatisk Scen* (A Dramatic Scene, "Late One Night," 1976), a single act chamber opera, was set to a libretto in Swedish by the composer. Commissioned by the Gothenburg Music School of Sweden, it was rehearsed but deemed too difficult for music students. It was never performed, and later withdrawn by the composer. The plot concerns Järnberg, a Swedish translation of Rautavaara's name, who becomes involved in a political protest through helping a friend, and then fears for himself and his family being

---

[3] Tiikkaja, 374, 425. Rautavaara was fluent in several European languages, as many Finns are through necessity, but he did not speak Hungarian. Scholars claim Hungarian to be closely related to other Uralic languages such as Finnish, Estonian, and some tribal Russian groups, originally from areas near the Ural mountains in Russia. Finns are often puzzled overhearing spoken Hungarian, finding the sounds familiar but not understanding the content. Rautavaara's performance as a narrator in Hungarian may have been reasonably close to being understood by the audience, if only vaguely by the speaker.

controlled by outside forces.[4] In 1970s Finland, Russia and communism were constant actual threats, politically, economically, and also in artistic matters. The characters of the opera included a wife named Maria and a teenaged son named Marko, all of whom really lived at Järnberg/Rautavaara's address in Westend. Rautavaara's marriage was unstable at the time. Perhaps the story was too close to his own, revealing too much. Musically, it was a return to the 12-tone row idiom, with two versions of a row used to distinguish various characters, and also employed a rhythmic row.[5] Neither the school nor Rautavaara were satisfied and the project and its hefty income was dropped.

*Annunciations*, Concerto for Organ (1976), is his most extensive concerto at thirty minutes. It was commissioned by the Stockholm Organ Festival, for a specific instrumentation which they requested. Three groups are opposed, the organ, a brass quintet acting as a concertino group and a symphonic wind orchestra. Though the title word "Annunciation" usually refers to the visit of the angel to the Virgin Mary, the use of the plural here conveys a realm of other mystical events, awesome, perhaps fearful. Rautavaara preferred to remain ambiguous about its programmatic intent, leaving it to the listener's imagination.

The work opens with a building organ cluster, evoking a "creation of the world," or, perhaps, the coming of a vision. The brass group enters with a slow stepwise chorale-type theme, establishing its typical musical role throughout. Flutes have a bird-like response, while the organ stop Zimbelstern with its tiny unpitched bells adds a rapid high sparkle. The groups alternate their motivic contributions. A brief organ cadenza follows, with organ figuration and brass fanfare interjections. Next comes a quiet section with a unique conclusion. The score calls for turning off the organ blower motor while holding down a massive chord. The wind sounds die away irregularly, some pipes sustaining longer than others. Obviously, this is an effect not possible on an electronic organ, since it depends on the actual wind pressure. In the final section, the organ figuration races above the affirmative brass chorale. When the brasses have finished, brief bird motives call from the organ until all have faded. The title, *Annunciations*, conveys the essence of this concerto, implying a mystical awe with the strong warm brass affirmation.

The song cycle *Matka* (Journey, 1977) might be singled out because of the poems written by the composer. Rautavaara provided both the Finnish and English translation of his texts. The texts are: No. 1 "Kuljin matkan aamupuolella yötä" (I took that trip); No. 2 "Mitä on silmäluomiesi taka syntymässä" (What is there?); No. 3 "Kuljen yli kevätlumisien puistikoiden" (I am walking over tiny

---

[4] Pekka Hako, *Finnish Opera*, trans. Jaakko Mäntyjärvi, (Saarijärvi, Finland: Finnish Music Information Centre, 2002), 98.

[5] Tiikkaja, 362.

spots of snow); and No. 4 "Yö on syvä" (Deep is the Night). Regarding these texts and songs, Rautavaara calls them "surreal, nightmarish, and personal," influenced by his return trip to New York City and a nighttime tour of the Bowery, a slum area, with a friend.[6] The words are nightmares, "I took that trip towards an early daybreak, walking holding someone's heart...on a hook..covered with ants...it lasted years and years." The atonal vocal part is accompanied by forearm clusters on the piano, punctuated by individual notes, appropriate for the horror. The second song also has a bizarre text, "What is there arising from behind your eyelids?...wicked fingertips...foam-covered dolphins...for the men to absent-mindedly cast an eye upon when they're drowning, down, down in the sea." The accompaniment is rippling cascades of notes and then striding triads over arm clusters. The third song, "I am walking over tiny spots of snow in springtime parks where gay and merry baby tigers roll and romp...snap at my fingertips; winged organ grinders...fly through my house...humming." The mood has two parts here, fast playful arpeggios accompanying the tigers' romp and a slow meandering piano melody in widely spaced intervals evoking the winged organ grinders. Number four, "Deep is the Night," uses word painting, with very low piano register for "deep," a descending vocal line for "From the top to the bottom," and "we are trying to awake from a dream called life" remains unsettled with the last repetitions of the piano's augmented fourth interval, a half step below the last note of the singer. The suite of songs was first presented by baritone Jorma Hynninen, later to become the lead singer in several of Rautavaara's operas, accompanied by concert pianist Ralf Gothoni.

In 1975, Rautavaara was impressed with the demonic playing of a young Romanian contestant in the Sibelius Violin Competition, Eugen Sarbu, who won the Third Prize. The idea for a violin concerto from Rautavaara was agreeable to both. Sarbu was in Finland attending a master class and was available to try out portions of the music as they were composed, helping Rautavaara with his work process. Completed in 1977, the last bit in New York City, again with Sarbu's help, the *Violin Concerto* was premiered by Sarbu with the Radio Symphony Orchestra of Helsinki during the Helsinki Festival week in August of 1978.

In style, it combines both broad Romantic melodies with virtuosity, light delicate textures with big dissonant climaxes. The concerto falls into two movements, "Tranquillo," and "Energico." A celeste is added to the usual orchestra, and is heard at the very beginning, adding to the ethereal high treble sound.

The first movement opens and closes with a Romantic cantilena which is contrasted with a concertante section of fragments from the soloist and other instrumentalists. The second movement tends to blend scherzo and finale elements. Its cadenza is partly left to the performer. A final display of

---

[6] Einojuhani Rautavaara, liner notes for *Rautavaara Songs,* BIS CD-1141.

virtuosity using a detached bow finishes the work. The recording of the violin concerto with soloist Elmar Oliveira and the Helsinki Philharmonic under Leif Segerstam on the disc *Angels and Visitations* took the Cannes Classical Award in 1998, giving Rautavaara worldwide recognition and admiration.

In 1978 the Finnish Radio Symphony Orchestra commissioned a series of three works from Rautavaara. The first of these was the overture *Angels and Visitations*. Regarding these "angels," Rautavaara tells of his boyhood nightmares and his later identification with the poet Rainer Maria Rilke's angels as figures of holy dread.

> *Angels and Visitations* (1978) is the first work in my "Angel Series." [*Angels and Visitations* 1978, an overture; *Angel of Dusk, Concerto for Double Bass* 1980, and *Symphony No. 7, Angel of Light*, 1994]. The first impetus for *Angels and Visitations* came when I read Rilke's verses "es nähme einer mich plötzlich ans Herz: ich verginge von seinem stärkeren Dasein" ("... should one suddenly press me to his heart: I would perish by his more powerful presence..."). A recollection surfaced in my mind, a vision that had troubled my dreams when I was seven or eight years old: again and again in my dreams, an enormous grey, powerful, silent creature would approach me and clasp me in its arms so that I feared its mighty presence would suffocate me. I struggled for dear life--as one is supposed to wrestle with an angel--until I awoke. The figure came back, night after night, and I spent the days fearing its return. Finally, after dozens of these battles, I learned to surrender, to throw myself into the creature, to become part of it, and after a while the nocturnal visits ended. This was a "visitation," a revelation and a scourge, an ordeal. And those words, "angel" and "visitation" remained engraved in my mind, repeated like a mantra, until in 1978 I composed *Angels and Visitations*. They bear some resemblance to the visions of William Blake, and are certainly related to Rainer Maria Rilke's awe-inspiring figures of holy dread: "ein jeder Engel ist schrecklich..." ("...every angel is terrible...").
>
> ... the Angel compositions have no program....For *Angels and Visitations* presents a world of sharp contrasts, in which a hymn rising up from the depths may be followed by what sounds like a riotous pack of demons...only to give way to a Palestrina-like violin texture hovering in the heights or the bright tinkling of the harp and celesta. The work is a set of variations on the theme of contrast, polarity, the logic of antithesis.[7]

---

[7] Einojuhani Rautavaara, Liner note for *Angels and Visitations, Viuluknosertto, Lintukoto*, Ondine ODE 881-2; also, www.fimic.fi/rautavaara.

The work opens with high string plucked glissandos, like drops of water, with ominous rustlings, building to an explosion. From the start we understand that this is no peaceful description of celestial fields. From the rustlings, a straightforward lyrical woodwind theme appears, building to a low brass hymn chorus. High strings and celeste tinkling takes us to celestial heights, but these are soon interrupted by dissonance from Rautavaara's "riotous pack of demons," leading on to the sound of a human male scream. Hymns and demons do indeed alternate. The celeste has a solo with ridiculing laughter suggested in the background strings. The triumphant return of the low brass hymn fades out into the receding sounds of the opening plucked string glissando.

*Angel of Dusk, Concerto for Double Bass and Orchestra* (1980), is the second work in the "Angel Series," the three works commissioned by the Finnish Radio Symphony orchestra (an overture, a concerto, and a symphony). The first impetus for *Angel and Dusk* was a request from Olga Koussevitsky in 1977, at a time when Rautavaara visited New York City, for a work in memory of her husband, famous conductor of the Boston Symphony and double bass virtuoso, Serge Koussevitsky. Rautavaara had been the recipient of the Koussevitsky scholarship given to Sibelius to award to his choice of a Finnish student in 1955 for his study at Tanglewood and Juilliard. Returning home to Finland by air after his 1977 trip to New York, Rautavaara gazed out at the clouds, gray and streaked with color, and thought of a possible title, "Angel of Dusk." When Madame Koussevitsky died unexpectedly, the work was postponed. Soon the young Finnish double bass virtuoso Olli Kosonen requested a concerto, the Radio Symphony Orchestra was agreeable to that kind of work, and the concerto was resumed. Rautavaara borrowed a double bass from the Sibelius Academy and tried out various techniques at home.

The first movement, titled "His First Appearance," opens with a brief hymnlike introduction for orchestra rising to a climax. The following low-pitched lyrical theme for double bass is balanced by use of harp arpeggios and high celeste. This solo line is interrupted by dissonances from the brasses, in what Rautavaara calls a "disturbance technique."[8] A dialogue between the two forces leads to a final quiet section of melody using glissando double stops. The middle movement, "His Monologue," consists of a long cadenza, with a variety of techniques, harmonics, plucking, sliding, double stops, bowing on the strings close to the bridge, bouncing on the strings, rough plucks combined with glissando, with only a few contributions from the orchestra, sometimes taunting, with sarcastic trumpet interjections. The third movement, "His Last Appearance," opens without break with a quiet swaying cantilena which

---

[8] Einojuhani Rautavaara, Liner notes for *Angel of Dusk*, BIS CD-910 Digital.

gradually ascends. Violent timpani strokes introduce a new section with full orchestra and rapid figuration for the soloist. The sliding glissando melody from the first movement leads back to the movement's opening mood, with an inconclusive fading ending. In 1993 the concerto was rearranged as a chamber work for solo double bass, two pianos, and a single percussion player for the Kuhmo (Finland) Chamber Music Festival of 1994.

Rautavaara hosted his own radio show on the Finnish Yleisradio station from 1975 through 1983. Entitled "New Finnish Music," the show reviewed and analyzed new Finnish compositions recorded in the previous year. The works reviewed were purchased and catalogued by the music department, important to young composers. Letters, cards, and telegrams came from listeners, with complaints, praise, even packages from ladies including such oddities as a pound of different buttons or burnt cake.[9]

---

[9] Rautavaara, *Omakuva*, 216-8.

CHAPTER SEVEN

# POSTMODERNISM, 1981-89

During the 1980s Rautavaara received many commissions for new works, enough so that he retired from his teaching position at the age of sixty, in 1988. Continuing the "Angel" motive, he wrote *Playground for Angels* (1981) for a brass ensemble, as well as a Fifth Symphony (1985). It was originally to be titled "Monologue with Angels" but he later dropped the title in the process of composition. His most important work of the period was his opera *Thomas* (1985), continuing his medieval period involvement with the world of the Kalevala. Its synthesis of a variety of tonal systems--modality, synthetic scales, octotonicism, and serial rows, all used separately and sometimes simultaneously-- was a remarkable example of a post-modern style. His opera on Van Gogh, *Vincent* (1990), was soon to follow, incorporating musical interpretations of famous paintings as well as a synthesizer to indicate the distortions of madness. Other outstanding works of this era include the Second Piano Concerto of 1989 and his autobiography, *Omakuva* (Self Portrait, 1989). Personally, his life became more stable and satisfying, with an end to his marriage after twenty-three years in 1984, and remarriage that August to the woman he called his muse, singer Sinikka Koivisto.

In 1981, Rautavaara received a commission for a brass ensemble work. *Playgrounds for Angels*, a twelve minute work for brass ensemble (4 trumpets, 4 trombones, horn, and tuba), was composed for the Philip Jones Brass Ensemble for the Helsinki Festival Weeks, in September of 1981. Rautavaara related that with the first rehearsal in Helsinki, the Philip Jones Ensemble declared the work too difficult rhythmically to perform as chamber music. Mr. Jones insisted on conducting it and sent off to London for an additional brass player to fill in for himself. The usual fare for this group was the "Flight of the Bumblebee," arrangements of Bach's D minor Toccata, and other light classics, hardly anything new or avantgarde. Obviously too difficult for the group, the first performance was terrible, but the ensemble went on to perform it elsewhere and eventually recorded it.[1]

The playground is evoked by opposing brass players in a taunting dialogue, like groups of boys shouting insults at each other. It opens with playful snatches of dialogue between two trumpets, echoes that with muted trumpets, and then the same material is passed to the lower brass. Special effects include trombone

---

[1] Rautavaara, *Omakuva*, 325-326.

glissandos, gruff comments from the tuba, a passage for trombones in clashing seconds, and the sounds of blowing air through the instruments. A contrasting slow and low-pitched middle section gives way to a return to the rapid opening style in the higher register of the trumpets. At times the French horn attempts to be a lyrical soloist unsuccessfully. Two final tuba notes deride the whole encounter.

In 1983, Rautavaara began divorce proceedings for his first marriage, after living separately for some years. The time of conflict soon was left behind and led to a productive time of new styles and successes with new works, as well as happiness in a new relationship with a young singer who became his wife in 1984. Sinikka Koivisto, born 1957 in Lahti, Finland, performed the role of Marjatta in Rautavaara's 1977 choral opera *Marjatta matala neiti* (Marjatta the Lowly Maiden) and later went on a European tour with this role to England, Hungary, and Germany. She completed her studies at the Sibelius Academy, with degrees in music education in 1983, in voice in 1986, and a Magister of Music in 1995. She went on to have featured roles in Rautavaara's operas *Thomas* (1985), *Vincent* (1987), and *House of the Sun* (1990), as well as to become a teacher at the Sibelius Academy.

In 1984 Rautavaara had the joy of commissioning his own work, *Häämarssi* (Wedding March, 1984), for organ for his wedding to Sinikka Koivisto in Helsinki on August 18. After Rautavaara's marriage to the twenty-nine years younger singer, they sought an apartment. The Finnish Singers and Performers' Union had a house available named "Hopiala," given to the organization in the will of Heikki Klemetti's widow, Armi. It came with Armi's neglected garden, some dead fir trees, and a big ants' nest in front of the trees, where Heikki, (according to Rautavaara) famous for his anger, was wont to stir with his cane on his way to work every day, in order to stimulate the angry ants into activity. The happy couple moved into the old wooden frame house, decorated with Swedish style "gingerbread" trim. Choral conductor and composer Klemetti had been the composition authority who had once advised Rautavaara that if he didn't succeed as a composer he could make a good living by driving a truck. Rautavaara kept Klemetti's old grand piano for a time and enjoyed having a garden in this suburban neighborhood. Domestic peace reigned, and Rautavaara referred to Sini as his muse.

In 1984 the opera *Thomas* was commissioned by the city of Joensuu for the 1985 Joensuu Song Festival celebrating the 150th anniversary of the *Kalevala* publication. Written at the request of baritone Jorma Hynninen, who performed the title role, it tells the medieval Finnish story of Bishop Thomas of the early 13th century. An Englishman, he arrived in Sweden-owned Finland about 1220 A.D., with strong connections to the Sorbonne University in Paris and with the papal court. As head of the Roman Catholic Church in Finland, he was also the only governing authority, since Sweden had not yet established any outposts. He organized a crusade against the Eastern Orthodox city of Novgorad and was routed by the forces of Alexander Nevsky. With few historical records, Rautavaara was free to add plot details. In Rautavaara's libretto, Thomas retreated to Finland's capital city of that time, Turku (Åbo in Swedish). He eventually resigned in 1244 out of guilt at having caused the torture and death of a colleague and of sending a false document to the Pope to gain support for his crusade. Thomas, in reality, was perhaps the first to have a vision of an independent Finland. In his attempt to make an independent Papal State of Finland, the early medieval Catholic world and the shamanistic Kalevala magic met and collided in a crusade against a third party--the infidel city of Novgorod to the east.

Rautavaara already had a plan for a Kalevala-era story *Kultaneito* (Golden Girl) as a symbolic opera and combined these ideas with the story of *Thomas* into a larger drama. Since very few facts were known about the historical bishop, secondary characters were invented with various singers in mind. The role of the Girl was written for Sini Rautavaara, with her light high voice quality. She materializes from a statue in the cathedral, is mute, but sings like a bird with trills and bird calls. She represents the Finnish people as either a pagan or angelic spirit, and at times either instructs or rescues Thomas. Among other characters, there is a Knight of the Sword, who is the leader of a Livonian group ordered by the Pope to join in the crusade against the Novgorods, and a merchant of Gotland who finances the crusade. These, plus Thomas and his two friars, represent the Roman Catholic west. A trio of three shaman or Magi represent paganism in Finland.

The main subject of the opera *Thomas* is the clash and synthesis of differing cultures. At times this results in a clash of languages, heard separately or even simultaneously. Latin appears in Gregorian chant, and in comments by the churchmen. Medieval English enters when Thomas is reflecting on his childhood playmates and his mother. The Magi, and also Thomas at times, speak in mystical Kalevala-like rhymes. Most memorable of the latter is the closing song of Thomas, which was twice sung in the prologue, summing up Thomas's ineffective vision of Finland's independence, some 700 years before it was actually attained:

"Suddenly sang the bird, the bird sang in the darkness.

In the dark it erred. It erred like a man

and sang the sounds of morning into the night,

across the evening and beyond time."

In the Finnish language it contains much alliteration, parallelism of verses, and repetition of material, as does the folk epic, the Kalevala. This alliteration and repetition can easily be heard even by the non-Finnish speaker.

"Äkkiä lauloi lintu, lintu lauloi pimeässä,

pimeässä se erehtyi, se erehtyi kuin ihminen

ja lauloi aamun äänet yöhön, iltaa pitkin, ajan taakse."

To represent the different protagonists, Rautavaara uses different tonal systems—diatonicism, modality, serialism, and atonality—like the use of different languages sometimes side by side, and often superimposed. Because of these varied tonal systems, each designed to evoke a distinct atmosphere, this opera has been called Rautavaara's first major Postmodern composition.

The clash of cultures also results in a clash of musical styles, sometimes layered together. The chorus, singing as Finnish people, use a pentatonic scale, representing antiquity, or whisper in sprechstimme. The monks sing in a modal Gregorian chant in parallel fourths. The English children and the mother sing in diatonic folk music style. The cathedral choir sings diatonically with imitative entrances. Music material for the three shamans derives from a given serial row having 12 tones, but with four repeated, making it not a traditional 12-tone row, sometimes appearing as an octotonic scale of alternating half and whole steps. The mute Finnish Maiden has an aleatoric and atonal wordless melodic line with bird trills, while Thomas, the friars, the knight and merchant all have twelve tone rows. At times, all appear together simultaneously, helped by similar intervals in all and underlying pedal tones. According to Rautavaara: "the need for synthesis, linking together of contradictory systems must of necessity come to break the taboos of each system...but then I also believe that all artistic taboos are evidence of short-sightedness (in time and space), and often of racism."[2]

In Joensuu on Johannesaatto (St. John's Eve, or Midsummer, the first day of summer) in 1985, all three of Rautavaara's Kalevala operas were performed on the same day, a most unusual event. Both Finnish and foreign critics gave *Thomas* favorable reviews. When it later appeared at Finlandia Hall in Helsinki, it was declared Rautavaara's most remarkable work to date. At the Joensuu festival, the director of the newly founded Finnish recording company Ondine, Reijo Kiilunen, made arrangements to record the first performance, though the festival usually did its own recording. This became the start of a long and fruitful recording relationship with Ondine as well as new connections with reviewers

---

[2] Einojuhani Rautavaara quoted in Sivuoja-Gunaratnam, 110.

**Example Nineteen:** The form of the Fifth Symphony (1985), in composer Kalevi Aho's graph. The half hour single movement has been described in several ways: sections of linked traditional symphonic movements [moderate, slow, scherzo, fast]; eight sections in symmetrical arrangement (A = H [Intro and Coda], B = G [Processional and Transition], C = E [Chorale 1 and Chorale 2 with development], D = F [Scherzo 1 and Scherzo 2]. Aho prefers to call it a "spiral," where similar moods marked by white or black lines return, serve almost as variations or reminders and then move on again. Graph used by courtesy of composer and writer Kalevi Aho.

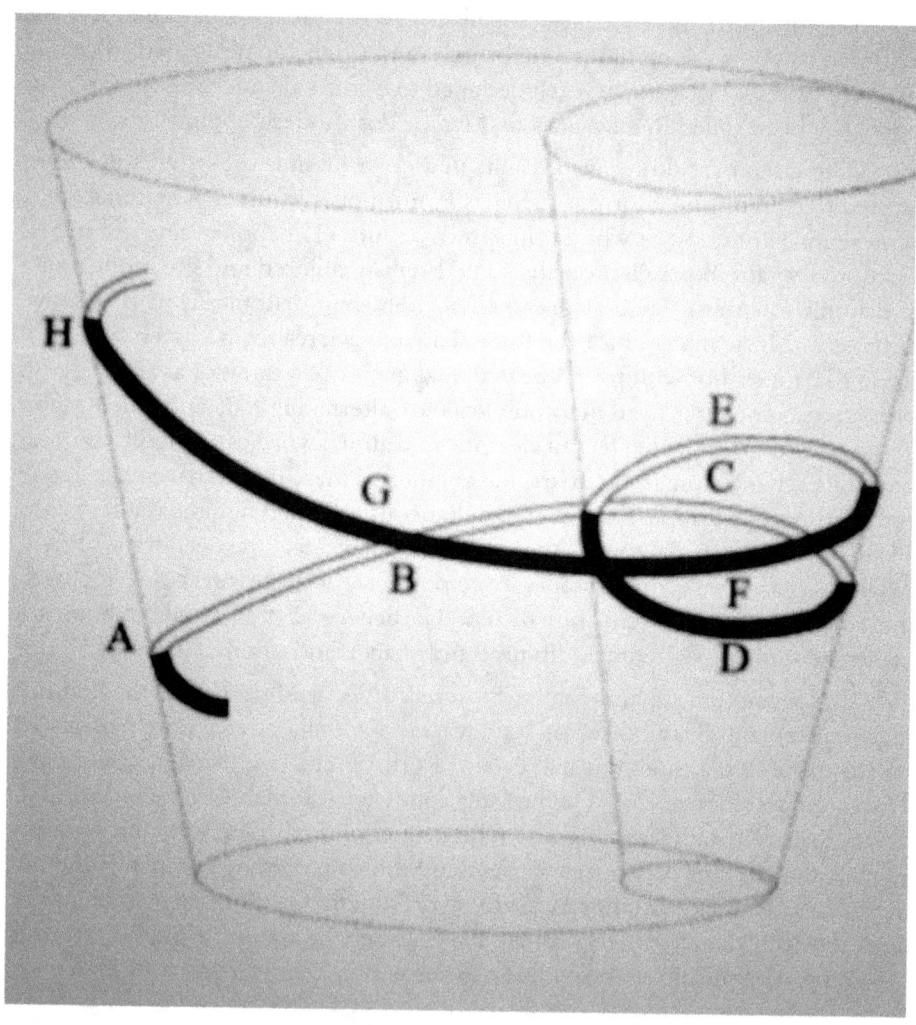

of other countries. *Thomas* was later presented in Germany in translation to German in the 1990s.

Wanting to complete the Angel Trilogy, begun in 1978 with the overture *Angels and Visitations,* and the concerto *Angel of Dusk* for double bass of 1980, Rautavaara originally planned the Fifth Symphony (1985) with the title "Monologue with Angels," later dropped. Taking up the genre of a symphony after a gap of nearly twenty years, Rautavaara created a half-hour single movement, with sections unlike those of the traditional symphony movements. Composer and writer Kalevi Aho has described the overall form as "a spiral."[3] Aho divided the work into eight sections that each mirror another section, first and last, second and seventh, etc. The spiral term refers to a return to earlier heard material that is now varied and moving forward to its final goal (Example Nineteen, Fifth Symphony, p. 84).[4] Other writers have found sections that compare to the usual four movement symphonic form, return of opening material, a traditional slow movement and scherzo, but all combined with variations or new development. The written score combines conventional notation with an unusual time-point notation where measures are given an approximate duration in seconds, also used by composers Berio and Penderecki.[5] Conductor Esa-Pekka Salonen, a former student of Rautavaara, recalled conducting Mr. Rautavaara's Symphony No. 5, which opens with a series of chords in radiant C major.

> "That kind of signal at that moment in history was like a huge exclamation mark: I'm starting a piece that is called 'symphony' — which is already outrageous — and I'm starting it in C major," Mr. Salonen said, laughing. "When I conducted the first rehearsal of that piece, I felt as if my grandfather had spotted me buying a porn magazine. It was an outrageous thing to conduct a new piece that started in C major."

Mr. Rautavaara had great patience for such feelings, Mr. Salonen said.

> "He was very gentle about these tendencies I had," he said. "He understood that a young person needed some kind of a tribal identity, to be against somebody and for something. He said when you get older you will learn that truth is more elusive than you think — and that maybe it's not even the point. Maybe we are trying to achieve something different."[6]

---

[3] Rautavaara, *Omakuva,* 328; Kalevi Aho, *Einojuhani Rautavaara Symphonist* (Helsinki: Pan, 1988): 98ff.
[4] Tim Howell, *After Sibelius: Studies in Finnish Music* (London: Ashgate, 2006), 125-126.
[5] Frank J. Oteri, *Rautavaara Orchestral Works* (Helsinki: Werner/Chappell Music Finland, 1999), 21.
[6] Corinna da Fonneca-Wollheim*Times,* "Einojuhani Rautavaara, Composer, Dies at 87; His Lush Music Found Wide Appeal," *New York Times,* August 3, 2016.

In 1986 Rautavaara was invited to submit his five symphonies to Edition Pan, a publisher of Finnish orchestral scores founded by his former student, composer Kalevi Aho in 1975. Preparing the scores for publication and a definitive version of the works caused Rautavaara no few problems. The Fifth Symphony had just been completed and was ready. The Fourth Symphony of 1964 had been withdrawn. With some thought, Rautavaara decided to substitute his *Arabescata*, his four movement totally serial work of 1962, and label it the Fourth Symphony. The Third Symphony of 1961 needed no revisions. The Second Symphony of 1957 had already been revised and material added for a larger orchestra in 1984. Rautavaara signed an agreement with Pan Editions for publication of the Second through Fifth symphonies. The First Symphony caused the most difficulties. A work of his student years, in 1957 Rautavaara was still having trouble organizing his themes into logical forms. In looking back on the work from his 1986 viewpoint, he wanted to fix what he saw as inadequacies but at the same time not destroy the youthful work. By 1988 he had his solution and the work could be published. The result was a combination of the first and third slow movements for the new first movement, retention of the fast third movement as the new finale, and discard of the original fourth movement. Though the work was then published with the other symphonies, Rautavaara still felt something was missing and in 2002 added a middle slow movement, "Poetico," based on a 1957 song "Die Liebende." With the completion of the publishing project, the publisher and editor Kalevi Aho wrote a series of analyses of the five works as *Einojuhani Rautavaara sinfonikkona* (Einojuhani Rautavaara as a Symphonist, 1988).

After the 1985 opera *Thomas*, baritone Jorma Hynninen suggested another subject for an operatic collaboration, one based on the life of painter Vincent Van Gogh, which became the opera *Vincent* (1987-1990). Hynninen was soon to become the artistic director of the Savonlinna summer opera festival, which was sponsoring a composition competition to celebrate the 350th anniversary of the city of Savonlinna (castle of Savo province, in Finnish) in 1989. The opera festival, founded in 1955 but based on earlier sporadic efforts dating from 1912, takes place in the picturesque courtyard of Olavinlinna (Olaf's Castle), built in 1475. This outdoor venue holds an audience of 2,200, with the stage at the foot of a forty-five foot stone wall. Though *Vincent* was written for that competition, it had to compete against the other two composers invited to participate, Kalevi Aho and Paavo Heininen. Heininen won with *Veitsi* (*The Knife*). Despite a good deal of disagreements and accusations during the competition, all three operas became successes. Heininen's work was performed both in 1989 and 1990 at Savonlinna. Aho's opera, *Hyönteiselämä (Insect Life)*, had a great success at the Finnish National Opera in 1996. Rautavaara's completed three-act opera *Vincent* was premiered at the Finnish National Opera in Helsinki in 1990, appropriately in the year of the Van Gogh centennial. Attracting some international attention, *Vincent* was later in the repertoires of two German opera houses, Kiel and Hagen, at the same time, in 1991, translated into German.

Rautavaara again wrote his own libretto, both in Finnish and in German. To do this he began a study of the painter's life using as many sources as he could find, not only the scholarly but the romanticized films and novels. He was especially impressed by the letters of Vincent to his brother and patron, Theo. Deciding that the opera should be a paraphrase of the life of Vincent van Gogh, rather than yet another attempt at factual reality, Rautavaara chose to use a series of flashbacks into Vincent's past to illustrate his main life stages, with references to several of the more famous paintings and to Vincent's letters to his brother about those events. Each of the three acts opens with an orchestral prologue titled after a Van Gogh painting, "Starry Night," "Wheatfield with Crows," and "The Church at Auvers."

The opening scene is the sanitarium at St. Rémy, with Vincent painting and surrounded by other patients. A quartet of other characters appear: a pompous doctor, his secretary futilely attempting to spell the words of the diagnosis, a stuttering hospital priest, and an authoritarian warden. The quartet reappears in each act, transformed into other people, but keeping the same personality traits. Claiming he needs to imitate Jesus, Vincent offers his body and blood at the dinner table to the repulsed patients. Voices from the wall, a trio of female singers, call to him. Despairing, Vincent sees his loyal brother Theo who tells him to look back into his past for explanations. This begins a series of flashbacks. Vincent begins by revisiting the poor Dutch village where he was a pastor and had to flee because of being accused of illegal political activities. Brother Theo tells Vincent that his gift is to bring light and life to the world through his painting, and to keep on.

In Act Two Vincent is painting during an art exhibit. The quartet is now a group of art critics. Paul Gaugin enters and suggests a party at a bordello with piano rag music. Left alone, Vincent dances with a female illusion to a waltz. The group return to celebrate a pagan ritual needing a sacrifice and Vincent cuts off his ear. The guests flee in horror and darkness falls bringing black birds flying at Vincent.

In Act Three Vincent is again back in the sanitarium. He offers his painting to his doctor and then to the others of the original quartet, but all are reluctant to accept something so unusual. Again rejected, he sings of his despair which then changes to a hymn of praise for the visions of life he has had. Rautavaara had difficulty deciding how the opera should end. But, after seeing a New York exhibit of the van Gogh paintings of his last months, he became impressed with the light and joy expressed in them. In the opera, Vincent's final words sum up his life and work: "The day of the sun! And he who dies today shall never disappear, but will join those who once had the courage to go on and live!"

The music mixes twelve-tone rows and synthetic modes, each one having its own sound characteristics. Rautavaara said of these that the rows can be compared to tubes of paint, "the music derived from each of the rows has its own interval color, its own character...the different colors could thus be mixed together in different ways, just as a painter does with his paints."[7] The vocal parts are not derived from the rows, allowing Rautavaara more expressiveness. Much of the instrumental part includes a synthesizer, to emphasis the inner distorted world of Vincent, contrasted with the normal world conveyed by the regular orchestra. Other styles of music are used to set the scenes, such as the ragtime piano, and the waltz rhythms of his dance with Gaby, the illusionary muse of "singing colors." Less apparent touches of other styles include a reference to the hymn of the Soviet Union when the text refers to "Mao and Lenin's theory of contradiction" from one of the art critics, and, in another place, chorale-like chords under the text "who do you think you are? A grand vice-Jesus?" in a parody of a Christmas tune.

Composed for pianist Ralf Gothoni, Rautavaara's Second Piano Concerto (1989) is more demanding than the first piano concerto, which he wrote for his own performance. Rautavaara began by determining his 12-tone row and its various forms. But he also gave the three connected movements expressive Italian titles: "In Viaggio" (On a Trip), "Sognando e libero" (Dreamlike and Free), and "Uccelli sulle passioni" (Birds with Passion). These are "not birds created from music...but music as birds."[8]

As a pianist, Rautavaara was not content to write sparse pointillistic passages for his instrument. High treble rippling passages for piano, representing the twittering of a flock of birds, open the work and continue on, with comments added from other instruments. The main theme is a stepwise melody from the violin section. A solo passage for piano takes over both the melodic aspect and the continual rapid passagework. When the ensemble joins in, all move to several climaxes. The movement ends quietly with the piano passages winding down.

The slow movement follows with little pause, in the style of a sentimental character piece dominated by the piano. This leads to an energetic section punctuated by occasional dissonances, whip lashes in the percussion, a long fermata, and then return to the slow movement's slower opening style, though gloomier in mood.

---

[7] Rautavaara, *Omakuva*, 335-336.
[8] Einojuhani Rautavaara, Liner notes, *Piano Concertos 1 & 2*, Ondine ODE 757-2.

A new section begins with the piano given single fast repeated pitches, wood block, and vibraphone interjections, perhaps the birds as musicians, as a segue into the finale. The main theme from the first movement returns in the low strings and brass while the high strings take over the bird chattering and the piano races on. In a quiet coda the twittering bird sounds fade, with pauses, into the distance.

By 1988, at the age of sixty, Rautavaara resigned his position as Professor of Composition at the Sibelius Academy, in favor of composition of the many commissions he was receiving. Paavo Heininen, the winner of the Savonlinna opera competition with his opera *Veitsi* (The Knife), was appointed as the replacement, though Rautavaara had recommended his former student Kalevi Aho, another of the Savonlinna competitors. Having more time for his own projects, Rautavaara was encouraged to write his autobiography, *Omakuva* (Self-Portrait, 1989), by music journalist Pekka Hako, who some ten years later became Rautavaara's biographer, with his own book *Unien Lahja: Einojuhani Rautavaaran maailma* (Gift of Dreams: Einojuhani Rautavaara's World, 2000). Rautavaara's autobiography, intended for a Finnish readership familiar with other such books written by Finnish composers, is fairly chatty in style, telling of his childhood, his education, and, often, the circumstances of the composition of his better known works. Rarely does he give technical details, knowing that they might be beyond his general readers. More information is given about the people involved, the stories of performers, the literary background of his choice of texts, what effect the various works had, occasional scandals, and amusing stories. Each chapter is headed by a quote from one of his opera librettos. The opening introduction is headed with: "Puhu tuolle! Ja huuda peilille! Eihän sinua muu kiinnosta kuin oma itsesi kuitenkaan! (Speak there! And shout to the mirror! No one but you is as interested in yourself anyway!), a quote from the opera *Vincent*. A later chapter has as its heading a quote from the opera *Thomas*, "Äkkiä lauloi lintu, lintu lauloi pimeässä" (Suddenly sang a bird, a bird sang in the darkness). Though in the opera this repeated text represents the futility of a medieval attempt at an independent Finland, the chapter in Rautavaara's autobiography discusses actual birds, the birds recorded in *Cantus Arcticus* (1972). Altogether, his self-portrait is a valuable source of information and fund of quotable material, unfortunately not available to English speakers, and also limited to the years before 1989.

CHAPTER EIGHT

# THE 1990s

During the 1990s decade Rautavaara produced a prodigious amount of work: three operas, three symphonies, orchestral works, a third piano concerto, and a string quintet, plus numerous smaller works. His 1995 Seventh Symphony *Angel of Light* brought him international fame and important commissions from performers and ensembles of high repute. Again his subject matter ranged widely, from a tale of two old ladies to shipwrecked sailors in Antarctica, from a classic short story of O. Henry to the struggle by Finland's first Finnish language novelist. His musical language showed no dramatic changes, moving within an expressive combination of serialism and free tonality. In a statement in 1992, he defined his use of rows at that time as a source of motivic relationships. Rather than a mechanical approach, it gave him both background structure and foreground expressive freedom:

> The function of the series was to act as a motivic automaton that creates coherence...because everything is derived from the series and the intervallic formations are everywhere in the piece, in the melodies and harmonies, in the vertical and intervallic figures. You don't need to pay any attention to it; you are free to consider other things, the larger formal entities and overall form.[1]

In 1990 his *Auringon talo* (The House of the Sun), a chamber opera in two acts, commissioned by the Finnish National Opera, presented its first performance in Lappeenranta, Finland. Inspired by an actual newspaper story, its two principal characters are two emigré sisters from Russia who maintained their pre-Revolution aristocratic lifestyle and finally froze to death. Fleeing from Russia in 1915 to an estate called the House of the Sun in rural southwest Finland, the family soon disintegrated. The father and brother were unable to establish themselves in the rural Finnish countryside, and committed suicide. The mother then died of a broken heart, two older sisters died early, leaving the two twin sisters to fend for themselves. The sisters lived on into their eighties, never leaving their house, unwilling to learn the Finnish language, and maintaining their childhood lifestyle. Eventually, without servants, they discarded their rubbish in an unused room, and spent their time reminiscing about their girlhood beaus in St. Petersburg. In Rautavaara's opera, using his

---

[1] Rautavaara, quoted in Sivuoja-Gunaratnam, 37.

own libretto, the setting is aptly conveyed in the first moments of the opening scene of the opera, when one sister throws an expensive Russian jeweled Easter egg at a rat. Bickering at each other for not being able to catch a rat or even their former young men, they imagine that the young men may well still come to restore them to their old lifestyle. When the postman arrives bringing a letter, they misunderstand it as an announcement of a visit from an English cousin, requiring them to hire two local boys as servants to answer the door. In a prank, the boys turn off the power, run away, and the two sisters slowly perish from the cold. Growing ever sleepier, they imagine their sweethearts and family of long ago come to invite them to dance, all singing "It is time; it is time to come, it is time to go…like a cloud passing, soon blown by the wind into oblivion."

The opera is structured as a series of conversations between the two old ladies, interrupted by dream sequences of their girlhood. This requires the roles of the sisters to be double cast, two singers for the old ladies and two singers for their teenage years. At times dream and reality blend, the two old sisters astonished at seeing themselves as young women, and the young girls frightened by the blurred vision of two old ladies sitting in arm chairs. Bits of comedy arise from the misunderstood Finnish postman and his references to classical Greek mythology, the training of the two farm boys to become footmen, and from the misinterpretation of visits from a real estate agent and a municipal home care lady. The music is continuous, with the orchestra dominated by the melodic voices. The dialogue is interspersed by lovely duets from the two sisters and ensembles with other cast members. The change into dream sequences is signaled by use of eerie background high-pitched synthesizer tones added to the orchestra, along with mention in the dialogue of an approaching light from outside, from a star or sun.

In 1992 Rautavaara used material from his opera *Vincent* (1987) to rework and develop into his Sixth Symphony *Vincentiana*. Each of the four movements has a title derived from one of the Van Gogh paintings musically described in the opera. The first movement, "Starry Night," is mostly derived from the orchestral prelude to Act One of the opera. Likewise, the second movement, "Crows," and the third movement, "The Church at Auvers," come from the preludes to Act Two and Act Three. The fourth movement, "Apotheosis," is developed from the closing scene of the opera, and was rearranged as a separate movement for string orchestra in 1996. Though dependent on the musical material of the opera but not identical, the symphony intends no dramatic program. The traditional symphonic contrasts of tempo and mood between movements do not apply, making the four movements more of a suite.

Unusual for a symphony, the scoring calls for a synthesizer, as does the opera. In the opera, the sounds of the synthesizer are linked with depictions

**Example Twenty:** Sixth Symphony, *Vincentiana*, (1992), II. "The Crows." Taking motifs from the opera Vincent, this symphonic movement is developed from depiction of Van Gogh's painting, "The Crows." Note the growling of the low synthesizer, timpani, and ratchet, all below the three parts of "cawing" of the trombones in clashing glissandos. ©Fennica Gehrman Oy, Helsinki. Printed with permission.

of Van Gogh's imagined reality, as contrasted with the real world, depicted by a normal symphony orchestra. Another contrasting style element is the Viennese waltz, near the end of the third movement, which comes from Vincent's dance with his muse in the opera. The waltz becomes more and more dissonant, eventually turning into the distortion of the synthesizer realm.

The opening movement depicts stars twinkling with its eerie string tremolos, and pointillistic entrances of bells, gongs, plus the dizzying vertigo of Vincent's madness expressed in a furious outburst of strings and a synthesizer. It continues on with broad lyrical melodies in the strings, creating a warm Neoromantic mood, interspersed with sections of the dissonant sounds of conflict, all ending in dissonance. The second movement, "Crows" (Example Twenty, Sixth Symphony, page 92), opens with cawing sound effects of ratchets, trombone glissandos, and pounding percussion, fading into synthesizer. Eventually it becomes a morose slow movement mostly in a low register, with faint high twittering bird sounds above. The lively third movement, "The Church at Auvers," seems to depict a busy village scene. A pause with harp arpeggios indicates a coming change, and the waltz emerges. The density and dissonance increase, a swarm of birds call, the synthesizer depicts church bells out of focus, and the music fades away into the blackness of Vincent's madness. The fourth movement, "Apotheosis," is a final affirmation of the value of Vincent's artwork as light and life with its soaring Romantic melodies and sweet harmonies. Bird calls appear again at its close.

In 1992 the Finnish Broadcasting Station commissioned *Canto IV for string orchestra* to be performed by the Keski-Pohjanmaan Kamariorkesteri (the Central Ostrobothnian Chamber Orchestra) under the direction of conductor Juha Kangas. Originally a folk fiddler, conductor Kangas founded this chamber orchestra as a sideline to his teaching at the regional music institute. Eventually it developed into an outstanding ensemble, known for debuts of contemporary music and winner of the Nordic Council Music Prize of 1993, in competition with all the young composers and performers of Scandinavia. Of this seventeen minute work, Rautavaara has said it was the inspiration of a morning, with no conscious effort to mold it in any shape. Rautavaara has often claimed that his works tend to have a mind and will of their own. From the opening, the narrow-ranged phrase is developed, inverted, and reworked, but keeps its recognizable length and motions. A second section contrasts a high treble melody of wider intervals with an arpeggiated accompaniment. After some pauses with dissonant interjections, a solo viola prevails. The work closes with the full strings, with high treble twittering above, in a passage later reused as the broad final section of the Seventh Symphony.

In the summer of 1992 the Rautavaaras were invited to Japan for a music festival featuring Rautavaara's works. Japanese pianist Izumi Tateno, who had been a piano instructor at the Sibelius Academy in the 1960s and 70s, had returned to Japan and supported Finnish music by his recordings and by arranging festivals featuring Finnish composers. In 1991 the festival included Rautavaara's *Ikonit* (Icons, 1955) for piano and his *Pelimmanit* (The Fiddlers, 1952, 1972) in its string orchestra arrangement. In 1992 the festival focused on works solely by Rautavaara. Soprano Sini Rautavaara performed *Funf Sonette an Orpheus* (1955) with her husband at the piano. *Cantus Arcticus* (1972) was presented by the Japanese Philharmonic Orchestra under the direction of Finnish conductor Osmo Vanska, the first sonata for cello and piano was performed by Finnish cellist Erkki Rautio with Izumi Tateno at the piano, and the *Cantos I* and *II* (1960) were directed by Juha Kangas with the Keski-Pohjanmaa (Ostrobothnian) chamber orchestra.

The Japan visit resulted in a new commission from the Tokyo Philharmonic Chorus for a set of choral songs based on a text suitable for the present day. Rautavaara's choice was three songs on texts by Frederico Lorca, *Canción de nuestro tiempo* (Song of our Time, 1993), performed the next year in Tokyo.

*Die erste Elegie* (1993) for a cappella mixed choir came as a continued interest in reading the poems of Rainer Maria Rilke. They had inspired him to set texts much earlier for his *Funf Sonette an Orpheus* (1954-55) and *Die Liebende* (1958). Rilke's *Die erste Elegie*, especially, made a deep impression on him, as it depicts a mysterious angel-like figure, which, if it clasps someone to its bosom, is terrifying, but refrains from destroying. This angel spirit, combined with an enormous gray smothering figure in his boyhood nightmares, became the reference point of his *Angels and Visitations* (orchestral work, 1978), *Angel of Light* (Seventh Symphony, 1994), *Angel of Dusk* (concerto for double bass, 1980), and *Playgrounds for Angels* (for brass ensemble, 1981). In 1993 when the international chorus Europa Cantat commissioned a large-scale choral work, Rautavaara decided it was time to set the *Die erste Elegie*. The basic pitch material is derived from four triads which together form a 12-tone row. The whole effect is of narration, with words set to reflect the inherent meaning. The six divisions of the text have no common musical factor. The opening is dramatic, with the high sopranos establishing a repeated note ostinato on "Who among the host of angels hears me?" while the male singers abruptly enter several times with "when I cry out." All join together in "the beautiful is but the start of terror which we can barely endure." A solo soprano emphasizes the last line, "Each and every angel is (pause) terrifying." The text goes on, speaking of the young dead, both they and the mourners have no places to turn in need, such as nature, but tells how angels move through both the living and the dead indiscriminately. The final lines, set in an exultant musical climax, state that music, though in legend said to have been born in mourning, is what bursts through the emptiness and sadness to support us and bring comfort.

    The Seventh Symphony, *Angel of Light*, (1994-95) was commissioned by conductor David Pickett for the Bloomington (Indiana) Symphony Orchestra for its twenty-fifth anniversary. Rautavaara, knowing that Indiana University in Bloomington, Indiana, had a famous music school, assumed the work was intended for a first class orchestra. He had a symphony of four movements in mind, at a fairly high commission. David Pickett, however, was a faculty member at the famous school who also conducted an amateur community orchestra. Pickett was hoping for a small scale work that would be easy for his group and for his listeners. Learning all the details, the community orchestra erupted into arguments about spending so much money on a work by a contemporary composer not known to them. Eventually, a reduced price was agreed upon. In the spring of 1995, Rautavaara was serving as a judge in a composition competition in Brussels, and was unable to attend the first performance of his new Bloomington Symphony. On receiving tapes of the orchestral rehearsals, he realized with great dismay that the work was too hard for the performers. On receiving the tapes, Rautavaara made some revisions, especially to the first movement, taking out a whole section which ended up in his 1994-95 opera *Tietäjien lahjassa* (The Gift of the Magi), based on the O. Henry short story. The Bloomington community orchestra gave the first performance under David Pickett on April 23, 1995, with little publicity and mild encouragement from a local newspaper.

    Rautavaara was able to hear his symphony performed in Helsinki that summer with the Helsinki City Orchestra under Leif Segerström for the music festival week. Again the reviews were moderate. The director of the Finnish recording company Ondine, Reijo Kiilunen, persuaded the composer to return to his originally considered name of *Angel of Light* as a title far more marketable than *Bloomington Symphony*. Though Rautavaara was doubtful of being associated with the new age concept of angels, Kiilunen was able to persuade him that it fit in with his earlier works, the overture *Angels and Visitations* (1978) and the concerto for double bass *Angel of Dusk* (1980), making a complete set of works forming a concert program of overture, concerto, and symphony. Before the release of the recording, an extensive ad campaign was mounted, even with a competition for a painting of an angel for the record cover won by Pekka Hepoluta. The result was that the seventh symphony became a commercial hit on the international market. It also received the Cannes Classical Award in 1997 and in 1996 a Grammy Nomination. By 2014 the recording had sold more than 25,000 copies and had received glowing reviews in the leading music journals BBC Music Magazine, Gramophone, and The Times. Ondine Recordings

**Example Twenty-one:** Seventh Symphony, *Angel of Light* (1995), its row and the theme derived from the letters of Bloomington. This symphony was the result of a mistakenly understood commission from an amateur orchestra in Bloomington, Indiana. Too difficult, too expensive, and too unappreciated for that group, the title was later changed from *Bloomington Symphony* to *Angel of Light*. A big ad promotion was made. and the work went on to great international success, receiving a Grammy Nomination in 1996 and a Cannes Classical Award in 1997. ©Fennica Gehrman Oy, Helsinki. Printed with permission.

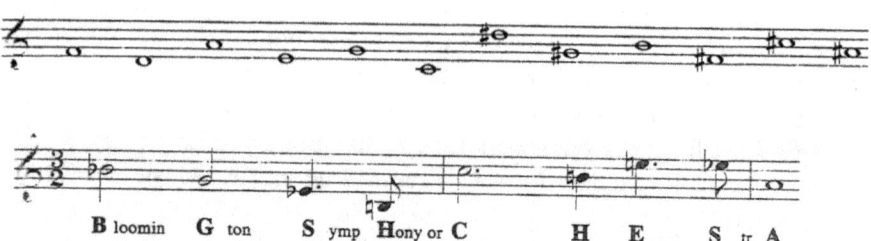

followed up with recordings of *Angels and Visitations* and the violin concerto with soloist Elmar Oliveira, winning a second Midem Classical Award the next year. Ondine purchased recording rights to future Rautavaara works, and the Helsinki orchestra appointed him composer-in-residence. International performances and commissions from prominent artists followed. The original disappointment caused by the commission became a great success.[2]

The work was generated from a twelve tone row used in several compositions of 1993, a series of tones forming four successive triads. Another pre-compositional decision came in making a theme that appears in all four movements, using the pitches derived from the words BloominGton SympHony orCHEStrA. Germanic notational customs allow B to become B flat, H represents B natural, and S equals E flat, resulting in B flat, G, E flat, B natural, C, B natural, E natural, E flat, and A. (Example Twenty-one, Seventh Symphony, *Angel of Light,* page 95).

The opening Tranquillo establishes serenity through low string arpeggio patterns. The Bloomington motif is introduced first by the glockenspiel and vibraphone, broken into several motives, and nearly unnoticeable over the harmonic string accompaniment. Soon an upper string melody progressively rising appears. The Bloomington theme is reserved for the loud brass chorale transition. The second theme is based on rising and falling thirds and its

---

[2] Tiikkaja, 487-491, 497-503 passim.

dialogues between single instruments. The motifs weave on, returning in new timbres, in a now yearning, now lush tonal harmony made possible by the triadic outlines in the row. Both the A theme, transition, and B theme return, much shortened. A coda brings an ascending bass solo from the trombone and horn, and restatement of the Bloomington theme in the glockenspiel and vibraphone. The overall form is ABABCoda, with the most memorable idea, the Bloomington theme, used as transition and final statement.

The fast second movement contrasts with its clashing seconds in short motives. It brings up an image of a scoffing antithesis to the heavenly strains of the first movement. Again, the Bloomington theme appears only as a transition to a set of variations on the opening motives. Dispute is conveyed by rapid notes sounding like verbal argumentation, dissonant clashes, tentative reminders of the hymn theme, now in clashing seconds, in the background, all ending in final schoolyard taunts from the trumpets in clashing seconds and bass growls.

The third movement, Come un sogno (Like a Dream), continues the heavenly atmosphere in the high registers of divisi strings. Various quiet wind solos enter with comments against the background of the strings. Growing to a climactic pause, the remainder is given to a high-pitched violin solo with quiet fluttering motifs interspersed, and a final soft reminder of the hymn tune in the French horn.

The finale opens with a fanfare of brass chords plus a few measures of a lyrical violin, both retaining the rhythms and leaps of the Bloomington theme but not the original pitches. A low-register modal sounding hymn begins in the strings with whirling flute comments at the end of each phrase. The B section is an arrangement taken from *Canto IV*, a work of the same year using the same triad-based row. A C section brings the Bloomington theme to the foreground, over a murmuring accompaniment similar to the first movement. The final section brings back the brasses on the B theme with the strings intensifying their activity and volume. At the climax, the Coda, the first movement's hymn theme returns in ecstatic restatement, and motion dies away as if the whole heavenly complex were moving out of sight and sound. Concerning this symphony Rautavaara has said:

> It has been described being serene, as having the feeling that the music all the time knows where to go and goes there peacefully...There are very strong moments, but the logic is very clear in a classical sense—not in the sense that there's a given form that it falls into rather that it searches for its own form and finds it.[3]

---

[3] Martin Anderson, "Einojuhani Rautavaara, Symphonist: The Finnish Composer Talks to Martin Anderson," *Fanfare* XIX/6 (1995-96): 63-71.

The forty-five minute chamber opera *The Gift of the Magi* (Tietäjien lahja) (1994) is based on the O. Henry short story about the giving and receiving of gifts at Christmastime. Not having much money, both husband and wife sell something of value in order to get the other a gift, only to discover that their gifts, a watch chain and hair clips, complement something that is now gone, sold in order to get the other a meaningful gift. Even so, they recognize and accept each other's gesture of love. Rautavaara set his version of the story in 1930s Helsinki. The plot follows the wife's actions, until the husband gives his gift at the end. New characters are invented from biblical references in the written tale: King Solomon becomes Mr. Saloman, the landlord, and the Queen of Sheba, a prostitute. A fifth character is the wigmaker, to whom the wife sells her hair. He is given an extensive aria meditating on love, with a line that sums up the story, "love can light the lowliest house, like a Christmas star." The wigmaker's aria reuses music from Rautavaara's Seventh Symphony, *Angel of Light*, composed two years earlier. The opening string arpeggios punctuated by vibraphone and bells now accompany a freshly composed vocal line. A chorus of townspeople and children add comments of their own as they watch the action unfold. Spoken dialogue appears here at times, always with orchestral accompaniment. As in his other operas, the music is continuous.

In 1995 Rautavaara composed *Lintukoto* (Home of the Birds, or, Isle of Bliss) for orchestra based on the poem by Aleksis Kivi (1834-72), Finland's first Finnish language poet and novelist. Composed for the Espoo Music Institute orchestra, it was inspired by Kivi's version of the island paradise, a place where time stops, youth is retained and death is defeated. The musical material came from the first act of Rautavaara's opera *Aleksis Kivi*, which though completed had not yet been performed. As in Kivi's poem, the musical version begins fast and cheerfully, moves to a more reflective section, and then fades away, reverting to the "crimson rise of dawn." Rautavaara also connected this setting with an island in the Baltic where he had spent several summers. There he saw a large bird walking back and forth on the shore at night and then found it dead in the morning. The fishermen told him that old seagulls often flew out to that island to die, making it "the last home of the birds."[4]

*Aleksis Kivi*, Rautavaara's opera, about the life of the first important Finnish-language author, was presented in 1997, again starring Jorma Hynninen. As in *Vincent*, Rautavaara returned to the theme of the tragic fate of an artist, here a Finnish writer. Rautavaara wrote the libretto for this opera in addition to composing the music. The premier took place in Punkaharju's Retretti caverns

---

[4] Einojuhani Rautavaara, Liner notes, *Angels and Visitations, Violin Concerto, Isle of Bliss*, Ondine ODE 881-2.

# The 1990's

**Example Twenty-two:** "Sydämeni laulu" (Song of My Heart), from the opera *Aleksis Kivi* (2000). The text comes from Finnish author Aleksis Kivi's (1834-1872) most famous poem, set as Kivi's dying song at the end of the opera. The phrases of the simple stepwise melody often end in a leap that lands exquisitely in a new key center. The accompaniment moves by triads with clashing seconds, ascending and descending in inversions, changing tonal centers each measure. ©Fennica Gehrman Oy, Helsinki. Printed with permission.

during the Savonlinna Opera Festival of 1997 and was later presented in English in 1999 in Minneapolis, Minn., at a festival of Rautavaara compositions.

Aleksis Kivi (1834-1872) is noted for his novel *Seitsemän Veljestä* (Seven Brothers, 1870), the best known literary work in the Finnish language. One reviewer has compared the status of Kivi's novel *Seitsemän veljestä* in Finland to that of Mark Twain's *Huckleberry Finn* in America.[5] Both deal with comic rural characters growing up. His other work includes plays, collections of poetry, and an earlier novel, *Nummisuutarit* (The Cobblers of the Heath, 1865), for which he won a national literary prize established by educator J. V. Snellman.

Prior to this time, the cultural life of Finland was almost exclusively carried on in the Swedish language, the language of the upper class landowners. Influenced by European nationalism, the Finnish Literature Society was formed in 1831 to collect folk material in the Finnish language. Its most important result was the collection and publication by Elias Lönnrot of the ancient oral sagas of the *Kalevala* in 1835. Eventually the first state supported public elementary schools taught in Finnish were founded in 1865. Nationalism convinced many educated Swedish speakers to switch languages and even change their surnames to the Finnish equivalent. By the end of the nineteenth century an acrimonious divide of languages split both the cultural and political scene. Kivi began his career in the middle of that. In addition, a mid-nineteenth century European-wide movement toward realism in art, even if crude, clashed with the older romanticism. Kivi's works, written in the still scorned language of the lower classes, and portraying rustic, uneducated people in their actual lifestyle, met resistance by the establishment, particularly by one perhaps overly influential university professor and literary critic, August Alhqvist.

In Rautavaara's libretto, the story begins in the Prologue with Kivi, at the end of his life, mentally ill, and drunk, being tormented by hallucinations, especially the imagined figure of Professor Ahlqvist and his harsh scorn. In Act One, the time returns to Kivi's days as a college student, when he is encouraged by the politically active Young Finns, and has an exchange of views with Professor Ahlqvist, who treats him dismissively. Kivi's patroness, Charlotta Lönnqvist, an older unmarried woman, and her assistant Hilda, are introduced. Possible romantic interest in Kivi, who lodges in their house, gets Hilda sent away, and Charlotta's interest is implied. In Act Two, the now mature Kivi visits Ahlqvist to request his help in publishing his works. The Young Finns, now opposed to Kivi, enter and degrade his writing. Ahlqvist ends by throwing a coin on the floor for Kivi to take his disappointment to the nearest bar. In Act Three, a drunken Kivi arrives in a

---

[5] John Kiltinen, *A Review of Rautavaara's Opera Aleksis Kivi*. From finlandia@lists.oulu.fi, available Thursday, Aug. 1, 1996.

theater lobby where his play *Nummisuutarit* (The Cobblers of the Heath) is being performed. Overcome by gruesome hallucinations, he slumps on a seat and falls asleep. Ahlqvist enters, pushing the very old poet laureate, J. L. Runeberg, in a wheelchair. Both ridicule Kivi. Two characters from the play then in progress, hallucinations, arrive and join Kivi in a drunken carouse. Charlotta comes and attempts to dissuade him from drinking, to no avail. A group of Young Finns enter with a covered statue, which Kivi thinks is of himself. But, unveiled, it is a decrepit and senile statue of Runeberg that comes to life, and at that point, all join in reviling Kivi's works. The final epilogue depicts the mad Kivi visited by Charlotta and by his younger self, played by another singer. Saying he cannot find his way home, both illusions tell him that home is near. Kivi then sings his most famous poem, "Sydameni Laulu" (Song of my Heart) (Example Twenty-two, *Aleksis Kivi*), about the peaceful place of death.

Rautavaara took excerpts of Kivi's writings in various plays for use in the libretto. Notable are excerpts from the epic *Isle of Bliss* at the beginning and end of the opera, two poems in Act One about the little squirrel and married life, and the final aria based on Kivi's most famous poem, Sydämeni laulu (Song of My Heart).

Tuonen viita, rauhan viita!

Kaukana on vaino, riita,

kaukana kavala maailma.


(Grove of Tuoni, peaceful woodland!

Far from hatred, far from struggle,

far from the evils of mankind.)


Another actual quote is taken from the poetry of Ahlqvist, who wrote melancholy verse under the pen name of A. Oksanen. The two imagined characters from the Cobblers play sing Oksanen's verse: "Ah, joy is fleeting like a gaggle of dreams. If it's happiness you want, only liquor has it for sure" (Ah, katovaista on riemu kuin unten häilyvä parvi, viina on aina vaan, joss' ilo varmana on). The words given to both Ahlqvist and to the senile poet Runeberg, revered, but in this situation outdated, are taken from their actual harsh criticisms, in Runeberg's case, words that had been long suppressed in some editions.

The music of the opera is continuous, with only a few portions set aside for distinct arias, notably those based on Kivi's poetry, the most famous being "Sydämeni laulu" (Song of My Heart). Both Ahlqvist and the aged Runeberg are given spoken roles, as a kind of demotion, a means of depicting them of being incapable of being musically inspired. As in the opera *Vincent*, a synthesizer is added to the orchestra at times when reality is exchanged for hallucinations. Rautavaara borrowed his own tune from the opening of *Pelimannit* (The Fiddlers) for the scene with the two folk musicians from *Nummisuutarit* (The Cobblers of the Heath), though it is somewhat hidden in the musical mayhem.[6]

In 1996 a commission came from the Kuhmo Chamber Music Festival, known for its two weeks of chamber music in the remote east area of Finland. Though originally commissioned as a string quartet, the resulting work, *Unknown Heavens* (1997) changed in the process of composition into a quintet. The third movement wanted to open as a duet for two cellos, changing the whole concept of the work. The subtitle, *Les cieux inconnus* (Unknown Heavens), recalled by Rautavaara as being from a poem by Rimbaud which he set for male choir in the 1970s, is actually from his setting of Charles Baudelaire's "La Morte des Pauvres" (The Death of the Poor), the second in a group of songs called *Neljä serenadia* (Four Serenades), of 1978. Baudelaire's text begins "Death is..." and, after several interpretations, ends with "It is the portal opening on unknown skies (le portique ouvert sur les Cieux inconnus)." A quote from this line in the song appears in all the movements of his quintet, another example of Rautavaara's finding more to say with a motif from a previous composition. It appears in the first movement, in the second bar, when the second violin responds with a descending melody to the first violin's ascending solo. Familiar bits from the "unknown heavens" melody, the descending motion, a four bar motif F-E flat-D flat-E, appear throughout, though it never is actually completely restated. The harmonic language of the work is lushly Romantic, often moving lyrically in parallel thirds and sixths. As one might expect with a work dealing with death and unknown heavens, the overall mood is quiet and pensive. The moderate tempo of the opening movement with its beautiful melodies at times becomes more agitated with a triplet figuration in its accompaniment. The slow second movement is a lovely elegy. The third movement opening with the cello duet develops the ascending melody of the first movement and adds fragments from the descending "heavens" motive. The finale, after bringing back the first movement's introduction in inverted intervals, is more passionate, faster, includes the first movement's triplet figuration in one section, and ends with a fading out of high string twittering, perhaps twinkling of stars. In the year 2000 Rautavaara rearranged the second movement for string orchestra with the title *Adagio celeste*. With the recording of this version, he made no mention of *Unknown Heavens* in his notes. Instead, he claims he was inspired by verses written by Lassi Nummi in 1982: "Then, that night, when you want to

---

[6] Einojuhani Rautavaara, Liner notes, *Aleksis Kivi*, Ondine ODE 1000-2D.

love me in the deep of the night, wake me...let me wake through old age and death...join us to the communion of the world."[7]

In 1997 Rautavaara began a new commission from Vladimir Ashkenazy for a third piano concerto. On his 69th birthday, October 9, the Helsinki Philharmonic Orchestra presented a concert in his honor featuring the overture *Angels and Visitations* under the direction of eighteen-year-old Mikko Franck. Franck was so impressed with the music that he became one of Rautavaara's most frequent presenters. The Turku Philharmonic Orchestra also featured Rautavaara at the same time, programming Rautavaara's First Piano Concerto with pianist Laura Mikkola. She too became known for Rautavaara piano premieres. After Rautavaara won the Cannes award in 1997 for *Angels of Light*, he received many requests for compositions and invitations to travel to concerts where his works were being performed. He also found time to publish a collection of his essays in *Mieltymyksestä äärettömään* (A Liking for the Infinite, 1998). Many of the short essays came from his radio show on new Finnish music during 1981-83, featuring works of Erik Bergman, Esa-Pekka Salonen, Magnus Lindberg, Kaija Saariaho, and others.

For his 70th birthday in 1998 a series of concerts honoring him was arranged. A concert of his sacred works was put together at the Helsinki Cathedral that included his organ works from the late 1960s, choral works including two parts of the *Vigils* (1972), *Credo* (1972), and *Canticum Mariae virginis* (1978), and ended with his brass ensemble compositions *Playgrounds for Angels* (1981) and *A Requiem in Our Time* (1953). Rautavaara commented that listening to the program was like sitting through a review of his compositional history, with the organ works especially noisy, dissonant, atonal, and, at this later date, just plain irritating to him. Later concerts that year presented his *Ikonit* (1955) and *Tulisaarnan* (Fire Sermon, Piano Sonata, #1, 1969) for piano; *Pöytä Musiikkin Herttua Juhanalle* (Table Music for Duke Johan, 1954), a work for recorder quartet rarely played; and two works for children's chorus, *The First Runo* (1984), and *Missa duodecanonican* (1963).[8]

In 1997 Rautavaara received a commission for *The Last Frontier* (1997), for chorus and orchestra, in honor of Rautavaara's seventieth birthday the following year. As a boy, Rautavaara remembered reading an adventure story by Edgar Allen Poe, *The Narrative of Arthur Gordon Pym*, known in Finnish as *Valtameren salaisuus* (The Secret of the Deep). Setting its ending to music caught his interest. The story tells of various exciting events likely to engage young boys, but the ending became eerie enough to be long remembered. A crew of a shipwrecked boat is drifting toward the South Pole, and fast approaching a

---

[7] Einojuhani Rautavaara, Liner notes, *Book of Visions*, Ondine ODE1064-5.
[8] Tiikkaja, 523.

gigantic curtain of fog. Like an unseen waterfall, a sound is oncoming from the fog, from which shrieking white birds emerge and reenter, disappearing into invisibility. Approaching at a frightening speed with powerful winds and waves, the sailors see the mist gaping open here and there to reveal black holes, some kind of an abyss. Helpless, they see or sense an enormous human figure white as snow, perhaps the angel of death.

The composition calls for a large orchestra and a large chorus. Both are equal protagonists with a form of continuous variation on two themes. The orchestra sets the scene with an ominous string passage in icy parallel motion, moving into thunderous waves, foaming bubbles conveyed by rapid flute figuration. A pulsation in the lower strings seems to imply fearful anticipation. The chorus then enters and gives a verbal description. Quiet interludes and sections of tension alternate. Tension builds, shrieking birds sound from the trumpets, and terror grows in the chorus and orchestra to a final epiphany.

At the end of the concert, the Finnish Culture Fund and American poetess Aina Swan Cutler gave a scholarship for the winner of a composition scholarship that Rautavaara had been allowed to select from four candidates, similar to the Koussevitsky scholarship that Sibelius had given to Rautavaara in 1955. The candidates were well thought of, Juha T. Koskinen, Johan Tallgren, Lotta Wennäkoski, and Jani Kääriä. Rautavaara announced the winner, Jani Kääriä, chosen for his originality and scholarship. Kääriä's interest in mysticism and historical eras likely resonated with Rautavaara.[9]

Rautavaara did a considerable amount of traveling in 1998, attending festivals of his music and premieres of his compositions in Stockholm, Berlin, and Innsbruck, Austria. At the end of 1998 Rautavaara travelled to Cannes to receive his Cannes Classical Award for the recording of *Angels and Visitations*, the violin concerto, and the orchestral work *Lintukoto* (Home of the Birds, or Isle of Bliss). While there he also arranged for a documentary video called *Unien lahja* (Gift of Dreams). He was honored that year by having three music festivals feature his compositions.

In March 1999, he was invited to Minneapolis, Minnesota, by the Plymouth Music Series and the University of Minnesota for a week of his compositions, including the U.S. premiere of the opera *Aleksis Kivi* performed in English, choral works *Vigilia*, *Nirvana Dharma*, commissioned for the festival, and a choral arrangement of songs from the Aleksis Kivi opera, *Under the Shade of the Willow*. There he received two commissions, one for a harp concerto and another work of his own choice. In June of 1999 the first Hampstead and Highgate Festival was held in London with a broad spectrum of Rautavaara's compositions, including

---

[9] Tiikkaja, 525.

*Cantus Arcticus* (1972) and *Angels and Visitations* (1978) for orchestra, *Pelimannit* (Fiddlers, 1952) for piano, and the first piano sonata *Christ and the Fishermen* (1969), two works for organ, the *Toccata per Organo* (1971/98) and the *Hymnus* (1998) for organ and trumpet, commissioned for this festival for the director of the festival, Barry Millington, an organist and his wife, Deborah Calland, a trumpeter, plus the *Lorca Suite* (1973) for a mixed chorus. In July his works were performed at the Hitzacker Musiktage, a summer music festival in north Germany. Also in July, his *Autumn Gardens* (1999) was performed at the London Proms. In August, his third piano concerto, *Gift of Dreams*, was premiered by Vladimir Ashkenazy as both performer and conductor in two Finnish cities.

*Autumn Gardens* (Syksyn puutarhat) (1999) for orchestra was commissioned by the Scottish Chamber Orchestra for the London Proms concert of 1999 for the orchestra's 25th anniversary. Rautavaara was inspired by the concept of an English garden, one freely growing and organized, but not like the French garden, geometric and strictly pruned into shape. The title is derived from a passage in the libretto of Rautavaara's opera *Auringon talo* (House of the Sun), "like a butterfly in a dark autumn garden." The motive from that passage became the theme for the variations of the first movement. The slow movement follows without a break, also on a theme from the opera. The finale, Giocoso e leggiero, is playful, depicting falling leaves, perhaps a "sarabande in honor of the dying splendor of summer," as Rautavaara described it, or as T. S. Eliot said, 'late roses filled with early snow.' "[10]

The Third Piano Concerto *The Gift of Dreams* (1998) was premiered by Vladimir Ashkenazy in the summer of 1999 in Tampere and Turku, Finland, with Ashkenazy as both performer and conductor. Rautavaara was introduced to Ashkenazy by his record company Ondine with which the pianist had recently signed a contract. Ashkenazy wanted a work which he could play and conduct. Already in 1997 Rautavaara and Ashkenazy had met and discussed the concerto's first movement while making a TV documentary. Though Ashkenazy played the first two movements at that time, having already received the score earlier, Rautavaara later made changes and cuts for those movement's final version.[11]

Overall, the need to have the pianist conduct from the keyboard required a fairly constant beat. The concerto combines an almost romantic lyricism with touches of atonality. But Rautavaara insists it is not 12-tone in the conventional sense, but related his symmetrically used four note motif to a Hindu or

---

[10] Einojuhani Rautavaara, Liner notes, *Autumn Gardens*, Ondine ODE 950-2.
[11] Tiikkaja, 534.

Buddhist mandala circular design, which uses balanced elements within a circle to represent a spiritual universe.

> While 12 tones are the vocabulary of the century, it is how to use those 12 notes that is important. Music needs structure just as humans need a back bone in order to survive but that structure should be appealing and moving.[12]

The subtitle *Gift of Dreams* derives from a 1978 solo song, "Le mort des pauvres," text by Baudelaire. In the poem, the words "le don des reves" appears with the notes F-E flat-D flat-E. This motive was used in the String Quintet, and then in the piano concerto in all three movements. It is part of the melody in the first movement, Tranquillo, dominates the slow movement, Adagio, and then is varied in the finale, Energico. Both the first and second movements build to an emotional peak and then return to their opening moods. The finale's speed and intricacy varies the motive with fanfares, and a variety of orchestral textures, difficult to perform without a conductor.

---

[12] Einojuhani Rautavaara, Liner notes, *Piano Concert No. 3 "Gift of Dreams,* Ondine ODE 950-2.

CHAPTER NINE

# AFTER 2000, THIS JOURNEY GOES ON

Though Rautavaara turned 70 in 1998, his energy and creativity showed no signs of slowing. Commissions continued to flow in, premieres of his works were connected with personal appearances, and the creation of large scale works seemed to present no problems. Orchestral works came forth, concertos, and yet another opera. At the conclusion of his 2004 *Book of Visions* with a movement entitled "Book of Fate," Rautavaara was suddenly struck down with an aortic rupture and hospitalized for months. Despite the long recovery period, further works continued to pour forth in the next few years, concertos, a *Missa a capella*, and other small compositions. A 2011 magazine interview wrote that he was in the middle of another opera, and several other works in planning stages. He once said that he composes every day, with an inner drive and desire to do so, saying "My wife would tell you I even compose on Christmas Day." Such an inexhaustible source of creativity is astonishing.

In 2000 Rautavaara traveled again, this time to Philadelphia and New York. The Eighth Symphony, *The Journey*, was commissioned and premiered by the Philadelphia Orchestra for the orchestra's 100th anniversary. The work was conducted by Wolfgang Sawallisch at three concerts in Philadelphia on April 27th, 28th and 29th and again at Carnegie Hall, New York City, on May 1, 2000. At the time, Rautavaara gave pre-concert talks to the audience. The Philadelphia Orchestra then took this work on its European tour to Birmingham, London, Paris, Zurich, Warsaw, Prague, Cologne, Turin, Rome, and Helsinki.

In commenting on this symphony, Rautavaara explained that his thinking about symphonic form had changed over the years, from a first symphony in a playful neoclassical parody of old-fashioned rules and structures, through serialism and aleatoric forms to a new concept of form as slow transformation of new aspects from the same basic materials. Or, it could be called "a journey through ever changing landscapes." Another reason for the title *The Journey*, is that the motive in the third movement comes from words in one of his operas, from *Thomas*, Act III, "This journey goes on...whose is it?...Of one who wanders from the end of the journey?...beyond time?..." [13]

The symphony is in four movements. The first is peaceful, proceeding

---

[13] Einojuhani Rautavaara, Liner notes, *Symphony No 8, The Journey*, Ondine ODE 978-2.

in long sweeps. The melody rising gradually from the low opening register is finally crystallized as a rising fourth motif in the French horns. This 'signature' motif is the identifying feature, as it were, running through the whole work. The symphony having been commissioned by the Philadelphia Orchestra, I was able to make the second movement an extremely virtuosic, technically demanding scherzo. The third movement is a slow, poetic episode beginning and ending with the 'signature' motif. The finale is a broad stream "con grandezza" in which the motif presented first by the horns and finally by the whole brass section is a downward variation on the fourth motif. My large-scale works have almost always ended in silence. The 8th symphony nevertheless wanted to end fortissimo--con grandezza.[14]

In the fall of 2000 Rautavaara went to Austria to hear his Third Symphony of 1961 performed at a concert at the Bruckner Festival in Linz, Austria, Bruckner's birthplace. Conductor Max Pommer, who had already recorded Rautavaara's first three symphonies, presented a concert with the Prague Symphony Orchestra with Rautavaara's Third and Bruckner's Fourth on the same program. With its many references to the style and orchestration of Bruckner, Rautavaara's work again caused controversy. In 1961, despite its combination of twelve tone structure and tonality, it was considered not modern enough. In 2000, the orchestra members from Prague discussed among themselves how much more they enjoyed the Rautavaara work than the Bruckner, which they had probably played many times. They were likely in a position to appreciate all the little references and modernisms.[15]

While in Minneapolis, Minnesota, in 1999 for a festival of his music, a harp concerto, *Concerto for Harp and Orchestra* (2000), was commissioned, with vague terms. The following year, while Rautavaara was in the United States for the premier of his Eighth Symphony, he returned to Minneapolis with a nearly completed concerto to finalize the terms and see to its first performance. No one seemed to know who commissioned the work. After some haggling by his Boosey and Hawkes agent, the work was accepted and scheduled. The harpist, Kathy Kienzle, was delighted, saying that the work seemed to have been composed by a master harpist. Unfortunately, she received no rehearsals with the orchestra, the orchestra either disappeared or drowned her out at times, and the work was placed before the featured soloist, Joshua Bell, playing the Sibelius violin concerto. In contrast to his earlier reception in Philadelphia and New York, Rautavaara was not interviewed nor asked to do any introduction to the work. Despite his weeklong festival in that city the previous year, his

[14] Ibid.
[15] Tiikkaja, 540.

reception in 2000 was cool. Later that year the work was performed in Helsinki with French harpist Marielle Nordmann and the Helsinki Philharmonic. The critics praised the work but complained that the orchestra was too loud.[16] The following year, two enthusiastic harpists performed the work in Finland. Kathy Kienzle came from Minneapolis to bring the work to Tampere, Finland, and Reijo Bister, who had earlier been a technical advisor to Rautavaara for the work, presented it in Helsinki, this time with the Radio Symphony Orchestra and conductor Hannu Lintu.

In order to have enough volume from the harp, the orchestra includes two additional harps to add to the harp sound when needed. The first movement opens with a slow introduction, followed by a more dramatic section with unusual harp effects and playing techniques such as "gushing chords," metallic sounds, and thunder effects. The second movement is a lullaby which grows into a cantabile melody along with arpeggios typical of the harp. The finale is solemn with the three harps in dialogue with the orchestra. A central dramatic section is followed by a return to the opening style, and includes the theme of the introduction from the first movement.

At the time Rautavaara was in Philadelphia and New York in 2000, the *Clarinet Concerto* (2002) was commissioned by three parties, Theodore Friedman, the International Arts Foundation, and the Washington National Symphony Orchestra, to be performed by Richard Stolzman.

> A year later [2001] Stoltzman came over to Helsinki…when we had played it [the *Clarinet Concerto*] through together goodness knows how many times together, something exciting happened: Richard Stoltzman executed a jubilant solo dance there in my living room.[17]

The first performance was given by Stoltzman with the National Symphony Orchestra in Washington, D.C., in 2002. Stoltzman brought the work to London and to Helsinki for later performances.

The first movement opens with an eruption of sound followed by figurations in the clarinet ascending in stages. The French horn introduces a melodic second theme taken over by the clarinet. The cadenza is partially left to the performer, which in the Stolzman performance includes some tone bending. The bass clarinet accompanies the soloist in the cadenza's final part, and all return to the melodic second theme. The slow movement is an unbroken song for the soloist. The Vivace finale was originally a short display of virtuosity, but

---

[16] Tiikkaja, 551.

[17] Einojuhani Rautavaara, "Some Reflections on a Symmetrical Year," *Nordic Highlights*, newsletter from Gehrmans Musikförlag & Fennica Gehrmann (No. 12/2002), www. Fennicagehrman.fi/highlights/archive.

later had rhythmic variants of the first movement's motifs added to unify the whole work together.[18]

In 2001 Rautavaara was working on several commissions simultaneously. The opera *Rasputin* had a deadline coming up, a piano piece *Narcissus* for the Maj Lind Piano Competition that each entrant was required to perform, needed to be available soon, and the Clarinet Concerto was underway. He also found time to write a book with his wife Sini, *Säveltäjiä ja muusa* (Composer and Muse, WSOY 2001), about their experiences together, each from his own view, alternating chapters. Sini wrote that she was annoyed at being asked if she were the composer's daughter. Rautavaara responded in their book that she was both mother and daughter to him, and he both father and son, and both were content. Reviews were mixed, for some were upset to learn more than they wanted to know about his disastrous first marriage with Mariaheidi Suovanen Rautavaara.

In 2001 conductor Mikko Franck was asked to plan a Helsinki Orchestra concert series for the spring of 2002 and requested Rautavaara to join him for a Rautavaara and Franck festival in May. The six concerts included the Third and Fourth of his symphonies, smaller orchestral works such as *Cantus Arcticus* and *Autumn Gardens*, chamber music, the first and second piano concertos performed by Laura Mikkola, a concert version of *Auringon talo* (House of the Sun), and arias from several other of his operas. *Adagio Celeste* for string orchestra was composed for this festival, a rearrangement of the second movement of his string quintet *Unknown Heavens*. With the recording of this version, he made no mention of *Unknown Heavens* in his notes. Instead, he claims he was inspired by verses written by Lassi Nummi written in 1982: "Then, that night, when you want to love me in the deep of the night, wake me...let me wake through old age and death...join us to the communion of the world."[19] These words he had already set, in German, in a choral song from 1966, *Dann, in jener Nacht* (Then in that night).

Yet another festival was devoted to the music of Rautavaara in 2002. The annual Luxembourgian festival "Classics of the 20th Century" of 2002 performed two concerts on November 29 and December 1. The first orchestral concert programmed the *Requiem for Our Time* (1954), the Piano Concerto #3 *Gift of Dreams* (1999) with Finnish pianist Olli Mustonen, *Pelimannit* (The Fiddlers, 1952), and the Seventh Symphony *Angel of Light* (1994). The second concert programmed the String Quartet No. 1 (1952) and the String Quintet *Unknown Heavens* (1997).

---

[18] Einojuhani Rautavaara, Liner notes, *Clarinet Concerto*, Ondine ODE 1041-2.
[19] Einojuhani Rautavaara, Liner notes, *Book of Visions*, Ondine ODE1064-5.

## After 2000, This Journey Goes On

Rautavaara became interested in the character of Rasputin, the spiritual advisor to the last tsar and tsarina of Russia, because of his dual nature as a great religious figure but also one of great lewdness and excess. The real Rasputin (1871-1916) was a nearly illiterate peasant from Siberia, an Orthodox lay preacher and spiritual father-figure, who gained influence at the court through healing the Crown Prince's hemophilia. He became involved in Russian politics about 1910. Opposed to war, he had ministers reassigned, appointed, or dismissed at will. He was murdered by a group of noblemen in December, 1916, just before the Russian Revolution of 1917.

All the characters in Rautavaara's own libretto for his opera *Rasputin* (2003) are depicted as a mixture of good and evil, strength and weakness. Rasputin, the main character, alternately charms us with his lullaby for the Crown Prince on the beauties of Siberia and repels us with his orgiastic dinner with his female sect members. The Tsarina, desperate to heal her hemophiliac son, gives Rasputin too much influence in political affairs. The Tsar Nicolas is a good father but a weak ruler. A subplot involved two noblemen, each aiming to gain power by marrying into the royal family while at the same time carrying on a homosexual affair. Three churchmen, one of whom stutters, oppose Rasputin and are involved in the unrest of the Russian people, a prominent chorus.

Act One lays down the base of the story with Rasputin soothing the ill Crown Prince and a scene with the two male lovers Dimitri and Felix discussing their scheme to gain power, part of which involves the assassination of Rasputin. In Act Two an Easter crowd of Russian people complain about the foreign-born tsarina, her ill son, and call for war against the Turks. The noblemen and churchmen begin to plot against Rasputin. A scene change brings Rasputin and his female diners onstage. Claiming that "only by sinning can one be cleansed of sin," Rasputin emerges from under the tablecloth where the women are dining and later takes one of them offstage. As party entertainment, nobleman Felix shows up in drag, dressed as a female gypsy with gypsy musicians. The churchmen then encourage one of Rasputin's women to stab him, claiming Rasputin is living in sin with the tsarina. The action in Act Three brings resolution. Rasputin recovers from stabbing, but sees the visiting daughters of the tsar as seductive women. Felix attempts to woo the princess Irina, tells her of his mission to kill Rasputin, but fails in all his plans by injecting himself with drugs. The Crown Prince has another attack and Rasputin uses it to gain political ends from the tsarina and the tsar. The noblemen poison and then shoot Rasputin. The people gather, the voice of the dead Rasputin prophesizes bloodshed and flames, the royal family is killed, and a small group of communists take the stage, pointing to the future of Russia.

The music of *Rasputin* is continuous in Rautavaara's modified serialism with many tonal references. Conventional tonality is used for the newly composed gypsy music in the second act. A Russian atmosphere is created by the dominant bass lead singer and the prominent chorus. Of the few solos or monologues, Rasputin's Siberian lullaby in the first act is the most memorable. The tsarina and tsar each have a turn, while small ensembles of duets and trios are added in. The work calls for an unusual array of twenty-five solo singers, chorus, and dancers.

The opera debuted on September 16, 2003, at the Finnish National Opera with soloists Matti Salminen (Rasputin), Jorma Hynnninen (Nicholas II), the choir and orchestra of the Finnish National Opera under conductor Mikko Franck and director Vilppu Kiljunen. It was taken to the Mariinsky theater in St. Petersburg in May of 2005. There was so much interest in the opera in Russia that screens were hung from four places on the roof to project a video of the opera to the outdoor audience in the spring weather.[20] In 2006 the opera was performed in Lubeck, Germany, shortened somewhat, revised for a baritone, and performed in German.

A year earlier, the dedicated presenter of his piano music, Laura Mikkola, requested a new piano piece. By fall of 2003 it was ready. As Rautavaara was in the middle of composing his opera *Rasputin*, he took themes from its second and third act for *Passionale*. In the opening, marked Agitato, a lyrical tenor register melody is accompanied by arppegios and then the hands exchange material. A slower more chordal section, Adagio dolente, intervenes, before the first melody and tempo returns. The whole lies easily for the hands and sounds romantically lush and passionate, and almost tonal, despite the constant chromaticism. A lack of key signature is truly functional, except for the long passages of sixteenths or even thirty-second notes where it is difficult to remember a sharp placed earlier among thirty two notes, deemed unnecessary to be repeated by editorial rules.

In 2003 the Åboa Musica Festival in Turku (Åbo in Swedish), Finland, concentrated in mid March on the works of Einojuhani Rautavaara during a four day span. During this weekend the festival focused on Rautavaara's wide repertoire of orchestral and chamber works. The works included were: *Serenades of the Unicorn* (1977) for guitar; piano works *Etudes* (1969), Sonata No. 2 *The Fire Sermon* (1969), and *Narcissus* (2002); orchestral works *Adagio Celeste* (1997/2000), and the *Violin Concerto* (1977), performed by Janne Martilla; string orchestral works *Pelimannit* (Fiddlers, 1952), and the *Epitaph for Bela Bartok* (1986); three sets of songs, the *Three Sonnets of Shakespeare* (1951), *I min äslingsträdgård* (In My Beloved's Garden, 1983) and *Maailman uneen* (Dream World, 1972/82); two

---

[20] Tiikkaja, 586.

chamber music works, *Octet for Winds* (1962) and *Quartet for Oboe and String Trio* (1957/64).

The orchestral suite *Book of Visions* was commissioned in 2003 by the Orchestre National de Belgique and its Finnish conductor Mikko Franck, who was dedicated to sponsoring Rautavaara works. The four movements have subtitles: "A Tale of Night," "A Tale of Fire," "A Tale of Love," and "A Tale of Fate." In his program notes to this work, Rautavaara related that the work emerged slowly, not as a description of these titles but as his personal response to them. Night was a time of omens, horror, and hidden treasures, as well as wrestling with the dark angel which appeared in his dreams. The movement opens with an ominous timpani roll, then settles into a slow moving string melody ascending stepwise. The general tone of unrest ends tonally in resignation, with dissonances unresolved in the background.

"The Tale of Fire" recalls for Rautavaara the flames of Helsinki during the Second World War, known in Finland as the Winter War of 1939 and the Continuation War of 1941-45, both with Russia. The melody in the strings evokes flickering flames in its gradual upwards motion. Sliding trombones and timpani pitch glissandos perhaps represent sirens and the roar of fire. The ending slows, the fire ending, leaving ashes and skeletal structural remains.

"The Tale of Love" features by turns, a solo violin, oboe, clarinet, or the violin section exchanging phrases with pairs of clarinets or oboes in thirds over a quietly pulsating background.

"A Tale of Fate" brings in the climatic full orchestra, with a string melody over brass accompaniment, affirming a triumphal outcome. The full divisi strings again use clashing seconds for color. At the end the melody from "Night" reappears, rounding off the work in a sigh.

On completion of the piano score of the work, Rautavaara suffered a near fatal heart attack with a ruptured aorta which hospitalized him for six months, from January of 2004.[21] After the initial repair, other complications arose: a blood clot, neuropathy with a paralysis of hands, legs, and lungs requiring a respirator, a tracheotomy and loss of speech, speech therapy, physical therapy, a move to a nursing home, and then home with caretakers. On finally arriving home he immediately went to his workroom, each day gradually increasing his energy to return to work.

About the time that Rautavaara was able to return home, still having care and using a wheelchair, his first wife, Mariaheidi, died of cancer in September of 2004. She had earlier sent a letter to ask for forgiveness and reconciliation, but

---

[21] Einojuhani Rautavaara, Liner notes, *Book of Visions*, Ondine ODE 1064-5.

Rautavaara wasn't able to make a response. During the time of his hospitalization, all three of his children came to see him there and began a new relationship. Markojuhani, a successful pop singer, had kept an off and on friendship with his father due to drug problems. Son Olof and stepdaughter Yrja had not spoken with him for twenty years, but now began again. In closing their mother's estate, the three found old Rautavaara manuscripts of unpublished works which were then returned to their father. To Rautavaara they were ancient history and of little interest.[22]

Despite being hospitalized for such an extended time in 2004, Rautavaara soon picked up his usual life style and produced a series of new compositions. One of these was a commission from violinist Midori Goto for a sonata for violin and piano, *Lost Landscapes* (2004), each movement dedicated to impressions and memories of one of the places where he had studied. The four were a peaceful "Tanglewood," a scherzo "Asconia" (Switzerland), a slow movement "Rainergasse 11, Wien," and a bustling finale "West 23rd Street, New York." In the last part of 2004 he regained enough strength so that he had not only completed the orchestration of *Book of Visions*, but he brought out his *Manhattan Trilogy* and *Before the Icons* in 2005, both works for orchestra.

For the centennial celebration of the Julliard School, Rautavaara was commissioned to write a work for the Julliard Orchestra, even though the board of commissioners were not aware that Rautavaara had studied there. Memories of his school year there in 1955 and 1956 were evoked in the three movements of the *Manhattan Trilogy* (2005). Though Rautavaara was still too weak to travel to the first performance in New York City, the third movement, "Dawn," was performed by the Juilliard Orchestra under James DePriest while on a tour to Helsinki in August of 2005. In October, the same orchestra and conductor performed the whole *Trilogy* in New York City, now including the movements "Daydreams" and "Nightmares." Rautavaara has described them as impressions of his youthful aspirations and doubts during those student years, rather than as portraits of New York City. "Daydreams" opens with a hymn-like passage, moves to several successive solos for oboe, clarinet, violin, and flute, all with quiet strings and plucked harp pulsations. Full orchestra returns with a chordal climax, now with timpani pulsations. The lilting solos return with the harp. "Nightmares" opens with hissing from brushes on cymbals, low register rumblings, conveying somewhat menacing dark city streets, slapping of bass strings, sliding trombones, muted trumpets for far-away car horns—a plethora of sound effects accompanying the main melodic motives in the strings. "Dawn" opens with a gentle rocking of low strings back and forth, bird

---

[22] Tiikkaja, 584.

sounds from flutes. The rocking continues while smooth melodies unfold in the strings, ever growing, adding brasses and timpani, then fading again, the sound of a bell faintly heard in the distance.

Rautavaara had planned to orchestrate his 1955-56 piano work *Icons* at the time of its composition, but did not get to that project until 2005. Creating a new setting, he added three "Prayers" in between the original six pieces describing Byzantine icons and also a concluding "Amen." The orchestral version, *Before the Icons* (1955-56/2005), was premiered by the Helsinki Philharmonic Orchestra under Leif Segerstam. An Australian premier was conducted by Vladimir Ashkenazy in March of 2009.

The original 1955 piano version of *Icons* uses quartal harmonies (chords based on superimposed fourths), polyharmonies, changing meters, motoric rhythms, triadic thirds and tritones, and massive superimposed triads on top of triads creating impressions of grandeur. The piano work has six movements, alternating slow and fast movements, titled after Orthodox icon paintings. These movements were composed in New York City when Rautavaara was still a student under Persichetti at Juilliard. He had not yet made any serious study of serialism, aleatory, or other of his later techniques. His works of that student era could better be described as neo-classical, sometimes modal, and often influenced by folk music.

The newly composed three "Prayers" and the final "Amen," composed fifty years later, could not conjure up the youthful style and deliberately set out to be something else. The result is an alternation of mood and style, and also of orchestration. The new *Icons* movements are orchestrated for full orchestra. The three new "Prayers" contrast with the old movements scored for strings alone, according to Rautavaara "to reflect the voice of the individual."[23] The tempos are slow and lines move smoothly, often by step, and in clear counterpoint to one or more other lines.

In 2006 he completed another work for violin and piano, *April Lines*, a single movement. Sketches for a violin concerto in 1970 had been used for a concerto for wordless soprano, chorus, and orchestra, *Meren tytär* (Daughter of the Sea, 1971). In 2006 he took thematic material from the old previous work and reused it for a commission from Finnish violinist Kaija Saarikettu.

Rautavaara received a commission from both the New Zealand Symphony Orchestra, under the leadership of Finnish conductor Pietari Inkinen, and from the Helsinki Philharmonic Orchestra for an orchestral suite, *A Tapestry of Life* (2007). Each of the four movements has a programmatic title, implying not so much a story as a descriptive mood. The first movement, "Stars Swarming," is

---

[23] Einojuhani Rautavaara, Liner notes, *Before the Icons,* Ondine ODE 1149-2.

based on a poem by Edith Södergran, "The Stars." In an Emily Dickinson style, it warns of stars falling into splinters on the garden grass, so don't go barefoot if you walk there. Rautavaara set this text as a song when he was a teenager, lost the manuscript, and later set it again for chorus in *Katedralen* (The Cathedral, 1983). The opening movement takes themes from his opera *Thomas* and his Third Piano Concerto. In this orchestral interpretation, brief opening cascades of falling notes depict falling stars and high plucked harp over strings conveys "twinkling" or "glitter." After its Helsinki performance, reviewers criticized him for reusing his old material perhaps too often.[24] "Halcyon Days," the second movement, is built on a constant repetitive triplet with an ascending melody line. "Sighs and Tears," the third movement, features the oboe and cor anglais in lyrical broad sweeps of melody. The final movement, "The Last Polonaise," a solemn dance, opens dramatically with timpani strokes, like the end of some drastic event. Rautavaara mentions in his notes that he has often used a polonaise as a symbol of finality to end his operas. In *The House of the Sun* the two old ladies freeze to death at the end, but their thoughts and imagined actions are that of dancing out the door with their long awaited suitors. The opera *Rasputin* also includes a polonaise as a sign of the declining power of the tsar.[25]

Honors continued to come Rautavaara's way. In 2007 he and composer Kimmo Hakola were nominated as the first honorary members of the Helsinki Chamber Choir, formerly known as the Finnish Radio Chamber Choir. In the 1990s the choir had recorded all of Rautavaara's choral works. Founded in 1962, the chamber choir is the only chamber choir in Finland made up of professional singers. The group specializes in new music, regularly commissioning new works, mostly from Finnish composers. The choir cosponsored the International Einojuhani Rautavaara Chamber Choir Composition Workshop and Competition in 2012, along with the Viitasaari Time of Music Festival. Young composers between the ages of 18 to 35 were invited to apply as participants to work with the Helsinki Chamber Choir and two renowned composers in a workshop before writing their final work for the competition. The competition took place at the Viitasaari Time of Music Festival on July 6 and 7, 2012. At the conclusion of the final concert, an international jury awarded the Einojuhani Rautavaara Prize to the composer of the work it deemed the best, Zesses Seglias, with an audience favorite award going to Mike Solomon.

About 2007, Rautavaara received a commission for a percussion concerto which became the Concerto for Percussion, *Incantations* (2008). Composed for percussionist Colin Currie, this work was commissioned by four orchestras from London, Rotterdam, Baltimore, Maryland in the U.S., and Tampere, Finland. A

---

[24] Tiikkaja, 595.
[25] Einojuhani Rautavaara, Liner notes, *A Tapestry of Life*, Ondine ODE 1149-2.

reviewer in London expressed surprise that the work was not "as one had feared, a massive crash-bang-wallop drum extravaganza…but of great expressiveness with the marimba and vibraphone carrying much of the solo writing."[26] The score calls for marimba, vibraphone, timpani, four rototoms (pitched drums without shells) three tam tams (small gongs), two bongos, two congas, crotales (tuned bronze disks), tuned bells, three gongs, thunder stick, and pedal bass drum. The title conveys the idea of Lapland shamans, but Rautavaara wished to avoid the usual repetitive rhythms associated with such chant, writing varying meters such as 7/8, 3 +2+3/8, 11/8.

In three movements, the concerto features the marimba in the first and last movements and the more expressive vibraphone in the slow middle movement. The final movement adds a cadenza meant to be improvised by the performer. *Incantations* opens with a repeated melodic motif in the orchestra. Then marimba comes in with a rhythmically capricious texture, replaced soon with rototoms, bongo, congas and a few lines for cymbals. The percussion character has been introduced gradually. In the second movement the vibraphone dominates and the atmosphere is brooding, expressive and poetic. The third movement could be a shaman's dance in a jerky rhythm…a 'grandioso' end based on the opening motive from the first movement, with virtuoso passages in the marimba and bells.[27]

Rautavaara's second cello concerto *Towards the Horizon* (2008-2009) was dedicated to Truls Mørk, Norwegian cellist of the Minnesota Orchestra. Unfortunately, Mørk was too ill to do the premiere, so the first performance was done by cellist Arek Tesarsczyk with the Minnesota Orchestra under conductor Osmo Vänskä in the fall of 2009. In the same season, the concerto was performed by yet two other soloists, Mario Brunello in Amsterdam, and then in Helsinki by the original dedicatee, Truls Mörk. Rautavaara described the work as "a becalmed view of the far horizon distracted by a series of energetic dialogues before the melody recedes into the distance."[28] A work in one continuous movement, Rautavaara deliberately restrains the orchestra so that the cello can be heard. The opening lyricism leads to a Furioso, then a development with a dialogue between the cello and instrumental groups, ending in a high pitched cello register, like birds, moving ever quieter toward the horizon.[29]

---

[26] Martin Kettle, Review of *Incantations*, The Guardian (London), Oct. 26, 2009.
[27] Einojuhani Rautavaara, Interview about new percussion concerto, www.boosey.com, (Sept. 2009).
[28] Einojuhani Rautavaara, Program notes to first performance of *Cello Concerto: Towards the Horizon*, Minneapolis, Minnesota, Sept. 30, 2009.
[29] Ibid.

The various reviewers have described it in positive, but usually imprecise and flowery terms such as "bittersweet" (Osmo Vänskä on YouTube), "meditative and lyrical" (Michael Anthony in the Minnesota Post),[30] and "soothing, far-reaching, essentially symbolist and dream-like" (Helsingin Sanomat, January, 2011).[31] The recording of the work received a Grammy nomination in 2012 as well as a Gramophone prize and an International Classic Music Award.

In between these larger works, Rautavaara, as usual, had many smaller compositions underway. During 2008, he completed a choral work, *Our Joyful'st Feast* (2008), for mixed a cappella chorus. The *Fuoco* (2007) for piano joined two other pieces for piano, the *Narcissus* (2002) and *Passionale* (2003), to make a set of three for a performance by Laura Mikkola at a birthday party for his wife, Sini Rautavaara. A work for a coloratura soprano and string quartet, *Eingang* (Entrance), was completed in 2009. An unusual chamber work, the *Fanfare per Fagotti* of 2010 was written for six bassoons.

In early 2011, his *Missa a cappella* (2010-2011) for mixed chorus a cappella was completed and then premiered in November of 2012 in Utrecht, Netherlands. By composing this large Catholic text, his largest of several earlier, Rautavaara added to the variety of his liturgical repertoire. Both his *Before the Icons* (2006) and His *Vigilia*, a vigil for the Orthodox Feast of John the Baptist, represent the Orthodox Church. *Vigilia* was highly praised and performed in a shortened concert version many times. His Lutheran church works dot his entire career, mostly in choral works. Finnish paganism is represented by *The Abduction of the Sampo*, *Marjatta matala neiti*, *Thomas*, and other works. *Nirvana dharma* (1979) deals with Hinduism and Lord Krishna's flute.

The seven sections of the Mass, the Kyrie, Gloria, Credo, Sanctus, Benedictus, and Agnus Dei, are a marvel of "vocastration," the art of orchestration using voices. Each movement has a new type of arrangement for the voices. The Kyrie opens with an animated pulsing cluster of voices in field technique, out of which voices emerge with melodic phrases. The Gloria opens with an exultant homophonic chorus, alternation of male and female voices, and softer sections. The Credo, composed in 1972 and incorporated into this work, opens with an animated pedal point of male voices and female voices on the melody, and juxtaposes homophony, slower, and faster sections according to the long text. The Sanctus features a melodic tenor solo over the homophonic choral accompaniment, while the following Benedictus gives the melodic lead to the sopranos over a slower male accompaniment. The Agnus

---

[30] Micahel Anthony, review of *Cello Concerto: Towards the Horizon*. Minnesota Post (Oct. 1, 2010).
[31] Ibid.

Dei is a slow homophonic section with sopranos in the melodic lead. All of Rautavaara's various choral techniques are put to use here.

In 2010 Rautavaara's first opera, *Kaivos* (1957-58), previously performed only as a TV drama with changes in the location of the rebellion to satisfy the political climate, was presented in concert version in Tampere. Its first fully staged performance took place in Budapest, Hungary, in October of 2016 in commemoration of the 60th anniversary of the Revolution. Performed as a one act opera, it was done in Finnish with English and Hungarian subtitles.

In 2011, Rautavaara completed *Into the Heart of Light* (2011), for chamber orchestra, a work commissioned by the Ostrobothnian Chamber Orchestra for their fortieth anniversary in 2012. This 15 minute work is also subtitled *Canto V*. The work was first performed by the orchestra's founder and conductor Juha Kangas in Kokkola, Finland, on September 8, 2012, then taken on tour in Scotland with the Scottish Chamber Orchestra under conductor John Storgårds, principal conductor of the Helsinki Philharmonic and principal guest conductor of the BBC Philharmonic.

Two sets of songs were commissioned by baritone Gerald Finley in 2010. *In the Stream of Life* (2013) contained new orchestrations of six Sibelius songs originally with piano accompaniment, with texts by Ernst Josephson, Richard Dehmel, J. L. Runeberg, and others. A song cycle, *Rubaiyat*, on the writings of Omar Khayyam, was also completed, in versions for voice and orchestra or voice and piano.

An opera on the life of Lorca was being considered by Rautavaara as early as 2006. He hoped to use the same approach as he had used for the opera *Aleksis Kivi*, reading all of his works and other people's commentary on him, and then including as much of the author's own words as possible. He wanted to do this in a Spanish libretto, because of the difficulty of translating poetry. Unfortunately, he could find little support for a Spanish language opera nor for one on Lorca. Since he already had a first act finished, he put it down. Later salvaging what he could, he produced the cantata *Balada*, in 2015.

*Balada* takes poems from several different Lorca sources, creating a somewhat ambiguous tale of a man going on a journey. There is a lost love of a gypsy girl, death personified entering a tavern to stab the speaker, two friends climbing to a balcony while both bleeding, the first saying he will go far away "on a ship without sails, But do not ask me to explain anything." A solo tenor alternates with the chorus.

In 2013 Rautavaara mentioned several works he had in progress: a string quintet with two cellos commissioned by the U.S. Library of Congress and the

Chamber Music Society of Lincoln Center, *Variations for Five*, and a piece, *Mirroring* (2014), for piano for the Hong Kong Vladimir Ashkenazy Piano Competition.

In 2015 *Fantasia for Violin and Orchestra* was commissioned by violinist Anne Akiko Meyers. A single movement work, the violinist described it as an elegy, very reflective. She made the trip to Helsinki in December of 2015 to perform the work for Rautavaara while it was still unpublished, pleasing the composer. She described the experience: "After I played *Fantasia*, he looked at me and repeatedly said, 'I wrote such beautiful music!' We laughed and agreed. I was amazed that he made no changes to any notes or dynamics. Everything was in place, just the way he wrote it."[32] That was fortunate, because Rautavaara passed away before her first public performance of it in March of 2017.

*In the Beginning* (2016), Rautavaara's last work for orchestra plus marimba, tom tom, and harp, is seven minutes in length, and was completed in 2016, before his death on July 27, 2016. The work was commissioned by Pietari Inkinen, Finnish conductor, as a concert opener. It received its first performance on September 8, 2017, by the Deutsche Radio Philharmonic Orchestra of Saarbrucken in Kaiserlaufen, Germany, as part of a world tour. Inkinen then took the work to Japan, Cologne, and Prague. The work begins with a low register string ostinato with clashing seconds. Woodwind motives spark out of the dense texture. Gradually rising in pitch, a lushly lyrical melody appears and is passed back and forth from the strings to the brass, sidesteps into a brief rhythmically agitated section and then climaxes with the return of the broad melody. This apparent depiction of the creation grows from darkness into a radiance of light ending abruptly, leaving listeners wanting more.

*Two Serenades for Violin and Orchestra* (2016), commissioned by Finnish conductor Mikko Franck, was left unfinished when Rautavaara died in July 2016. The second serenade remained in a piano score. Franck was able to persuade Radio France to sponsor its completion by Finnish composer and former Rautavaara student Kalevi Aho. The work was scheduled for its first performance with Hilary Hahn, violin, Mikko Franck, conductor, and the Orchestre Philharmonique de Radio France in Paris in February of 2019.

The two movements are titled "Serenade pour mon amour" and "Serenade pour la vie." The first calls for solo violin and strings and has a lyrical barcarolle style, while the second adds woodwinds and horn, in a faster sectional arrangement.[33] Both are similar in style to several Rautavaara late works for violin and orchestra or violin and piano, the *Fantasia* of 2015 and *Whisper* (2010) for violin and piano, requiring lyrical playing rather than virtuosity.

---

[32] Anne Akiko Meyers, Liner Notes, *Fantasia*, Avie Records.
[33] www.boosey.com/cr/news/Rautavaara-s-last-work-premiered-by-Hilary-Hahn.

## GIVING RAUTAVAARA THE LAST WORD:

"If people ask me what I hope will happen to my own pieces, of course it would be nice if they lived on and people were able to receive them for a long time to come. But on the other hand, I don't hope they'll get an unlimited reception, because that would mean the world had stood still and would never be anything but what it is now."

"Nothing in the world goes on forever. That is what's so terrific."[34]

---

[34] Hako, Peka, Teostory article of 3/2013, at www.fennicagehrman.fi (1/7/2014).

# PART TWO

# WORKS BY GENRE

# CHAPTER TEN
# OPERAS

## *Isä-Peikko ja Simpukka-Ukko* (Father Troll and Old Man Clam) (1952)

This music, for flute and piano, was written to accompany a children's play by Pirkko Karppo-Salonen, and was first performed in Helsinki on December 26, 1952. The music included an overture and entr'acte music of songs and dances. The overture employed a whole tone scale while other pieces were constructed from octotonic scale steps, of alternating half and whole steps. Though mostly tonal and not abrasive, the new scales lent the sound of modernity.

## *Kaivos* (The Mine) (1957-58.1960/63), Op. 15

Rautavaara's first opera began as an entry in an opera composition competition. Deciding to write the libretto himself to better make the words and music interconnect, he based his story on the Hungarian uprising of 1956 and stories heard from Hungarians while attending the contemporary music festival in Zürich in 1957. Though the competition jury wanted to award it first place, the political policy of not offending their big neighbor, the Soviet Union, and self-censorship by the Finnish media and the arts determined that the award went to another. With some revisions—moving the setting to Franco's Spain of 1930 and removing Communist terminology--the opera was performed in 1963 on public television, the first such television opera in Finland. The opera was subsequently withdrawn and material from *Kaivos* later found its way into *Cantos* I and II (1960) and the String Quartet No. 3 (1965). In 2010 the opera was performed in concert version in Tampere, Finland, and recorded. Its first fully staged performance took place in Budapest, Hungary, in October of 2016 in commemoration of the 60th anniversary of the Revolution. Performed as a one act opera, it was done in Finnish with English and Hungarian subtitles.

Act One introduces the striking miners' capture of the Commissar, the manager of the mine appointed by the ruling Party and the reluctant recruitment of Simon, a former rebel leader, to head the strike. Simon's girlfriend Ira, who has her own self-centered agenda, arrives with him. In Act Two Ira sings that all is vain against a jazz radio background, releases the Commissar and temporarily becomes his hostage. The Commissar escapes to gather his forces while the wives and miners flee into the depths of the mine. The Third Act takes place in a cave in the mine. The Priest administers Communion to the hopeless crowd. Some of the miners take up drinking. One panics and leads a scuffle in which Ira is shot. The bullets weaken a retaining wall of an old tunnel that gives the group a means of escape. While Simon mourns Ira's death, the Commissar and his troops rush in, bayoneting Simon against the wall in the shape of a crucifix, as he has chosen his own sacrifice to give the miners time to get away.

In this 3-act opera, the music is in an expressive 12-tone technique, even in the jazz from the radio that forms the background for Ira's song. There are no distinct arias, though expressive solos and duets develop in the ongoing drama. The influence of Rautavaara's Swiss instructor Vogel can be seen in the spoken choral techniques of speaking, shouting, and whispering, often as background to a sung part. Contrasting musical styles, called for by the libretto, are heard in the jazz band playing on the radio in the background of Ira's solo, tonal music in the communion scene, and in the drinking song of the miners.

### *Kiusaukset* (The Temptations, 1969), a ballet

The ballet *Kiusaukset* (The Temptations, 1969), on a pantomime drama by the composer, was composed for a 1971 composition contest, and was first performed in 1973. Even before the performance the work was criticized in the press for portraying Jesus as dancing, one even calling it blasphemy. Based on the three temptations of Jesus in the wilderness, the work was difficult for Rautavaara to compose. Although he capably wrote his own libretti for his opera and set his own poems as solo songs, he had never worked with a speech-less pantomime before. The main characters were that of Jesus and a snake-like Satan, aided by the corps de ballet. One reviewer criticized the music as a backward step and pedantic, sounding like piano music, not realizing, or perhaps being more astute than he knew, that, indeed, Rautavaara had borrowed material from his 1969 piano pieces, *Etydit* (Etudes).

### *Apollo contra Marsyas* (1970)

In 1969 the Swedish author Bengt V. Wall approached Rautavaara about collaborating on an opera on an Edda saga topic. Much discussion later, the intertwined myths of Apollo and Marsyas and that of Daphne were decided upon. The musical competition between the satyr Marsyas playing the loud and raucous aulos, an instrument with an internal double reed similar to a bagpipe, and the god Apollo playing the more conservative lyre gave a good opportunity to contrast two styles of music and their supporters.

Rautavaara's opera divides the musical styles between the setting in antiquity of the first and third acts, and the present day setting in the second act. In this second act the protagonists are a contemporary pop musician, but with his own standards (Apollo), his girlfriend Daphne, and a pop music manager (Marsyas), who arranges to have him killed in a car accident. In the second act Rautavaara changes his usual style into that of a musical, with pop or light music. From this score he submitted two movements, *Helsinki Waltz* and *Helsinki Blues*, combined into a suite entitled *Helsinki Dancing*, to a composition contest with a light music category. Though the suite won the prize, he evidently was not particularly proud of it and later withdrew it from his catalog of works.

## *Runo 42: Sammon ryosto* (The Abduction of the Sampo) (1974, rev. 1981)

*The Abduction of the Sampo* is a choral opera in one act. The libretto was written by the composer after the Finnish epic Kalevala. Originally entitled *Runo 42*, it was a work for vocal soloists, three grand pianos, one of them a "prepared" piano, and percussion intended for the Helsinki Festival Week of 1976. Not satisfied with it, Rautavaara put it aside. In 1981 he was commissioned to compose a work for the 100th anniversary in 1983 of the Helsinki University chorus (the Ylioppilaskunnan Laulujat), a male choir. Pulling the score back out, he added choruses, electronics, recorded tape, and both a prologue and epilogue.

The three Kalevala heroes, Väinämöinen, Lemminkäinen, and Ilmarinen, set out for Pohjola, the North Farm, to win back the magic mill, the Sampo. Though made by the smith Ilmarinen, it was stolen by Louhi, the mistress of Pohjola. This magical machine can grind out grain, salt, and coins. The three heroes charm the inhabitants to sleep with song, steal the Sampo back, and flee by sea. Louhi, the mistress of Pohjola, pursues them, turns herself into an eagle, and smashes their ship with her terrible energy, at which time the Sampo is lost in the sea.

The Sampo can be presented dramatically or as a concert work, and contains an important tape part. Selecting from Runo 42 of the Kalevala, Rautavaara compiled his text, and added a prologue and epilogue musing on the parallelisms of the quests of men in both ancient and modern times. The tape has spoken narrative, distributed among several speakers spatially arranged, and performs as an accompaniment, with material ranging from thematic ideas heard in conjunction with the choral writing, to various sound effects, distorted voices, and whisperings. Though the work has four vocal soloists, the chief protagonist is the chorus. It undertakes a variety of roles, helping both to tell the story and to create an appropriate atmosphere for the myth.

In this opera we see two widely contrasting elements: live voices versus electronically distorted voices with unusual electronic sounds. The live voices have mostly traditional styles of melody and harmony, with canons, and tone clusters. The tape has the distorted sounds of the sorceress Louhi, actually Rautavaara's own distorted voice, and of the farm at Pohjola. Rautavaara had already done some work with tapes and electronic manipulation of sound in his works *True and False Unicorn* (1971) and in *Cantus Arcticus* (1972), *Concerto for Birds and Orchestra*.

## *Marjatta Matalan Neiti* (Marjatta, the Lowly Maiden), (1975)

*Marjatta matala neiti* is an opera in one act based on the Finnish folk version of the coming of Christianity to Finland. Rautavaara wrote his own libretto based on the final story, Rune 50 of the Kalevala, Finland's collection of heroic tales of the pagan pre-Christian era. The performance calls for children's chorus, four soloists, a small instrumental group with a technically difficult part for solo flute, plus narrator with a spoken prologue, comments on the way, and a conclusion. Commissioned by the city of Espoo for the Tapiola Children's Choir, it is a 22 minute long work.

In this folk version of the Virgin Mary and the birth of the Christ Child, Marjatta is a young country girl taking care of her family's sheep. She hears a lingonberry calling to her, the berry climbs up her body, slips into her mouth, then her belly, making her pregnant. Wanting to hide this from her parents, she continues on until the ninth month. She then sends her maid to the manor house of Ruotus, the local landowner, to beg for the use of a village sauna near running water to use for the birth. Ruotus is a Finnish corruption of the name Herod. The wicked Mistress will only grant the use of an old sauna, now used as a stable. The tradition of using of a sauna to give birth was because it was usually the cleanest place on a farm and could be warmed. Marjatta cries but accepts, finding the breath of the horse has warmed the small building, and there is an awaiting manger for a cradle. At the end of the opera, Marjatta sings a song comparable to the Magnificat, "I am your creation, come Thou to my aid, Creator." The narrator concludes with the interpretation of the old legend as the coming of "a new age, a new faith, a new hope, and goodwill towards men."

The musical materials combine old and new elements. There are settings in stanzas using the old modal scales of Finnish folk music and hymns. Among the modern elements are newly invented scales, aleatoric elements in the flute part, and speaking choir effects. The children are asked to baa like sheep or hiss, to create the warming breath of the horse. The spoken part for the narrator not only opens and closes the work, but is woven between choruses. The first performance took place on Sept. 3, 1977, Tapiola Church, Espoo, with the Tapiola Choir.

## *En dramatisk Scen* (A Dramatic Scene, "Late One Night") (1976)

*En dramatisk Scen* was commissioned by the Gothenburg (Sweden) Music School. A single act chamber opera in a 12-tone idiom, it was rehearsed but found to be too difficult for music students. The performance was put aside and the opera later withdrawn by the composer.

The plot, in Swedish on a libretto by the composer, concerns Järnberg, a composer, who becomes involved in politics. Afraid of being controlled by outside forces, he wants to withdraw from a union.[1] Järnberg, a Swedish translation of Rautavaara, also has a wife, Maria, and a teenaged son Marko, and lives in Westend, actual facts from Rautavaara's own life. In the opera, Järnberg's friend Mikael comes to his door asking for a place to stay for himself and his friends after being involved in a violent demonstration. Though allowing them all in, Järnberg fears for his wife Maria and son Marko. He calls the police telling them where to find the demonstrators. His foreboding is realized when the police take the teenage son Marko along with the demonstrators.

The prologue has the character Järnberg, acting as the real composer, telling the audience that the plot is fiction. Why Rautavaara chose to make fiction using himself and his own family so thinly veiled is a bit peculiar. Rautavaara returned to a 12-tone technique in this work after some years away. The characters of Järneberg and Mikael use a tone row full of seconds. Maria and the son Marko are given a quinten row, full of fourths by virtue of its construction. The Quintenreihe, learned from studies with Vogel, takes the original row's first note to begin a chromatic scale, then replaces every other tone with a note a fifth above. The new substitute notes then replace those pitches in the original row, wherever they are found. Since Rautavaara's original row had minor seconds in succession, the result would be leaps of fourths in the new version. In addition to these two rows, there is a rhythmic row.[2]

No suitable singer could be found at the music school to sing the role of the composer. Rautavaara was also unsatisfied with the musical aspect, put away the music, and gave up the hope of the commission income.

---

[1] Pekka Hako, *Finnish Opera*, trans. Jaakko Mäntyjärvi, (Saarijärvi, Finland: Finnish Music Information Centre, 2002), 98.
[2] Tiikkaja, 362.

## *Thomas* (1985)

Written at the request of baritone Jorma Hynninen, who performed the title role, *Thomas* tells the medieval Finnish story of Bishop Thomas, who led a crusade against Novgorod and Alexander Nevsky. The opera was commissioned by the city of Joensuu for the 150th anniversary of celebration of the Kalevala publication and first performed on June 21, 1985, in Karelia Hall, at the Joensuu Song Festival, in Joensuu, Finland. Rautavaara wrote his own three-act libretto, in both Finnish and German.

Bishop Thomas, an Englishman, arrived in Finland by way of Sweden about 1220 A.D., with strong connections to the Sorbonne University in Paris and with the papal court. He was perhaps the first to have a vision of an independent Finland, at that time loosely a part of Sweden, and mounted a crusade against the Novgorods of early Russia. Crushed by the forces of Alexander Nevsky, Thomas retreated to Turku, Finland's early capital city. In 1244 he resigned from his position as bishop as he blamed himself for the torture death of a colleague and for forging a papal dispatch. Taking the meager historical facts, Rautavaara's libretto envisions a three-way conflict: Thomas's attempt to make an independent Papal State of Finland in the early medieval Catholic world, the shamanistic Kalevala magic, and the Eastern Orthodox world represented by the city of Novgorod to the east.

Rautavaara invented various representative characters. Two friars help to clarify the thoughts and actions of the Bishop. Members of the attacking forces are represented by a merchant supporting them and a Knight of the Cross from Germany, sent by the Pope. The role of the Finnish Maiden, who represents the Finnish pagan people and a supernatural muse, was written for Sini Rautavaara, with her light high voice quality. She materializes from a statue in the cathedral, is mute, but sings like a bird with trills and bird calls. In the story line, she is threatened with rape by the knight, later appears on ship as an unexplained companion of the bishop, a woman on a ship as a sign of unluckiness, and rescues Thomas from certain death in battle.

The Finnish language libretto includes bits of Latin, Chaucerian English, wordless birdsong, and echoes of the Finnish Kalevala style of verse using repetition and alliteration. At times these languages are layered. In the opening Prologue, the Gregorian chant begins by itself and soon retreats into the background. We hear the chant, the Old English of the children's chorus, the mother's voice in English calling Thomas in from play, and, finally, added to all those, two friars singing simultaneously in Latin and Finnish, "Why hast thou forsaken us?" A similar layering of languages happens at the end of the opera.

The most memorable of the Kalevala style verses is the closing song of Thomas, which was twice sung in the prologue, summing up all the action of the opera, mourning that thoughts of independence came too soon:

"Suddenly sang the bird, the bird sang in the darkness.
In the dark it erred. It erred like a man
and sang the sounds of morning into the night, across the
evening and beyond time."

In the Finnish language it contains much alliteration, parallelism of verses, and repetition of material, as does the Kalevala. This alliteration, repetition of the same letter and sounds, and repetition of words can easily be heard even by the non-Finnish speaker.

"Äkkiä lauloi lintu, lintu lauloi pimeässä,
pimeässä se erehtyi, se erehtyi kuin ihminen
ja lauloi aamun äänet yöhön, iltaa pitkin, ajan taakse."

In *Thomas* Rautavaara uses different tonal systems—diatonicism, modality, serialism, and synthetic scales—side by side, and often simultaneously, to represent the different protagonists. Because of these varied tonal systems, each designed to evoke a distinct atmosphere, this opera has been called Rautavaara's first major Postmodern composition. Its compositional language stretches from Gregorian chant to 12-tone and aleatory field. The use of similar intervals in each system and underlying pedal tones ties all the different tonal systems together..

Musical styles, languages, and tonal systems change as needed by the plot. An ancient pentatonic scale depicts the chorus of Finns. The chorus changes identity as needed, from ancient Finns, to monks chanting in modality, to a cathedral choir, singing in diatonic tonality with imitative entrances. At times, they whisper the curses of the people or add successive layers to create big static sound blurs. The English children and mother sing in a very simple folksong style. The three shamans have music based on an octotonic scale of alternating whole and half steps, the mute Finnish Maiden has an aleatoric wordless melodic line with bird trills, and for the westerners--Thomas, his friars, a knight and a merchant--twelve tone rows are created. When required by the plot, these separate language styles and separate music styles are fitted together, a remarkable feat of synthesis. The text requires the various tonal systems, and the tonal systems then influences the text. Drama and composition were done at the same time, one often leading the other.

## *Vincent* (1987-1990)

After the 1985 opera *Thomas*, baritone Jorma Hynninen suggested another subject for an operatic collaboration, one based on the life of painter Vincent Van Gogh. Using a series of events from Vincent's life in flashbacks to show the course of his life, Rautavaara again wrote his own libretto, both in Finnish and in German. Besides the main characters of Vincent, brother Theo, and artist Paul Gaugin, lesser parts include an early wife originally a prostitute during his failed pastor days in Belgium (named Maria Hoornik referring indirectly and unflatteringly to his ex-wife Maria Heidi), two bordello prostitutes Rachel and Magdalena, and Gaby, the inspirational muse written for Sinikka Rautavaara. Each of the acts includes a quartet, the same singers but playing new roles as hospital employees, police, and then critics. Sometimes they sing together, as in a chorale, sometimes making comments individually. Each of the three acts opens with an orchestral prologue titled after a Van Gogh painting, "Starry Night," "Wheatfield with Crows," and "The Church at Auvers," all later incorporated in his Sixth Symphony *Vincentiana*, along with a final fourth movement "Apotheosis" based on Vincent's final monologue.

As in the opera *Thomas*, characters are distinguished by their own twelve-tone rows or synthetic modes, each one having its own sound characteristics. The vocal parts are free from the rows. An unusual touch is a synthesizer, which is used to show the inner distorted world of Vincent, contrasted with the normal world accompanied by the regular orchestra. Other styles of music are called for by the libretto, such as the ragtime piano of the bordello and the waltz of Vincent and Gaby. Hidden references appear, too, such as the hymn of the Soviet Union when the text refers to "Mao and Lenin's theory of contradiction" from one of the art critics, and a hymn-like setting under the text "who do you think you are? A grand vice-Jesus?" in a parody of a Christmas tune.

## *Auringon talo* (The House of the Sun, 1990)

In 1987 Rautavaara was captivated by a newspaper article about two elderly sisters brought from Russia by their family during the Revolution of 1917. In a rural setting near the port city of Turku, they maintained their old pre-Revolutionary aristocratic life style and never adapted to their new conditions. Rautavaara's libretto attempted to keep their story intact, with the failures of their aristocratic family who expected to return to Russia shortly, making no attempt to learn Finnish or Swedish. Rautavaara, though considered to be primarily a composer, is certainly to be admired for his literary skills and dramatic pacing. His libretto is well-structured and alternates bits of comedy with profound philosophy.

The father failed to establish a business, finding that knowledge of Russian, German, and English was not enough in rural Finland. His suicide was followed by the son's, the mother's, and then deaths of two daughters, leaving the twin sisters essentially living in the past, in their memories. Rautavaara remarkably condenses the family's tragic deaths into a single scene with the servant repeatedly entering from the garden saying "I have the honor to announce that Mr. John has shot...Master Victor is hanging...Madam Victoria has departed."

Act Two adds a lighter contrast. The chatty mailman jokes with references to Greek mythology, uncomprehended by the sisters. A letter from a realtor is mistaken for an announcement of a visit from an English cousin, requiring the hiring and training of two farm boys to act as footmen, A social worker is confounded by the inexperienced footmen.

While taunting each other about not catching a beau earlier in St. Petersburg, one sister says "he may still come," while the other says, "perhaps, in a wheelchair and with smacking false teeth." As in Rautavaara's *Vincent* opera, the composer had difficulty deciding how to end the opera's story. His wife, Sinikka, suggested that it end in a waltz. The light changes, the synthesizer indicates that the setting has returned to the dream world of the past, and all the characters of the past come forth to be announced by the long-departed servant, now a major domo. They take their partners and go through the garden door into the ballroom singing "It is time; it is time to come, it is time to go...like a cloud passing, soon blown by the wind into oblivion." This text is a recapitulation of the sisters' earlier duet:

> When will this end, when will the world be empty enough for us,
> Like a person is empty when stripped bare?
> When only the soul remains, weightless and wind-tossed,
> Blown like a leaf off the ground into oblivion?[3]

Their story of misunderstandings, inability to interact with their neighbors or even to care for themselves led to their deaths. A cruel prank by local boys in turning off their electricity caused them both to freeze to death in their eighties.

The opera takes place in both the past and the present, with the old ladies at times replaced by their younger versions, four cast members in all. Duets in close harmony from the sisters and ensembles with the other characters combine with continuous orchestral music. Moving back to the past is indicated

---

[3] Rautavaara, *The House of the Sun* libretto, Ondine CD ODE 1032-2D, 34. (In Finnish, Milloin tämä päättty, million maailma on kyllin tyhjä meille.)

by the addition of a high-pitched synthesizer to the orchestra as well as mention by the sisters of an approaching light from outside, a star or a sun, which might even have been the light from a nearby gas station.

*Auringon talo* was commissioned by the Finnish National Opera and had its first performance on April 25, 1991, in Lappeenranta, Finland, with the Finnish National Opera and the Lappeenranta Symphony Orchestra. The same production was taken to Stockholm in 1992. The opera was presented in German in Greifswald, Stralsund, and Mönchengladbach, Germany, during 1994-1995, in English at the Opera of the Ozarks in Fayetteville, Arkansas, in 2004, and in Vienna in 2004.

## *Tietäjien lahja* (The Gift of the Magi) (1994)

This forty-five minute chamber opera produced on television is based on the O. Henry short story about the giving and receiving of gifts at Christmastime. The wife sells her hair to a wigmaker to buy her husband a watch chain. The husband sells his watch to buy her hair clips.

The setting of the story is in 1930s Helsinki. The wife's story leads, until the husband gives his gift at the end. Besides the two main characters, others are invented. King Solomon becomes Mr. Saloman the landlord, the Queen of Sheba is a prostitute, and there is the wigmaker, who buys the wife's hair. He is given an extensive aria, "love can light the lowliest house, like a Christmas star." A chorus of townspeople and children add comments of their own, sometimes spoken, as they watch the action unfold.

The work was delayed by choice of the leading soprano. Rautavaara wanted his wife Sini to do it, and the producer had someone else in mind. Sini asked Rautavaara to let it go, so that the work could be finished and performed. Both Sini and Einojuhani appeared in the show, dressed in furs as Russian aristocrats among the townspeople.[4]

The style of the music is similar to Rautavaara's other works of the early 1990s, *Cantos IV*, *Die Erste Elegie*, and *Angel of Light*. Spoken dialogue appears here at times, always with orchestral accompaniment. The wigmaker's aria reuses music from Rautavaara's Seventh Symphony, *Angel of Light*, composed two years earlier. The symphony's opening string arpeggios punctuated by vibraphone and bells now accompany a freshly composed vocal line. As in his other operas, the music is continuous.

---

[4] Tiikkaja, 495.

## *Aleksis Kivi* (1995-96)

Jorma Hynninen, the baritone who had sung the lead in Rautavaara's operas *Vincent* and *Thomas,* suggested an opera on the tragic fate of Aleksis Kivi, the first important Finnish-language author. Hynninen, as the artistic director of the Savonlinna opera festival, wanted another opera to star in and had the ability to make it happen. Rautavaara wrote the libretto for this opera in addition to composing the music. The premier took place in Punkaharju's Retretti caverns during the Savonlinna Opera Festival of 1997 and was later presented in English in 1999 in Minneapolis, Minnesota.

Rautavaara took excerpts of Kivi's writings in various plays for use in the libretto, from the epic *Isle of Bliss* at the beginning and end of the opera, two poems in Act One about the little squirrel and married life, and the final aria based on Kivi's most famous poem, "Sydämeni laulu" (Song of My Heart), taken from his novel *Seitsemän veljesta* (Seven Brothers).

> Tuonen viita, rauhan viita!
> Kaukana on vaino, riita,
> kaukana kavala maailma.
>
> (Grove of Tuoni, peaceful woodland!
> Far from hatred, far from struggle,
> far from the evils of mankind.)

Ahlqvist, the antagonistic Swedish language critic of Kivi both in reality and in the opera, wrote melancholy verse under the pen name of A. Oksanen. The two drunken imagined characters from the Kivi's play *Cobblers of the Heath*, referred to in the Third Act, sing Oksanen's verse: "Ah, joy is fleeting like a gaggle of dreams. If it's happiness you want, only liquor has it for sure." The music of the opera is continuous, with only a few distinct arias, notably those based on Kivi's poetry. Rautavaara later published four orchestral songs from the opera: "Ikävyys" (Melancholy), Kivi's opening aria; "Laulu oravasta" (The Squirrel), from Act One where Kivi is requested to read one of his poems to Hilda and Charlotta; "Oi mailma, elämä sä ilmeellinen" (O World, Life, Thou Marvel), Kivi's song from the opening of Act III; and "Sydämeni laulu" (Song of My Heart), Kivi's final aria about the peace found in the grove of Tuoni, the land of the dead. Rautavaara has mentioned several times his original reluctance to set this last song, since the setting by Sibelius was well-known and loved. But, since this poem is so tied to Kivi, it was essential to the opera. Rautavaara's setting of this strophic poem sounds apparently simple but is exquisitely expressive (Example Twenty-two, p. 99). A fifth orchestral song was also published as Charlotta's Monologue, "Eron hetki on kalveakasvo" (The Moment of Parting is a Pale Mask), from the scene where Charlotta movingly realizes she must let Kivi go. Both Ahlqvist and the aged Runeberg are given spoken roles, depicting them as unmusical. As in the opera *Vincent*, a synthesizer is added to the orchestra at times when reality is changed for hallucinations. Rautavaara borrowed his own tune from the opening of *Pelimannit* (The Fiddlers) for the scene with the two folk musicians from the *Nummisuutarit* (The Cobblers of the Heath), though it is somewhat hidden by other themes going on. The opera was first performed at the Savonlinna Opera Festival in 1997, and later performed at Strasbourg, Opéra du Rhin, France.

## *Rasputin* (2003)

The opera *Rasputin* tells the story of the spiritual advisor to the last tsar and tsarina of Russia. The real Rasputin (1871-1916) was a nearly illiterate peasant from Siberia, an Orthodox lay preacher and spiritual father-figure, who gained influence at the court, particularly through the Tsarina, by healing the young Crown Prince of his hemophiliac attacks. Rasputin was allowed to become too involved in Russian politics about 1910 and was murdered by a group of noblemen in December, 1916, just before the Russian Revolution of 1917. The actions and feelings of all the characters involved are well-depicted. The distraught royal parents search for any possible help for their son, and are easily taken in by Rasputin. The healer claims miraculous powers through his faith while indulging in orgies of drunkenness and his power over his female followers. Two noblemen represent their class in scheming to regain political power through royal marriages while enjoying their own homosexual affair. The people in the chorus are caught up in decisions made by others, helpless to change their circumstances except by violence.

Serialism and tonality are combined in continuous music, with the gypsy music definitely tonal. The bass aria of Rasputin singing about the wonders of Siberia to calm the the sick child is the most memorable solo. Other characters, the tsarina, the tsar, the two male conspirators, also get solos and featured parts. Twenty-five solo singers are called for, as well as chorus and dancers. A Russian atmosphere is created throughout by the dominant bass lead singer Matti Salminen and the prominent chorus. Understandably, the opera created a sensation in St. Petersburg, Russia, where the overflow crowd was catered to with outdoor video screens and a picnic atmosphere.

# CHAPTER ELEVEN
# ORCHESTRAL WORKS

### *Dramaattinen alkusoitto* (Dramatic Overture) (1951) (withdrawn)

A student work, later prohibited from performance, this orchestral work was first performed at the Ung Nordisk Musik-festivaali (Young Nordic Music Festival) in Copenhagen on October 19, 1951. The festival, begun in 1946, included seven representative works chosen from each Nordic country. Though Rautavaara had still not begun composition study, the fact that his professors encouraged him to submit this work and its acceptance shows that they were impressed with his ability and future promise.

### *Tema con tre variazioni* (Theme with Three Variations) (1952), for orchestra (withdrawn)

A student work removed from performance, this work was first performed in Oslo, on October 10, 1952, for the Young Nordic Music festival of that year. It may be identical to the *Tema con variazione for piano*, which Rautavaara included in his first composition recital at Raisio, a town near Turku, on May 8, 1954.

### *Andante moderato* (1952) for orchestra (withdrawn)

This student work was performed by the radio orchestra in 1952 and was then withdrawn.

### *Divertimento* (1953)

This student work for string orchestra suggests folk music in both its modal melodies and rhythms, similar to works of Bartok. An eighteen minute work, it develops its material into one long form, rather than a string of short movements. It was first performed by conductor Jorma Panula at the Sibelius Academy in 1953.

## *Sinfoninen sarja* (Symphonic Suite) (1953) (withdrawn)

First performed in Tampere by the City Orchestra under conductor Usko Meriläinen on May 20, 1955, this early composition completed as a student at the Sibelius Academy is classified as not to be performed.

## *Adagio and Toccata* (1954), orig. for piano, arr. for orchestra (withdrawn)

Originally for piano, this orchestral version was performed by the Helsinki City Orchestra under Tauno Hannikainen in Helsinki on February 18, 1955. The piano composition was performed as part of Rautavaara's composition recital on May 8, 1954. Both were withdrawn from performance and lost.

## Symphony No. 1, Op. 5 (1956/1988/2003)

In 1956, Rautavaara attempted his first symphony using a standard format in four movements, working with composer Persichetti at Juilliard. Though the work was accepted for performance in Helsinki the next year, Rautavaara withdrew it. In 1988 he was offerd a chance to publish five of his symphonies by Pan Editions and decided to revise this first symphony. After more than thirty years, it was difficult for him to avoid changing his youthful style into one using his mature techniques. He chose to combine the two slow movements, use the fast second movement for the finale, and omit the original final movement.

Some previously composed songs were used for themes. The *Orpheus Sonnets* composed during his study in Vienna the previous year gave him his opening, "Da steig ein Baum" (A Tree Arose), but was cut in the revised version. In 1988 the new finale used the ascending scale and triadic leaps of the third song from *Three Sonnets of Shakespeare* (1951), "Shall I Compare Thee to a Summer's Day."

In the first movement, Andante, the timpani stroke and roll announce the opening romantic unison string melody with leaps to a climatic note, often a minor 9th. The music flows unobtrusively through a wide variety of metric changes, such as 3/8, 5/8, 7/8, 5/4, 4/4, 2/4, 5/4. Long pedal tones ground temporary tonal centers and added seconds brighten triadic sounds. With the combining of the two original slow movements, the resulting form is difficult to follow. Two ideas are presented and alternated, plus a dotted note idea that later predominates at the end. A half step chromatically descending accompaniment and the dotted note pattern tend to unify the whole. A fourth theme, an ethereal solo for violin, is later repeated by a solo flute. The opening theme has disappeared in the process and only the dotted note pattern receives development. Though this movement was revised in 1988, Persichetti's comment in 1956 that Rautavaara had yet to learn to control his form was accurate. Yet, the melodies are enticingly lovely and deserve their continued performance (Example Five, page 22).

The finale begins with a motoric pulsation. The ascending scale theme in the strings is quickly answered by high winds in a descending scale. Comedy and mad-cap adventure sounds from the finale's various solo passages for bassoon, tuba, piccolo, and clarinet, all cut off by a final rim shot on a snare drum.

The original version was first performed in Helsinki by the Radio Symphony Orchestra under Nils-Eric Fougstedt on January 22, 1957. Withdrawn and then revised in 1988, the work was performed by the Radio Symphony Orchestra under Jukka-Pekka Saraste during the Helsinki Festival Week, on August 24, 1990. In 2002 "Poetico," a new middle movement was officially added, based on his solo song "Die Liebende," the third song in his song cycle, *Die Liebenden*, of 1958.

## Second Symphony, Op. 8 (1957/1984)

After the first performance of Rautavaara's First Symphony, he felt that the critics found him too conservative. He wanted to demonstrate his ability to write modern styles. He took four movements from his *Seitseman preludia pianolle* (Seven Preludes for Piano, 1957) and reworked them into much longer orchestral movements. Rautavaara described the Preludes and their later manifestations in his Second Symphony as "bare, sketchy, aphoristic, unconventional, ascetic, and dissonant but still supported with tonality." Besides being developed further into far lengthier symphonic movements in his Second Symphony, they were also later transformed into a work for string orchestra, the *Finnisch, heute* (Finnish, Today) of 1970.

Like the Preludes, the movements are tonal but dissonant, not developmental nor repetitious. The opening somber firstt movement derives from the fourth and sixth preludes. The second fast movement comes from the fifth prelude, a fugato. The third movement connects with the second prelude, titled "Kyllin hiitasti" (Slowly Enough). The last movement has many changes of meter in a fast Presto (Example Six, p. 26).

The final version of this symphony, dating from 1984, differs from the original in that it is scored for a slightly larger orchestra, adding more brass and strings, as well as further thematic material for the strings in the third movement. The original version was first performed by the Helsinki City Orchestra under Tauno Hannikainen in Helsinki on October 11, 1957. The revision came as a request from conductor Jorma Panula to play the work with the Sibelius Academy orchestra in 1985.

## *Modificata* (1957)

*Modificata* was partly composed under the supervision of teacher Wladimir Vogel, with elements taken from the earlier 1956 string trio begun under Persichetti. The first movement "Recitatio" was written as an exercise for Vogel, originally for string quartet but later for orchestra. The original row is symmetrical so that it has the identical intervals in its retrograde version, divided in half as a palindrome. After his return to Helsinki, Rautavaara added two further movements not in serial technique, "Meditatio," and "Affectio." All the movements are unified by a short melodic figure at the opening, C, E♭, B, B♭, a trill or tremolo motive appearing prominently in the first and second movement, and by repetition of sections only slightly changed (Example Seven, page 30).

Modificata was presented at a concert by conductor Tauno Hannikainen with the Helsinki City Orchestra, in April of 1958. Rautavaaara's Finnish compoisition teacher Aarre Merikanto praised it, but his Ascona teacher, Vogel, who happened to be in Helsinki for another event, was disappointed that the second and third movements were not in serialism. Rautavaara withdrew the work and then in 1964 reworked it for a *Quartet for Oboe and Strings*, which gained little notice.

## *Praevariata* (1957)

In the same year as *Modificata*, Rautavaara decided to try his hand at total serialism, where not only the tones were in a serial row, but also rhythm, dynamics, orchestration and form. With all these decisions made before the start of his composing, Rautavaara felt it should be named what it was, a set of variations decided before or "pre" variation.

The 12 tone row contains four patterns of a major third plus a minor second, two in the first hexachord and two in the symmetrical second hexachord (the first hexachord, C-E-F-G♯-A-C♯, and the second hexachord, E♭-B-B♭-G-F♯-D.) In orchestration, the xylophone begins as a solo, has a single note, the next bar has it playing two notes, moving to 5 notes per measure and then reverses, and starting again. The number of beats in a measure start at 9 sixteenths, grows to 13 beats in a measure and then reverses back to 9. Dynamics in a pattern begin with the xylophone at pp, grows to ff, and reverses back to pp. In the eleven variations, the climax occurs in the seventh, with the most instruments and thickest texture, then reverses to the quiet xylophone ending (Example Eight, page 31).

On completion the work had a varied history. In 1958 it was selected as the Finnish contribution to the ISCM (International Society of Contemporary

Music), and was recorded by the Strasbourg Radio Symphony under Charles Bruck. In 1964 Rautavaara made it a part of his Fourth Symphony, as a second of two movements, now titled "Variazioni." It was presented by the Helsinki City Orchestra under Jorma Panula in 1965. Revised, it was performed in 1970 by the Finnish Radio Orchestra under Paavo Berglund and then withdrawn. When it came time to publish his first five symphonies in 1988, he substituted another work, *Arabescata*, naming it the Fourth Symphony. If one wants to find the original *Praevariata*, it remains only in old recordings, one from the Strasbourg performance and one from the Helsinki Fourth Symphony performance of 1965.

## *Canto I*, Op. 16, and *Canto II*, Op. 17 (1960)

In 1960 Rautavaara produced two orchestral works, *Canto I*, Op. 16, for string orchestra and *Canto II*, Op. 17, for full orchestra, four Wagner tubas, celeste, and harp. The name of the composition refers not only to Ezra Pound's poetry, but also to vocal song.[1] Ezra Pound's *The Cantos* was a long poem of 116 sections or cantos written between 1915-62, touching on historical, geographical, and mythological events in an experimental style of writing, apparently without structure or ending. What Rautavaara meant by adopting this vocal and poetic term he never fully explained. Perhaps it was referring to his own stream of consciousness, that he considered it his right to rework and develop his own earlier material from his opera *Kaivos* (The Mine, 1957-58, 1960- 63). Perhaps it was his concept of such a work as experimental and showing his current state of approach to composition. Or, perhaps it was his rationalization that his vocal lines could equally well serve as orchestral themes.

*Canto I* is based on material from Acts One and Three of the opera *Kaivos* (The Mine). *Canto II* comes from the first half of Act Two, reproducing the ABA form of bars 102-149 of the second act. Another work, the *Third String Quartet* (1965), also draws material from *Kaivos*, from the second half of Act Two.[2]

About the time of composition Rautavaara spoke of three ˆCantos," one for for string orchestra, the second for strings, brass, and timpani, and the third for a large orchestra. In later years, he revised them, reversed their order, to keep the material of the opera *Kaivos* (The Mine) in the right sequence, and then omitted one. Musicologist Anne Sivuoja-Gunaratum claims, however, based on thematic content, that, of the three mentioned in 1961, it is the original third

---

[1] Rautavaara, quoted in Sivuoja-Gunaratnam, 190-1.
[2] Sivuoja-Gunaratnam 95.

Canto that was reorchestrated for string orchestra which became what is now the first Canto and the original second Canto that has disappeared. The three original Cantos were written in 1960, using materials from the opera *Kaivos* dating from 1957-58, and a year after Rautavaara's marriage to Mariaheidi. After her death in 2004, long forgotten compositions and sketches were returned to him, including the original Canto II, proving Sivuoja-Gunaratum's theory. The puzzle, long forgotten by Rautavaara himself, was solved. The later works designated as *Third Canto* (1972), *Fourth Canto* (1992), and *Canto V* (2010) are thematically unrelated to the earlier two.

## Third Symphony, Op. 20 (1961)

The Third Symphony, Op. 20 (1961), evokes the spirit of Anton Bruckner's Fourth Symphony and at the same time mixes 12-tone serialism with consonant music. The row, C-F-E♭-A♭-D♭-E-B♭-G-D-A-F♯-B, contains three tonal triads. Tonality is implied by many octave doublings and thirds, the horn motif in fifths and fourths, temporary pitch centers, such as D, at the beginning, as well as the serially unlikely immediate repetitions of tones and of small groups of tones. In the program notes to the first performance Rautavaara declared the work entirely twelve-tone, saying:

> the horn theme heard at the beginning is the series which functions for all melodic and harmonic events, even the most tonal ones...The symphony signifies a logical step in evolution whereby the twelve tone technique has gained...the status of providing tone and intervallic material, which is conceived as music basically relying on tonal laws.[3]

The first movement opens with a horn melody based on the row. The horn motif, full of fifths and fourths, is set against a string tremolo, borrowing the opening texture and orchestration from Bruckner's Fourth Symphony (Example Eleven, pages 43-44). The second movement evokes a lullaby with its melody placed over a rocking string ostinato pattern. The third movement's scherzo has fanfare melodies and repeated rhythmic motives. Concluding and summarizing, the finale weaves together the main material from the previous movements and comes to rest in the tonal center of the opening, D minor, at the same time bringing back a recall of the opening horn melody, string tremolos, and flute flutters. Other Bruckner trademarks can be seen in the use of the Wagner tuba, themes and motives in sequences, and performance marks in German.[4]

---

[3] Rautavaara, quoted in Sivuoja-Gunaratnam, 63.
[4] Kimmo Korhonen, *Finnish Orchestral Music* (Jyväskylä: Finnish Music Information Centre, 1995), 39.

## Symphony No. 4 *Arabescata*, Op. 24 (1962)

This four movement work, though composed in 1962, was named the Fourth Symphony in 1986 after the original Fourth Symphony (1964), Op. 25, a two movement work, was withdrawn. The only totally serial symphony to have been composed in Finland, the parameters of pitch, rhythms, durations, dynamics, timbre, density and miniature forms are all predetermined by rows.

The first movement is organized by ABA forms, at both the large and small levels. Both contain two hexachords, the second a transposed retrograde of the first. The two rows are also expanded by their Quinten variants, offering new intervals logically derived from the original rows.[5] The score calls for an orchestra plus saxophone, Wagner tuba, harp, celeste, and piano divided into five groups: the woodwind, brass, strings, percussion, and a fifth group composed of celesta, harp, and piano.

The second movement has five sections, each accompanied by a graph included in the score. Each graph is intended to show how the instrumentation, the rhythmic values, the density of events happening at the same time, and dynamics all relate to each other. For example, the first section "Quadratus" has eighteen measures, subdivided into 6+6+6. Volume increases and decreases in each 6 measure unit. Pitch is controlled like that, too. Part of the graph shows how each of the five groups of instruments are to deal with all these elements simultaneously before the next group of eighteen measures changes all the relationships.

The second section of eighteen measures, titled "Zigzag" has a graph showing two lines, formed from single notes showing how each of the five groups provides one note, the next note coming from a different group to make up the line. Two lines like these, formed of notes of different timbres, creates the "Zigzag." One of the lines moves in slower note values than the other. Both arrive at their middle and then reverse.

The third section, "Figurae" gives each of the five groups its own figure, pitted two against each other, and then changing to other groups with their own separate figuration.

---

[5] To create a Quintenreihe, a chromatic scale beginning on the same first note of the original row is laid out, above every second note is a fifth higher than the first note, creating an augmented fourth tritone interval. The higher pitch replaces every other normal chromatic note in the chromatic scale, in whatever position it falls in the original row. For example, in a chromatic scale starting on C, the next note is C♯ and will have a G (the fifth above the previous C) sitting above it. In the original row, the C♯, no matter where it occurs in the row, will be replaced by a G. This process of substitution for every other note of the original row continues until all twelve tones are used. This provides a logical means of derivation, and the result is a new row that relates to the original, though more remotely than the usual transpositions, inversions, and retrogrades of a serial row.

The fourth section looks like a canon in descending metric measures, 4/4. 3/4. 2/4. 6/8.

The Fifth section has a graph with four small round circles in the middle of a larger circle. It is meant to show that each circle touches and propels another. Such graphs may have helped Rautavaara with his planning, but may or may not have meant anything to the conductor.

The last movement is aleatoric, with each group given a number of sections and waiting for the conductor to indicate when they should begin each section, before, in the middle, or somewhat at the end of the other; groups doing their prescribed parts. When all have entered and completed the numbered section, they all move on to the next.

The actual scheduled conductor declined to conduct the work, suggesting the composer do it himself. Words were exchanged and the newspapers turned it into a scandal (Example Thirteen, p. 48).

Without repeated melodic motifs, either tonal or atonal, the listener is required to concentrate on the entries and combinations of the five groups of instrumental sounds, and the opposition of dynamic or duration values. Fortunately, much of the score is in a thin chamber-like texture. The breakup of a group's figuration between various instruments, with the next note in the figuration passed to a new instrument in the group, makes the chamber music style even harder to recognize.

## Symphony No. 4, original version (1964/68)

Rautavaara completed his original Fourth Symphony, in two movements, "Sonata," and "Variazioni." As in *Arabescata* of 1962, he divided the orchestra into groups. This work has four quartets: four woodwinds, four brass, four percussion, and four strings."[6] The string group had four players: a violin, a viola, a cello, and a double bass. The second movement is based on his earlier 1957 serial work, *Praevariata*, newly orchestrated into the four quartets, and with a new inserted variation. The symphony was withdrawn and then revised in 1969 as *Quarto sinfonia per quattro quartetti*. The changes were made to the first movement, which became shorter, had longer melodic lines, and contains temporary tonal centers, evidence of Rautavaara's stylistic shift from serialism to neotonality. Performed in February, 1970, Rautavaara was still disappointed with it. In 1986 when the scores of his symphonies were to be published, he discarded this work, naming his *Arabescata*, Op. 24 of 1962 as his Fourth Symphony.

---

[6] Rautavaara, quoted in Sivuoja-Gunaratnam, 104.

## *Helsinki Fanfare,* Op. 31 (1967/87)

The *Helsinki Fanfare,* a one minute long work for orchestra, won the first prize in the Helsinki fanfare composition contest of 1967.

## *Lahti Fanfare,* Op. 35 (1967)

The following year, Rautavaara won a similar contest sponsored by the city of Lahti with his *Lahti Fanfare.*

## *In memorium J. K. Paasikivi,* Op. 38 (1967)

Commissioned by the Suomen Sinfoniaorkesterit ry. (Finnish Orchestral Union), this work, based on the first symphony, was first performed in Vaasa by its city orchestra under the direction of Eino Haipus on March 9, 1968 and later withdrawn. It honors the memory of Juho Kusti Paasikivi (1870-1956), President of Finland 1946-1956, and chief architect of Finnish post-war foreign policy.

## *Anadyomene* (Adoration of Aphrodite), Op. 33 (1968)

The orchestral work *Anadyomene* (1968), one movement about thirteen minutes long, was the beginning of Rautavaara's Neo-Romantic period. Rautavaara intended to write a serial work based on ideas from James Joyce's *Finnigan's Wake.* The music, however, seemed to have a will of its own, abandoning serialism. The letters H-C-E (B natural-C-E), were used prominently throughout James Joyce's work, and the descriptive opening sentence offered further letter pitch possibilities for a row: "riverrun, past Eve and Adam's, from swerve of shore to bend of bay, brings us by a commodius vicus of recirculation back to Howth Castle and Environs." The concept of flowing water recirculating became the opening measures of successively added layers of divisi strings, murmuring in a symmetrical polyphony in a pattern of alternating half steps and thirds and their retrogrades. Bassoons and oboes soon refer to H and C+E in longer duration values and then are merged into the murmuring swell of the river. The brass enter with prominent half notes spelling out "Eve and Adam's" (E-B-E, A-D, A-D-A-B-E♭), referring to the garden of Eden. At that point, the music left James Joyce and rippled on independently.

The harmonies of the polyphony often result in static repetitive sonorities like pedal points which are occasionally tonal. The flute and bass clarinet interject the calls of sea birds and arpeggiated harp adds the color of foaming waves. The orchestration shows the influence of Debussy's *La Mer.* In his book, Joyce later wrote "Sir Tristram, violer d'amores, fr'over the short sea." Rautavaara chose to hide the opening motifs of Wagner's *Tristan and Isolde* into the polyphony as a compositional joke. The subtitle, according to Rautavaara, probably came from his fleeting interest in studying Greek, in order to read Homer's *Odyssey* in its original language.[7] Since he composed it at his recently purchased summer house by the ocean, he said that "like Aphrodite, the composition rose from the sea" (Example Fourteen, page 55).[8]

### *Sotilasmessu* (A Soldier's Mass), (1968), for wind band

A wind band composition was commissioned that same year, to celebrate the Finnish Army's 50th anniversary, founded the year of Finland's independence in 1917. *Sotilasmessu*, for winds and percussion in a free tonal style, was first performed by the Finnish Army Festival Band. Its four movements follow a Roman Catholic mass arrangement: Kyrie, Miserere, Gloria, In hora mortis. The Finnish military text is a variant: Sotajoukkojen Herra (Lord of the Troops, have mercy), Armahda meitä (Have mercy on us), Kunnian kentillä (Glory from the Field); Kuolemamme hetkellä (In the Hour of our Death).

The music was taken from a 1968 attempt at an opera, *Hippios Koiranos*, based on a gloomy Greek myth about a man rescued from shipwreck by dolfins, and later killed. Since Rautavaara had difficulties with the opera, he abandoned it and used the music, namely a march, a grotesque waltz, and a gloomy part for the wind band commission.

### *Finnisch, heute* (Finnish, Today) (1970), for string orchestra

Based on material from the *Seitsemän preludia pianolle* (Seven Preludes for Piano, 1957), Op. 7, this work was a further outgrowth from the symphonic movements of the Second Symphony (1957), itself a longer version of the piano pieces. The five movements in the string orchestra adaptation are titled in German: 1. Die traditionelle Landschaft; 2. Zwei nervösse Tänze; 3. Choral mit Variation; 4. Zitternd, im Herbst, and 5. Fugato mit Schlussmusik.

### *Helsinki Dancing*, Op. 48 (1971), for orchestra (withdrawn)

*Helsinki Dancing*, an orchestral work in two movements, "Blues" and "Waltz," won a first prize in a light music composition contest sponsored by Finlandia Hall. This suite came from the second act of his 1970 *Apollo contra*

---

[7] Rautavaara, 222-225.
[8] Tiikkaja, 273.

*Marsyas* opera, which contrasts both the ancient and modern versions of conflict between light and serious music composers.

The first movement, "Blues," was scored for four saxophones, four trumpets, four trombones, drums, viola, cello, and double bass. The "Waltz" calls for a full orchestra plus saxophones. The work received its first performance at Finlandia Hall with the Helsinki Philharmonic Orchestra under conductor Jorma Panula. Despite this very respectable reception, Rautavaara later withdrew the work from performance.

### *Säännöllisiä yksikköjaksoja puolisäännöllisessä tilanteessa* (Regular Sets of Elements in a Semiregular Situation), Op. 60 (1971), also called *Garden of Spaces*

This aleatoric work for orchestra was inspired by the Finnish architect Reima Pietilä's 1971 exhibition, entitled *Tilatarha* (Garden of Spaces). Pietilä's buildings were designed "of regular materials" but the shapes altered to fit in "irregular" landscapes. In Rautavaara's composition, the conductor can order the precisely notated "sets" (regular elements) belonging to five different instrument-groupings to be played in any order (semiregular situations) either overlapping, or in strict succession. The five instrumental groups must play their numbered portions in the prescribed sequence in each of the sets. Scored for a 17-player orchestra, revised for full orchestra in 2003, the work actually has a Neoromantic sound and an overall arch form. This is achieved by arranging the sets in different textural density, dynamics, tuttis, and registral extremes. Each new set provides a forward motion, the work moving to a climax and then fragmenting again as at the beginning, creating a sense of large form to the whole.[9] Knowing what each instrumental unit is doing in a particular set, even when entering at unpredictable times, actually gave Rautavaara quite a bit of control in his planning for the combined results.

Rautavaara's *Arabescata*, fourth movement, from a decade earlier in 1962, used a similar aleatoric arrangement of five groups in a numbered sequence of sets, each group to play its materials when the conductor asks, but with all groups needing to finish their numbered unit before all move on to the next set. But his compositional style had changed in that time, one in an atonal serial context and the later one, in a style with tonal references.

---

[9] Tim Howell, *After Sibelius: Studies in Finnish Music* (Hants, England and Burlington, Vermont: Ashgate, 2006), 124.

## Canto III: A Portrait of the Artist at a Certain Moment (1972), for string orchestra

Though the title makes reference to James Joyce's *A Portrait of the Artist as a Young Man*, Rautavaara disclaimed any particular "Certain Moment" of his own in this ten minute work in one movement. However, his opening use of symmetry with two mirroring melodic lines reflects one of his own early technical interests. The top line is harmonized in parallel triads and the second line with the cellos and basses in unison moves exactly opposite in intervals. Bits of imitation on a contrasting motive of upward leaps serve as introduction to the main theme, a narrow melodic motive turning back on itself using one pitch and its upper and lower neighbors. This receives much development by placing it at different pitch levels or in different instruments, by varying its rhythm, or in sequences ever higher. An added busy accompaniment with tremolo strings in mirror symmetry adds to the density of activity, a crescendo leads to a climax, a pause, then a growling rhythmic motive in the basses and cellos, another climax and a fade away. Some of the material was borrowed from an incomplete violin sonata of 1969, that had a neoBaroque style and an actual quote of Bach's D Minor Toccata and Fugue.

The *Portrait of the Artist at a Certain Moment* shows a break with twelve tone technique, references to tonality but not to a specific key, interest in mirror interval writing, lengthy motivic development with expressive climaxes that seem to be organic rather than controlled and plotted, contrast with an opposing rough rhythmic section, and a rounding off of a nontraditional form with a return to earlier motives. This was the artist in 1972.

## Pelimannit (The Fiddlers) (1952/1972), orig. for piano, arr. for string orchestra

This eight minute set of pieces for string orchestra is an arrangement of Rautavaara's piano suite from his early student days twenty years earlier. Intended for the Ostrobothnian Chamber Orchestra founded by Juha Kangas, it displays Rautavaara's skill in contrasting the different timbres and registers available in the small group of string players. The melodies are seventeenth century Finnish folk music preserved in a notebook by a fiddler, Samuel Rinda-Nickola. The folk customs of the day are depicted in the arrival of fiddlers to accompany a bridal party's walk to the doors of the church, an organist practicing, bell ringing, a clockmaker, a fiddler practicing in the woods, and dance tunes.

Rautavaara, at the time not yet having had any composition classes, set the melodies tonally but added modernisms of his own often adding clashing seconds. The Gregorian church modes intrude now and then, scale steps altered to Mixolydian, Lydian, or Dorian, a long lasting trait in Finnish folk music.

The first piece, "Närböläisten braa speli" (The Fiddlers of Närbö Arrive) presents a steady C major scale descending melody as a fanfare, marked Pomposo e rustico. for the full ensemble. It is answered by a faster motive in sixteenth notes with a reduced number of strings. A contrasting quieter section follows. The opening flourish returns, marked Pesante, with the bass octaves partly in a whole tone scale, partly Phrygian mode descent.

The second piece, "Kopsin Jonas," the fiddler practicing in the woods, opens with a solo violin, accompanied by low basses. A high string ostinato twitters in the background, with full strings joining for melodic passages, each group acting their separate roles. The meter changes from 3/2 to 2/3 at cadences.

"Jacob Könni," the clockmaker, alternates a high mechanical pulsation with a low string solemn chordal answer, earlier borrowed for use as "Doubt and Creed" in *Requiem in Our Time* (1954) for a brass ensemble. "Klockar Samuel Dikstrom," a sexton and organist, practices broken triads and wedding tunes. "Pirun polska" (Devil's Polska) starts and ends with a mournful solo cello recitative enclosing a fast dance in Lydian mode with octave echoes and full ensemble. The final piece, "Hypyt' (Hopping Dance), a 45 second piece marked "burlesco," has a clear G major melody harmonized with clashing minor seconds, wide-spread registers, abrupt interjections, and sparkling chromatic scales in contrary motion.

A piano suite arranged for string orchestra, *Pelimannit* went through a further transformation into an accordion suite for performer Matti Rantanen in 1992.

### *The Finn Way,* Op. 67 (1973) (withdrawn)

This march for a big orchestra was first performed by an orchestra under George de Godzinsky and aired on the Finnish radio, December 3, 1975. It was later withdrawn.

### *Three Meditations for Orchestra* (1973), for string orchestra

The three orchestral interludes from the 1973 *Lapsimessu* (Children's Mass), Meditatio super Kyrie, Meditatio super Gloriam, and Meditatio super Agnum, can be performed separately.

### *Kasvaa—kehittyä—muuttua* (Growth--- Development— Variation), Op. 81 (1974), (withdrawn)

This seven minute work for strings, piano and celeste was commissioned by the Pellervo Society, an organization promoting cooperatives, mostly banks. It was later withdrawn. Originally, it was composed as a one movement continuous work titled *Adriatica*, submitted to a composition competition in Trieste. Having no success there, Rautavaara reused his material and gave it a new title. It was performed by the Helsinki City Orchestra for its 75th anniversary in 1974. Still not satisfied with the work, Rautavaara withdrew it.

### *Fanfaari Lahden hiihdon maailmanmestaruuskisoihin* (Fanfare for the Lahti World Champion Skiing Competition) (1978)

This one minute work for the opening ceremonies was recorded by the Radio Symphony Orchestra under the direction of Leif Segerstam on February 17, 1978, and the performance was heard from the tape at the event.

### *Suomalainen myytti* (A Finnish Myth) (1977), for string orchestra

This seven minute work for string orchestra was commissioned by the Jyväskylä conservatory and first performed by their string orchestra. The piece opens with an ominous low register cluster, widening into a field of sound. The slow melody that emerges is harmonized with dissonant clusters, high string arpeggios, and harmonic glissandos.

### *Angels and Visitations* (1978), overture

In 1978 the Finnish Radio Symphony Orchestra commissioned a series of three works, later known as Rautavaara's "angel" works. The first of these was the overture *Angels and Visitations*. Regarding these "angels," Rautavaara told of his boyhood nightmares and his later identification with the poet Rainer Maria Rilke's angels as figures of holy dread. Despite the works' later great popularity, often called New Age music, with easily imagined religious significance, Rautavaara disclaimed that kind of interpretation.

> These angels are not figures out of a children's fairytale, and nor are they religious kitsch; they spring from a conviction that other reali-

ties, quite different modes of consciousness exist outside our everyday awareness...that could be denoted as angels. They are possibly reminiscent of the visions of William Blake and they are almost certainly akin to the horrifying figures of Rainer Maria Rilke bursting with saintly fury.

...the Angel compositions have no program...*Angels and Visitations* presents a world of sharp contrasts, in which a hymn rising up from the depths may be followed by what sounds like a riotous pack of demons--only to give way to a Palestrina-like violin texture hovering in the heights or the bright tinkling of the harp and celesta. The work is a set of variations on the theme of contrast, polarity, the logic of antithesis.[10]

The overture is a one movement work in an overall arch form, lasting about twenty minutes. In the middle are sections that introduce new melodic or chorale ideas and then return, varied in orchestration or registration, in a symmetrical reverse order. It could be diagramed as Intro, A, B, C, D, C, B, A, Coda (Intro). Material from previous compositions is borrowed: a cadential theme in the A section and its return at the end is taken from the Third Symphony and also used in *True and False Unicorn*. The music here is used without the words which were originally sung by the *Unicorn* saying "I am the unicorn, but is that I?" In the third theme, C, a quiet melody is taken from a choral work written about the same time, *Lehdet lehtiä* (Leaves Are Leaves). Often when Rautavaara takes a theme or motive from a work with words, there is some meaning implied beyond the musical notes. "Am I the Unicorn?" may be Rautavaara questioning whether he is really the creator of the music or just the intermediary writing down what has been given. *Lehdet lehtiä* (Leaves are leaves), based on a poem by Paavo Haaviko, speaks of pages in a book: books last, are not intended for a specific person, and like a breeze that shreds leaves, a book's pages are forgotten (or shredded mentally) as soon as read. The musical borrowing occurs in a tranquil setting for high strings, an unemotional Phrygian mode in a "Palestrina-like" polyphonic texture, implying a celestial setting or church. Did Rautavaara intend some meaning here? How much to read into these or how little is speculation.[11] Another chorale-like short stepwise motive in clashing seconds is taken from the Second Symphony's finale.

The overture is truly a work of contrasts and oppositions. Hymns and demons do indeed alternate. Melodic chorales in full phrases are opposed and disrupted by short dissonant motives. Sections are often not clear cut,

---

[10] Einojuhani Rautavaara, Liner note for *Angels and Visitations, Viuluknosertto, Lintukoto*, Ondine ODE 881-2; also, www.fimic.fi/rautavaara.

[11] Wojciech Stepien, *The Sound of Finnish Angels: Musical Signification in Five Instrumental Compositions by Einouhani Rautavaara* (Hillsdale, NY: Pendragon, 2011), 103-118 passim.

while returns of themes are somewhat hidden by changes in orchestration or in register.

The first introductory section introduces melodic lines based on Messiaen's modes one and six, scales rearranging the whole and half steps in symmetrical intervals. It opens with high string plucked glissandos ascending, like drops of water, with ominous rustlings underneath growing in intensity, low pitched growls, and noise added by glockenspiel, xylophone and celeste.

The A theme section has a brass chorale with clear phrases and unrelated harmonic triads, giving brief tonal centers. Its diatonicism and tonal sounds in the slow moving chords contrast to the introduction. At one point there is a borrowing from his Third Symphony (1959-1961), also used in his *True and False Unicorn* (1971). Woodwinds have a stable triadic set of arpeggios as countermelody, actually an accompaniment. The strings take over the chorale. The brass A theme is reaffirmed over the bustling woodwinds and the *Unicorn* motive is heard briefly.

The B theme has an expressive melody for violins in a wavy motion with tonal references and then passes the melody to the brass. The A theme brass chorale returns and passes its melody to the strings.

The Palestrina-like C theme is for high strings alone, in a polyphonic Phrygian mode, cool and celestial. The strings pass it on to the brass chorale. Returning to the high strings again, the melody is interrupted by short angry motives from the lower brass and winds, attempting to disrupt it in an aleatoric manner, building in volume and climaxing with a human scream. The snare drum and low register instruments establish a military march over a constant pedal point. The strings whizz short circular motives above.

At theme D, a step-wise brass chorale melody enters, very loud, clashing with seconds, a theme taken from the finale of the Second Symphony. Passed to the high woodwinds the interruption motives are frantic, the "riotous pack of demons."

The C theme enters with a new orchestration of two oboes and English horn, with many blasts of dissonant interruptions. The C theme reappears calmly in celeste, glockenspiel, and harp. Disruption adds the D theme.

The opening woodwind arpeggios reappear and earlier ideas are brought back not in their earlier order. The *Unicorn* motive reappears in affirmative statement, the woodwind arpeggios return with quiet interruptions, then the brass chorale theme A. The B theme makes a short appearance, the Third Symphony finale makes a triumphant entry. Xylophone and celeste become temporary soloists. Finally the material from the intro, the rising plucked glissandos, now is given to the harp and the music dies away.

New sounds and techniques are required from many of the instruments, such as blowing through the brass without making a tone, notable at the quiet beginning and end, as well as plucked glissandos, harmonics, microtones, and adding a human scream.

In summary, one can say that this is not a beautiful piece of music; it is a drama. The more details that emerge show the intricate symmetry of successive entries, the careful change of registers, opposition of free tonal areas with aleatoric dissonance. The title suggests angels and threatening demonic forces, yes. But it is also what Rautavaara claimed: a study in contrast, polarity, and the logic of antithesis.

## *Pohjalainen polska* (Ostrobothnian Polska) (1980)

In 1980 Rautavaara returned to a favorite folk tune, *Piru ja juomari* (The Devil and the Drunkard), for this orchestral work commissioned by the city of Vaasa's orchestra. A version for string orchestra was later set in 1993. A setting of the same folk song for piano solo was evidently sketched as early as 1952 but not published until 1976, and later rearranged for accordianist Matti Rantanen in 1992. The same folksong is the basis for a set of variations for two cellos and piano, *Polska*, composed in 1977. The folksong actually comes from Rantasalmi, in southeast Finland, but is sometimes called an Ostrobohnian folksong (northwest Finland). The term "polska" is also confusing, as it usually refers to a triple meter dance, originally from Sweden and further back, influenced by a Swedish Queen from Poland. Usage probably turned it into a term for a rustic dance, sometimes in duple meter.

## *Hommage à Zoltán Kodály* (1982), for string orchestra

In 1982 the Kodály Society commissioned a work in honor of the composer's centenary. Rautavaara commented about the structure of this work in his CD liner notes:

> ...I made use of thematic material based on the letters from the title: H(omm)AGE A (ko)DA(ly) Z(olt)A(n). My none-too-serious approach to selecting these note-names should at least be evident from the use of Z for the note E flat (=Es). The resulting motive appears only in a stylistic pastiche cast in Hungarian rhythms. It is not given a structural role to play. In fact, no melodic motives as such are used in the work. Instead I use different textures which relate to one another through opposition and contrast. A new texture may come to displace the for-

mer one, or it may transform into another one....The composition is prefaced by the words: In the beginning there was time; the expanse, the plains of Hungary, eternity.

The simple melody of a violin makes its appearance, soon to be joined by others...And time begins to beat and become itself. A short melody starts to form, h-a-g-e-a, and then much later another one: d-a-es-a. Words which demand to be clothed in beauty, colour, rhythmic twists, expansive and variegated surfaces like bird gardens and country estates. For all around can be heard the sound of these words, in transformation, growth, and evolution: Hommage à Kodály Zoltán.[12]

From a swirling sound field of low string sounds, the violin opens with a simple diatonic figuration, joined by others on a similar pattern out of phase. Several crescendos lead to short melodic motives and a dense cadential passage of sliding notes. A sustained melody emerges accompanied by ostinato arpeggios in the cellos, which in turn evolves into a quieter section of twittering upper strings. Another melody is then opposed to the twittering, gradually growing in volume and the density of the divisi string parts, while passing the melody to the cellos. A dance-like section follows, begun with a rhythmic ostinato in the low strings. A final section has a chorale in the high strings played without vibrato, with opposing conversational-like interjections. The chorale endures to the end, fading, with final comments made by plucked cello notes and high-pitched final bird chirps.

## Fifth Symphony (1985)

Rautavaara originally planned the Fifth Symphony with the title *Monologue with Angels*, wanting to complete the Angel Trilogy begun in 1978 with the overture *Angels and Visitations*, and the concerto *Angel of Dusk* for double bass of 1980. The angel title was dropped in the process of composition. The symphony is a half-hour single movement, with sections unlike those of the traditional symphony movements.

The work begins with an eleven bar Introduction. A long sustained C major chord expands and adds timbres to end in a striking dissonance, moving and repeated several times, putting emphasis on a new triad/pitch class. Theorist Howell summarizes its importance:

This Introduction has been carefully constructed. In its use of varied

---

[12] Einojuhani Rautavaara, Liner notes, trans. by Andrew Bentley, *Complete Works for String Orchestra, Vol. 1*, Ondine ODE 821-2.

repetition of events, manipulations of musical timescale and deployment of pitch class centres, it sets up in miniature a structural shape that is to be reflected by the progress of later concerns.[13]

The work then moves into the next long lyrical melodic section, accompanied soon by polyphony of other moving lines and by twittering high passages. Composer and writer Kalevi Aho has described the overall form as "a spiral"[14] (Example Nineteen, page 84). Aho labels the eight clearly defined sections as: Introduction, Processional, Chorale, First Scherzo, Chorale/development, Second Scherzo, Transition, and Coda. He shows that there are similarities between sections: the Introduction and Coda, the Processional and the Transition, the two Chorales, and the two Scherzi. Howell describes the interrelationships:

> ...a widening spiral where the listener may return to a place that seems familiar, but it is, nevertheless, one revolution further up and out on a journey that presses ever forward. More subtle processes of recollection and recall have replaced structural repetition... This carefully judged technique preserves just enough of its model to permit large-scale connections, while at the same time, the material is varied and extended in an ongoing succession.[15]

The written score combines conventional notation with an unusual time-point notation, where each measure is given an approximate duration in seconds, also used by composers Berio and Penderecki.[16]

## *Epitaph for Béla Bartók* (1986), for string orchestra

In 1986 Rautavaara reworked his 1955 *Prelude and Fugue on the name of BEla BArtók*, originally for cello and piano, as a work for string orchestra. The Helsinki Junior Strings under the direction of Czaba Szilvay, performed the new version in Helsinki. Szilvay, a Hungarian cellist, brought Kohdály teaching methods to Finland. Rautavaara, studying in Vienna in 1955, had found himself attracted to Bartok's mysticism, formal structures, and incorporation of folk elements into his music. The pitches B-E-B-A are announced dramatically at the beginning and pervade the following material, homophonically in the prelude and polyphonically in the fugue.

---

[13] Tim Howell, *After Sibelius: Studies in Finnish Music* (London: Ashgate, 2006), 127.

[14] Einojuhani Rautavaara, *Omakuva* (Self Portrait), 328.

[15] Howell, 125-126.

[16] Frank J. Oteri, *Rautavaara Orchestral Works* (Helsinki: Werner/Chappell Music Finland, 1999), 21.

## *Hommage à Liszt Ferenc* (1989), for string orchestra

*Hommage à Liszt Ferenc* is the third string orchestra work dedicated to Hungarian composers. The earlier works were the *Epitaph for Béla Bartok* (1955, revised 1986), and the *Hommage à Kodály Zoltán* (1982), all three works either commissioned by the Helsinki Junior Strings or first performed by them, led by the Hungarian conductor and string educator, Czaba Szilway. Rautavaara wanted to convey the romanticism and virtuosity of Liszt in a string medium. The intervals of the augmented fourth and later the perfect fourth unify the work both melodically and harmonically.

## Sixth Symphony, *Vincentiana* (1992)

Rautavaara used material from his opera *Vincent* (1987) to rework and develop into his Sixth Symphony. In the opera, each of the three acts is preceded by a musical prelude bearing the title of one of Van Gogh's famous paintings. These three preludes, "Starry Night," "Crows," and "The Church at Auvers," seemed to make their own separate suite. When the Helsinki Philharmonic asked for a new work, Rautavaara offered them a work based on the *Vincent* material. The first three symphonic movements are based on thematic material from the opera's preludes, but they are reworked and expanded. The fourth movement, "Apotheosis," is developed from Vincent's monologue in the closing scene of the opera, rearranged later as a separate movement for string orchestra in 1996. The reuse of the operatic material is not intended to tell the story again nor does it make any attempt to become the usual symphonic movement structures of sonata allegro, slow movement, scherzo, and final rondo or sonata form.

Much of the music is still quite programmatic. The synthesizer added to the orchestra in the opera is retained in the symphony as is the Viennese waltz of Vincent's dance with his muse. The opening movement, "Starry Night," depicts stars twinkling with its eerie string tremolos, and pointillistic entrances of bells and gongs. The second movement, "Crows," opens with cawing sound effects of ratchets, trombone glissandos, and pounding percussion, fading into synthesizer (Example Twenty, page 92). At the end of "The Church at Auvers" the orchestra suggests a swarm of birds, the synthesizer depicts church bells out of focus, and the music fades away into blackness and dissonance. The fourth movement, "Apotheosis," is a final affirmation of the value of Vincent's artwork as light and life with its soaring Romantic melodies and sweet harmonies. Bird calls appear again at its close.

## *Canto IV* (1992) for string orchestra

In 1992 the Finnish Broadcasting Station commissioned a work for string orchestra to be performed by the Keski-Pohjanmaan Kamariorkesteri (the Central Ostrobothnian Chamber Orchestra) under the direction of conductor Juha Kangas. Rautavaara chose to use the title *Canto* again for this seventeen minute one movement work. His first two *Cantos,* using material from his opera *Kaivos* (The Mine, 1958), were originally single movement works for string orchestra, later rearranged and reorchestrated. The reference was to Ezra Pound's *The Cantos*, a long poem of 116 sections or cantos in an experimental style of writing. *Canto III: A Portrait of the Composer at a Certain Moment* (1972) was also a single movement work for string orchestra. Twenty years later he used the same title for a string orchestra work, though there is no further motive nor style connection between the four *Cantos.*

Rautavaara devised a twelve tone row made of major and minor seconds, and minor thirds. The quiet main theme, moving in undulating half steps, is developed, inverted, and reworked, but keeps its recognizable length and motions. A second section based on a quinten version of the row with wider intervals offers a contrast with a slow moving high treble melody with an upper strings arpeggiated accompaniment, a celestial effect. After some pauses with dissonant interjections, a solo viola reigns, with a lyrical passage. The work closes with the full strings, with high treble twittering above, a passage of thirds and whole steps which later became the final section of the Seventh Symphony's finale.

## Seventh Symphony, *Angel of Light* (1994-95)

The Seventh Symphony was commissioned by the Bloomington (Indiana) Symphony Orchestra, a community orchestra of amateurs, for its twenty-fifth anniversary. Despite serious misunderstandings on both sides regarding commission price and the abilities of the players, that group gave the first performance under David Pickett on April 23, 1995, to nearly unnoticeable publicity and reviews. Through the help of the Finnish Ondine Recording Company and the Helsinki City Orchestra, the work soon became an international success.

*Angel of Light* was based on the same twelve tone row as several earlier works of the previous year, the *Canto IV* for string orchestra, *Canción de nuestro tiempo* (Song of our Time) a choral work, and *Notturno e Danza* for violin and piano. The row was designed to outline four successive triads, F-D-A, E-G-C, D♯-G♯-B, F♯-C♯-A♯, making many references to tonality possible.

Rautavaara also devised a theme based on musical pitches from the name of the Bloomington Symphony Orchestra. The prominent brass theme repeated in all four movements (Example Twenty-one, page 95) is created from the words Bloomington Symphony Orchestra, taking the pitches from the letters applicable.

| B♭ | G | E♭=S | B♮ =H | C B E E♭=S | A |
|---|---|---|---|---|---|
| Bloomin | Gton | Symp | Hony | orC H E S tr | A[17] |

The opening Tranquillo first movement establishes its heavenly serenity with a mid range string arpeggiated accompaniment, and then, subtly, brings in the important Bloomington theme in glockenspiel and vibraphone. Divided into four separated motives, it is nearly hidden by the slow harmonic motion in the strings. The upper strings eventually become a stepwise melody with no contribution from the Bloomington theme. Growing to a climax, four horns enter majestically with the descending broken triad Bloomington theme in thirds, several times repeated, acting as a transition to the second theme area. The second theme area introduces a motive that outlines the four triads in the main 12 tone row, with a dialogue of solo instruments. The A theme returns, varied, with two brief references to the Bloomington theme, the four horns return with that theme in another appearance of the transition, and section C, a coda, begins. A solo trombone climbs from the depths up through a minor scale, answered by a similar motive in the French horn, the opening bars of the Bloomington theme intrude several times, then all fades into a G minor chord ascending in its inversions played by the harp.

The Molto allegro second movement with its sprightly theme in clashing seconds is similar to Rautavaara's earlier *Playground for Angels* for brass ensemble, sounding like school yard taunts. There are arguments, clashes, partial returns of the Bloomington theme, and some final sneers. Instruments are paired in short motives throughout. Five distinct sections seem to be variations of the first section. The Bloomington theme appears in the first transition from A to B in the French horn. Section B has a short upswept motive. Section C murmurs smoothly in a small range, shifting into triplets for a transition to section D in staccato triplet motives. Section E begins as a loud coda but abruptly stops for a very slow entry of the Bloomington theme in the glockenspiel and vibraphone followed by the "disturbance technique," the trumpets in clashing seconds, actually a reworking of the opening motive.

---

[17] Tiikkaja, 489.

Essentially, the trumpets thumb noses and call out the equivalent of "Nah, nah, na-nah, nah" in childish fashion and then fade away. Little angels? Imps? The listener can invent his own story.

The third movement, "Come un sogno" (Like a Dream), continues the heavenly atmosphere in the high register triads of divisi violin, while the accompaniment calls for violas to be divided into six parts. Material for this movement came from his earlier composition *Nocturno*, of *Nocturno e danza* (1993) for violin and piano. The central part of this ABA form contains motives again given to pairs of instruments. The Bloomington theme appears as a transition back to the opening material and a final appearance of the Bloomington theme from the French horn.

The finale opens with a majestic brass chordal fanfare and a lyrical six measures for the first violins, both of which hide the Bloomington theme rearranged. A low-register modal sounding hymn begins in the strings with whirling flute comments at the end of each phrase. Brasses alternate with the main melodic lead, with ever increasing swirling accompaniment. At section B, m. 55, the horns introduce a new theme, taken from *Canto IV*, passing it to the trombones and back. The strings take up the whirring motion from the first movement's transition. At C, m. 75, the opening sounds of the symphony return in the arpeggiated string accompaniment and the Bloomington theme returns in the slow chordal motion of the upper strings. The brasses return with their B melody. At the climatic Coda, m. 109, the first movement's Bloomington theme returns in ecstatic restatement, and all motion dies away.

## *Lintukoto* (Home of the Birds, or Isle of Bliss) (1995)

In 1995 Rautavaara composed the ten minute orchestral work *Lintukoto* (Isle of Bliss) based on the poem by Aleksis Kivi (1834-72). Composed for the Espoo Music Institute orchestra while waiting for the first performance of his opera *Aleksis Kivi*, Rautavaara drew on Kivi's poetic version of the island paradise, a place where time stops, youth is retained and death is defeated. The music material came from the first act of his opera *Aleksis Kivi*. Rautavaara maintained that his earlier themes often came back to him, wanting further development in new fashions. The music begins fast and cheerfully, moves to a more reflective section, and then fades away, perhaps programmatically reflecting the story of the dying sea gulls told to Rautavaara by the fishermen.[18]

---

[18] Einojuhani Rautavaara, Liner notes, for *Angels and Visitations, Viuluknosertto, Lintukoto*, Ondine ODE 881-2; also, www.fimic.fi/rautavaara.

## *Apotheosis* (1992/1996), for string orchestra

Arranged for string orchestra, this piece was originally the fourth movement of the Sixth Symphony *Vincentiana*, which in turn was based on music from the opera *Vincent* (1986-87).

## *Autumn Gardens* (Syksyn puutarhat) (1999)

Rautavaara has compared his composition work to gardening, saying that his music is similar to an English garden, freely growing yet organic, unlike the geometric and rectangular French garden. *Autumn Gardens* is dedicated to an English orchestra, actually the Scottish Chamber Orchestra, for an English festival, the famous Proms concert series in July of 1999. The title is derived from a passage in the libretto of Rautavaara's opera *Auringon talo* (House of the Sun), "like a butterfly in the garden of black autumn." The motive from that passage became the theme for the variations of the first movement. Without a break, the following slow movement takes its material from the dream scene in the opera when the two old ladies see themselves as young women in the past. The finale, Giocoso e leggiero, comes from the final dance music of the opera when the old ladies, hallucinating while freezing to death, are invited into their past ballroom days.

## Eighth Symphony, *The Journey* (1998-9)

With the international success of his 1995 Seventh Symphony *Angel of Light*, and awards for his Violin Concerto, Rautavaara began to get international commissions. One came from the Philadephia Orchestra for a new symphony to celebrat the orchestra's 100th anniversary. Conductor Wolfgang Sawallisch presented the work at three concerts in Philadelphia on Apr. 27, 28, 29, in 2000, and again at Carnegie Hall, New York City, on May 1, 2000. The Philadelphia Orchestra then took this work on its European tour to Birmingham, London, Paris, Zurich, Warsaw, Prague, Cologne, Turin, Rome, and Helsinki, giving the work a broad international exposure and much publicity.

Material for the eighth symphony included bits of works Rautavaara had composed years earlier. The first movement establishes a motif never used before of four ascending fourths that appears in all the other movements. As well, the first movement includes passages from his *Nirvana dharma*, a work for mixed chorus, soprano, and flute of 1979, and from his choral song "Ciudad sin sueño" in *Cancion de nostro tiempo* of 1993. The second movement takes portions from the first and third movements of the *Unknown Heavens* string quintet of 1997. Both the third and fourth movements of the symphony use a motif from the opera *Thomas* (1985), likely referring to the "journey" words. The fourth movement quotes from the Gregorian chant opening Thomas's reflections in Act One of *Thomas,* then collects all these previous movements references with the motif of the fourths, now proceeding downwards.[19] In a sense, this symphony is a partial musical autobiography. Rautavaara had frequently maintained his reasons for reusing his own material as finding more to say, new ways to express, to develop ideas still wanting to be written out, as though they had a life of their own.

From the peaceful first movement, the fast second movement becomes a virtuoso tour-de-force for the world famous orchestra. The slow third movement begins and ends with the rising fourths motif. The finale, unusual for Rautavaara's works, concludes with a fortissimo rather than dying away.

## *Adagio Celeste* (1997/2000), for string orchestra

In the year 2000 Rautavaara rearranged the second movement of his string quintet *Unknown Heavens* for string orchestra with the title *Adagio Celeste*. With the recording of this version, he did not acknowledge the borrowing from *Unknown Heavens* in his notes. Instead, he claims he was inspired by verses written by Lassi Nummi written in 1982: "Then, that night, when you want to love me in the deep of the night, wake me…let me wake through old age and death…join us to the communion of the world."[20]

In the string quintet there is a quote from a Rautavaara song appearing in all the movements, another example of Rautavaara's finding more to say with a motif from a previous composition. The quote comes from his setting of Charles Baudelaire's *La Morte des Pauvres* (The Death of the Poor), the second in a group of songs called *Neljä serenadia* (Four Serenades), of 1978. Baudelaire's text begins "Death is…" and, after several interpretations, ends with "It is the portal opening on unknown skies (le portique ouvert sur les Cieux inconnus)." Familiar bits from the *Unknown Heavens* melody, a descending motion with a four bar motif F-E$^b$-D$^b$-E, appear throughout, though it never is actually completely restated. The harmonic language of the work is lushly Romantic, often moving lyrically in parallel thirds and sixths. The overall mood is quiet and pensive, equally suited to a poem about unknown heavens after death or, as here, love through old age and death.

---

[19] Tiikkaja, 540.
[20] Einojuhani Rautavaara, Liner notes, *Book of Visions,* Ondine ODE1064-5.

## *Book of Visions,* (2005) suite for orchestra

This orchestral suite was commissioned by the Orchestre National de Belgigue, and conducted by Finnish conductor Mikko Franck. The four movements have subtitles: "A Tale of Night," "A Tale of Fire," "A Tale of Love," and "A Tale of Fate," with each depicting some scene from his own memories. Some thematic material came from his opera *Rasputin* and other snippets come from the clarinet concerto.[21]

"A Tale of Night" described a fearful time, nightmares. There's an ominous timpani roll, a slow moving ascending string melody, a swirling of strings, a menacing bass section, clashing seconds, chime and brass call interjections. "The Tale of Fire" recalls for Rautavaara the flames of Helsinki during the time of the Second World War, seen by Rautavaara as a boy. The music evokes flickering flames, sirens from the sliding trombones, the roar of buildings on fire and an ending of silent smoking ashes. "A Tale of Love" pairs off usually solo instruments, playing in warm thirds over a pulsing accompaniment. "A Tale of Fate" employs the full orchestra, a string melody supported by the brass, triumphantly. With the completion of the piano score, fate met Rautavaara with a ruptured aorta, hospitalizing him with other complications for six months. When at last home, he finished the orchestration in time for the performance date.

"The Tale of Fire" recalls for Rautavaara the flames of Helsinki during the Second World War, seen by Rautavaara as a boy. The melody in the strings flickers gradually upwards in climbing patterns with sliding trombones and timpani pitch glissandos perhaps evoking sirens and the roar of fire. The ending slows, perhaps evoking the desolation of destruction.

"The Tale of Love" exchanges solo instruments on the melody with pairs of clarinets or oboes in thirds over a quietly pulsating background.

"A Tale of Fate" brings in the climatic full orchestra, with a string melody over brass accompaniment, affirming a triumphal outcome. The full divisi strings again use clashing seconds for color. At the end the melody from "Night" reappears, rounding off the work in a sigh. On completion of the work in piano score, not yet orchestrated, Rautavaara suffered a near fatal aortic rupture which hospitalized him for six months.[22] Fortunately, he was able to complete work on the score in time for the requested date in 2005.

---

[21] Tiikkaja, 586.
[22] Einojuhani Rautavaara, Liner notes, *Book of Visions,* Ondine ODE 1064-5.

## *Manhattan Trilogy* (2005)

For the centennial celebration of the Julliard School, Rautavaara was commissioned to write a work for the Julliard Orchestra. Memories of his school year there in 1955-1956 were evoked in the three movements of the *Manhattan Trilogy*. The third movement, "Dawn," was performed by the Juilliard Orchestra under James DePriest while on a tour to Helsinki in August of 2005. In October, the same orchestra and conductor performed the whole *Trilogy* in New York City, now including the movements "Daydreams" and "Nightmares." Rautavaara has described the movements as aspects of his student years, rather than as portraits of New York City.

The first movement, "Daydreams," is quiet with hymn-like meditation, possibilities are suggested by various solo instruments, and it then closes with bold hymn chords, augmented by timpani. Most of Rautavaara's time in New York was a time of optimism, productive study, and plans for performances in Finland. "Nightmares" suggests late night street sounds, hissing from brushes on cymbals, rumbling of subways done with low bass instruments, sliding trombones and muted trumpets for sirens and police cars, all mixed with melodic strings. "Dawn" has a rocking motion, bird calls, a growing intensity of activity and sound level. Reversing to a lower energy, a bell sounds, far away, perhaps calling to school or to morning prayers.

## *Before the Icons* (1955-56/2005)

Rautavaara had planned to orchestrate his 1955-56 piano work *Icons* at the time of its composition, but that project waited until 2005. Among the old manuscripts found after his first wife Mariaheidi's death were sketches for the *Icons*, reminding him that he had forgotten his original intention to orchestrate the pieces. The original six pieces described Byzantine icons, alternating slow and fast movements. With the new orchestration of those for full orchestra, he added three "Prayers" for a contrasting string orchestra in between each piece and also a concluding "Amen."

The original piano version had been an early work begun in New York in 1955. Looking back on it, Rautavaara could see his old style of quartal harmonies built from fourths, polyharmonies, changing meters, repetitive rhythmic patterns, triads, tritones, and triads on top of other triads. There was no way he could duplicate that old style. He chose to set the original six movements with a full orchestra. Inbetween he added three "Prayers" for string orchestra, contrasting in mood.

The new *Icons* movements are orchestrated for full orchestra. The comparison of piano and orchestra versions show how well the orchestra brings out the character of each motive. Fortissimos are emphasized with full brass, call and answer phrases are set with contrasting sounds, the rather comical "Two Village Saints" has a melodic phrase given to piccolo, and the martial character of the "Archangel Michael" is interpreted by a tuba bass line melody and bits of snare drum. One reviewer commented that the orchestral version lost the pianistic bell-like sonorities.[23] True. There is little given to the bells in the new orchestration. But, one need only imagine hearing the orchestral version while watching slides of the painted icons to experience a glorious fully Technicolor production.

The three "Prayers" contrast with the old movements by orchestration for strings alone, according to Rautavaara "to reflect the voice of the individual."[24] The tempos are slow and lines move smoothly, often by step, and in clear counterpoint to one or more other lines. A repeated rhythm pattern of long-short-short-long-long underlies both the first and second "Prayers." The third "Prayer" does not have this pattern, but builds its melody around two alternating pitches or upper and lower neighbor tones. The final short "Amen" brings back the rhythmic figure as its main focus, adds the full orchestra, and builds to a climax.

## *A Tapestry of Life* (2007), a suite for orchestra

Rautavaara composed this orchestral suite on commission from both the New Zealand Symphony Orchestra, under the leadership of Finnish conductor Pietari Inkinen, and from the Helsinki Philharmonic Orchestra. The first movement of four, "Stars Swarming," is based on a Swedish poem by Edith Södergran, "The Stars." It warns of stars falling into splinters on the garden grass that could cut feet. Liking this text, Rautavaara set it several times, an early song and then a chorus in *Katedralen* (The Cathedral) (1983). In this orchestral interpretation, the material comes not from either of those but from his opera *Thomas* and his Third Piano Concerto. Falling notes depict falling stars and high plucked harp over strings conveys "twinkling" or "glitter." A central lyrical section rises to a climax and the opening mood returns. "Halcyon Days," the second movement, is built on a constant repetitive triplet. Growing more animated, the melody in the strings moves with an added major seventh, rather than his more common minor seconds. In "Sighs and Tears," the third movement, the oboe and cor anglais dominate in sweeps of melody. Two harps provide an animated arpeggiated background for the melody, just before the return section. The final

---

[23] Andrew Mellor, BBC Review of *Before the Icons*, www.bbc.co.uk/music/review ((2010/05/26).
[24] Einojuhani Rautavaara, Liner notes, *Before the Icons*, Ondine ODE 1149-2.

movement, "The Last Polonaise," is a solemn dance used by Rautavaara several times to end an opera.²⁵ The polonaise rhythm can be heard in the background played rather ominously by the brasses, while the strings and woodwinds press on. Harps create a whirlwind sound, the brasses continue to intone, and the strings tell of emotional struggle, all left unresolved at the end.

## *Canto V, Into the Heart of Light* (2011), for chamber orchestra

Commissioned by the Ostrobothnian Chamber Orchestra for their fortieth anniversary in 2012, this 15 minute work is also titled *Canto V*. The work was first performed by the orchestra's founder and conductor Juha Kangas in Kokkola, Finland, on September 8, 2012. Both the orchestra and its conductor had premiered Rautavaara's *Canto 4* in 1992. In December, 2012, the work was taken on tour in Scotland with the Scottish Chamber Orchestra under conductor John Storgårds, principal conductor of the Helsinki Philharmonic and principal guest conductor of the BBC Philharmonic.

It opens with fast string arabesques set against long sustained chords in the bass register, then string melodies take over in octaves and piquant clashing seconds. Toward the end the energy winds down while themes join together. In the coda, a solo cello brings back the main melody in a low register with the other strings in static long chords, fading away "into the heart of light."

## *In the Beginning* (2016), for orchestra

In 2016 Rautavaara completed a short single movement for orchestra, before his death on July 27, 2016. The seven minute work was first performed the following year by the Finnish conductor Pietari Inkinen. who had commissioned it. Inkinen took it on a world tour with his various postings as guest conductor, beginning in Kaiserlaufen, Germany. The score calls for a full orchestra plus marimba, tom tom, and harp.

Apparently a creation story, it begins with dense dark low strings with a good deal of dissonance. Gradual growth with woodwinds move ino higher pitches, brings more light and a lyrical melody for strings and then brass. A brief rhythmically agitated section perhaps indicates that even a Divine creation of the world did not always go smoothly. The return of the broad ecstatic melody grows to a climax and ends abruptly. The listener would likely wish this were only the beginning of another symphony or further extension to Rautavaara's musings.

---

²⁵ Einojuhani Rautavaara, Liner notes, *A Tapestry of Life*, Ondine ODE 1149-2.

# CHAPTER TWELVE
# CONCERTOS

## *Konsertto puhaltimille* (Concerto for Winds), (1950) (withdrawn)

In 1950 the Ung Nordisk Musik (Young Nordic Music) festival was held in Helsinki. Rautavaara's first orchestral work, for winds and percussion, was performed under conductor Jussi Jalas at the Sibelius Academy, on October 23, 1950. This student work in three movements, I. Allegro, II. Tema con variation, III. Finale, was likely influenced by similar works by Stravinsky (perhaps the Concerto for Piano and Winds of 1924?). The conservative reviewer panned the work by saying "Tässä nähtiin nuori mies, joka yrittää latvasta puuhun mutta pudota romahtaakin päälaelleen"[1] (In this we saw a young man who was trying to climb to the top of a tree but fell with a great crash...). Rautavaara revised the work and it was probably performed in Stockholm in 1951 as *Concerto grottesco* and then withdrawn. In 1953 a march was resurrected from it and became the "Dies Irae" movement in *A Requiem in Our Time* (1953), Op. 3, a work also scored for winds and percussion. The concerto's second movement also became a resource for the piano piece *Tema con tre variazioni*, performed by Rautavaara at his composition recital in 1954.

## Piano Concerto No. 0, (1955), withdrawn

Though Rautavaara wrote a piano concerto in 1955 during his student years, he later withdrew it. Despite his rejection of the concerto, he won a third prize with the work in the Suomen Kultuurirahasto (Finnish Cultural Prize) composition competition that year. His composition teacher at Tanglewood, Roger Sessions, had criticized it for formlessness. Among Rautavaara's harmonic techniques were those he had used previously: symmetrical structures, added tones to triads, octotonic scales, mixed meters, and ostinato patterns.

---

[1] Rautavaara, 77.

## First Cello Concerto, Op. 41 (1968)

The first of three movements opens with a lengthy solo cello passage in double stops, in sixths, introducing the main theme recognizable later by its falling minor third motive. It ascends through several measures implying triads on A, F♯ and E♭. Eventually the orchestra comes in, led by trombones and pizzicato strings, building to a climax. A contrasting area gives arpeggiation to the cello and melody to the flutes. A growling cadenza on the opening idea leads to a lovely passage of smooth harmonics and a climatic reprise of the opening theme for everyone. Besides the singular shape of the form, the movement gives great attention to the soloist where the accompanying instruments either fade to the background or are completely missing.

A lyrical largo follows. Rautavaara wrote that he sat at his desk, writing an "a" for the cello and did not know how to continue.[2] The end result is exactly the random inspiration of an improviser. The melody starts with a turn, using the opening pitch's upper neighbor and lower neighbor. This simple but memorable motive then dominates the continuation. After the orchestral reiteration and arpeggiated cello harmonics, the cello has a solo passage which combines the turn motive with the falling minor thirds from the first movement. After the restatement of the opening themes and orchestration, and play on the combined motives, the harp repeats the tonic, the arpeggiated cello harmonics continue, and both fade away.

The third movement is a dance-like Vivace with the cello in a rhythmic pattern including fast triplets against the steady pulse of the orchestra. A broadening into to a slow lyrical melody becomes a transition into a cello cadenza. The dramatic cadenza refers to the first movement in its low register of double stops and virtuosic figuration, but includes the falling thirds only briefly. The opening Vivace returns and includes the lyrical transition. It ends with a codetta with the cello and flute exchanging segments of falling minor third patterns, the flute following the cello in a canonic echo, lulling each other, closing with cessation of movement rather than a cadence. Overall, the homophonic texture and the triadic and tonal references combine with dramatic, lyrical, and virtuosic playing from the cello, to make a very attractive Neo-Romantic work.

## First Piano Concerto (1969)

Rautavaara's first summer at Tanglewood in 1955 saw the beginnings of a piano concerto, under the guidance of Roger Sessions. Completed at Juilliard

---

[2] Tiikkaja, 280.

in the fall, the work won a competition prize in Finland. But after working with composer Persichetti and learning more about formal organization, he was dissatisfied with it and withdrew the work. In 1969 he wrote another piano concerto for his own performance and gave it the title of First Piano Concerto.

Not much of a concert pianist, he wrote for his own capabilities. In addition to Romantic melodies and big washes of arpeggios, he included a technique he had not used before. Full clusters of notes are played by the flat of the hand on the keys, or by using his full forearm. The clusters, the top melodic notes moving by descending steps, are accompanied by arpeggios covering the whole range of the piano (Example Fifteen, page 55). A second lyrical idea arrives with a single note melody with expressive leaps, still accompanied by arpeggiation, with brass motivic interjections. A cadenza develops both themes and includes clusters and dissonant harmonic sonorities. The slow movement has a chorale-like melody and keeps the accompaniment in arpeggiation. After the strings have had a turn, the piano moves on into a dissonant cadenza leading to the finale. The fast third movment establishes a rhythmic 3+2+3 samba-like dance. The perpetual motion was termed by critics as Gershwin material. Despite the criticism of that rhythm pattern, Rautavaara used it several times more, in his two piano sonatas of 1969, and in his 1970 concerto for textless soprano, *Meren tytär* (Daughter of the Sea).

## *Meren tytär* (Daughter of the Sea) (1970), concerto for soprano, choir, and orchestra

This textless four movement work won a first prize in a composition contest of the Finlandia Hall, for a work for the opening concert of that hall. The music was taken from an unfinished violin concerto of that year, and much later, was reused for *April Lines* (2006) a one movement piece for violin and piano. The four movements of *Meren tytär* have symphonic titles: Andante, Allegro, Andante assai, and Allegro assai. The fourth movement is notable for its 3+2+3 rhythmic pattern, similar to the finale of the First Piano Concerto (1969) and the *Fire Sermon* (1969) piano sonata's opening movement. The performers were Rautavaara's wife, Mariaheidi Rautavaara, the Academic Choral Society (Akateeminen Laulu), and the Helsinki City Orchestra under conductor Jorma Panula, on December 2, 1971. The work was later withdrawn by the composer but is still available in print.

## *Cantus Arcticus, Concerto for Birds and Orchestra* (1972)

When Rautavaara was commissioned by the University of Oulu in northwest Finland to write a cantata for its first degree-granting ceremony, he could not find a text that inspired him. He was also too aware that such a choral work would likely be performed once and then forgotten. Familiar with Oulu and its surroundings through his maternal relatives living there, the idea came to him to use tapes of arctic birds with an orchestra. From Oulu it was a short distance to the Leminka Bay region known for its nesting waterfowl and as a resting place during their fall migration. He recorded the sounds he wanted and then edited the tapes in Helsinki at the Finnish Broadcasting Company.

Since bird calls cannot easily be regulated into consistent bar lines or pitches, the composition became partly aleatoric. The first movement, "The Bog," opens with a flute duet based on motives harmonically stable. The bird tape is soon added to the flutes, with the twittering of small marsh birds and the call of the arctic cranes in a descending minor third or a single note. According to the conductor's choices, the orchestral instruments join in, imitating the bird calls. Eventually the orchestral introduces a quiet step-wise melody over a slow triadic low string support which moves often by thirds, rather than in functional harmony. Several repeats at different pitches and with different orchestrations lead to a final cello solo version and the fading away of both birds and orchestra.

The second movement, "Melancholy," begins with melodic warblings of the arctic shore larks, entering in what could be called a natural canonic imitation, but with the recording slowed down to drop the pitches by two octaves. The entrance of the upper strings in an ethereal divisi at a very slow speed creates a mystical aura. The rest of the orchestra is added for harmonic support underneath the continuing high strings, with trombones picking up the minor third motive of the cranes' call. Both the orchestra and birds build to a climax and then retreat into the opening calm.

The third movement, "Swans Migrating," opens with the sounds of many migrating swans, created by layering the original tape with many copies. At the conductor's signal, the flute begins a repetitive melody similar to the opening of the first movement, with a pulsing pedal point below. The trombones add a quiet theme moving around a central pitch with alternating neighbor tones. The strings take over the melody, bells tinkle, the solo trumpet continues with the strings, and the whole complex of swans, flutes, and orchestra swell and then fade out, leaving the swans calling as they disappear in the distance on their journey.

In 2017 a transcription was published for birds and piano, *Cantus Arcticus: Duet for Birds and Piano*. This arrangement was first suggested by pianist Laura Mikkola, a frequent performer of Rautavaara's works. The project was accomplished by Peter Lönnqvist, also a Finnish pianist. Rautavaara commented on the work saying "I think he knew how to demand more of the pianist than I would have dared to do."[3] The recorded tape of the birds, inflexible in its time span, must be downloaded from the publisher for performance. The pianist must keep to the suggested tempos and time limits. In the first movement the pianist imitates the flutes' duet alone. When the birds enter, the pianist must also decide how to ensure that the aleatoric passage lasts exactly two minutes to coordinate with the next thematic section in a fixed tempo, since the bird sounds do not noticeably give any clue. The second and third movements call for birds alone at the beginnings, for a specified amount of time, requiring use of a stopwatch. Starting the bird tape after the pianist has begun in the first movement calls for an assistant who can deal with the required amplifier, watch the score, and who must also increase the birds' volume at times. Attempting to include all the important orchestral contributions in a piano version leads to unusual techniques. One passage calls for octave descents beyond the normal range of the piano keyboard, if possible. Although this can be done on a Bösendorfer Imperial concert grand with its extended bass keys, routine practice of that effect might well lead to finger injury when another piano brand is all that is available. Rautavaara's love of independent whirling chromatic passages for flute duets makes the third movement near impossible for a pianist to master. At times, the various simultaneous orchestral effects call for reading on three lines, which combine the impression of a sharp key in one hand while reading a flat key in the other, sorting out the sharps and flats in clusters, and remembering chromatic alterations written perhaps some 30 notes earlier, but technically still in the same measure. The arrangement is not for the faint-hearted pianist, but is still a delight to the listeners' ears!

## *Tuulten tansseja* (Dances of the Winds) (1973), concerto for flute and orchestra.

*Dances of the Winds* was commissioned by Robert von Bahr, owner of BIS recordings, for his first wife, the Swedish flautist Gunilla von Bahr. The work calls for four different sizes of flutes, and for the rare flautist who is not only able to play each one but can change easily from one to another within a movement, having to reset his mouth's embouchere. The orchestration is remarkable, carefully scored to allow for the quiet low tones of the larger flutes, making much use of alternating comments so as not to overpower the flute.

---

[3] Rautavaara, Preface to the score, *Cantus Arcticus: Duet for Birds and Piano*, arr. Peter Lönnqvist.

The first movement, Andantino, calls for the standard flute and, in the middle, the bass flute. The soloist begins with rippling statements, often repeated inverted in mirror image, soon answered by growling low orchestral instruments, responding in antagonistic replies. After a crashing climax, a long pause on sustained quiet strings brings in a new section. Each flowery flute phrase is followed by a quiet brass chorale line. The two thematic ideas dominate the whole concerto. A lengthy section for homophonic strings allows the flautist time to exchange instruments to the bass flute. The bass flute's comments on the chorale theme are carefully accompanied by a restrained orchestra. The movement is rounded off by brief returns to the opening standard flute's figuration, its grumbling accompaniment and then the chorale.

The second movement, a scherzo, requires a piccolo. Patterned after a medieval fair show of a dancing tamed bear, it opens with drum beats and a picolo fast folksong in a stanza form: the first line repeats twice and then has a closing line. The next stanza is similar, but the melody, actually a rapid version of the first movement's chorale, is now inverted, three lines identical, and a closing line. The ongoing development is chaotic, with instrumental "raspberries" blurting, and a change of meter to depict the slow lumbering steps of the bear. The original melody begins again in augmentation, and is built up by stretto to a climactic end.

The third slow movement asks for an alto flute. Its steady walking melody stays in a narrow range and constantly turns back on itself. Though Rautavaara took this melody from the choral cantata *The Book of Life* (Elämän kirja), "Song of Myself," the winding and turning back of the melody on itself is a common trait in many of his other works. In the middle, the orchestra contributes the Beethoven Fifth fate motive, da-da-da-dum. The low brasses intone the chorale melody. The opening material returns at the end.

The finale brings back elements from the earlier movements. The opening martial introduction brings back the character of the orchestral gruffness in the first movement. After a pause, the bass flute brings in a call and response loosely based on the chorale theme, again alternating the bass flute with the orchestra because of its low quiet range. A particularly unlikely orchestration happens in the pairing of the low bass flute in a tenor register and a countermelody in the soprano register done by a muted trumpet, supported by soft strings. The martial material returns, followed by a cadenza for bass flute with orchestral interjections. With a brief return to the standard flute and some Beethovenesque fate motives, the work fades away.[4]

The concerto was later revised to omit the rare bass flute. Both versions

---

[4] Tiikkaja, 346-347.

were recorded by Israeli flautist Sharon Bezaly von Bahr, the second wife of Robert von Bahr, in 2016, some forty plus years after its premiere.

## Concerto for Organ, *Annunciations* (1976)

*Annunciations* was commissioned by the Stockholm Organ Festival, directed by organist Erik Lundkvist. The requested instrumentation called for three groups in opposition, the organ, a brass quintet, and a symphonic wind orchestra. The title word *Annunciations* here refers to mystical events, rather than the New Testament experience of the Virgin Mary. Rautavaara prefers to remain ambiguous about its programmatic intent, leaving it to the listener's imagination.

> Behind this work stands a powerful personal vision, strictly musical in nature. This said, it is possible for listeners to experience visual images when listening to this music, and its unbroken arc of half an hour's duration has a narrative feel to it. The introduction is slow and exploratory, like the creation of the world. In a way it lays out various symmetrical structures which invite further development. Fast passages in the organ trigger off a 'domino' form in which various sections follow one another in succession, laid end to end as it were. A dense 'forest of birds' is followed by a cantabile canon, which in turn culminates in a boisterous scherzo. After another cantabile passage the music quiets and a long, slow climb begins which eventually leads to the climax of the whole work. At this point the organ motor is switched off, leaving the notes of a dense chord swimming around in the hall and individually dying out over shorter or longer periods, depending on the acoustics. A swiftly moving finale then spurs on the work's 'annunciations' to a furious conclusion. One critic, commenting on this finale, once remarked that it reminded him of a Pasolini movie in which 'drunken aristocrats writhe over the organ keys.' I rather liked this analogy.[5]

Each group adds its own characteristic motive: the organ opens with a building of a cluster, the brass group introduces a chorale-like theme, flutes have a bird like response, and the tinkling of the revolving small bells of the organ stop Zimbelstern adds its own unusual color. The groups alternate, each continuing its motivic contribution. Low register saxophones add ominous sounds, fast figuration in the organ whirr above a sustained pedal tone with

---

[5] Einojuhani Rautavaara, trans. Jaakko Mäntyjärvi, web site of the Finnish Music Information Centre. www.fimic.fi.

timpani and dissonant trombone slides, all moving to some catastrophe. What sounds like a brief organ cadenza follows, with organ figuration and brass fanfare interjections. Next comes a quiet section with motives alternating between the groups, which then climaxes with a unique conclusion. The score calls for turning off the organ blower motor while holding down a massive chord. The organ sounds die away irregularly, some pipes sustaining longer than others. In the final section, with the organ blower turned back on, the organ figuration races above the affirmative brass chorale. When the brass have finished, brief bird motives call from the organ until all have faded.

The brasses often move in romantic triadic harmony, the organ contributes clusters, the flutes exchanges bird sounds with the organ, the wind band adds volume and dissonances. The organ itself adds its own specialties: the small unpitched bells of the tinkling Zimbelstern, the sustained bass organ pedal tone, its registral changes from full wind band sound to high crisp rapid figuration or flute imitation. The title, *Annunciations*, conveys the essence of this concerto, implying a mystical awe with the strong warm brass affirmation.

## Violin Concerto (1977)

In 1975, Rautavaara began a violin concerto intended for a young Romanian contestant in the Sibelius Violin Competition, Eugen Sarbu, who won the Third Prize. Sarbu was in Finland attending a master class and was available to try out portions of the music as they were composed, as well as again in New York City in 1977. The work was premiered by Sarbu with the Radio Symphony Orchestra of Helsinki during the Helsinki Festival week in August of 1978.

The violin concerto falls into two movements, "Tranquillo," and "Energico." A celeste is added to the usual orchestra. Rautavaara has provided a good description of the events. In the first movement:

> The solo violin seems to be travelling, encountering new landscapes and new situations time and again. At the very beginning, a sustained cantilena glides on, forming ever-expanding rings of intervals…An energetic sequence follows, featuring the violin's call and response with the French horn, until the music culminates in a heavy orchestral undulation.
>
> A new 'concertante' section begins, in which the two-part progression [double stops] of the violin line, surrounded by flute figuration, soars ever upward, then descends in a cascade of broken chords…there is a capricious violin cadenza, into which conversational comments by

various instruments are woven. The final section again opens with a slow melody, joined by the orchestra with its own variations...The work closes with a backward look, a quiet reminiscence of the opening motif.

The second movement:

If the opening section can be seen as a blend of classical principal movement and slow movement, the closing section is a synthesis of finale and scherzo. The brisk opening features constantly shifting rhythms; it is energetic music, in which the solo is driven impatiently forward by the blows of the orchestra...A quieter bridging passage... a solo cadenza. The composer left the closing bars of the cadenza for each soloist to compose anew, in the traditional classical manner. Once the orchestra returns, the violin climbs to romantic heights, then quickens its pace for the final stretto, in which the soloist must display sure control of the bow hand in a repetitive détaché.[6]

The recording of the violin concerto with soloist Elmar Oliveira and the Helsinki Philharmonic under Leif Segerstam on the disc *Angels and Visitations* took the Cannes Classical Award in 1998.

## Concerto for Double Bass and Orchestra, *Angel of Dusk* (1980)

*Angel of Dusk* is the second work in the Angel Series, the three works commissioned by the Finnish Radio Symphony orchestra (*Angels and Visitations*, 1978, an overture; *Angel of Dusk*, concerto for double bass, 1980; and Symphony No. 7, *Angel of Light*, 1995). Originally a commission from Olga Koussevitzky to honor the memory of her husband, famed conductor and bass player, Serge, the work was put aside on her death. When Rautavaara received a new commission for such a work from the Finnish Broadcasting Corporation, the concerto was revived and renewed by suggestions from the bass virtuoso Olli Kosonen. Rautavaara borrowed a bass and experimented at home with new techniques.

The first movement, titled "His First Appearance," opens with a brief hymnlike introduction for orchestra rising to a climax. The following lyrical theme for double bass explores its wide range and is balanced by use of marimba, glockenspiel, celeste, and harp arpeggios. The solo line is interrupted by dissonances from the brass, in what Rautavaara calls a "disturbance technique."[7] These short chromatic motives of interruption are ascending in the upper brass and descending in the lower, a kind of mirror writing. After a complete disruption from the brass, the bass takes up the chromatic motive. A dialogue

---

[6] Einojuhani Rautavaara, Liner note for *Angels and Visitations, Viuluknosertto, Lintukoto*, Ondine ODE 881-2; also, www.fimic.fi/rautavaara.

[7] Einojuhani Rautavaara, Liner notes for *Angel of Dusk*, BIS CD-910 Digital.

between the two forces, a quiet bass line and abrupt brass interjections, leads to a final quiet section of melody from the introductory hymn using glissando double stops in seconds on the bass.

The middle movement, "His Monologue," consists of a long cadenza, with a variety of techniques, harmonics, plucking, sliding, double stops, bowing on the strings close to the bridge, bouncing on the strings, rough plucks combined with glissando, with only a few contributions from the orchestra, sometimes taunting, with sarcastic trumpet interjections. Written without bar lines, it is divided into six sections by rehearsal numbers. In a symmetrical arrangement, both the first and last sections are for bass alone. Most of Rautavaara's unconventional bass techniques appear in the opening section, such as the first col legno (the back of the bow) tremolo while plucking twice on the open lower E string at regular intervals. The middle sections include bits of orchestral involvement, such as violin clusters moving in glissando. Almost at the end comes a Phrygian melody in high harmonics sounding like a Finnish folksong. The opening tremolo returns with the regular plucking on the E string and the bass ends with a passage in double stops leading directly into the final movement.

The third movement, "His Last Appearance," opens without break with a quiet swaying cantilena based on the intervals of seconds and thirds and gradually ascending. The accompaniment, two pizzicato basses and timpani roll, also includes the blowing of air through the brasses without a tone, sounding like a wind machine or ocean waves. The cantilena moves on with motion in clarinets and chords in the strings. Violent timpani strokes introduce a new rhythmic section with full orchestra, and rapid figuration for the soloist. The ongoing solo rhythmic section ends with full orchestra disturbances like those in the first movement. The sliding glissando melody from the first movement leads back to the movement's opening mood. The opening of Movement II is recalled with the paired plucked notes on the E string. A coda begins with celeste, vibraphone, harp and then strings playing ascending chords to accompany the soloist's melody to a fading ending.[8]

Reviews of the double bass concerto were mixed. Some said it was Rautavaara's most important work to date, while others recommended it be rearranged for cello, or commented on its "uninteresting sawing."[9] In 1992 the work was performed in Germany, Sweden, and Hungary. The following year, 1993, the concerto was rearranged as a chamber work for solo double bass, two pianos, and a single percussion player for the Kuhmo Chamber Music Festival of 1994.

---

[8] Stepien, 119-135 passim.
[9] Tiikkaja, 402.

## Second Piano Concerto (1989)

Composed for pianist Ralf Gothoni, Rautavaara prefaced the score saying that the titles of the three movements give its intended meaning. He gave the three connected movements expressive Italian titles: "In Viaggio" (On a Trip), "Sognando e libero" (Dreamlike and Free), and "Uccelli sulle passioni" (Birds with passion). These are "not birds created from music...but music as birds." To clarify this, he refers to the style of a restaurant's menu, saying "Musique à l'oiseau."[10]

According to Samuli Tiikkaja, the 12-tone row moves through all its possible variants, in its original form, introversion, retrograde, and retrograde inversion, in a dazzling array of spiraling appearances.[11] Since much of the writing for piano is in thirty-second notes to invoke the twittering of birds, an analyst would be hard pressed to identify each variant.

The first movement begins with high treble rippling passages for piano, with soft accompanying comments added from other instruments. The main stepwise melody appears in the violin section, below the piano's register. As a soloist, the piano takes over both the melodic aspect and the continual rapid passagework. The ensemble joins in, reaching a high register climax. Various brass squawks interject, like birds, into the piano figuration. The strings take up the main melody again. A further climax is reached by the combined forces, and the movement ends with the piano passages running out.

The lengthy slow movement follows with little pause, in the style of a sentimental character piece, though atonal, led by the pianist. Woodwinds and strings are added to the dominant piano, creating an ethereal setting. An energetic middle section is punctuated by occasional dissonances, whip lashes in the percussion, repetitive bird-like chirps, a passage that repeats its motive slowing down more each time, ending with a long fermata. The slow movement's opening style then returns, though gloomier in mood.

A transition, perhaps intended as a partially accompanied cadenza, gives the piano single fast repeated pitches, wood block, and vibraphone interjections, perhaps the birds as musicians, as a segue into the finale. The first movement's stepwise melody returns in the low strings and brasses. The high strings take over the bird chattering while the piano races on. The bird sounds fade into the distance.

---

[10] Einojuhani Rautavaara, Liner notes, *Piano Concertos 1 & 2*, Ondine ODE 757-2.
[11] Tiikkaja, 463.

## Third Piano Concerto, *The Gift of Dreams* (1998)

The Third Piano Concerto was premiered by Vladimir Ashkenazy in the summer of 1999. Rautavaara was introduced to Ashkenazy by his record company Ondine with which the pianist had recently signed a contract. As a conductor as well as pianist, Ashkenazy wanted a work which he could lead from the piano. This set certain limits on the composer to keep the beat reasonably steady in order to make the coordination of solo and orchestra easier.

The subtitle *Gift of Dreams* derives from a 1978 solo song, "Le mort des pauvres," text by Baudelaire. The words "le don des reves" appear with the notes F-E♭-D♭-E. This motive, with its available major third, minor third, whole step, and half step, allowed for diatonic, whole tone, or chromatic usage, was also used in the *Unknown Heavens* String Quintet (1997), and then in the piano concerto in all three movements. Rautavaara related that his symmetrical use of this motive in the construction of form was similar to a mandala, a circular religious symbol of a balanced spiritual universe in both Hinduism and Buddhism; his use of the twelve tone row in that manner united all elements of melody and harmony in an enclosed universe, a circle.[12] The motive is part of the melody in the first movement, dominates the slow movement, and then is varied in the finale.

The first movement, Tranquillo, is lyrical but grows to an emotional outburst. Based on a concerto's traditional ritornello structure, it adds in a dualism, splitting the ritornello by a soloist's repetition of it. The ritornello alternates with episodes of other themes in dialogue between the two forces rather than a development. Throughout, the piano ripples in arpeggios. The second movement, Adagio, in an ABA form, takes the motive from calmness to a violence of chromaticism and back again. The finale, Energico, varies the motive with fanfares and a variety of orchestral textures, then to a cadenza referring to the first movement. Near the end a restatement of the lyrical theme from the first movement is reset with a version of the motive underneath in long bass notes, the ending of the first movement's ritornello appears, and the final coda concludes it all.[13]

## Concerto for Harp and Orchestra (2000)

While in Minneapolis, Minnesota, in 1999 for a festival of his music, a harp concerto was commissioned. Knowing from past experience composing his *Ballad* for harp and string orchestra that a quiet harp solo could well be

---

[12] Tiikkaja, 535.
[13] Howell, 140-141.

overwhelmed by the orchestra, Rautavaara sought advice from two professional harpists to help with the balance and with possible harp techniques. With an orchestra including woodwinds, brass, and percussion he decided to add two additional orchestral harps to increase the harp sound when needed. The first movement opens with a slow introduction for the strings and a solo French horn. The harp takes up the narrow range melody, in a gentle way with accompanying arpeggios, with the orchestra downplayed in the background. A more dramatic section follows, with unusual harp effects and playing techniques such as "gushing chords," metallic sounds, and thunder effects, punctuated by orchestral outbursts. The harp returns to its gentle theme, dominating the orchestra. The second movement is a lullaby which seems to relate to the first movement's theme by inversion. The movement grows into a cantabile with brilliant arpeggios typical of the harp. The finale opens with full orchestra with added vibraphone and chimes plus the three harps in dialogue with it. A central dramatic section is followed by a return to the opening style, where the introduction from the first movement ends the work. The first performance was given by Kathy Kienzle and the Minnesota Orchestra under Osmo Vänskä.[14] The work was later performed and recorded in Helsinki with French harpist Marielle Nordmann and conductor Leif Segerstrom.

## Clarinet Concerto (2002)

The clarinet concerto was written for Richard Stolzman and commissioned by three parties, Theodore Friedman, the International Arts Foundation, and the Washington National Symphony Orchestra. The first performance was given by Stoltzman with the National Symphony Orchestra in Washington, D.C., in 2002. Stoltzman, delighted with the work, brought it to London and to Helsinki for later performances.

The noticeable features of the first movement are an opening burst of sounds followed by ascending clarinet figurations, with a French horn to introduce a melodic second theme. The cadenza was likely well discussed with the performer, because it is partially improvised. An unusual touch is the addition of a bass clarinet to accompany the soloist in the cadenza's final part. The melodic second theme returns to close the movement. The second movement is an unbroken song for the soloist. The rhythmic final movement, Vivace, brings back motifs of the first movement and sets off a display of virtuosity.[15]

---

[14] Einojuhani Rautavaara, Liner notes, *Harp Concerto,* Ondine ODE 978-2.
[15] Einojuhani Rautavaara, Liner notes, *Clarinet Concerto,* Ondine ODE 1041-2.

## Concerto for Percussion, *Incantations* (2008)

Composed for British percussionist Colin Currie, this work was commissioned by four orchestras from London, Rotterdam, Baltimore, Maryland in the US, and Tampere, Finland. The score calls for marimba, vibraphone, timpani, four rototoms (pitched drums without shells) three tam tams (small gongs), two bongos, two congas, crotales (tuned bronze disks), tuned bells, three gongs, thunder stick, and pedal bass drum. Though the title refers to pagan chants, often repetitive and limited in range of pitches, Rautavaara wrote varying meters such as 7/8, 3+2+3/8, 11/8, and uses the marimba and vibraphone for a predominance of melody.

In three movements, the concerto features the marimba in the first and last movements and the more expressive vibraphone in the slow middle movement. The first movement opens with orchestra, continues with marimba and then alternates with entries from various other percussion in such a fast and rhythmically complicated manner that the player has no time to change mallets. The slow movement's vibraphone turns the mood into a poetic one, accompanied mainly by strings. In the jerky rhythms of the finale the marimba revels in virtuosity and adds an improvised cadenza. The marimba takes one theme from the last part of his *Notturno e Danza,* and the vibraphone sounds like a melody from *Book of Visions* "A Tale of Night." It ends with a grand restatement of the first movement's opening.[16]

## Cello Concerto, *Towards the Horizon* (2008-2009)

Rautavaara's second cello concerto was dedicated to Truls Mørk, Norwegian cellist of the Minnesota Orchestra. Though Mørk was too ill to do the premiere, he later performed and recorded the work in Helsinki. Rautavaara described the concerto as a one movement "becalmed view of the far horizon distracted by a series of energetic dialogues before the melody recedes into the distance."[17] It was this receding concept that gave him the title, *Towards the Horizon.* Rautavaara gives details in his program notes:

> After an introduction, the cello presents the main theme, a cantilene, where woodwind solos and strings join in, ...a Furioso passage leading to a development,...dialogues between the soloist and instrumental groups (solo horn, then flutes). (Toward the end) the cello sings in the

---

[16] Tiikkaja, 597.

[17] Einojuhani Rautavaara, Program notes to first performance of *Cello Concerto: Towards the Horizon,* Minneapolis, Minnesota, Sept. 30, 2009.

highest possible range which brought to my mind the view of a far horizon. The energetic Vigoroso section alternates with the "horizon" idea until only the "horizon" is left.[18]

## *Fantasia* (2015), for violin and orchestra

Commissioned by violinist Anne Akiko Meyers, this fifteen minute single movement work did not receive its first performance until March 2017, nearly a year after Rautavaara's death in July of 2016 at the age of 87. The work was first introduced by Meyers and the Kansas City Orchestra under conductor Michael Stern and then recorded by Meyers with the London Philharmonic Orchestra with conductor Kristjan Järvi in October of 2017 for Avie Records.

Meyers has described the score as

> transcendent and has the feeling of an elegy with a very personal reflective mood. Rautavaara's signature soulful sound permeates throughout the piece, with fluid harmonies and deep moods--much like flowing large movements of water and majestic scenes from nature.[19]

In December 2015, Meyers performed the yet unpublished work for the composer at his home in Helsinki. She describes the experience:

> After I played *Fantasia*, he looked at me and repeatedly said, 'I wrote such beautiful music!' We laughed and agreed. I was amazed that he made no changes to any notes or dynamics. Everything was in place, just the way he wrote it.[20]

With a brief orchestral introduction, the violin begins and continues without pause or breath with a mournful, mesmerizing tale. The violin dominates the quiet orchestral strings which act as sympathetic listeners murmuring in the background. The orchestra makes no attempt to dialogue or comment in its own sections. Various solo woodwinds emerge from the flow of the strings to offer small counter melodies. Toward the end the violin becomes more agitated, reaching a climax. The orchestra has an equally passionate and dissonant interlude, then both rejoin solemnly and rise again to a climatic end.

---

[18] Ibid.
[19] Anne Akiko Meyers, Liner Notes, *Fantasia*, Avie Records
[20] Ibid.

The consistent mood of the unceasing melody seems to call out for some poetic interpretation, perhaps a deeply felt grief.

## Two Serenades for Violin and Orchestra (2016)

Commissioned by Finnish conductor Mikko Franck, the work was left unfinished on the composer's death in July 2016. Radio France commissioned Finnish composer and former Rautavaara student Kalevi Aho to finish the orchestration of the second serenade which remained in a piano score. Aho, a highly respected composer, composition teacher, essayist and publisher of Finnish compositions, was also known for his arrangements or reconstructions of other Finnish composers' works, such as the Eric Tulindberg string quartets of the late 1790s and the Uuno Klami ballet *Pyörteitä* (Vortices, 1960). As such, he was the best possible choice for the completion of the Rautavaara *Serenades*. The work was scheduled for its first performance with Hilary Hahn, violin, Mikko Franck, conductor, and the Orchestre Philharmonique de Radio France in Paris in February of 2019.

The first *Serenade*, "Serenade pour mon amour," is scored for violin and strings and has a lyrical barcarolle mood. The second, "Serenade pour la vie," has added woodwinds and horns to the strings, likely a combination of both Rautavaara's and Aho's tastes. It falls into three sections by tempo markings: an opening andante, a middle faster section, and a closing agitato. Both movements are not intended as virtuosic display pieces, but are melodic and melancholy.[21]

---

[21] www.boosey.com/cr/news/Rautavaara-s-last-work-premiered-by-Hilary-Hahn.

# CHAPTER THIRTEEN
# SOLO VOCAL WORKS

### *Hunnuton* (Unveiled) (1947), lost

A song on a text by Aila Meriluoto, it won a second prize at the Suomen teinliito (Finnish Teen League) composition competition of 1947.

### *Lauluja Paul Verlainen ja Aila Merluoden runoihin* (Songs to the poetry of Paul Verlaine and Aila Meriluoto) (1947), lost

### *Lauluja Kaarlo Sarkian ja Edith Södergranin runoihin* (Songs to the poetry of Kaarlo Sarkia and Edith Södergran) (1948), lost

### *Ensi lumen aikaan* (Time of First Snow) (1947), for voice and piano

This song on a text by Kaarlo Sarkia, was given away as a gift to friends and forgotten. About the year 2000, a copy was sent to Rautavaara anonymously. A review of it shows that it had an ABA form, contrasts of dynamics, some modality, and seventh chords.[1]

### *Nu så dansa denna världens barn* (Tanssihin käyvät lapset mailman, The Children of the World go to Dance) (1948)

This is a song on a text by Harriet Löwenhjelm, which shows the influence of Debussy in its harmonies and a mixolydian mode in its melody. This song and two others, *Tähdet* (Stars) on a text by Editin Södergran, and *Erottua* (Difference) probably on a text by Kaarlo Sarkia, were presented on the radio in February of 1950 in a young composers' concert and subsequently lost.

---

[1] Tiikkaja, 53.

## *Galgenlieder* (Gallows Songs) (1949), for voice and piano, lost

Three songs on nonsense poems by Christian Morgenstern, "Galgenbruders Lied an Sophie, die Henkersmaid" (Gallows Brothers' Song to Sophie the Executioner), "Galgenkindes Wiegenlied" (The Gallows Child's Cradle Song), and "Galgenbruders Frülingslied" (Gallows Brothers' Spring Song). A fourth song, "Geiss und Schleich" (The Goat and the Lizard), lost, was mentioned in a handwritten manuscript, along with the notation that it belonged to a set of variations for baritone and string quartet, evidently never completed. The first performance in Stockholm at the 1949 Nordic Music Days, performed by baritone Matti Lehtinen and pianist Kerstin Peterson, received a cool reception by the critics.

## *Three Sonnets of Shakespeare* (1951, 1973) for voice and piano

The Shakespeare songs include: 1. Sonnet LXXIII "That time of year thou mayst in me behold," 2. Sonnet XII "When I do count the clock", and 3. Sonnet XVIII "Shall I compare thee to a summer's day?" Rautavaara, learning by copying other composers' works by hand, had been impressed with Benjamin Britten's use of bitonality in his *Seven Sonnets by Michelangelo* and used that technique in his own setting of Shakespeare sonnets.

The first sonnet depicts old age. There are three musical sections, andantino, larghetto, andantino, each with a textual analogy: [in me thou seest] that time of year [autumn], in me…twilight, in me…glow of an expiring fire. The melody allows the singer to recite the words clearly in constant eights, in simple steps or thirds, focusing around an F♯ or C♯. The accompanying bitonal material includes superimposed triads of different keys in half notes. The opening sound in the four measure introduction piles up thirds, using a G major triad in the left hand, and an F major in the right. The next few sonorities successively move both triads up a minor third. With the entry of the voice the piano style changes to harmonize the melody in thirds and a descending single note bass line in steps, fifths or fourths, stressing final phrase endings on F♯ or C♯ (Example Two, page 12).

The piano part in the second song follows the declamation of the voice with slow diads of open octaves with the bass note and the third above it, all moving non-tonally. It opens with the ticking of the clock conveyed by the vocal pitch repetitions that begin almost every phrase. With a change in the lyrics from depicting the effects of aging to a question of why "thy beauty… must go," the accompaniment changes to an even slower chordal style with grating triads in cross-relationships. After many chromatic shifts, both the singer and piano end in G major.

The last song "Shall I compare thee to a summer's day" is marked Vivace. It establishes a clearly tonal B♭ major, leaps through a cheerful melody, and then throws in a countermelody in B major. Its brief slower middle section has the bass line calmly climbing or descending in interval ladders of thirds, depicting the words "too hot the eye of heaven." The opening Vivace returns with the words "But thy eternal summer shall not fade," ending in the opening key of B♭ (Example Two, page 12). The first performance was with Matti Lehtinen, baritone, and Rautavaara, piano, at the Young Nordic Music festival in Copenhagen, Denmark, on October 21, 1951.

## *Pyhiä päiviä* (Sacred Feasts, 1953) for voice and piano

The *Sacred Feasts* group are a set of four songs on the Laestadian poetry of K. Lounasheimo from a conservative religious group in Lapland, northern Finland. Originally conceived as congregational hymns, they evolved into more complex solo songs. The four songs were: "Suuri pitkäperjantai" (The Great Good Friday); "Iltarukous" (Evening Prayer), added later with a text by Aaro Hekkaakoski, "Kynttilänpäivä" (Candlemas, a Christmas carol), and "Joulun virsi, elämän virsi" (Christmas Hymn, Hymn of Life). The last one was rearranged for male chorus as well as for a children's chorus in 1978 and in 1995 Rautavaara made an arrangement of it for mixed chorus with an English text. The first performance was in Turku, Finland, on May 8, 1954 with Hannu Heikkilä, bass, and Rautavaara, piano.

## *Kaksi nokturnoa* (Two Nocturnes) (1951), lost

These two songs on texts by Rautavaara were first performed by Rautavaara with baritone Matti Lehtinen in Copenhagen, presumably at the Nordic Music Days, in 1951, and then again at Rautavaara's composition recital in 1954 with baritone Hannu Heikkilä. The manuscripts have been lost.

## *Madrigalen* (1952), unpublished

"Quando il giorno da l'onde apporta il sole," on a text by Gabriele Fiamma, and "Danza, danz fanciulla gentile, al mio cantar," on a text by an unknown author, may both have been influenced by Benjamin Britten's *Seven Michelangelo Sonnets*, using the Renaissance Italian texts and polytonality to dramatic effect.

## *Fünf Sonette an Orpheus* (Five Sonnets to Orpheus, 1954-55), Op. 9, for voice and piano

The five songs on texts of Rainer Maria Rilke were: 1. Da stieg ein Baum (A Tree Arose); 2. Und fast ein Mädchen wars (A Maiden Almost); 3. Ein Gott vermags (A God Can Do It); 4. O ihr Zärtlichen (O Tender Ones); and 5. Errichtet keinen Denkstein (Raise No Memorial). Completed before his first neoclassical symphony and his first twelve-tone compositions, these songs are still mostly tonal and full of bits of word-painting, such as in the first song, a rising melodic line for "A tree arose, O wonderful rising!," tentativeness in "not in stealth nor in fear," and bass tones at "somber." In the second song, "A Maiden almost," a light texture portrays wonder and pauses portray the questioning. "A god can do it" is ominous recitative, denying that song is yearning, and culminating in exclamation that song is "a breeze of god." In the fourth song, "O tender ones, step sometimes into the breath" has a repetitive ostinato figure illustrating walking for two stanzas. Then tenderness gives way to heaviness in harmonies and discords, until a final light last line depicting "air," and "space." In the last song, the poet entreats us not to raise any memorial to Orpheus, because…he comes and goes. The gentle melody lies over a constant back and forth motion in the accompaniment. Although the first three songs had been presented on his 1954 composition recital, the whole set of five received their first performance by Peter Roberts, tenor, and Rautavaara, pianist, at Tanglewood in the summer of 1955. In 1960 Rautavaara arranged the set for voice and orchestra. His first wife Mariaheidi Rautavaara was the soloist, with the Helsinki City Orchestra in 1961.

Three further *Orpheus* songs were composed but never performed or published. In 1958 came "Nur wer die Leier Schon hob" (Only he who has lifted his lyre) and "Fruhling ist wiedergekommen" (Spring has come again), and in 1961 "Wandelt sich rasch auch die Welt" (The World is also rapidly changing). The three were later arranged into a piano work entitled *Rilkeadi*, but it, too, was never performed or published.

## *First Sonnet From the Portuguese* (1957), lost

Based on an English text by Elizabeth Barrett Browning, this song was first performed by Peter Roberts, Rautavaara's Tanglewood roommate, with Olive Roberts, piano, in Norwich, Connecticut, in 1957. Though it probably was intended to be part of a suite, no further songs were ever completed.

## *Hajoaminen* (Disintegration, 1957), a set of four songs on texts by Lassi Nummi, unpublished.

These four songs on gloomy texts were never published nor performed at the time of their composition. The first song, "Déluge," took its motives from his earlier song, *First Sonnet from the Portuguese*, and lent the set its title from words in the first verse. The second, "Requiem," was later set in a version for piano, voice, and obligato cello. The third song, "Elegia," was perhaps Rautavaara's first attempt at the twelve tone method of composition. The fourth song continued the style of the first two in its use of ostinatos and repeated motives.

After the death of Rautavaara's first wife, Mariaheidi, in 2004, Rautavaara's three children gave him a stack of his old manuscripts, including these four songs. Two of the songs received their first performance in March of 2018 at the Finnish National Theater in Helsinki as part of the Black Box series run by the Finnish newspaper, Helsinkin Sanaomat, featuring talks about journalism. Journalist and musicologist Samuli Tiikkaja spoke about his research for his book *Tulisaarna* (The Fire Sermon, 1914) and the finding of these long lost songs. Besides the talk, Tiikkaja arranged the performance of two of the songs, including the third one, "Elegia." The performers were mezzo soprano Essi Luttinen and pianist Kireill Kozlovski. "Elegia" was Rautavaara's first attempt at using twelve-tone rows, before his study with Vladimir Vogel, and resulted in his ability to create longer spans and continuity in his works.

## *Orpheus Sonnets, Zweiter Zyklus* (1958-1961) three songs for voice and piano.

In 1958 Rautavaara continued writing additional songs by Rainer Maria Rilke intended to join the previous five. "Nur wer die Leier Schon hob" (Only he who has lifted his lyre) and "Fruhling ist wiedergekommen" (Spring has come again), were joined in 1961 by "Wandelt sich rasch auch die Welt" (The World is also rapidly changing). At some point Rautavaara rearranged these songs into a piano set, *Rilkeadi*, but neither the songs nor the piano work were ever published or performed.

## *Die Liebenden* (The Lovers, 1958-59), Op. 13, song cycle for high voice and piano or orchestra, later reorchestrated for full orchestra with celeste and harp.

The set of songs called *Die Liebenden* on four poems of Rainer Maria Rilke include: 1. Liebes-Lied (Love Song); 2. Der Schauende (Man Looking); 3. Die

Liebende (Woman Loving); and 4. Der Tod der Geliebten (Death of the Beloved). The protagonists, the woman and the man, take turns in their songs. Her songs, the first and third, are quiet and lyrical while his songs, the second and fourth, are more dramatic. The four songs were composed in a modified twelve tone technique. The first song's row is built of six pairs of seconds. The expressive melody moves in a smooth conjunct style, freely taking its pitches from the row presented first in the accompaniment. By contrast the piano accompaniment is more angular in its leaps. Harmonic areas are implied but not realized. The dream-like harmonic instability is grounded by the constant quarter note pulse.

Some word-painting appears throughout, as in "die Stürme" (the tempests bluster) of the second song, the importance of the reference to the angel by giving the word the highest melodic pitch, "durchsichtig wie eines Kristalles" (transparent as glass) in the third song. Rautavaara later reused material from two of the songs in the String Quartet No. 4 (1975), with the second movement based on the third song, "Die Liebende," and the third movement based on the second song, "Der Schauende." The first performance of the songs was by Mariaheidi Suovanen Rautavaara, soprano, and the Chamber Orchestra of the Sibelius Academy. In 1962 the pieces were performed at the Nordic Music Festival in Copenhagen.

## *14 Sånger till dikter av Bo Setterlind* (1962), unpublished

In 1962, Rautavaara completed some fourteen songs on texts of Setterlind but did not publish them at that time. Some became part of the *Guds väg* (God's Way) set, some were used in the *Maria I Norden* set, and some were used as material in the *Itsenäisyyskantaatti* (Independence Cantata) of 1967.

## *Guds väg* (God's Way) (1964), for solo voice and piano

These four Swedish songs on texts by Bo Setterlind, "Guds väg," (God's Way), "Barnet" (The Child), "Pingst" (Pentecost), "Dröm I katedralen" (Dream in the Cathedral), were first performed by Jorma Hynninen, baritone, in 1980. Besides the austere music with tonal references, the settings are programmatic, with slow broad movement illustrating God's way over "wastes of space," rapid passage work for the piano illustrating "the child plays" while the Magi adoringly present their gifts, the agitation of dreaming of attacking soldiers on horseback while listening to a priest in a cathedral.

## *Maria I Norden II* (Maria of the North II) (1964)

This set of three songs on Swedish texts by Bo Setterlind are now either withdrawn or lost. Only the first title is known, "Vad du är vacker" (How Beautiful You Are).

## *I vinternatten* (In a Winter Night) (1969), for voice and piano

A single song set to a Swedish text by Bo Carpelan (1926-2011), a well-known Finnish author.

## *Kaksoiskotka* (Double Eagle) (1972), song cycle for voice and piano, withdrawn

This set of songs on a text by Paavo Haaviko was withdrawn.

## *October*, Op. 75, later retitled *Mailmaan uneen* (Dream World) (1972, 1982/1997), a song cycle for voice and piano

Entitled *October* on Finnish texts by Aaro Hellaakoski, this set of songs won a first prize in the 1973 Finnish Broadcast song composition contest. Originally two songs, "Tulen" (I Approach Thee) and "October," a third song was later inserted into the middle in 1982, "Viatonten valssi" (Waltz of the Innocents), an arrangement of a choral work for children's chorus, violin, and piano. With that addition, the name of the set changed to *Mailmaan uneen* (Dream World).

## *Almanakka kahdelle* (Almanac for Two) (1973/1998), duet for two voices, a male and a female, with piano

Commissioned by baritone Jorma Falckin and his wife, alto Ritva Määttänen-Falckin, the four seasons are depicted in four songs of different poets, each in a different language. "Vårvisa" (Spring Song) with a text in Swedish by Olaf V. Dalin, "Kesäyö" (Summer Night) with a text in Finnish by Aaro Hellaakoski, "Herbsttag" (Autumn Day) with a text in German by Rainer Maria Rilke, and "Winter" in English by William Shakespeare.

## *Ilmarisen lento* (The Flight of Ilmarinen) (1976), for voice and piano

The text of this song comes from the Kalevala.

## *Matka* (The Trip) (1977), for baritone or mezzosoprano and piano

The Finnish Public Radio commissioned this set of songs on texts by Rautavaara, originally intended for an abandoned 1968 opera *Hippios Koiranoksen*. The original gloomy and surreal text was about an ancient Greek sailor rescued from a shipwreck and brought to shore by dolfins. The four songs include "Kuljin matkan aamupuolella yötä" (I took that trip), "Mitä on silmäluomiesi taka syntymässä?" (What is there?), "Kuljen yli kevätlumisien piuistikoiden" (I am walking over tiny spots of snow), and "Yö on syvä" (Deep is the Night). Surreal images show a trip through hell, repulsive animals, of a nightmare, while trying to wake up.

The first song tells of a heart covered with ants, snakes with wings dropping down, all of this lasting for years. The unconventional piano accompaniment changes at each image, closing with forceful tone clusters. The second song depicts the last irrelevant images seen while drowning. Ripples from the piano end in low bass clusters. The third song tells of baby tigers romping through bits of snow in new grass, fast figuration setting the mood. "Deep is the Night" is slow, deep in pitch, with the last two lines, strangely, no longer in Finnish, but in English, "we are trying to awake from a dream called life." The songs were first performed on May 26, 1978, taped for a radio performance by Jorma Hynninen, baritone, who sang lead roles in several Rautavaara operas, accompanied by Ralf Gothoni. They were sung in Finnish at the Minneapolis week-long Rautavaara festival in 1999 by Vern Sutton, a music professor, a fan of Finnish music, and co-arranger of the festival. Sutton wished to include Rautavaara's opera *Aleksis Kivi* in the festival, having seen it performed in Finland, and translated the whole libretto into English, despite no knowledge of Finnish. He himself took the spoken role of the harsh Swedish critic, August Ahlqvist. Perhaps it was just as well that the nightmarish words of the *Matka* songs were covered up by the awkwardly pronounced Finnish language. Rautavaara included the songs in a collection of his solo songs published in 2001 by Warner/Chappell.

## *Två stranddikter* (Two Beach Poems) (1982), for voice and piano, withdrawn

Dedicated to Sini Rautavaara, these settings in Swedish of the poetry of Edith Södergran were "Mitt liv" (My Life) and "Mellan gråa stenar" (Among the Grey Stones). The second song was later included in the set *I min älsklings trädgård* (In My Beloved's Garden).

### *I min älsklings trädgård* (In My Beloved's Garden) (1983-87), for voice and piano

Another set of Swedish texts by Edith Södergran also inspired Rautavaara at this time and were dedicated to Sini Rautavaara, about the time of their courtship and marriage. The three songs were: "I de stora skogarna" (In the Great Wild Woodlands); 2. "Mellan gråa stenar" (In Between Grey Stones); and 3. "Lyckokatt" (Lucky Cat). Rautavaara had set these as a teenager but lost the manuscripts. The cheerful first song tells how the wanderer often went in the woods seeking fairy tales and dream castles, but in the lover's garden he never needed to go wandering, for there sat the merry cuckoo which his yearning followed. Each pair of two lines of text is set like a verse of a folksong, with a pause on a chord before the light-hearted motion begins again. At the end, the piano adds a final "cuckoo."

The second song is mournful, "In between grey stones thy white body lieth still and mourneth." The final song bounces, cat-like, asking the cat to tell the future. In 1993 the three songs were rearranged for a female choir, the Florakören of Turku, Finland, under the title of the first song, *I de stora skogarna*.

### *Minä en puhu minä laulan* (I Don't Speak, I Sing) (1986), for voice and piano

This song for solo voice and piano on a text by the composer was commissioned by the Lappeenranta Solo Song Competition, and was a required song for all contestants. The Lappeenranta Singing Competition, a national competition for young singers in Finland, is held every two years. Many of Finland's internationally known opera singers got their start there, including Jorma Hynninnen, Soile Isokoski, and Karita Mattila.

### *Sinulle minä antaisin auringonkukka* (To You I Would Give Sun Flowers) (1986), for voice and piano

This song on a text by Rautavaara was first performed at the Lappeenranta Song Festival of 1987.

### *Eron hetki on kalveakasvo* (The Moment of Parting is a Pale Mask) (1997), for female voice and piano or orchestra

This aria was rearranged from "Charlotta's Monologue" in the opera *Aleksis Kivi*, with text from the poetry of Aleksis Kivi. Charlotta, Kivi's patroness, movingly realizes she must let Kivi go.

## *Nelja laulua oopperasta Aleksis Kivi* (Four Songs from the opera Aleksis Kivi) (1997), for voice and piano or orchestra

Rautavaara later published four orchestral songs from the 1996 opera: "Ikävyys" (Melancholy), Kivi's opening aria; "Laulu oravasta" (The Squirrel), from Act One where Kivi is requested to read one of his poems to Hilda and Charlotta; "Oi mailma, elämä sä ilmeellinen" (O World, Life, Thou Marvel), Kivi's song from the opening of Act III; and "Sydämeni laulu" (Song of My Heart), Kivi's final aria about the peace found in the grove of Tuoni, the land of the dead (Example Twenty-two, page 99). Three of the songs (the third omitted) were rearranged for a cappella mixed chorus for a festival of Rautavaara's works in Minneapolis, Minnesota, in March, 1999, under the new title of *In the Shade of the Willow*, words that come from the first song where Kivi asks to be buried anonymously under a willow.

## *Eingang* (Entrance) (2009), for soprano and string quartet

This song on a text by Rainer Maria Rilke was begun in 1952 on a translation by poetess Aila Meriluoto titled "Ken lienetkin." The original song was written for voice, piano, and cello. In 2008 Rautavaara revised it using the German text, some of the old material, an added intensity, and much high coloratura to suit the singer.[2] A four minute work, it was completed in 2009 for the Turku Music Festival and performed by virtuoso coloratura soprano Piia Komsi with the Zagros Quartet.

## *In the Stream of Life* (2013), seven Sibelius songs for solo baritone and orchestra, orchestrated by Einojuhani Rautavaara.

The Finnish, German, and Swedish texts are by a variety of German, Swedish, and Finnish poets listed below. The settings were commissioned and first performed by baritone Gerald Finley in Bergen and Oslo, Norway, in March of 2014. The seven Sibelius songs are:

#1. "Die Stille Stadt" (The Quiet City), Op. 50, #5, text by Richard Dehmel

#2. "Jägargossen" (The Young Sportsman), Op. 13, #7, text by J. L. Runeberg

#3. "Hjartats morgen" (The Heart's Morning), Op. 13, #3, text by J. L. Runeberg

---

[2] Tiikkaja, 601.

#4. "Älven och snägeln" (The River and the Snail), Op. 57, #1, text by Ernst Josephson

#5. "Näcken" (The Elf), Op. 57, #8, text by G. Wennerberg

#6. "Jag är ett Trad" (The Tree), Op. 57 #5, text by Ernst Josephson

#7. "Svarta rosor" (Black Roses), Op. 56, #1, text by Ernst Josephson

The choice of songs reflect Sibelius's broad stylistic range from full-blooded Romanticism to austere modernism. Rautavaara's orchestral versions call for a fairly small orchestra with much given to the timpanist. In the opening 'Die stille Stadt' ('The Silent City'), Rautavaara gave the accompaniment undulations to clarinet and flute rather than harp, with bits of glockenspiel.[3]

## *Rubaiyat (*2013), song cycle for voice and orchestra or voice and piano*

Commissioned by baritone Gerald Finley, this work is based on the poems of Omar Khayyám (1048-1131), the Persian poet, as translated by Edward FitzGerald, a Victorian British poet. Each of the five songs continues without break into an orchestral interlude leading into the next song, but the songs can also be performed separately. The first performance was by Gerald Finley in London's Wigmore Hall, on May 31, 2014.

The songs are "Awake," "And lately," "Here with a Loaf of Bread," "We are no other than a moving row," and "Oh, make haste." The intervening interludes are labeled only 1, 2, 3, and 4. The first song is richly orchestrated and melodic. The next few are lyrical and full of melancholy, while the faster finale meditates on eternity, how the speaker wishes to experience all of life before mortality overtakes him.

---

[3] Daniel Gutman, Review: *In the Stream of Life: Sibelius Songs*, in Gramophone, The Weekly Newsletter (2016?).

# CHAPTER FOURTEEN
# CHORAL WORKS

### *Suomalainen Rukouskirja* (*A* **Finnish Prayerbook) (1952, pub. 2013)**

These three choral works were found in an unpublished manuscript buried in a file under the name of Rautavaara's father, Eino Rautavaara, in the Sulasol (Suomen Laulajain ja Soittajain Liitto [The Finnish Amateur Musicians' Association or FAMA]) archives and published in 2013. Based on folk poetry collected by Martti Haavio, the titles are: "Tuo'os mettä kielelläsi" (Honey on Your Tongue) meaning "May your response to my prayer be sweet," from a Kalevala verse; "Saunarukous" (Sauna Prayer), also related to a Kalevala verse describing the physical delights of the sauna; and "Taivahan ilohon" (Heavenly Joy), this last apparently published separately at an earlier date. Originally a set of four songs written for a competition, the fourth, "Laulupuu" (Tree Song), was the only one returned to Rautavaara and was probably lost. The other three were first performed by the Ahjo Ensemble in the spring of 2013.

### *Laulupuu* **(Tree Song) (1952) unpublished**

This choral song was originally part of a set of four choral songs submitted to the Sulasol competition (see entry above), and was the only one returned in 1952. In a hurry to submit *Requiem in Our Time* (1952), the work was orchestrated and used as the first movement, "Hymnus." As a choral work, it was performed only in 2013 with a group of other rediscovered choral works by the Ahjo Ensemble.

### *Lapsen virret* **(Children's Tunes) (1952), unpublished**

The three songs "Kaikki kuuset kukkimahan" (All the trees bloomed inside the stomach), "Tuuti, tuuti tummaistani" (Hush, hush, my little darling), and a third lullaby "Tuudi lasta nukkumahe" (I sing a child to sleep), were recorded in 1953 with the title *Kehtolaulu Suistamosta.*(Lullaby from Suistamo [Karelia]) by a violinist friend, Tauno Tiikkainen, with piano accompaniment though composed for voice and piano.

## *Lauluja* (The Singer) (1956), for male chorus

This choral work, on a text from the Kalevala, was originally composed in an easy style for a male chorus of expatriate Finns in New York, the Laulumiehet (Men of Song). Rautavaara met the conductor while a student at Juilliard and became interested in this group, even substituting as conductor on occasion.[1] *Lauluja* actually received its first performance by the Helsinki University Singers (Ylioppilaskunnan Laulajat) under Ensti Pohjola in May of 1956. This choral song about the singing of a skylark keeps the constant alliteration of the Kalevala rhymes. The harmony is tonal, and word painting prevails, such as the repetitions on "pahasti" (ill or blame), "vihaisen äänen" (angry voice) set for basses, "lapsi" (child) set for a single male soprano, and the ascending crescendo on "nuorisossa nousevassa" (among the rising young people).

## *Two Preludes by T. S. Eliot*, Op. 42 (1956, revised 1967), for male chorus

Originally four preludes for mixed choir and percussion, Rautavaara revised the set in 1967 for male chorus and removed both the percussion and two of the preludes. Its two remaining movements are "Winter Evening" and "The Morning Comes."[2] "Winter Evening" charms with its icy vocal pizzicato on "winter evening," "six o'clock," and "lighting of the lamps." A simple two part texture with a repeated descending pattern on the bottom quietly sets the mood of withered leaves and newspaper scraps, burnt-out ends of smoky days. "The morning comes" has fast repeated notes on the same pitch, a patter song, depicting "smells of stale beer," "raising dingy shades," and "masquerades that time resumes." The revised version was first performed in Helsinki by the YL chorus on May 20, 1969.

## *Ludis verbalis* Op. 10b (1957), for speaking choir

While studying in Anscona, Switzerland, with Vladimir Vogel, Rautavaara applied the newly learned techniques of *sprech chor* (speaking choir) to a set of choral pieces. In *Ludus verbalis*, the text contains only four different categories of German words, each in its own separate movement. For example, the first short movement is titled "Personalia" and the text is "Wer? Er, Sie, Du und Er, Jemand, Niemand, Wer?" The second movement, "Temporalia," uses the German for time words like "when, then," etc. The third is based on Qualitative words

---

[1] Rautavaara, 151-2.
[2] Rautavaara, 152.

like "such, what sort," and the fourth is Quantitative, "A little, more, enough." Pitch is not notated but is indicated on a relative scale of low-medium-high, with some register changes from alternation of female and male voices, but rhythms and dynamics are precisely notated.[3] *Ludus verbalis* was performed in 1958 by the Kammersprechchor Zürich, conducted by Ellen Widman.

### *Ave Maria* Op. 10a (1957), for male chorus

Newly enthusiastic about twelve-tone composition from his study with Vladimir Vogel, Rautavaara was eager to try out this new technique. His friend, Eric Bergman, asked him for a choral work on the text of the Ave Maria, for the male choral group he conducted, Muntra Musikanter (Merry Musicians), a Swedish-speaking chorus. Rautavaara busily constructed his tone row, and also a Quinten row and a Quarteten row as taught by Vogel. Exploring all possibilities, the row was used in its original, inversion, retrograde, and retrograde forms, with the Quinten and Quarten forms of the row giving new sounds to a contrasting section. The texture is an imitative polyphony with homophonic climaxes, and a clear and consistent 4/4 meter. The first performance, despite Rautavaara's promptness, was not given by Bergman's group until May 10, 1960.

### *Missa duodecanonica* (1963), for children's choir

Just over two minutes in length, this Mass is a work based on the traditional Catholic text and is set for a cappella children's choir with three voices. Each of the brief three movements, Kyrie, Sanctus, and Agnus Dei, is a canon based on one of the forms of the tone row. It received its first performance more than thirty years later, in 1998, by the Kiimingin Kiurut (The Larks of Kiiminki) under conductor Liisa Räisänen in Helsinki.

### *Nattvarden* (Ehtoollinen in Finnish, Communion) (1963), for mixed chorus

*Nattvarden* is a suite of four brief songs for a cappella four-voiced mixed chorus on texts by the Swedish poet Bo Setterlind, using a symmetrical basis of organization. The songs, which take four minutes to perform, are Psalm vid Nattvarden I, Psalm vid Nattvarden II, Kyrie, and Herdepsalm (Shepherd's Psalm). Conductor Harald Andersén and the Radio Chamber Choir gave their first performance in Helsinki in 1964.

---

[3] Rautavaara, program notes for *Works for Mixed Chorus*, Ondine CD ODE 851-2.

## *Lu'ut* (Magic Verses) Op. 27 (1965), for mixed chorus, withdrawn

This ten minute choral work was based on the shamanistic Kalevala magic verses. It was performed in Helsinki in 1965 and then withdrawn. The work called for vocal techniques such as whispering, speaking, normal singing, and falsetto at high volume. One choral conductor complained that it was damaging to the voices.

## *Syksy virran suussa* (Autumn at the River Mouth) (1965/95), for male chorus

A freely tonal setting of a Finnish language text by T. Pekkanen, this work was first performed by the male choir Laulu-Miehet (Men of Song) in 1965, and was later revised in 1995. A depiction of nature, its opening words translate as "Scream, O great gulls, at the autumn windstorm!"

## *Itsenäisyyskantaatti* (Independence Cantata) Op. 29 (1967), for soloist, reciter, mixed choir, and orchestra

In 1967 Finland celebrated the 50th anniversary of her 1917 independence from Russia and sponsored an Independence Cantata Competition. Rautavaara composed the prize-winning entry during the summer of 1966 while at the family's summer rental place. The music was borrowed from some of his unused 1962 set of fourteen songs on texts of the Swedish poet Bo Setterlind The Finnish texts in the fourteen movements, however, came from various Finnish writers: Paavo Haavikko (1931-2008), one of Finland's most outstanding writers; V. A. Koskenniemi (1885-1962), poet and critic; and from the speeches of historical figures at the time of the 1917 independence. The music has expressive thematic material with inversions and mirror symmetry. A kind of free tonality pervades the whole, established with modal melodic progressions with third-based harmonies, chorale-like chord progressions, and triads in non-tonal relationships. The choral techniques call for Sprechchor, some aleatory, and, new for Rautavaara, choral clusters or field technique.

The importance of the occasion can be seen in the size of the performance group, collected for the May 10, 1967 performance at Tampere, Finland. A reciter was needed, Veikko Sinisalo, a well known Finnish movie and TV actor, Mariaheidi Rautavaara, the composer's wife, was the soprano soloist, with Matti Tuloisela, a leading opera baritone and professor of voice at the Sibelius Academy. Three city orchestras were combined, from Lahti, Tampere and Turku, and combined mixed choruses and speaking choir from southern Finland.

### *Kaksi psalmia* (Two Psalms, 1967/1971), for mixed choir or male chorus

These two settings of Psalms 23 and 130 were originally for mixed choir and later arranged for a male chorus. Psalm 23, "The Lord is My Shepherd," was commissioned by the Hämeenlinna Vahan Säästöpanki (Old Savings Bank) 125th anniversary and is fairly tonal. The Psalm 130, "From the depths of despair I cry unto you, O Lord," contains many augmented fourths to create the mood. As in English, the text has no recurring lengths or rhymes, making these through-composed Finnish language settings difficult to arrange for other languages.

### *Praktisch Deutsch* (Practical German) (1969), for speaking choir

In the style of *Ludis verbalis* of 1957, written while studying with Vogel in Switzerland and performed in German by a Zurich chorus, a second set of pieces for speaking choir was commissioned by a Helsinki choral group in 1969. Remembering the Ionesco play "The Bald Soprano," in which two visiting couples speak and reply without relationship to each others' stories, Rautavaara found a text that allowed him to finish his composition in two days. The useful but unrelated conversational texts were taken from a German language tourist guide on the topics of "The Hotel," "Shopping," "At the Tailor," and "At a party." The unrelated sentences and repetitions of words or syllables without logical connection are intended as elements of articulation and intonation. The singers are required to alternate female and male voices, avoid normal spoken intonation, slide indefinite pitches, repeat pitches, and whisper. The final piece, "At a party," conveys the sound effect of several dozen people speaking at once, some audible, others blurred. Rather than traditional pitches and a musical heightening of a poetic text, the work exploits the varied possibilities of vocalizing or using the voice as an instrument, with sliding intonations, percussive consonants, hissing sibilants, contrasting timbres, and varied rhythms.

### *True and False Unicorn* Op. 58 (1971, 2000), cantata for three reciters, chamber chorus, and orchestra, plus piano and sound effects (or tape for the 1971 orchestral interludes)

This forty-six minute work in twenty movements was commissioned by a Danish conservatory's chamber choir, Holstebro Musikhøjskolen, specifically requesting taped or electronic instrumental components. The cantata was originally for three reciters, chamber chorus, and instruments including piano, tape, string quartet, and a siren. Rautavaara limited his use of electronic instruments to the introductions to the four cantata sections, so that the student coordinators would not need to synchronize the tape with the actual performers. In 2000, Rautavaara removed the taped portions and rewrote them for orchestra and later for chamber orchestra. Following the needs of the texts, the music combines many styles: jazz, gospel, swing, and national anthems from various countries combined polyphonically, as well as his own contemporary style and techniques. A wide range of percussion instruments are used for sound effects, such as xylophone, bells, wood blocks for unicorn prancing, chimes to indicate the virgin's somewhat religious environment, loud piano clusters for the "cosmic" origin of the unicorn's immortality. The vocal and choral techniques include Sprechstimme, clusters, and whispering.

James Broughton's English language text is called "a tapestry of voices." The characters portrayed in the seven Arras tapestries of the New York City Cloisters museum, *The Hunt of the Unicorn,* and its mythical animals speak one by one about the unicorn, which symbolically represents the artist. The four sections each have a short orchestral introduction, originally performed by electronic instruments and taped. In Part I, Before the Arras, the "Lion," speaks through the singing of the male chorus about the unicorn as an indestructible king of the beasts doing miraculous things. A whole tone scale predominates. "Sigmund of Vienna," a nobleman, declares in a bass Sprechstimme alternating with a female choral refrain that we are all hunters of the unicorn, dreaming of possessing the fabulous. "The Unicorn" seeks his own meaning, by way of male chorus, asking "I am the unicorn. But who am I?" In Part II, Horn and Hounds, "Young Sagittarius," the name referring to the centaur, a half man half horse archer, describes the playful land where the unicorns grow up, with orchestral accompaniment including a toccata-like piano and xylophone. "A Virgin Waiting" tells of her hopes and fears in taming the unicorn and in so doing, breaking the spell he is under. "The Empress of Byzantine" is a low-pitched and rough female Sprechstimme role demanding the horn. "Queen Victoria" promises treats; the music has the chorus singing "O Pretty Pony, naughty pet," to the tune of *God Save the Queen,* with interjections and overlays of the French, Austrian, and American nation anthems. "His Honor the Mayor" speaks in Sprechstimme accusing the unicorn of being a highbrow jackass, with sound effects, a hee-haw and a police siren. In "Big Black Sambo" the chorus tells of a black man in the American south wanting an exceptional racehorse, with musical quotes of "Swing Low, Sweet Chariot." In Part III, Snare and Delusion, "The Unicorn, Wounded" laments his capture through the chorus, "Where am I truly or falsely at home?" Then looking at his reflection in a well, saying "He is my unicorn, he is not I." Part IV, Mon Seul Désir, has "Sigmund of Vienna" return with Sprechstimme speaking of the capture as a mix of curse and blessing. "The Lion" returns to tell the unicorn he will outwit and outlive the hounds. "The Unicorn" asks the lion to "burn bright his irresolute cold." "Tom Fool" in Sprechstimme tells of time's furiously fast revolving cycle of light and dark, death and rebirth. "The Virgin's Lullaby" uses the female voices to tell the unicorn "dream again of when you rise again, again for beauty's eyes." "The Unicorn" sings of his wonder but acceptance of his reality, "I am my unicorn and so is he." His previous musical motifs return to round off the whole work.

## *The Water Circle, An Homage to Lao-Tzu* (1972), for chorus, piano and orchestra, withdrawn

In the summer of 1972 the Rautavaara family moved to their summer home and found it vandalized. In the confusion of repairs and moving, Rautavaara happened to only have the collected poems of James Broughton with him. Under pressure to work on a new commission, he chose Broughton's *The Water Circle*, based on Lao-Tzu and Daoism, and stressing the recirculation of water as a metaphor for life. Broughton claimed his work was inspired by the music of Corelli. Rautavaara was in turn inspired by the thought that poetry born of music might well be recirculated back into music. This second large work on a text by James Broughton was performed in Copenhagen in December, before the first performance of *True and False Unicorn* in 1973. Because the *Unicorn* did better, *The Water Circle* was withdrawn and quietly put away.[4] Broughton made a three minute movie on this in 1975.

Rautavaara described the musical features of this work in a letter to the Copenhagen conservatory, saying that the piano sometimes plays in traditional styles, such as in the manner of a fugue, and sometimes plays aleatorically, choosing when to play himself. The choral techniques include four part harmony, Sprechchor, glissandos, and clusters.[5]

## *Vigilia* (All-Night Vigil, 1971-72, 1986), for soloists and a cappella mixed choir

This setting of the Vigils service for the Feast Day of John the Baptist of the Orthodox church was jointly commissioned by the Helsinki Festival and the

---

[4] Tiikkaja, 337.
[5] Ibid. 338.

Orthodox Church of Finland. Because of the nearly three hour length of the whole service, the premiere of the first part, the Evening Service, took place at divine service in the red brick Uspenski Cathedral in central Helsinki in 1971, and the second half, the Morning Service was delayed until the same feast day in 1972. The concert version of 1997 is an independent work later adapted and much reduced in length from the original.

The text follows the liturgy of the day dedicated to John the Baptist. The Finnish language is used, partly because the Orthodox Church of Finland broke its ties with the Russian Orthodox Church at the time of the 1917 Independence, and also because the Orthodox Church required the use of the local language. Rautavaara's reduced concert version has 34 composed movements that include psalms, hymns of both of the normal regular use and those pertaining to the topic of the day, and prayers. Six of the movements refer to the story of John the Baptist, the sinful dancing of Salome, and the beheading of John. Other items focus on the Resurrection of Jesus, thanksgiving to the Mother of God, and reference to other saints.

Since no instruments are used in the Orthodox Church, the *Vigilia* calls for a variety of solo chant and choral settings. Solo chant from a deacon or priest may involve a choral response or a quiet harmonic background during the chanting. The solo chants best display the odd sounds of the microtones of the early chant modes, but also are not confined to repetitive recitation tones nor to any prescribed narrow range. The basso profundo solos near the opening stand out, evoking the sound world of the deep Russian basses as well as the chant of the Orthodox priest. The very low bass is also required of the chorus, at one point calling for a long sustained low B♭. The varied choral techniques include choral homophonic chant, choral glissandi, whispering, the pyramid-like building of rising or descending clusters, microtones derived from the early Byzantine modes, and parallel intervals of fifths or fourths. The glissandi was a traditional part of the earliest Orthodox liturgy, written here for both soloists and the chorus. The variety of the choral settings, including solos from the soprano, alto, tenor, bass, and basso profundo, alternating duets between female or male singers, solo chant and choral response, keep the interest of the audience on the ever changing musical activity in the lengthy service. A variation structure holds the whole work together, often through use of the same text as response.[6] The *Avuksihuutopsalmi* (Psalm of Dedication) (Example Seventeen, pages 65-66) and the *Ehtoohymni* (Evening Hymn) were later published separately.

---

[6] Einojuhani Rautavaara, Liner notes to *Vigilia*, Ondine ODE 910-2 (1998).

## *Elämän kirja* (Book of Life) (1972), for a cappella male chorus

*Elämän kirja*, for a cappella male chorus, has eleven movements and is in five different languages. The work was commissioned by the Helsinki Y.L choir (Ylioppilaskunnan Laulujat, University Singers) to take on an international tour. The request was for a major work of a half hour or so of short individual songs, each song should be able to be used separately, each of the movements should be easy enough for an amateur chorus and, for convenience while traveling, should be a cappella.

Rautavaara decided on the theme of life from childhood to old age, using a variety of poets and languages. The poems are well chosen: "Kindheit" (Childhood) by Rainter Maria Rilke, "Ma bohème" (My Bohemian Life) by Arthur Rimbaud,"L'Amoureuse" by Eugene Grindel, "Vanitas vanitatum" a strophic drinking song by Goethe, "Hope is the thing with feathers" by Emily Dickinson, "Are you ready" by James Broughton, "Huojuva keula" (The Swaying Prow) text by Aaro Hellaakoski, "Le Bain" by José-Maria de Hérédia, "Me emme kuole koskaan" (We shall never die) by Paavo Haaviko, "Så var det" (So it was) by Dag Hammarskjöld, and "Song of Myself" by Walt Whitman. The choice of the poems, fitting each portion of a person's life, shows Rautavaara's remarkable command of poetic literature. The choice of the different languages pays respect to the audiences of the international tour while still including some Finnish poetry.

Musically, some of the songs stand out. The first song, "Kindheit" (Childhood) by Rainer Maria Rilke, contrasts dreary school, loneliness, being led firmly by an adult's hand, with the delight of gardens, fountains, play. The choir sings in parallel intervals, in symmetrical opposition, with plodding rhythms giving way to bright faster rhythmic complexity. "Vanitas vanitatum," though a strophic drinking song by Goethe, allows for variants required by the text. A musical repeat of the first line often turns to a slow minor depicting a sad outcome, such as "I put my bet on women, Oho, And gained a lot of trouble, Oho." "Are you ready" by James Broughton, a short strophic text, divides the choir into two lines successively distinct in different rhythms and pitches, but both moving within a narrow range and turning back on themselves. Both go again over the same range, essentially illustrating the text "are you ready for the journey going nowhere?" "Huojuva keula" (The Swaying Prow) text by Aaro Hellaakoski, describes life's course as a ship finding its way to port through storms, with the forcefulness of the whole choir. "Le Bain" by José-Maria de Hérédia, in French, has an underlying ostinato of a galloping horse, and choir above "defying danger in the foaming waves." "Me emme kuole koskaan" (We shall never die) by Paavo Haaviko, is a boastful song of a Finnish farmer defying death by speaking of his strength and that of his sons carrying heavy burdens. It is set in defiant major with a refrain "we laugh at the death of apple trees without cause." Doubt enters in the next portion as he remembers seeing his father die, and the black crows of death have now come, set partly as a unison for basses. But the refrain returns in a major key, "we laugh...I and all my sons." "Song of myself" is a through composed setting of the long text of Walt Whitman's poem, saying there is really no death, that life cycles on like the smallest sprout of grass on graves, death is different from what anyone supposed and luckier, with a final exultant choral exclamation on "luckier."

## *Credo* (1972), for a cappella mixed choir

In 1972 Rautavaara began the composition of a Catholic Mass, starting with what he considered the hardest part, the Credo. This a cappella mixed choir piece uses the Latin text of the Catholic Mass and was later included in the 2011 *Missa a cappella*. The long list-like text became a set of three variations on a group of motives. It opens with an animated pedal point of male voices with the female voices declaiming the text "Credo in unum Deum." Female and male voices lead and join through the next statements, coming to a pause of "descendit de caelis" (descending from heaven), a long held note followed by a falling fourth "descending." A second section begins with the most solemn and mystical part of the text, "Et incarnates est," describing the incarnation of the Holy Spirit, birth, crucifixion, and resurrection of Jesus. Its slow buildup of voices creates a setting of awe and wonder. A third section resumes the animation of the opening at "Et in Spiritum Sanctum" (and in the Holy Spirit). The words "Et unam sanctum catholicam et apostolicam ecclesiam" (And in one holy Catholic and Apostolic Church) are underlined by the homophony and unified rhythm of the chorus. The end comes almost as a surprise, in a slow tempo, just two final syllables of the quiet homophonic Amen.

## *Viatonten valssi* (Waltz of the Innocents) (1973), for children's choir, violin and piano

This choral work on a text by Aaro Hellaskoski was composed for the Tapiola Children's Choir, whose members provide their own instrumental accompaniment when needed. In 1982 an arrangement of the choral work as a solo song was inserted into a song cycle of 1973 entitled *October* with other Finnish texts by Aaro Hellaakoski. With that addition, the title of the song set was changed to *Mailmaan uneen* (Dream World).

### *Lapsimessu* (Children's Mass, 1973), for a cappella children's choir

When the Tapiola Children's Choir held a competition for a new composition, it offered an unusual opportunity. The children were not only widely recognized for their singing but for their training in orchestral instruments, in order to provide their own accompaniments. Rautavaara chose to compose a work alternating a cappella choral movements with orchestral interludes. The three Mass movements in Latin, "Kyrie," "Gloria," and "Agnus Dei" were each followed by a string orchestra Meditatio, with a final "Halleluja" with chorus and orchestra combined. The choral parts are usually homophonic and tonal, with the more active "Gloria" adding a descant to the middle portion. The orchestral meditations are based on each of the earlier choral movements. Each set of three pieces, the choral and the orchestral, can be performed separately.

For the same competition Rautavaara also submitted a set of four songs called the *Lorca Suite*. The suite received only a third prize, in contrast to the first prize *Lapsimessu*, but went on to be far more famous and widely performed and recorded internationally.

### *Kolme kappaletta vokaaliyhtyeelle* (Three Pieces for Vocal Group) (1973), for vocal group and instrumental group, withdrawn

The three pieces of this set were composed for the Finnish National Opera's concert for children and the child-like and were performed by a group of children associated with the opera house and soloists from the opera company. The first, "Kolme Gothamin viisasta miestä" (Three Wise Men of Gotham) is based on the Finnish translation of the English nursery rhyme: "Three wise men of Gotham went to sea in a bowl, and if the bowl had been stronger my song would have been longer." The second song was "Viimeinen enkeli" (The Last Angel) on a text by Leena Krohn, and the last was "Lintujen hautajaiset" (The Bird's Funeral), on a text by Aale Tynni. Despite the performance and a recording by Columbia records, the work was withdrawn by the composer.

### *Lorulei* (1973), for a cappella children's choir

This a cappella setting of three Finnish children's songs won a first prize in a composition contest celebrating the 100 years of public education in Finland. The three songs are "Mistä on pienet pojat tehty" (What are Little Boys Made Of?), "Hus sika metsään" (Hus Swine into the Forest), and "Peukaloputti sai sian" (Thumb Putti was Pig).

### *Kaksi taloa* (Two Houses) (1973), for unison chorus and piano

This brief one minute work calls for a unison chorus and piano, and is subtitled "psalm" with text by Rautavaara.

### *Kaksi kelmiä* (Two Rogues) (1973), for a cappella children's choir

This a cappella setting of a Finnish folksong was dedicated to another well-known children's choir, the Cantores Minores boys choir, based at the Helsinki Cathedral.

### *Herran rukous* (The Lord's Prayer) (1973), for mixed chorus

This piece, like *Lorulei* (1973), was also dedicated to the public education celebration.

### *Isontalon Antti ja Rannanjärvi* (Big House Andy and Lakeshore) (1973), for male chorus

Arranged for the Ylioppilaskunnan Laulujat (University Singers), this is a folksong about two hot-tempered woodsmen who get back at the mean local sheriff by wrecking his house and threatening his life. It is dedicated to Rautavaara's Ostrobothnian grandfather, Gustaf Jernberg, who had been the chief constable in Ilmajoki, Finland.

### *Hallin Janne* (Janne of Halli) (1973), for male chorus

Again written for the male chorus Ylioppilaskunnan Laulujat (University Singers), this is a folksong about a rural man whose efforts to be rich enough for marriage get him thrown in prison for robbery and murder.

### *Lorca Suite* (1973), for children's chorus

Submitted to the Tapiola Children's Chorus competition, the third place winner *Lorca Suite* (1973) is a set of four Spanish-influenced songs for mixed choir or children's choir on texts by Federico Garcia Lorca (Example Eighteen, page 67). Competing against his other submission, *Lapsimessu* (The Children's Mass) which won first place, the *Lorca Suite* went on to become internationally successful. In "The Rider's Song," death stares down on the fearful horse rider's gallop, evoked by the ostinato of the rhythm. A vocal glissando equals a mysterious scream in the hills, unexplained, in "The Scream." A Phrygian scale in "The Moon Peeps Out" conveys iciness and isolation. "Dance from Malaga" has the excitement of a stamping dance accompanied by guitar, but it is death who goes in and out of the tavern.[7] Rautavaara was surprised at the international success of this set, saying that he received programs listing it from Japan, Israel, Cuba, Macedonia, and that it had been recorded four or five times by 1985.[8]

## *Morsian* (The Bride) (1975), for mixed choir a cappella

Written for a choral competition honoring the centennial birth of the conductor Heikki Klemetti, *The Bride* is based on ancient wedding poetry of the folk tradition, in which the bride is first mocked in a light-hearted way and then praised. The text is from the Kalevala. The division into two halves is easy to hear. The first half sprightly mocks the bridegroom, saying, "Shame! You've brought a bride...from the swamp you bring a lapwing...from the field a scarecrow." The mood changes to slow and ethereal, with solo voices here and there contributing to the praise---"Handsome is she...like a ripening cranberry...noblest of all the country."

## *Lähtö* (Departure) (1975), for mixed choir a cappella

Also written for the Klemetti choral competition, *Departure* is a setting of a poem from the 1930s by Toivo Pekkanen. It is based on the same motive as "The Bride" in inverted form, F-E♭-G♭. An ostinato portrays the galloping horse taking the rider to redemption and freedom from torment.

## *Kettu ja sairas kukko* (The Fox and the Sick Cock) (1975), for male choir a cappella

A third work composed for the Klemetti competion was based on a text by Kristfrid Ganander, an eighteenth century Finnish author on many topics, including fairy tales. Here, the rooster outsmarts the fox.

---

[7] Einojuhani Rautavaara, Liner notes to *Works for Mixed Chorus*, Ondine CD ODE 851-2.
[8] Rautavaara, 261.

### *Sommarnatten* (Summer Night) (1975), for mixed choir

Based on a folk melody from Swedish-speaking areas of Finland, Ernst Victor Knape's text depicts youthful memories of dancing and yearning during the warm, light nights. The three-part structure follows the words. "Might he dance with me?" has slow, yearning, polyphony against a repeated line, then lively dancing with a chordal summation on the words "summer night!" Then follows a return to the slowness, now "years faded…memories…a summer peace to her who yearned." The conclusion is another chordal return of the words "summer night."

### *Hammarskjöld-Fragment* (1975), for tenor soloist and male chorus a cappella

This choral work based on a text from a posthumous collection by Dag Hammarskjold, former Secretary General of the United Nations, was another composition prize winner. The occasion was the one hundredth anniversary of the Muntra Musikanter (Merry Singers) chorus, a group originally formed of Swedish-speakers. The short chorus uses texts that are a mixture of aphorisms and bits of free standing poetry: "The road, thou shalt follow it," "Moonlight on a warm autumn night, On this path, Far away a heart stops," "While the shots rang out…For the one that believes the last miracle will be greater than the first." Rautavaara unites them all with a rhythmic ostinato in the basses.

### *Puusepän poika* (The Carpenter's Son) (1975), for a cappella children's choir

The Tapiola Children's Choir took part in a film on the poetry of Sanelma Kuusisto in 1975, with a setting of this poem. The choral work was later rearranged as electronic music for the film *Hiilivalkea* (Coal White), named for a set of poems written by poet V. A. Koskenniemi. This short piece opens peacefully with an underlying ostinato depicting the carpenter at work and his son playing. As the text proceeds, the music builds, and the wooden shavings transform into a crown of thorns, pointing to the son's future.

### *Kainuu* (1975), a cantata for mixed choir, reciter, and percussion.

Kainuu is a district in the middle of Finland, with several hundred miles of border with Russia, known for its dense forests and rugged landscape. It was in this region, rather remote from the influence of the Lutheran church's attempts to stamp out paganism, that the verses of the pagan-era Kalevala remained to be collected in the nineteenth century from rural singers. Rautavaara's cantata was commissioned for the 250th anniversary of the Paltaniemi church, a wooden parish church built in 1726. This very small town's best claim to fame is as the birthplace of nationalist poet Eino Leino (1878-1926).

Rautavaara wrote his own text, paraphrasing the Finnish poems of various authors. For this he did a considerable amount of historical research. The five songs relate to the church community with topics on its remoteness, an invocation, the poor, chant, and pallbearers. The first song "Kaukamoisen" (Remoteness) refers to a perhaps mythical king of the Kainuu area, Faravid, mentioned in an Icelandic saga. "Ihmisparka" (Poor Wretch) tells of hardships during the time of the Great Northern War of the early 1700s between Sweden and Russia, known in Finland as Isoviha (The Great Wrath). Other texts refer to eighteenth century hymn verses and the fighting during the Winter War of 1939-40, between Finland and Russia.

Much of the long text is given to a reciter. The mixed chorus, too, is often similar to recitative or chant. Percussion invokes a shamanistic ostinato.[9] Matti Lehtinen, by that year a successful opera baritone and instructor at the Helsinki Sibelius Academy, was invited for the celebratory performance. Though perhaps not a composition designed for an international concert stage, for the local audience and dignitaries at the event it must have been overwhelmingly personal and emotional.

## *Yxi ja kaxi* (One and Two) (1975), for unison chorus

Rautavaara wrote his own text for this one minute work.

## *Marjatan jouluvirsi* (Marjatta's Christmas Hymn) (1975/1995), for mixed chorus

This Christmas hymn was arranged from the last chorus in the opera *Marjatta matala neiti* (Marjatta, the Lowly Maiden) of 1975, with a text written by Rautavaara after the Kalevala story.

## Joulun virsi, elämän virsi (Christmas Hymn, Hymn of Life) (1953/1978), for male chorus

Arranged from the last in an earlier set of songs, *Pyhia päiviä* (Sacred Feasts, 1953) for voice and piano, this work was based on the Laestadian poetry

---

[9] Tiikkaja, 364.

of K. Lounasheimo from a conservative religious group in Lapland, northern Finland. Originally conceived as congregational hymns, the set evolved into more complex solo songs. The style being not too far from a congregational hymn, the last of the four songs was easily adapted for male chorus, for children's chorus, and, in 1995, for a mixed chorus with an English text.

## *Neljä serenadia* (Four Serenades) (1978), for male chorus

The first. of these four songs commissioned by the Y.L. (Ylioppilaskunnan Laulujat/University of Helsinki Singers) is the "Serenadi oluelle" (Serenade to Beer), based on a Finnish folk song. The second, "La Mort des Pauvres" has a text by Charles Baudelaire. Number three, "Serenade für meine Frau," has a text by Stefan George, and the fourth returns to a Finnish folksong. "Serenadien serenadi" (Serenade to a Serenade).

## *Canticum Mariae Virginis* (1978), for mixed chorus

This eight minute work uses the Catholic Latin texts for Ave maris stella and portions of the Magnificat and was commissioned by the Suomen Laulu (Finland Sings) mixed chorus. It is deliberately archaic in style, yet very modern. The inner voices form a constant sound field over a pedal tone, intoning the Ave maris stella text. The sopranos soon enter with a melodic and rhythmically more active line, overlaying the first group with the second text of Gaude Maria virgo. The basses then enter, echoing the sopranos with the Gaude text. At one point the whole group, including the pedal point inner voices, shift harmonically up a step, perhaps emphasizing the text "intercede pro nobis" (pray for us). The Magnificat text predominates over the background Ave maris stella, and the opening word "Gaude" (Rejoice) appears again and again.

## *Odotus* (Waiting) (1978), for mixed choir, reciter, and organ

A twenty-five minute cantata, on Biblical texts from the liturgy for the first Sunday of Advent and newly written words by Rautavaara, it was first performed for the dedication of a church in Lahti, Finland. Partly based on a non-traditional scale, it also incorporates a 12 tone row.

## *Lehdet lehtiä* (Leaves are Leaves) (1979), for tenor soloist and male chorus

A choral piece on a text by P. Haavikko, it was commissioned by the Finnish Library Association for its fiftieth anniversary, and then revised in 1992.

It calls for a tenor soloist and an a cappella male chorus. Material from a chorale in *Angels and Visitations* (1977) is set in a contrapuntal style. Its first performance was given by the Ylioppilaskunnan Laulujat (University of Helsinki Singers).

## *Magnificat* (1979), for mixed chorus and soloists

The *Magnificat* is a five movement work for a cappella mixed choir based on the Latin Biblical text. Like the *Canticum Mariae Virginis* of 1978, it also has a sound field of the middle voices around which the soprano and bass weave their lines.

## *Nirvana dharma* (1979), for mixed chorus, soprano, and flute

*Nirvana dharma* combines two English language poems from a collection titled *Knots* (1970) by R. D. Laing, a psychiatrist and poet. Laing was a radical thinker, explaining schizophrenia as not a genetic problem but one of inability to deal with contradictory environmental information. A psychotic attack was an attempt to communicate distress, and could be a potential break-through, or rebirth. The two Laing poems chosen by Rautavaara tell of going to Nirvana, the heaven of both Hinduism and Buddhism, as passing through a gate which some say doesn't exist; however, there is no way of knowing except to go through it.

According to Rautavaara, the solo flute at the beginning represents the Hindu god Krishna who is often depicted as a blue-skinned young man playing the flute. Each voice of the choir gradually enters, forming a large tone cluster, including all the pitches of an octave and a half. The text is obscured by the tone cluster and by the very slow tempo, "Although innumerable beings have been led to Nirvana no being has been led to Nirvana." After a climax (the gate), the tenors emerge from the pervading cluster with an animated and clear declamation of the second text, "Before one goes through the gate one may not be aware there is a gate…" A soprano soloist then declaims the first poem again above whispering female voices, which Rautavaara calls "an enlightenment."[10] The background tone cluster, soprano, and tenors singing the second text, at times whispering, continues to the end. Rautavaara depicted the musical form in a graph, showing the individual lines meeting at the gate and then roiling in a circle, enlightenment. The choral song was commissioned by the Luleå Chamber Choir of Sweden and flautist Gunilla von Bahr, for whom the earlier *Dances with Winds* flute concerto was composed in 1973.

---

[10] Einojuhani Rautavaara, Liner notes for *Works for Mixed Chorus*, Ondine ODE 851-2; Tiikaja, 375.

According to Samuli Tikkaja, the work grew from an earlier unperformed work, *En arkhee* (Greek, "In the Beginning [was the Word]," designed for the same forces as in *Marjatta, the Lowly Maiden* of flute and children's chorus. The Greek text from the New Testament, John 1:1, was stretched out, with the opening words lasting a minute and a half, actually unintelligible, with the remainder only a series of consonants.

### *Ylistyspsalmi* (Psalm of Praise) (1979), for mixed chorus and organ

This short cantata, based on an 18$^{th}$ century hymn of praise, was commissioned and first performed by the Espoonlahti Church for its dedication in 1980 and then withdrawn by the composer.

### *Parantaja* (The Healer) (1981), for mixed choir and orchestra

In 1981 Rautavaara was commissioned to write a choral work for the conferring of doctoral degrees at the Faculty of Medicine at Helsinki University. The result was a set of four songs for a narrator, chorus and orchestra on texts adapted from various Finnish language sources by the composer. The titles included were: 1. "Matka on niin pitkä" (The Journey is So Long); 2. "Näin opetti Hippokrates" (So taught Hippocrates); 3. "Parantaja, hämmästy" (The Healer, Surprised); 4. "Tietomme on tänään sopivasti suuri" (Our Knowledge Today is Suitably Large). For the first performance, leading musicians of the day were involved, including Matti Lehtinen as narrator, the Academic Choral Society which was the choir of the Finnish National Opera under the direction of Ulf Söderblom, and orchestral conductor Esa-Pekka Salonen. To fit the ceremony, the cantata opened with a procession and the remainder was integrated with the program.

### *Rakkaus ei koskaan häviä* (Love Never Faileth) (1983), for a cappella children's choir

This four minute work was commissioned by the Finnish Broadcasting Company and first performed by the Tapiola Choir in 1983.

### *Katedralen* (The Cathedral) (1983), for mixed chorus and soloists

The Finnish Broadcasting Company and the Swedish national radio company jointly commissioned yet another choral work, for mixed chorus and soloists, on poetry by Edith Södergran. Her Swedish-language poems had appealed to Rautavaara since his teenage years and his first attempts at composition, long lost. The poems set included: "At Nietzsche's Grave," "The Stars," "The Whirlpool of Madness," and "Am I A Liar?" In these poems, Sodergran combines a sense of infinity as well as the mundane, respect for an earlier writer as well as self-doubt. The reader can smile at the similarity to Emily Dickinson's style in "Hör, en stjärna föll med en klang! Gå icke ut I gräset med bara fötter, min trädgåtf är full av skärvor." (Hark! A star falls with a sound! If you go out on the lawn, do not go barefoot; my garden is full of splinters.) According to Rautavaara, the combination of these poems represent a walk through a cathedral, where a sarcophagus represents "the death of romanticism," through the roof one can see "meadows of stars," the very atmosphere contains "the frenzied absurdity of godliness," and the walker is forced to consider "the ultimate questions of man and artist."[11] Rautavaara described the musical construction of the piece:

> Arches which reach for the stars are created out of polyphonic textural masses. Symmetries are to be found everywhere in the melodic and harmonic structures, just as they are in the symmetrical parity of a cathedral's transepts on either side. A melodic figure which appears at the opening of the work may turn up later in intervallic inversion. By the end of the work we arrive at an altar "On the Steps of the Himalayas", and the words "The garland which never adorned my brow" in the tenor find continuation in the bass soloist's line "these shall I lay silently at your feet," this time in melodic inversion: the brow, the honor of being laid on earth or at the feet--in essence they are the same and we find parity here too.[12]

The work opens with the a cappella sound field of female voices, "stars swarm in hosts above the garden," with high-pitched "stars" jumping abruptly from the dense field. Male voices enter with the main text in calm narrative, pausing to change mood with the exclamation "a star falls with a sound!" The sopranos warn of the splinters, in clashing seconds. "Trees ... mirrored by water" are sung in alternation by the male and female voices. The next section concerns "your boat in whirlpools of lunacy—save yourself," with each line changing character by the new text. At the words "On the steps of the Himalayas great Vishnu sits and dreams" we hear an evocation of Tibetan chant, many

---

[11] Einojuhani Rautavaara, Liner notes, trans. by Andrew Bentley, *Works for Mixed Chorus*, Ondine ODE 851-2.
[12] Ibid.

repeated notes on the same pitch with sustained fifths below. Women's voices take up the rapid pleading "we have traveled long to get here and are hungry for your wisdom," followed by solemn male voices in "Almighty power, hold my life for one fleeting moment." Solo voices emphasize certain texts here and there. Although an effective setting of the words, the listener needs to follow the text (or translation) carefully to glean the meanings of the varied musical settings.

### *The First Runo* (1984), for women's a cappella choir

The Kodály Institute Chamber Choir of Kecskemét, Hungary, commissioned this work based on the first runo of the Finnish epic, the Kalevala. The text was translated into English and concerns the creation of the world through Luonnatar, daughter of Ilmatar, goddess of the air. Luonnatar floated on the sea for several hundred years and caused the creation of the world through shifting off and breaking of the eggs of a tern, and later gave birth to the Kalevala hero Väinämoinen.

### *Legenda* (1985), for male choir a cappella

The Mieskuoroliiton (Male Choir Association) requested this work on the poetry of Eino Leino for their fortieth anniversary. Dedicated to choral song publisher Uolevi Lassander, it was first performed by the Amici Cantus male chorus under the baton of Sakari Hildén in Helsinki.

### *The Virgin's Lullaby* (1971/1986), for female choir

Arranged from the cantata *True and False Unicorn*, this excerpt on a text by James Broughton was published separately.

### *Katso minun kansani on puu* (Behold, My People are a Tree) (1991), a cantata for mixed chorus, orchestra with accordion

A second commission from the Joensuu Song Festival was a 14 minute cantata, also honoring the seventy-fifth Finnish Independence celebration. For a mixed choir and orchestra, it called for an accordion in addition. The text was written by the composer. Its first performance was on June 14, 1992, with the Joensuu Symphony Orchestra conducted by Jukka-Pekka Saraste. Later, an excerpt from the cantata, *Hymn*, was arranged for a cappella mixed choir, with an ad lib piano accompaniment.

## *I de stora skogarna* (In the Great Wild Woodlands) (1983-87/1993), for female choir and piano

A set of Swedish texts by Edith Södergran, which earlier had been composed as solo songs under the title of *I min älsklings trädgård* (In My Beloved's Garden) (1983-87), were arranged in 1993 for a female chorus, the Flora-kören of Turku, Finland, under the title of the first song, *I de stora skogarna*. The three songs were: "I de stora skogarna" (In the Great Wild Woodlands); 2. "Mellan gråa stenar" (In Between Grey Stones); and 3. "Lyckokatt" (Lucky Cat). Rautavaara had set these as a teenager but lost the manuscripts, recomposed them as solo songs, and then arranged them for female choir.

## *Canción de nuestro tiempo* (Song of Our Times) (1993), for a cappella mixed choir

These three songs are based on texts by Federico Garcia Lorca. The first song, "Fragmentos de agonia" (Fragments of Agony), is based on a poem called "Oda a Walt Whitman." The second is "Meditacion primera y ultima" (First and Last Meditation) and the third is "Ciudad sin sueho/ Nocturno del Sarajevo" (Sleepless City/ Nocturno of Sarajevo), based on a poem entitled "Cuidad sin sueho/ Nocturno de Brooklyn Bridge."

The Tokyo Philharmonic asked for an extensive choral work "with text and music relevant to the world of today."[13] Rautavaara took these three surreal poems, written in the 1920s and 1930s, considering them apt to the present day to describe the anguish of war and the inhumanity of the industrial society. He substituted the name of the 1990's war-torn Sarajevo for the Brooklyn Bridge in the last title, though neither place is mentioned in the actual poem. The first song alternates textures between a mechanical ostinato in the male voices plus bass recitative, telling of wheel, oil, leather, hammer, and a faster strophe with the whole chorus saying none could sleep. Calm reigns briefly with a soprano telling of the moon rise, but the machines and war return. The second song, about time having gone to sleep, features dense clusters of sound fields entering aleatorically, with slow solo voices contrasted against them. "Sleepless City" divides the choir into three elements, again low male voices in an ostinato "No one sleeps," female voices burst in with "lunar creatures...crocodiles," while a solo soprano voice soars above them all. Images of corpses still complaining, a boy crying while being buried, bear's teeth, all mix, ending with "no one sleeps."

---

[13] Einojuhani Rautavaara, Liner Notes, *True and False Univorn*, Ondine ODE 1020-2.

## Och glädjen den dansar (With Joy We Go Dancing) (1993), for mixed chorus

The choral work *With Joy We Go Dancing* is based on a folk melody from Swedish-speaking Sundom parish of Finland. *With Joy We Go Dancing* is an old wedding tune to which Alexander Slotte later penned words. Commissioned by the Jubilate chorus, it was first presented by that group under the direction of conductor Astrid Riska in Helsinki, in 1994. The tonal melody accompanied by more dissonant harmony is presented in several stanzas, the first by the whole choir, the second for soprano soloist and the final stanza for the male voices with a female countermelody. Each stanza tells of seasonal changes, joys and sorrows, birth and death, but ends with the same summation: "And the lilies they bloom in the springtime." Rautavaara gives this last line some stress by repeating a portion or by changing the vocal setting.

## *Die erste Elegie* (1993), for a cappella mixed choir

In 1993 when the international chorus Europa Cantat commissioned a large-scale choral work, Rautavaara decided to set the *First Elegy*, of Rainer Maria Rilke's *Duino Elegies*. His twelve tone row outlined four triads, allowing for bits of tonality, the same row as that used in several other works he composed about the same time---the *Canto IV* (1992) for string orchestra, the *Canción de nuestro tiempo* (Song of our Time) in 1993, *Notturno e Danza* (1993), and the Seventh Symphony (1994-95).

The words are set clearly, in an ornamented homophony, at times varying the choral sound between the male and female singers, and raising a line or two to prominence by giving it to a solo soprano. The six divisions of the text have no repeated musical motives, have no repeated text, and also do not make any effort at being programmatic. The sopranos open with "Who among the host of angels hears me?" set as an ostinato. The male singers interrupt with "when I cry out." The section ends with a solo soprano, "Each and every angel is (pause) terrifying." The text, continuing on through five more sections, mourns that there is no help in need and the newly dead cry. In consolation the ending affirms s that angels move through both dead and the living and that music brings support through sadness and brings comfort.

## *Wenn sich die Welt auftut* (When the World Opens Up) (1996), for female chorus

A commission came from the Mädchenchor Hannover (Women's Choir of Hannover) for a set of songs for the 2000 EXPO. Rautavaara chose five poems of

Lassi Nummi's translated from the Finnish into German. The songs were: "Freude steigt in uns auf (Joy Rises Up in Us)," "Meine Liebe (My Love)," "Dann, in jener Nacht (Then, in that Night)," "Der Brief (The Letter)," and "Flüstern (Whisper)."

## *The Last Frontier* (1997), for chorus and orchestra

When Rautavaara came across a copy of the collected works of Edgar Allen Poe, he recalled reading an adventure story as a boy called *The Narrative of Arthur Gordon Pym,* known in Finnish as *Valtameren salaisuus* (The Secret of the Deep). Finding it again, he chose to set it to music for orchestra and chorus for his 70th birthday celebration concert with the Helsinki City Orchestra. In the story, sailor Pym tells tales of far off lands and adventures. But the ending became something quite different, eerie and terrifying. A crew of a shipwrecked boat is drifting toward the South Pole, and fast approaching a gigantic curtain of fog. In the gloom there is the sound of an unseen waterfall with shrieking white birds emerging from the fog. Powerful winds and waves propel them toward some kind of abyss. Looming above, they see or sense an enormous white figure, the angel of death.

The large orchestra and large chorus are equal protagonists. The form of the work has been described as having two main themes and five sections plus coda in a continuous variation form, a cyclic arrangement of variations, similar to Rautavaara's Fifth Symphony.[14] Though the music is ongoing, the themes reoccur, varied. The orchestra opens with ominous strings portraying thunderous waves and breaking wave crests through flute figuration. The wrecked ship, beyond control, appears in a stepwise string melody. The lower strings pulsate, creating fear. The text of the chorus then tells of the looming ghostly figure, the sound of a hidden waterfall, the windblown gaps in the mist showing an abyss, the terror of the ship's crew. Two themes, one of quietness with various solo or duets of instruments alternate, with growing tension. The sound of the shrieking birds moving in and out of the fog is conveyed by the trumpets. Both chorus and orchestra build in terror to the inescapable end.

The work was commissioned by his publisher Warner Music Finland, Ondine recording company, and the Helsinki Philharmonic Orchestra in honor of Rautavaara's seventieth birthday and premiered in 1998 under conductor Leif Segerstam.

[14] Tiikkaja, 528.

### *Halavan himmeän alla* (In the Shade of the Willow) (1998), a song cycle adapted for mixed chorus from the opera *Aleksis Kivi*.

Rautavaara published four orchestral songs from the opera *Aleksis Kivi*: "Ikävyys" (Melancholy), Kivi's opening aria; "Laulu oravasta" (The Squirrel), from Act One where Kivi is requested to read one of his poems to Hilda and Charlotta; "Oi mailma, elämä sä ilmeellinen" (O World, Life, Thou Marvel), Kivi's song from the opening of Act III; and "Sydämeni laulu" (Song of My Heart), Kivi's final aria about the peace found in the grove of Tuoni, the land of the dead (Example Twenty-two, page 98). Three of the songs (the third omitted) were rearranged for a cappella mixed chorus for a festival of Rautavaara's works in Minneapolis, Minnesota, in March, 1999, under the new title of *In the Shade of the Willow*, words that come from the first song where Kivi asks to be buried anonymously under a willow. In the same year he set three of the four songs for male chorus and added "Olven kunnia" (In Praise of Beer) (1998), also from the opera.

### *Nelja romanssia oopperasta Rasputin* (Four Romances from the Opera *Rasputin*) (2003/2006), for male chorus a cappella

These four choral songs from the opera *Rasputin* include "Loista kimmeltävän yön" (Through the Glimmering Night), "Kaukana on minun maani" (Far Away Lies My Homeland), "Troikka kiltää" (The Troika Speeds), and "Kuu kelmeä vain virtaan kuvastuu" (Moonlight is Pale Upon the River). The first performance of these arrangements were given by the Talla Vocal Ensemble, a ten-man group founded by Pasi Hyökki from members of the Ylioppilaskunnan Laulujat (University Singers).[15]

### *Our Joyful'st Feast* (2008), for mixed a cappella chorus

These three songs on Christmas, two by Shakespeare and the third by George Wither (1588-1667), are performed without a break. The first performance of *Our Joyful'st Feast* was commissioned and performed by Nils Schweckendiek and the Helsinki Chamber Choir in December of 2008, for the European Broadcasting Union (EBU) Christmas concert. Rautavaara chose these texts, saying, "These have a robust Renaissance joyfulness which I feel suits a European Christmas, even five hundred years later."[16]

---

[15] Samuel Tikkaja, Liner Notes, *Rautavaara: Complete Works for Male Choir*, Ondine ODE 1125-2D.
[16] Jaakko Mäntyjärvi, Program notes, *Our Joyful'st Feast*, Hyperion CDA67787.

### *Unsere Liebe* (Our Love) (2010), for mixed chorus

Commissioned by the Helsinki Chamber Choir, this set of songs is a rearrangement of the Lassi Nummi songs published in 1996 as *Wenn sich die Welt auftut* (When the World Opens Up), for children's chorus or female voices.

### *Missa a cappella* (2010-2011), for mixed chorus a cappella

Commissioned by an Australian chorus, the premiere of this twenty-two minute work on the liturgical text was premiered in November of 2012 in Utrecht, Netherlands. Its seven sections, Kyrie, Gloria, Credo, Sanctus, Benedictus, and Agnus Dei, are all varied in vocal arrangement and offer contrast with the others. All of Rautavaara's various choral techniques are put to use here.

The Kyrie's field cluster of voices maintains its pulses while the short bits of text and melody come from it, "Kyrie eleison, Christe eleison, Kyrie eleison" (Lord have mercy, Christ have mercy, Lord have mercy). The Gloria is homophonic with jubilant praise, quieter sections, changing the registers with male or female voices. The Credo, taken up from one already composed in 1972, has a long text wth many suitable settings, pedal points, homophony for statements of unity, female voices alone in awe, tempo changes. A tenor solo sings the Sanctus over a choral background, with the forces reversed for the Benedictus, a soprano lead and male accompaniment. Agnus Dei again features the sopranos in a slow homophony.

### *Tapanin Virsi* (Song of Stephen) (2011), for mixed choir a cappella

This ten minute work is based on texts from the *Kanteletar* (1840), a collection of Finnish lyric folksongs, a companion publication to the national epic *Kalevala* (1835), both compiled and published by Elias Lönnrot. *Tapanin virsi* relates to events surrounding the birth of Jesus. In it, Tapani (Stephen), a stable hand at the house of Ruotus (Herod), goes to water his horse. Instead of drinking, the horse begins snorting, which makes Tapani wonder. Looking for the cause, he sees a star reflected on the water. He runs to Ruotus and proclaims that the star signifies the birth of a new king, Kiesus (Jesus). Ruotus says that he will believe it if the cock prepared for his meal starts crowing, the ox bones on the floor starts bellowing and the wooden handle of the knife starts sprouting golden leaves. All these miracles do, in fact, occur.

The song remained part of the December 26 (Feast of St Stephen) ceremony: young men went from house to house, one dressed as Tapani in a straw suit, others as Christmas bears, billy goats or cranes. They sang and danced *Tapanin virsi*, ending with a request for beer and food for their own feast.[17]

Rautavaara's version was first performed by the Cantores Minores boy's choir at the Helsinki Cathedral on November 2, 2012, in celebration of their 60th anniversary. The choir, based at the Lutheran cathedral, was founded in 1953 by Pastor Tarmo Nuotio and Dr. Ruth-Esther Hillila, a Finnish-American musicologist and specialist in boys choirs.

## Nelja laulua oopperasta *Rasputin* (Four Songs from the Opera *Rasputin*) (2003/2006), for mixed choir and orchestra (2012)

Although Rautavaara had already extracted four songs from the opera *Rasputin*, in 2007, he set four more for mixed choir and orchestra in 2012, with only one overlap, "Troika trotting," now used as the opening song. The four were: "Troika kiitää" (Troika trotting), "Koston aika" (The day of vengeance), "En pelkää nyt" (I fear not), and "Loista, Sion, loista!" (Shine, Zion, shine!). The first song is brisk, depicting a snowy journey. The second is ominous with male voices dominating with a heavy tread. "I fear not" is for females and is lighter, more lyrical. The last song, "Shine, Zion, shine!" is a climax for all of the pulsating declamations, frequent repetitions, and a religious frenzy ending in near chaos.[18]

## *Hommage vanhalle säveltäjälle* (Hommage to an Old Composer) (2014) for a cappella male chorus

This male chorus work was commissioned for the Ylioppilaskunnan Laulujat (University Singers) for the Sibelius 150th year celebrations of Sibelius's birth in 2015. Sibelius had a long association with this chorus, founded in 1882. The text describes a man on a road in a foggy landscape, calmly moving toward a goal, eternity, in the midst of other activities, bells ringing, flags flying. Close harmony, sometimes using a whole tone scale, conveys this peace.

---

[17] Transforming Folklore, http://www.helsinki.fi/lehdet/uh/499b.html
[18] Kimmo Korhonen, Program notes, for Rautavaara, *Rubaiyat, Balada, Canto V, Four Songs from Rasputin*, Ondine CD.

## *Balada* (2015), cantata for tenor soloist, choir, and orchestra

Based on words by Federico Garcia Lorca, the cantata was commissioned and premiered in Madrid. The poetry came from several different collections and was newly combined. The story line is vague, but involves a journey, a Gypsy girl, love, death as Death leaves a tavern with a dagger, climbing with Death to a balcony leaving a trail of blood, and a final farewell, "Fear not, I will go far away…But do not ask me to explain anything…" The tenor soloist alternates with the choir, perhaps once a part of the never completed *Lorca* opera Rautavaara worked on until 2007. Though Rautavaara had recovered from his ruptured aorta and six month hospital stay enough by the end of 2004 to resume work, an opera in Spanish was discouraged and support for the work could not be found.

## *Orpheus singt* (2016), for a cappella chorus

Rautavaara's last premiered work was these settings of texts by Rainer Maria Rilke, performed June 25, 2016 by the SWR Vokalensemble at the Ludwigsburger Schlossfestspiele, under the direction of Marcus Creed. #1. Da Stieg ein Baum (A Tree Arose), #2. Und fast ein Mädchen wars (A Maiden Almost). #3 Ein Gott vermags (A God Can Do It). Rautavaara had composed these songs for solo voice and piano in 1954, *Funf Sonette an Orpheus*. Completed before his first neoclassical symphony and his first twelve-tone compositions, these songs are still mostly tonal and full of bits of word-painting Although the original version of the first three songs had been presented on his 1954 composition recital, the whole set of five received their first performance by Peter Roberts, tenor, and Rautavaara, pianist, at Tanglewood in the summer of 1955. In 1960 Rautavaara arranged the set for voice and orchestra, for his first wife, Mariaheidi Rautavaara, with the Helsinki City Orchestra in 1961. Then again, in 2016 he rearranged the first three songs for a cappella choir.

# CHAPTER FIFTEEN
# SOLO KEYBOARD WORKS

### *La première neige* (1947), lost

Written as a teenager, Rautavaara won a first prize in the Suomen teiniliito (Finnish Teen League) Composition Contest with his performance of the work, and a second prize in the Suomen nuoriso kulturipäivä (Finnish Youth Culture Day) competition of 1947. Rautavaara studied piano at that time with Astrid Joutsenon, accompanist to the internationally concertizing violinist, Kerttu Wanne. He had also studied music theory with Arvo Laitenan at the Sibelius Academy during the summer of 1946. Though Rautavaara probably needed exposure to a wide range of piano literature and styles, he was most interested in the contemporary repertoire Ms. Joutsenon was willing to teach, including compositions of Debussy, Ravel, Hindemith, and Respighi. This piano work likely was influenced by Debussy and was given a title in French to suit.

### *Kaupungissa sataa* (Snow Falling in the City) (1948), lost

First performed by Rautavaara in Turku, December 1, 1948, this piece may well have been influenced by Debussy's "The Snow is Dancing" from the *Children's Corner Suite*. During the year of its composition, Rautavaara continued to study with pianist Astrid Joutsenon.

### *Kolme symmetristä preludia* (Three Symmetrical Preludes) (1950)

Completed before any formal study of composition, this work shows Rautavaara's first interest in symmetrical construction, a technique which continues even to one of his last piano works, *Mirroring* (2014). The fast first movement is set as two moving lines in strict opposite motion, widely separate in register, four octaves apart. The main motive, based on an octatonic scale, appears in the first two measures. It is divided not only in meter, usually five eighths in the first measure and three quarter notes in the second, but by articulation, slurred legato eighth notes in the first followed by three staccato quarter notes in the second. The second movement, a consistent 3/8 meter, is similarly fast with two opposing arpeggiated melodies sparkling with varied articulation which then end phrases with strong chords. Again, the phrases sometimes open with a separation of five octaves between the hands, then move closer. The third movement in 6/8 meter combines single note lines with thirds in opposite motion. It also makes use of a four octave separation as a unifying device with the previous movements.

Rautavaara performed the work at a student recital at the Sibelius Academy on May 14, 1950. At that time the student concerts were reviewed by the local newspapers. Well-known composer and critic Uuno Klami complimented the performer but noted, among other generalities that the work was in a "difficult style." Another critic labeled it atonal. In August that year, Rautavaara was one of three students who represented the Sibelius Academy at the Jeunesse Musicale Festival in Bayreuth, where he performed the work again. Though the preludes were dedicated to fellow student pianist Kauko Kuosma, also performing at Bayreuth, Rautavaara did his own performance, and Kuosma, hating the work, never performed it.[1]

## *Pelimannit* (The Fiddlers) Op. 1 (1952), for piano

Composed before taking any composition classes, *Pelimannit* was Rautavaara's first important work and the first published. The melodies for the six movements are taken from seventeenth century Finnish folk music set down in a notebook by fiddler Samuel Rinda-Nickola, describing fiddlers and country organists of the coastal region of Ostrobothnia in western Finland. In the process of revision five earlier included movements, "Könnin faari," "Hullu Sakari," "Johans Ylinickola," "Ostinato," and "Duo" were deleted. The Finnish folk songs *Aleksanteri Könni* (1952, 1976), and *Piru ja juomari* (The Devil and the Drunkard, 1952,1976), composed at the same time, were perhaps meant for the suite, but were later published separately.

The six short movements that remain last about eight minutes in all. The first, "Närböläisten braa speli" (The Fiddlers of Närbö arrive), depicts the arrival of the festival or wedding musicians who accompanied the wedding party and guests as far as the door of the church in a procession. A simple C major melody is presented as a fanfare, marked Pomposo e rustico. This melody is filled out with full chords in the right hand which all include a dissonant minor second. The left hand marches in very low piano register in open octaves up through what seems like a C major scale, but with a flat seventh, implying a Mixolydian medieval mode, and then proceeds back down, now with a flattened

---

[1] Tiikkaja, 62-63.

third and flattened second, a Phrygian mode. The first phrase is answered by a faster motive in sixteenth notes, set in parallel octaves and fifths, evoking either the violinists' flourish or perhaps the scurrying of a rustic audience. A contrasting quieter section in a middle register follows, then the opening idea returns. The whole cadences "pesante" with the opening material, now with bass octaves in a partly whole tone, partly Phrygian mode descent.

A study of both the original folk melody and Rautavaara's composition by Kimberley J. Scott shows that the original tune was divided into units of four or eight measure phrases, contained repeats, and had an overall ternary form.[2] Rather than quoting the melody and the design, Rautavaara altered the meter between sections from 2/4 to 3/4 and sometimes even within phrases. The original opening's even note values are altered, doubling their length of some in a melodic line for added interest. The repeats are omitted, but the ternary form is kept by composing his own contrasting middle section.[3] The harmonies which Rautavaara added are tonal but dissonant with clashing added seconds in the first phrase and by added fifths in the second phrase (Example One, page 11).

The second piece, "Kopsin Jonas," depicts a fiddler practicing in the woods on a midsummer night with a high ostinato passage over a low register Phrygian melody, shifting from 3/2 meter to 2/3 meter at cadences. The differences from the original folk tune lie in the ostinato derived from the folk melody used throughout and also as introduction, transition, and coda. A sharp $6^{th}$ tone added to the Phrygian tune blurs the identity of the mode. Scott points out the use of the original refrain intact as a remnant of the folk tradition of improvisation, refrain, improvisation, refrain.[4]

"Jacob Könni," the wizard clock maker, alternates a single line melody resulting in a mechanical pulsation by use of alternating hands with a slower solemn chordal phrase, a plan which works well for Rautavaara's later wholesale use of that material as "Doubt and Creed" in his *Requiem in Our Time* for brass and percussion (Example One, page 11).

"Klockar Samuel Dikström" (Sexton or Bellringer Samuel Dikström), described as an organist practicing his daily Bach and old wedding tunes, contains broken triadic figuration and a Dorian melody.

---

[2] Scott, Kimberly J., Unity and Pluralism: A Stylistic Survey of the Compositional Techniques of Einojuhani Rautavaara as Reflected in Selected Works for the Piano, DMA diss., University of Kentucky, 2009, 88.

[3] Ibid..

[4] Ibid., 89.

"Pirun polska" (Devil's Polska) has an active Lydian mode melody, introduced and ended with a bit of melancholy recitative.

"Hypyt" (Hopping Dance) concludes with a quick dance all of 45 seconds long, even with the repeat. Its clear G major melody is accompanied by clashing minor seconds. Marked "burlesco," its contrasting wide-spread registers, abrupt dissonant chord interjections, and sparkling chromatic scales in contrary motion create its verve. Rautavaara later arranged the suite for string orchestra in 1972, and then again, for accordion, to be performed by Matti Rantanen in 1992.

### *Aleksanteri Könni* (1952, 1976), for piano

This is a separate piano piece perhaps also derived from the Samuel Rinda Nickola notebook, but published separately years later. Könni is a village outside Ilmajoki in southern Ostrobothnia.

### *Piru ja juomari* (The Devil and the Drunkard) (1952, 1976), for piano

This arrangement of a folksong from Rantasalmi, a town in southeast Finland, appealed to Rautavaara so much that he later used it for two further works, *Polska*, for two cellos and piano, and a version for orchestra entitled *Pohjalainen polska* (Ostrobothnian Polska, 1980), later rearranged for string orchestra in 1993.

### *Tema con variazione* (1953), for piano, lost

This piano piece was performed by Rautavaara at his composition recital on May 8, 1954. It was probably derived from the revised but discarded *Konsertto puhaltamille* (Concerto for Winds, 1950), the second movement, a theme with three variations.

### *Adagio and Toccata* (1954), for piano, lost

First performed by Rautavaara at his composition recital in 1954, it was later rearranged for orchestra and performed by the Helsinki City Orchestra under conductor Tauno Hannikainen in 1955 and then withdrawn. The toccata had a mix of 3+2+3 meters, later copied in the finale of *Ikonit*, the first and second piano sonatas, and the first piano concerto.

## *Ikonit* (*Icons*) Op. 6 (1955), suite for piano

The piano suite *Ikonit* (Icons) was perhaps begun in Niinisalo during his military service in 1954-55 with a piano piece called *Tot der Muttergottes*. Though not musically related to "The Death of the Mother of God" in *Ikonit*, the idea for a work on the Orthodox icons had begun. In Manhattan a year later, a random find of a book on icons in the New York Public Library brought back memories of his 1939 trip to the Orthodox monastery in Valamo on Lake Ladoga. Not surprisingly, the piano work is dedicated to the memory of his parents. He found himself already composing "The Death of the Mother of God" on the subway home. The rest of the pieces came as quickly.[5] The work has six movements, alternating slow and fast movements, titled after Orthodox icon paintings.

The first, "Jumalanäiden kuolema" (Death of the Mother of God) opens with polytonality, combined $E^b$ and $D^b$ triads, to evoke the tolling of bells at the beginning introduction. The central Tranquillo passage of modal chant moves in constant quarter note parallel triads, now diatonic, now chromatic, now in the treble, now in the bass. A solo tenor chant appears, keeping the quarter note pulse but adding in faster irregular note groupings as though declaiming text. The bells in polytonality come back, growing in intensity, then fading away. The icon painting itself is described as the Mother of God lying on a purple bed surrounded by the apostles, now garbed in splendor with gold and jewels as princes of the church. Jesus stands by the bed holding the tiny soul of his mother in his hands.

The second piece, "Kaksi maalaispyhimystä" (Two Village Saints), marked Giocoso, places a single line Aolian mode or A natural minor simple melody against a constantly moving and leaping chromatic accompaniment, also a single line. A broadening augmentation of the tune into parallel triads, often with an added dissonant tone, provides contrast before the return of the opening tune, now an octave higher, in the opening texture. An added touch is the brief descent into $A^b$ Aolian minor, recommended by Perschetti and endorsed by Rautavaara as a kind of "parting bow to the saints," before the final A minor cadence, A and E, plus an added quiet clash of F and $B^b$. The painted icon is described as two saints in solemn joy on either side of the bright green icon cabinet looking down on countless village weddings.

---

[5] Rautavaara, *Omakuva*, 142.

The third icon, "Blakernajan musta Jumalanäidin" (The Black Madonna of Blakemaja), is a musical depiction of the famed icon in Constantinople, blackened by centuries of candle smoke, the Madonna gazing out with compassionless black eyes having seen too much sorrow. Marked Lugubre, the high parallel triads of the theme and its marcato bass octave accompaniment in polytonality are echoed by a pianissimo chordal response in a middle register. A similar fortissimo passage is followed by the opening theme, now pianissimo. The mood conveyed is one of solemnity, sorrow, and darkness.

The fourth piece, "Kristuksen kaste" (The Baptism of Christ), includes a musical depiction of the Jordan River. A flowing pattern of 3+2+3 eighth notes, alternates with a maestoso section of polytonal chords conveying solemn dignity and, later, a recitative section, depicting the figure of God blessing his son with the Holy Spirit in the form of a dove.

"Pyhät naiset haudalla" (The Holy Women at the Grave) calls up the image of women in mourning, hearing the far tolling of a bell. Musical phrases of triads with added tones and hands moving in contrary motion pause to hear the deep bass bell tolling.

In "Arkkienkeli Mikael kukistaa Antikristuksen" (The Archangel Michael Fighting the AntiChrist), St. Michael calmly rides his winged horse over the hairy enemy, wielding a spear, a censer, the Book of Books, and blows a trumpet. The music depicts the battle as an unrelenting aggressive motion of sixteenth notes in the right hand, moving through the church modes, while the left hand, also modal, is in slower note values carrying the main melody. The work climbs to a fortissimo, and builds again from a pianissimo to a final fortissimo conclusion (Example Four, page 30).

Rautavaara's teacher Persichetti was especially interested in quartal harmonies, polyharmonies, alternating meters, triads in thirds and tritone relationships, and church modes which carried a light or dark effect. All of these techniques were already apparent in Rautavaara's earlier works and were incorporated into *Icons*.[6]

The work was first performed by a fellow student, Arlene Zallman, in New York on August 10, 1956. In 1997 the work was arranged for accordion, for the Finnish virtuoso Matti Rantanen. In 2005, Rautavaara orchestrated the pieces and added three "Prayers" for strings to go between the icons and a final solemn "Amen."

---

[6] Rautavaara, as quoted in Wojciech Stepien, 96.

## *Seitsemän preludia pianolle* (Seven Preludes for Piano) Op. 7 (1957)

Begun at Tanglewood in 1956, Rautavaara dedicated them to Arlene Zallman, a fellow composition student at Juilliard and source of some helpful comments on his works. Although dealing with logical growth under his teachers, these short works did not adhere to those instructions, but were determined to follow their own path, described by Rautavaara as "bare, sketchy, aphoristic, unconventional, ascetic, and dissonant but still supported with tonality."[7] The seven miniatures last only eleven minutes.

The short pieces alternate fast and slow tempi. The first, "Kimmoisasti vasaroiden" (Elastically hammering), has a violent energy from fast alternation of the hands that ranges over the whole keyboard. The second, "Kyllin hitaasti" (Slowly enough), contrasts with its slow single line walking bass ostinato in the left hand and simple melody in the right, all in a transparent texture. The third, "Hermostuneesti mutta rytmissä" (Nervously but in rhythm), reminds one of Stravinsky's irregular rhythms. Its motive is built from a repeated note rhythmic pattern followed by a fast flight of notes upwards. The fourth, "Koraali ja muunnelma" (Chorale and Variation), is slow with a walking bass line and a chordal theme in regular chorale phrases. Its variation follows the chorale and its phrasing with a full texture of dissonant chords. The fifth is a fugue full of wide leaps and distinctly staccato jabs, in a style recommended by friend Arlene. The sixth, "Väristen" (Shivering), another slow movement, shivers with repeated notes in the bass and cold treble faster reactions. The last, "Alla finale," concludes energetically with a full texture of rhythmic dissonant chords followed by a faster answer.

Besides being developed further into far lengthier symphonic movements in his Second Symphony, the preludes were also later transformed into a work for string orchestra, the *Finnisch, heute* (Finnish, Today) of 1970.

## *Apotheosis* (1957), for piano (unpublished)

Originally for piano, this work was reshaped into *Fantasy for violin and piano* (1960), then rearranged into a violin concerto, a string quartet, a string orchestra, and in 1962 as a work for a full orchestra, named the Fourth Symphony, but never performed.

---

[7] Rautavaara, 174-175.

## *Partita for Piano*, Op. 34 (1958), original version 1956 for guitar unfinished and lost

The open string sonorities of the guitar, E-A-D-G, permeate the work as a chord, especially in the slow section, often combined with triadic material derived from the top three strings, G, B, E. Later, in Helsinki, in 1958, he used the guitar material for three character pieces for piano, all from the same theme, depicting the three children of some friends. These remained in private use, until they were again reworked and published in 1980, for the original medium of guitar. The guitar pieces bear a second title of *Luonnekuvaa* (Nature Pieces): 1. Meri (Sea); 2. Maarika; and 3. Markku.[8]

## *Ta Tou Theou,* (That Which Comes from God) Op. 30 (1967), for organ

The organ piece *Ta Tou Theou* was a composition competition winner, inspired by an enthusiasm for all things Greek. Sponsored by the Helsinki Cathedral, its first performance was given by Tapani Valsta, the Cathedral organist. Its two movements, "Nomen Patris et Filii et Spiritus Sancto," and "Gaudet in Filio Pater Spiritu Sancto," were in Rautavaara's earlier atonal serial technique.

The composition had a long and tortuous history. In 1957 Rautavaara wrote to his teacher Wladimir Vogel that, in addition to writing the pan serialist orchestral work *Praevariata*, he was also writing a piano work in a similar style with the title of *Apotheosis*. By August of 1960 the piece had become transformed into a violin and piano work, *Fantasia*. Efforts to turn the material into a violin concerto, a string quartet, or a string orchestra version did not succeed. In 1964 the work became the first movement of the original Fourth Symphony, later discarded, and then eventually in 1967 settled into the organ work *Ta Tou Theou*.[9]

## *Etudes for Piano* (1969)

The *Etudes*, Op 42 (1969), include six movements. Each has a tight, strict, structural idea, based on a given interval and is set in a Rachmaninov-like piano texture with rapid arpeggios ranging from top to bottom of the piano's register. The six movements are arranged not in intervallic sequence, but in an order by musical relevance: thirds, sevenths, tritones, fourths, seconds, and then fifths. According to Sini Rautavaara, the composer's wife, each one has its own mood.

---

[8] Rautavaara, 149.

[9] Tiikkaja, 180.

The thirds etude is brilliant and egotisical, the sevenths seeking rest but in vain, the tritones anxious, the fourths like forces of nature, the seconds expressive, and the fifths airily rhythmic."[10] The etude on fifths has a 3+2+3 beat pattern as in other of Rautavaara's works of that year, his first piano sonata and the first piano concerto. They were first performed in 1970 by pianist/conductor/composer Ralf Gothoni, in an incomplete version of five movements, and then, the same year, in complete form by pianist Izumi Tateno, a long time Finland resident and teacher at the Sibelius Academy. Some of the etudes' material found its way into the ballet *Kiusaukset* (The Temptations), also of 1969.

## *Christ and the Fishermen* (1969), sonata for piano

This sonata in three movements musically depicts the atmosphere of Christ calling the fisherman in the first movement, the exhilaration of the men working and learning from the Christ in the second, and, lastly, an extremely slow chorale of adoration with three verses and a coda that brings back the first movement's theme.

The first movement, marcato, con gravità, proceeds in quarter notes, in a walking tempo, with descending wide-spaced chords in the right hand made from two perfect fifths superimposed, or a fifth and a ninth, often descending in step-wise motion. The left hand accompaniment is a pattern of single quarter notes ascending by fifths. These repeat each time the melody comes back, establishing B♭ as an anchoring pitch. These first few measures are answered by three quieter measures marked Tempo II, slightly faster, in close spaced superimposed triads, both hands diverging in contrary motion, seeming to be a frisson of awe in response to Christ's words. Both ideas are repeated and then reappear altered, the melody in an ascending form in the left hand and the accompaniment pattern of fifths descending in the right hand. The movement concludes with a section of the opening ninth chord melody supported by rapid arpeggios, evoking waves, and ends with both forearms in very loud tone clusters. The tone clusters then fade into an E♭ major chord of overtone harmonics, barely heard.[11] The opening ninths call for a pianist with large hands. An octave stretch on white keys for the left hand with a clashing major seventh on a black key is near impossible for a small hand. The final tone cluster calls for use of forearm on black keys two octaves and a minor sixth (a low B♭ in the bass reaching to a G♭ in the treble), with a similar stretch for the

---

[10] Kimmo Korhonen, *Finnish Piano Music*, FIMIC1997, 57.

[11] The harmonics, or sympathetic vibrations, are created from the upper harmonics of a bass note. For example, a low C note played loudly can make the strings vibrate on a higher C, E, G, and other notes, to a lesser extent, if that higher key is pressed down (which raises the felt damper and allows the strings to vibrate freely).

right forearm on white keys in the same register, but from A, one note lower in the bass to a G, one note higher in the treble. An accurate rendering may be physically impossible, depending on the length of the player's forearm, but with such a mass of sound, no auditor is likely to notice a few missing notes. The mass of clusters then need to resolve to notes of the E♭ major chord, still held on the pedal and fingers transferred without resounding, in order to extend the harmonics of those notes after the piano pedal is raised.

In the restless second movement the hands rapidly alternate in chord clusters, set in a 13/8 meter with uneven groups of three, two, three, two, three eighth notes. This soon is shortened to 8/8, with groups of three plus two plus three eighth notes. The movement ends in a slowly rising bass line of single notes, climaxing in an enormously loud bass range tone cluster. These notes linger on in a retained E♭ major chord of harmonics, not restruck, of notes selected from the massive cluster.

In the finale, an other-worldly sense of awe is created. A slow chorale of triadic chords not related in tonal fashion, notated in quarter notes, moves often in parallel octaves against a contrapuntal part, mostly in eighth notes. These two textures are passed back and forth in the hands. Rautavaara marks two motives with the notation Hauptmotiv (Main motive), showing how he wants these emphasized, sometimes alternating, sometimes in stretto, overlapping. The final measures bring back the ninth chords of the first movement in their ascending version, again starting from a B♭ anchoring pitch, but ending on a G minor chord plus an added second on A, not E♭ as in the earlier two movements. An orchestrated version was entered in the Spanish Óscar Esplá competition but did not win.

## *Tulisarna* (The Fire Sermon), op. 64 (1969), piano sonata no. 2

This three movement work opens with an energetic rhythmic pattern in 3+2+3, using alternating hands, depicting the fire of the "fire sermon." A second lyrical idea has modal contours and modal harmonies, using a scale with alternating major and minor seconds, while keeping the energetic accompaniment going. Rapid and wild arpeggios, clusters, and scales intrude, thematic ideas return, then climax in a slow chordal passage, repeated three more times in ever higher registers.

In the second movement, Andante assai, a calm and simple melody attempts to establish itself but several times is contradicted by a gloomy theme which turns violent, and climaxes in clusters. The lyrical theme makes a final statement which dies away, slowing, having been beaten into submission. The third movement, Allegro brutale, begins in the bass with a spiky fugato, reiterates the subjects of the first movement, and ends fortissimo with a series of chords, a final D major chord of harmonics remaining from the last big cluster.

## *Laudatio Trinitatis* (1969/1970?), for organ

The three sections of this work deal with the Trinity of the Father, Son, and Holy Ghost. "In nomine Patris" has bitonal chords in a hymn-like setting. "Et Filii" begins quietly and builds. " Et Spiritus Sancti" continues energetically with an ostinato.

## *Toccata per Organo* (1971/98)

The *Toccata per Organo* (1971/98) has a seventeenth century baroque toccata form. It features a fast artistic texture and dramatic chords. Its free tonal melody lies over symmetrically built harmonies. Rautavaara arranged a new version for its performance at the week long Hampstead and Highgate festival of his compositions in London, in 1999, performed by Paul Dean. The same organist also performed a commissioned work for trumpet and organ, *Hymnus* (1999), at that festival.

## *Music for Upright Piano* (1976)

Wanting something fresh for these piano commissions, Rautavaara thought of a novel by Lassi Nummi (1928-2012) called *Maisema* (Landscape), with fantastic strange flowers, trees, and animals. Rautavaara wanted to create a dreamlike soundscape where comparable strange plants and animals lived. Part of this effect is created by exploring the sounds produced from the overtones series of a single note.[12] Each pitch includes its own pitch plus the lesser sounds of its octave, then a fifth higher, a flat seventh, second octave, and then pitches moving higher stepwise (C, C, G, C, E, G, B♭, C, D, E, F♯, G, A. B♭, B, C). As a parlor trick, this can be demonstrated on a piano when the sustaining pedal is put down, raising the dampers on all the strings. A higher key in the series is pressed down silently, and the lowest note from the same overtone series is then played strongly on the keyboard or plucked from the strings. This activates the strings of both the silent and played notes together, the overtones of the struck key and the silent key in a sympathetic resonance. The work was first performed by pianist Ralf Gothóni in March of 1976, along with *Music for Upright Piano and Amplified Cello* (1976), with cellist Erkki Rautio.

---

[12] Tiikkaja, 376.

### Second Music for Upright Piano (1976)

The second work for upright piano includes triads, glissandi, and pizzicatos. The work was dedicated to J. S. Bach's G major prelude in the Well Tempered Clavier, Bk. 1, Rautavaara's inspiration. This second piece, though composed also in 1976, waited until 1990 for its debut given by pianist Erik T. Tawaststjerna, son of the famous biographer of Sibelius.[13]

### Music for Upright Piano and Amplified Cello (1976)

Pianist Ralf Gothóni and cellist Erkki Rautio presented this work at the same time as the first piece for upright piano. Rautavaara attempted to expand the sounds of the cello in keeping with the new effects done on the upright piano. In these works for upright piano Rautavaara experimented with the effects of playing the piano both from the keyboard and directly on the strings.

### Ces Bons Soirs de Septembre (1976), for piano, lost

This three minute work for piano was performed by Kurt Walldén in Helsinki, in 1976, but was lost.

### Häämarssi (Wedding March) (1984), for organ

In 1984 Rautavaara had the joy of commissioning his own work, for his wedding to Sinikka Koivisto in Helsinki on August 18, 1984. Themes from the opera *Marjata matalan neiti* (Marjata the Lowly Maiden) were included, since the opera and their joint roles in its performance, Sinikka as soloist and Einojuhani as narrator, was the starting point of their marriage. Combining work and honeymoon, the newlyweds went to Hungary in the fall of 1984, when the Tapiola children's choir took *Marjata* there on tour. The local bookstore was selling a translation of the Kalevala at the time. With the new local enthusiasm for the Finnish epic, Rautavaara received a commission while there for another work for children's chorus based on it, *The First Runo* (1984), using the English translation of W. F. Kirby of 1907.[14]

---

[13] Tiikkaja, 377.
[14] Tiikkaja, 424.

## *Narcissus* (2002), for piano

This work was commissioned by the Helsinki International Maj Lind Piano Competition, as a required piece for the second round of competitions in Helsinki, August 14-16, 2002. According to Rautavaara's notes on the published piece, the work is so full of mirrored virtuosic motifs that the title *Narcissus* seemed to fit perfectly.

## *Passionale* (2003), for piano

Commissioned by the Iitti Music Festival and dedicated to pianist Laura Mikkola, this work is marked Agitato. Thematic material came from the opera *Rasputin's* second and third acts. A soaring melody of arches in the left hand is set against sextuplet arpeggios in the right hand. The pattern is reversed, with melody now in the right hand in octaves, plus the fifth and major seventh as added sonorities. The left hand moves faster, with eight notes against each quarter note of the melody, murmuring in and out of scale or chromatic scale passages. A slower middle section, Adagio dolente, settles into an expressive melody in octaves plus major sevenths, Rautavaara's signature clashing seconds, against triadic but not functionally related chords. Tempo I brings back the first melody with arpeggiated accompaniment, and the ending swirls down to a final "almost" D major chord, spelled D, F##, G#, A, and D.

## *Fuoco* (2008), for piano

Dedicated to pianist Laura Mikkola, this work was intended to complete the previous two single piano works of this decade. Laura Mikkola was invited to perform the three at a party both for Sini Rautavaara's birthday and for their wedding anniversary. Rautavaara's notes on the published work state that "like the first two pieces, this finale of the trilogy displays virtuosic feroce passages, symmetry, and cantando melodic moments." The piece has a three part structure, with an opening in 8/8 which falls in alternating hands as 3 + 2 + 3 eighths. This motoric section gives way to a central Cantando melodic area. The right hand quarter note melody is harmonized throughout in fourths, each note with its lower half step (for example, G# and A plus C# and D.) Arpeggios in the left hand include some of the same half steps. The Feroce section returns, briefly, followed by a return of the slower Cantando ideas.

## *Mirroring* (2014)

This piano piece was commissioned for the Vladimir Ashkenazy Piano Competition in Hong Kong as a required performance piece. The first performance of many was on Oct. 4, 2014.

# CHAPTER SIXTEEN
# CHAMBER MUSIC

## String Quartet No. 1 *Quartettino* (1952)

Rautavaara related in his autobiography[1] that he composed his String Quartet No. 1 in 1952 while a student at the Sibelius Academy, before having had any composition classes. The outer of the three movements are brief and rhythmic, while the slow movement puts an emphasis on melody. The melodies of the first two movements are constructed on a symmetrical or octotonic scale, an eight note scale of alternating whole and half steps. Rautavaara had not yet been introduced to this scale in his music classes but chose it for its melodic interest. The influence of Finnish folk music can be heard in the virtuosic final movement, Vivace assai (alla giga), as well as ideas gleaned from a counterpoint class in its brief fugato. It was first performed in Helsinki on December 12, 1954 by the Helsinki Quartet consisting of Anja and Jouko Ignatius, Arno Salmela, and Penti Rautawaara, Rautavaara's cousin who was a cellist. Later, Rautavaara arranged the first string quartet for string orchestra by adding a double bass, and gave it the title *Suite for String Orchestra*, using the same opus number. In this format it received its first performance in Tampere, Finland, in 1953 under conductor Jorma Panula.

## *A Requiem in Our Time*, Op. 3 (1953), for brass choir and percussion

Under Aare Merikanto's supervision Rautavaara wrote his *A Requiem in Our Time* to enter an American competition and dedicated it to the memory of his mother. The scoring required was for thirteen-part brass choir with percussion. In 1954 the work won the first prize in the Thor Johnson composition competition in Cincinnati, Ohio, and was performed there by the Cincinnati Brass Choir.

The *Requiem* contains four movements. Short on time before the deadline, Rautavaara adapted several earlier compositions. In the opening "Hymnus," marked Festivamente, a quartet of trumpets alternates with a quartet of horns,

---

[1] Rautavaara, *Omakluva*, 48.

tossing phrases back and forth, while the three trombones, baritone, tuba, and various percussion act as support for either group. Grounded in the key of E♭ major, the melody, taken from his choral work *Laulupuu* (Singing Tree), is accompanied by clashing parallel minor seconds in a harmonic style like that in *Pelimmanit*. The second movement, "Credo et Dubito," comes from the earlier "Jacob Könni" movement in the *Pelimannit* suite for piano. As Jacob Könni was a wizard clockmaker, the original work contrasted two sections, one a mechanical pulsation with the other a solemn slow chordal phrase. This may have been intended to simulate the winding of the mechanism and the serene slow march of time once it was set. Here, the two sections are used to depict nagging doubt and the serene faith. Faith has the last word, if only in the final chord. A march-like theme in the "Dies Irae" third movement derives from Rautavaara's *Concerto for Winds* (1950), a student work with awkward instrumental registers. The French horns have a steady chant that reminds of the Gregorian Dies Irae melody. Passages of syncopated brass interjections and horn glissandi, along with heavy snare drum evoke the terror of the Last Judgement. The lovely slow last movement, "Lachrymoso," establishes a muted brass section accompaniment with a quietly oscillating trumpet and then brings in the solo baritone horn in a high register, attractive but uncomfortable for the performer.[2] The solo lead passes to a French horn to solo trumpet, then back to the baritone, ending with the trombones.

### *Pöytämusiikki Herttua Johanalle* (Table Music for Duke Johan) Op. 4 (1954), a suite for recorder quartet.

Duke Johan was Finland's only royal resident, who established a court at the castle of Turku from 1556-63, and later became King Johan III of Sweden. These five short historical dances include Air allegretto, Gigue en rondeau, Air lent, Caccia, and Galliarde. Simple and repetitive motives unify the whole suite. The suite was commissioned and first performed by the Egil Cederlöf Quartet, in Helsinki in 1957.

### *Two Preludes and Fugues on BEla BArtok and EinAr EnGlunD* (1955), for cello and piano

These two preludes and fugues on letters from the names of the two composers, Englund, a Finnish composer (1916-1999),[3] and Bartok were

---

[2] Rautavaara, 75-76.

[3] Englund, some ten years older than Rautavaara, gained renown with his neoclassical works in the 1950s, withdrew from music life for a decade or so during a twelve-tone era in the 60s in Finland, and later returned to favor.

composed during Rautavaara's study in Vienna. Not yet serial, these works make much of the themes based on the extracted letters. Originally these works were three fugues, one on the name of a fellow student Cynthia Troxell, using the letters c-b-a, referring to Cynthia mit den Blauen Augen, a second fugue on Bartok, using the letters b-e-b-a, and a third fugue on the name of father Eino Rautavaara, e-a-a-a-a-a. Before the first performance in 1957 the first fugue became a tribute to his colleague Einar England; the third was discarded for having a monotonous theme of too many "a's." The aspects of Bartok which Rautavaara admired and wanted to emulate in his work were a well-constructed formal structure, interest in folk music, mystery, and pathos. A string glissando provides an interesting effect in the opening declarative homophony, before the polyphony of the fugue. Both preludes and fugues were first performed in 1957 for the 75th anniversary of the Sibelius Academy with cellist Eeva-Liisa Hirvonen and Rautavaara, piano. The Bartok fugue underwent several transformations, into a work for piano, for string trio, for orchestra, and also for accordion and cello in 1995. In 1986 a string orchestral version became *Epitaph for Béla Bartók*.

## The Second String Quartet, Op. 12 (1958)

The Second String Quartet was composed during Rautavaara's 1958 summer study under Rudolf Petzold at the Cologne Musikhochschule, a conservatory. Within a year after beginning serial composition under Vogel, Rautavaara had produced the choral song *Ave Maria*, the orchestral work *Modificata*, and the panserialist work *Praevariata*. Working with Petzold, Rautavaara was beginning to feel comfortable with his own materials, constructing his rows so as to combine the twelve-tone structure with tonality and allowing for his own style of expressiveness. The Second String Quartet's symmetrical serial row has four segments, each with a minor third and minor second. For contrast he constructed a Quintenreihe (fifths) row that provided four possible triads. The polyphonic opening of the first movement features a motive introduced by the violin, with a memorable rhythmic shape and wide-spaced intervals. A quieter section using the Quinten row contrasts with triadic ingredients and has an abundance of melody in the style of the late Romantics. The four movements are unified by the same melodic motives, but in different rhythms and aspects: a contrapuntal opening movement in moderate tempo, a dance-like scherzo, a melodic slow movement, and a fast finale.

## Octet for Winds (1962)

In 1962 Rautavaara's Octet for Winds, Op. 21, was written for the Pro Arte Intima Ensemble, to be performed in the 1963 Chamber Music Days program. Scored for four woodwinds (flute, oboe, clarinet, and bassoon) and four brass (trumpet, 2 cornets, and trombone), the second movement was later arranged for clarinet and piano as *Sonetto* (1969). It had a varied history, beginning as a work for flute and string quartet, then for a wind quintet, and finally, upon a commission, for a wind octet. The fifteen minute work has three movements: Allegro, Largo, and Prestissimo.

## Quartet for Oboe and Strings, Op. 11 (1957/64)

The 1964 quartet for oboe and strings reworked the thematic material of *Modificata* (1957).[4] Of this quartet's four movements, only the third movement, "Interludio," is new and the remainder are either shortened or exact copies of the *Modificata* movements. This new metamorphosis had as little success as the original.

## String Quartet No. 3 (1965)

The Third String Quartet, a single slow movement, is based on material taken from the second act of the opera *Kaivos* (The Mine), and uses the same serial row and its Quintenreihe. It won a first prize in the Camden Composition Contest of 1966 and was first performed by the Delmé Quartet in London, in 1967.

## Sonata for bassoon and piano (1965/68)

Dedicated to bassoonist Emanuel Elola, and first performed in 1965, the work was revised in 1968 and the first version withdrawn. Originally, the materials began in 1962 at the same time as Rautavaara was working on his Fourth Symphony (1962) as *Erstesspiel*, a work for flute, bass clarinet, violin, cello, and piano, and, at one point, also included voice. In a framework similar to his orchestral *Praevariata* (1957) where many of the parameters of beats, measures, orchestration, etc., are rigidly controlled, *Erstespiel* had a repetitive eleven beat structure. Little of the original remained after the various revisions.

---

[4] Rautavaara, 150-1.

## *Pentecost* (1967), for percussion, withdrawn

Composed for a competition arranged by a New York State University, this work won no prize.

## Sonata for Solo Cello (1969, 2001)

At the same time of the cello concerto composed for Erkki Rautio, Rautavaara wrote a four-movement cello sonata for Rautio, but not completed. Rautavaara kept the score, but mislaid it. The work was discovered about 2000 by Rautio's son, Martti Rautio, a pianist, among his father's music collection. The sonata was finished and first performed by Erkki Rautio, cellist, and his son, Martti, a pianist, at the Kemiö summer music festival in 2001. Unusual for Rautavaara in the late 1960s was the NeoBaroque style and the actual quotation of Bach's BWV 565 famous D minor fugue. Portions of the original were reused in Rautavaara's *Cantos III: Portrait of the Artist at a Certain Moment* (1972) for string orchestra. Rautavaara has described the musical contents as beginning with quiet bitonal chords in the piano. The cello adds a cantabile gesture following a more passionate development. There is a more poetic middle section with a dialogue between the cello and the piano. The final section is a more dramatic allegro, ending with the cello motive underlying the ebbing of the cello's tremolo.[5]

## *Sonetto* (1969), for clarinet and piano

Written for clarinetist Martin Fagerlund, this single movement work is based on the Largo second movement of the Octet for Winds (1962). It begins in an icy manner with smooth chords in the high register of the piano with clarinet single note staccato punctuations. Some lyrical phrases with wide-spaced intervals from the clarinet continue on, incorporating the staccato repeated note idea now in the piano. A new section takes the piano into a low register and leading the melodic flow, with comments by the clarinet. Both instruments press on, in a lyrical manner, to a climax. The opening idea returns at the end, rounding off the movement.

---

[5] Einojuhani Rautavaara, program notes for the July 10, 2001 performance (Second Cello Sonata).

### *Dithyrambos* (1970), for violin and orchestra or piano

*Dithyrambos* (1970), for violin and orchestra or violin and piano, was first performed by Manfred Gräsbeck with the Aarhus (Denmark) orchestra in 1972. The title refers to the solemn odes and hymns sung to Dionysus/Bacchus at his festivals, which usually involved exchanges between a leader and a chorus. This five-minute work in one movement, though it obviously has interplay between the soloist and orchestra, was never listed as a concerto by Rautavaara.

### *Ballade* (1973/80), for solo harp and string quintet

*Ballade* was later rearranged for solo harp and a string orchestra in 1976. Not usually considered a concerto, the work has a single movement. Rautavaara would later compose a true harp concerto in 1999, devising at that later time a means of having a harp solo without its being overwhelmed by the orchestra.

### *Ugrilainen dialogi* (Hungarian Dialogue) (1973), for violin and cello

This work was composed for Lajos Garam, violin teacher at the Sibelius Academy, and his cellist brother, Károly Garam. The brothers were born in Hungary but raised primarily in Finland, the home of their mother, Sole Kallioniemi, concert pianist and pianist of the Helsinki Philharmonic for many years. In 1975 Rautavaara reused this material in his Fourth String Quartet, for its first movement. The quartet's second and third movements were based on his 1958 song cycle, *Die Liebenden*, from its third and then second songs.

### *Cantilena* (1974), for cello and piano, lost

### *Variétude* (1974) for violin

The *Variétude* won the first prize in the International Sibelius Violin Competition composition contest and became a required performance piece for all the violin contestants in the 1975 third competition. The Competition was established in 1965, in honor of the centennial of Sibelius's birth year, and is held every five years. *Variétude* was later arranged for guitarist Ismo Eskelinen in 2006. A technical tour-de-force, it requires secure double stop playing from the performer, along with high range bowed passages interrupted by pizzicato interjections, double stops with one voice being in harmonics, echo effects, and high range pitch accuracy.

## Sonata for Flute and Guitar (1975)

After writing *Dances of the Winds* (1973), a flute concerto for four different sizes of flutes, Rautavaara wrote a sonata for flute and guitar for the same flautist, Gunilla von Bahr, with Diego Blanco guitarist, for a Stockholm performance in 1976. This sonata exploits the four sizes of flutes within the six-minute single movement. The work has four sections, with brief interludes for the accompanying guitar to allow for the flautist to change instruments. The opening graceful melody for the standard flute in a mid-range is laid over a fairly simple syncopated guitar accompaniment. With a few measures of guitar interlude a second more restrained low pitched melody for the alto flute takes over, with the guitar in a constant single note counterpoint. With some dramatic guitar strums, the flautist changes to bass flute and the two instruments echo each other's motives. The fourth section for piccolo moves to a high register for both instruments and concludes in an animated finale in triplets. The work is tonally anchored with frequent returns to a tonal center, but otherwise harmonically free. The guitar texture is often a single plucked note, sometimes a series of clashing seconds, sometimes melodic, but makes little use of the usual strummed chords. Though it is always present, it never dominates the flute.

## String Quartet No. 4 (1975)

The Fourth String Quartet was composed in the late summer of 1975 for the Voces Intimae Quartet. Its three movements have material from previous compositions, but are tied together with the motif heard at the very beginning, a dialogue between the viola and cello. The first movement comes from the *Ugrilainen dialogi* (Hungarian Dialogue) of 1973, a duet for violin and cello for two Hungarian Finnish brothers, Lajos and Károly Garam. The last two movements derive from two songs of the song cycle *Die Liebenden* of 1958, the third, "Die Liebende," and then the second, "Der Schauende,"

## *Tarantará* (1976), for solo trumpet

*Tarantará* for solo trumpet was commissioned for a wind instrument competition.

## *Music for Upright Piano and Amplified Cello* (1976)

Composed in the 1970s during a period of experimentation with other electronic sounds such as the *Sampo* opera, this work was first performed by Ralf Gothoni, pianist, and Erkki Rautio, cellist.

## *Serenades of the Unicorn* (1977), for guitar

In 1977 guitarist Josef Holecek of Gothenberg, Sweden, commissioned a work for solo guitar. The four sections of the resulting work, *Serenades of the Unicorn*, were: 1. "A Nervous Promenade and Dance (With His Own Reflection)"; 2. "Serenading a Pair of Giggly Nymphs (Drunk of Night)"; 3. "Serenading the Beauty Inobtainable (Too Far in Time)"; and 4. "Having a Grand Time (With Some Scythian Centaurs)." The first of these has a jerky arpeggio pattern with irregular accents and some glissando effects. The second of these has a background of two parts in an eerie ostinato of ascending and descending harmonics, the pair of giggly nymphs, with a plucked single note melody line in the foreground. The third is a slower melody over an arpeggiated figure, Romantic in style, except for the lack of tonal harmony. The boisterous finale contains loud strumming, and a final loud plucked sliding pitch.

## *Polska, Variations on a folksong from Rantasalmi* (1977), for two cellos and piano

In 1977 Rautavaara wrote this work for two cellos and piano, for cellists Erkki Rautio, first performer of Rautavaara's 1968 Cello Concerto, and Arto Noras. The folksong, "Piru ja juomari" (The Devil and the Drunkard), comes from Rantasalmi, a town in the southeastern lake district of Finland, near the border with Russia. Rautavaara returned to this melody twice, liking its unusual question and answer dialogue. It has two similar phrases, each with its own ending. The folksong was also the subject of a work for orchestra, *Pohjalainen polska* (Northern Polska, 1980), commissioned by the city of Vaasa, and rearranged later as a work for strings, *Ostrobothnian polska* (1993), Ostrobothnia being the northwestern coast of Finland on the Gulf of Ostrobothnia between Finland and Sweden. Though the usual polska is a triple meter folkdance from Sweden, with accents on the first and third beats, dotted rhythm patterns, two-measure phrases, triadic outlines, and a wide-ranging melody, Rautavaara's folksong is in a duple meter. The term "polska" eventually came to mean a folk dance, either in triple or duple meter. The traditional polska came to Finland in the 1700s when the landowners, predominantly Swedish-speaking, imported it from Sweden, where it, in turn, likely imported it from Poland along with a Polish Queen in the late sixteenth century. The aristocratic dances soon spread by way of the fiddlers to the countryside. Both title words in the last version of this tune could arguably be called misnomers, as the tune is neither a true polska nor from northwestern Finland.

The writing for cello calls for unusual harmonics, an aleatoric variation with a repeated cello pattern against an unmetered piano part, tone clusters in the piano, and clashing dissonances against the tonal folk melody. The words of the folksong imply the tempting of the drunkard by the devil with one more drink, and the music aptly conveys reeling hallucinations.

## *Electropus* (1977), for two winds, percussion, guitar, lutes, and piano

Improvised at an Instant Composition Workshop in Hämeenlinna in 1977, the performers included Jarmo Sermilä on an electronically altered trumpet, Seppo Keskinen on clarinet, Tim Ferchen on percussion, Kari Koivula on guitar, Herman Rechberger on sitar and bazooki (Indian and Greek lute-type instruments), and Rautavaara on piano.

## *Luonnekuvaa* (Nature Pieces) (1980), for guitar

Originally commissioned by a guitarist and begun as a guitar partita in 1956, the pieces remained unfinished until reworked into three piano character pieces in 1958, depicting the three children of friends. These remained in private use, until they were again reworked and published in 1980 under the title of *Luonnekuvaa* (Nature Pieces), for the original medium of guitar.[6] The open string sonorities of the guitar, E-A-D-G, permeate the work as a chord, especially in the slow section, often combined with triadic material derived from the top three strings, G, B, E.

## *Monologues of the Unicorn* (1980), for guitar

After *Serenades of the Unicorn* (1977) for guitar, Rautavaara composed a second work for the same guitarist, Josef Holecek of Gothenberg, Sweden, with allusions to older composers and their styles. The first is titled "Monologue with JSB (He gets slightly annoyed with the beast)," referring to Johann Sebastian Bach, and starting off like an inversion of the C major Prelude from the Well-Tempered Clavier. The second is "Monologue with Claude-Achille (Poeticized by the whiteness)," referring to Claude-Achille Debussy. Another type of arpeggio pattern appears, somewhat patterned after the opening of Debussy's *Arabesque No. 1* for piano. The third is "Monologue with Ad Schbeg (With occasional remarks by his son Aba Beg)," a reference to Arnold Schoenberg and his student Alban Berg, perhaps motives in twelve tone style and Berg's return to occasional triads.

---

[6] Rautavaara, *Omakuva*, 149.

The fourth is "Monologue with Igor (The horn gets on his nerves)," referring to Igor Stravinsky and a motoric neoclassical style of arpeggios.

## *Playgrounds for Angels* (1981), for brass ensemble

*Playgrounds for Angels*, a twelve minute work for brass ensemble (4 trumpets, 4 trombones, horn, and tuba), was composed for the Philip Jones Brass Ensemble for the Helsinki Festival Weeks, in September of 1981. The first performance was a disaster, with portions unrecognizable to the composer. Though not at first enthusiastic about the work, the ensemble went on to perform it elsewhere and eventually recorded it.[7]

In the ensemble's defense was Rautavaara's intention to write a work that would explore all the possible effects on the instruments--overtone notes, fast arpeggios, glissandi, playing and singing simultaneously on the trombone, combination tones—all requiring virtuoso players. While exploring these possibilities with local trumpet and trombone players, he had been assured the Philip Jones Ensemble was the best.

> The structure of the composition derives from the technical features of the trumpet, trombone, horn, and tuba. Those features guide the process, variations, details, and overall form of the music. Each group of instruments has its own musical playground.[8]

The work can be divided into four sections. The ensemble is divided into three groups, the four trumpets, the four trombones, a French horn that often solos, and a tuba that provides accompaniment. The first section, A, is dominated by the trumpets with interruptions from slow trombone and horn chords. The work opens with a rapid solo trumpet motive on a major chord. The trumpets, two in C and two in B-flat, at times muted, toss varied motives back and forth, at times playing in seconds apart. The second section, B, features a horn melody with the trombones sometimes singing while playing and tuba accompaniment, with interruptions from the trumpets. The third section, C, is marked Largo, and features a slow melody for the trombones in seconds, joined by the tuba. A few passages of wind blowing through the instruments appear here as well as trombone tremolos and glissandi. Trumpets provide quiet repetitive motives in a harmonic accompaniment. The final section regains the original tempo, all the groups participate in dense rhythmic layers. Solo horn attempts to dominate. The trumpet motives get shorter, with pauses. The final event is two notes by solo tuba marked as "lion's roar."[9]

---

[7] Rautavaara, *Omakuva*, 325-6.
[8] Rautavaara, Program notes to *Playground for Angels*, Ondine 957-2 (2000).
[9] Stepien, 158-167 passim.

In this work one could well imagine a playground scene of younger and older boys jeering at each other. It opens with playful snatches of dialogue between two trumpets, reminiscent of Mussorgsky's music depicting chattering women in the market place in *Pictures at an Exhibition*. Lower brass (perhaps the older boys?) soon get involved with similar material, while a solo horn tries to speak lyrically, unsuccessfully. The special effects, a slow and gloomy low-pitched middle section, a return to the rapid trumpet style, and final pair of derisive tuba notes all suggest some sort of antagonistic story line. According to Rautavaara's comments on angels, they seem not to be religious symbols, but are spirits that represent a kind of unachievable perfection, not judgmental, not emotional, but "terrifying" to mere mortals. Imaging this type of persona, *Playground for Angels* could well be an intellectual game of chess, a debate contest presenting and rebutting topics, or, perhaps Olympic tennis contestants. Both of the terms in his title, "playgrounds" and "angels," are left open to the listener's imagination by the composer.

## *Notturno* (1981), for flute and string quartet, withdrawn

*Notturno* was written as a concert piece for an evening program after the graduation of the new doctors from the Faculty of Medicine at Helsinki University in 1981. The ceremony earlier in the day was accompanied by Rautavaara's cantata, *Parantaja* (The Healer), with a large group of well known musicians.

## *Serenade in Brass* (1982), for 4 French horns, 5 cornets, 3 baritone horns, 2 tubas, and one percussionist

The Swedish brass ensemble, Solna Brass, requested a new work for a Stockholm brass festival. Rautavaara was in the process of writing *Playgrounds for Angels* and turned them down. Eventually he decided to put together a piece using materials from his *Magnificat* (1979) and *Lähtö* (Departure, 1975), both a cappella choral works. The work was performed in Stockholm in 1983 and then withdrawn.

## *Fanfare for EMO* (Espoo Music Institute) (1983), for two trumpets, 2 trombones and tape

The work was performed along with a prepared tape by Otto Romanowski at the electronic music studio of the Espoo music school (Espoo musiikkiopisto, or EMO).

## *Fanfaari* (Fanfare) (1991), for four trumpets

In honor of the 75th anniversary of the independence of Finland, achieved in 1917, Rautavaara was commissioned to write a trumpet fanfare for the opening ceremonies of the Joensuu Song Festival, *Suomi 75 soi!*, This one-minute work was first performed on June 6, 1992, in Joensuu.

## *Vantaan Hämeenkylän kuvakirkon kirkonkellojen musiikki* (The Music of the Hämeenkylä Church Church Bells) (1992)

Commissioned by the Vantaa church for its inauguration on December 20, 1992, it is not clear whether this work is for carillon or for bell ringers. Its three pieces are: 1. Kutsu jumalanpalvelukseen (Invitation to Worship); 2. Juhlasoitto (Celebration Piece); and 3. Hautajaissoitto (Funeral Piece). For the dedication of this new church, Rautavaara chose to use six bells in his melodies. For the celebratory section the peal was joyful and light. For the funeral peal he used four tones, similar to an old Lutheran funeral chant, so slow that they convey a slow entering into eternity.[10]

## *Pelimannit* (The Fiddlers) (1952/1992), orig. for piano, arr. for accordion

In 1992 Rautavaara arranged several works for the Finnish accordion virtuoso Matti Rantanen, including the six pieces of *Pelimannit*, *Piru ja juomari* (The Devil and the Drunkard), and in 1997 two more works, *Ikonit*, *Kaksi preludia ja fuugaa* (Two Preludes and Fugues on the names of EinAr EnGlunD and BEla BArtók).

## *Notturno e Danza* (1993), for violin and piano

This eight minute work was commissioned by the Musiikkiopisto Juvenalia (Youth Music School) of Espoo, a suburb of Helsinki, for a chamber music competition. Its material was based on the third movement of Rautavaara's Seventh Symphony, *Angel of Light*. *Notturno* is dreamy nightmusic using the same twelve tone row as *Die erste Elegie* and *Fragmentos de agonia* from *Cancion de nuestro tiempo* (Song of our Time) for a cappella mixed choir, composed the same year. *Danza*, however, is freely composed without any twelve tone row.

---

[10] Tiikkaja, 487.

## *Angel of Dusk* (1980/1993), for double bass, two pianos, and one percussionist

In 1993 the original concerto was rearranged as a chamber work for solo double bass, two pianos, and a single percussion player for the Kuhmo Chamber Music Festival of 1994.

## String Quintet *Unknown Heavens* (1997), for two violins, viola, and two cellos

In 1996 or 1997 a commission for a string quartet came from the Kuhmo Chamber Music Festival, held for two weeks in the remote east area of Finland. In the process of composition the third movement wanted to open as a duet for two cellos, changing the whole concept of the work, and at times adding a bass line. The subtitle, *Les cieux inconnus* (Unknown Heavens), came from his setting of Charles Baudelaire's *La Morte des Pauvres* (The Death of the Poor), the second song in *Neljä serenadia* (Four Serenades, 1978). Baudelaire's text begins "Death is…" and, after several interpretations, ends with "It is the portal opening on unknown skies (le portique ouvert sur les Cieux inconnus)."

The musical quote from Rautavaara's song, the descending four bar motif F-E♭-D♭-E, appears in all the movements of his quintet, though only in fragments. The harmonic language of the work, though based on a twelve-tone row, is lushly Romantic, often moving lyrically in parallel thirds and sixths. The overall mood is quiet and pensive. The moderate tempo of the opening movement with its beautiful melodies at times becomes more agitated with a triplet figuration in its accompaniment. The slow second movement is a lovely elegy. The third movement opening with the cello duet develops the ascending melody of the first movement and adds motifs from the descending "heavens" motif in a more direct narrative style. The finale, after bringing back the first movement's introduction in inverted intervals, is more passionate, faster, includes the first movement's triplet figuration in one section, and ends with a fading out of high string twittering, perhaps twinkling of stars. In the year 2000 Rautavaara rearranged the second movement for string orchestra with the title *Adagio celeste*.

### *Hymnus* (1999), for trumpet and organ

Commissioned by the Hampstead and Highgate Festival and dedicated to Deborah Calland and Barry Millington, a husband and wife duo of organ and trumpet, the first performance was given by Deborah Calland, trumpet, and Paul Dean, organ. Barry Millington was not able to be the director of the festival and also a performer. Rautavaara took material from his earlier *Guds vag* song cycle of 1964.

### *Con Spiritus di Kuhmo* (1999), for violin and cello

Dedicated to Seppo Kimanen, founder of the Kuhmo Music Festival (Kuhmo, Finland), this work was first performed by Yoshiko Arai, violin, and Martti Rousi, cello, in Helsinki, February 7, 1999.

### *Sydämeni Laulu* (*Song of My Heart*), (1996/2000) for cello and piano

This arrangement comes from the final song in the opera *Aleksis Kivi* (Example Twenty-two, page 98).

### *Lost Landscapes* (2004), for violin and piano

Commissioned by violinist Midori Goto and first performed in Munich in 2006, the four movements are meant to describe the four main places that Rautavaara lived in as a student: Tanglewood, Massachusetts; Switzerland, Vienna, and New York. A New York Times reviewer, Steve Smith, remarked that the first three movements were filled with ambiguous post-Impressionist harmonies and songful melodies, with such a dreamy luminosity that virtually guaranteed an emotional response. "Tanglewood" is peaceful, "Ascona," where Rautavaara studied twelve tone technique, is like a fast scherzo, "Vienna" is slow and melancholy. The fourth movement, "West 23rd Street, NY," offered a dazzling blur of near-constant motion reminiscent of Prokofiev.[11]

---

[11] Steve Smith, Review of Midori [performance of *Lost Landscapes* in New York], New York Times, April 28, 2007.

## *April Lines* (1970/2006), for violin and piano

Although Rautavaara began this piece as a violin concerto in April of 1970, the manuscript was lost and forgotten. Themes from it were reused in the concerto for voice, chorus, and orchestra, *Meren tytär* (Daughter of the Sea, 1970). When the original sketches were rediscovered, the composer decided to finish it, completing it in April of 2006. A single movement, it has contrasting sections taken from *Meren tytär's* movements three, two, and first movements. It opens briskly with repeated notes in the violin, interjections from the piano, and some pizzicato playing. A contrasting slow melody is accompanied by piano arpeggios and then the two exchange roles, piano playing the slow melody and the violin taking arpeggios up into harmonics. Rautavaara commented in his program notes, saying "the sharp contrasts between different textures could perhaps be understood as depicting the changing moods of the 'cruelest month'."[12] The first performance was given by Kaija Saarikettu, violin, and Teppo Koivisto, piano, in 2008.

## *The Last Rune* (2007), for flute and string quartet

The first performance of this eight-minute work was given by the New Helsinki Quartet in February of 2009 at the Ateneum Art Gallery in Helsinki.

## *Summer Thoughts* (1972/2008), for violin and piano

A short single movement work, the whole piece is dominated by a violin melody accompanied by varied piano accompaniments, like a vocal setting. The accompaniment changes from passages made of scale segments to arpeggios, to motives repeated in several octaves. The middle section is slower and includes a part where the violin plays without any vibrato, creating, along with the open octaves and fifths of the piano, a brief icy moment. The work was written for a summer music festival in Kemiö, Finland.

## *Whispering* (2010) for violin and piano

Violinist Hilary Hahn took on a project of commissioning small encores from a wide variety of contemporary composers, and then recorded *Twenty-Seven Pieces, The Hilary Hahn Encores*. Rautavaara's three minute *Whispering* became part

---

[12] Einojuhani Rautavaara, Liner notes, *April Lines*, Ondine ODE 1177-2.

of the set in 2010 and was first performed in Cincinnati, Ohio, in October of 2011. The music unfolds its minor mode melody in smooth eighth notes over pulsing quarter note chords in the piano. A brief rapid passage for both players breaks out before returning to the original style to close. Hilary Hahn has commented:

> Well, this piece by the Finnish composer Einojuhani Rautavaara. And he's written some really beautiful music for violin in different combinations of instrumentation. And I love the lyricism of this particular piece. It's called "Whispering" and he writes about that title, that he wanted to show that there is virtuosity even in quiet passages. There's an idea of the encore being a virtuosic showpiece. And I found that a lot of composers in this project wanted to redefine the term encore, and they wanted to create a different kind of virtuosity, or they wanted to create a lyricism, or a thoughtfulness that they had missed in certain kinds of encores in the past.[13]

### *Fanfare per Fagotti* (2010), for six bassoons

This composition was first performed by the Avanti ensemble at Porvoo Cathedral, in Porvoo, Finland, in July of 2010. The Avanti Summer Sounds music festival was founded in 1986 and specializes in contemporary music. Each year a new composer is asked to write the opening fanfare. As well, each year a new artistic director is invited

### *Variations for Five* (2013), string quintet

Commissioned by the Chamber Music Society of Lincoln Center, this quintet for two violins, viola, and two cellos was first performed at the Library of Congress in Washington, D.C. on April 10, 2014. The performers were the Amphion String Quartet with the addition of the second cellist Nicolas Altstaedt. The music is lush and Romantic, and gives the first cellist solos at the beginning of each movement. Each movement seems to flow seamlessly into the next.

---

[13] Hilary Hahn, Interview with Audie Cornish on November 13, 2011, copyright 2018 NPR.

# CHAPTER SEVENTEEN
# MUSIC FOR ELECTRONIC TAPE

### *Hiilivalkea (Coal Fire)* (1975), electronic music for a children's film

*Hiilivalkea* (Coal Fire) is a film based on V. A. Koskenniemi's poem from 1913. Rautavaara's fifteen minutes of music for it was arranged from a children's choral piece, *Puusepän poika* (The Carpenter's Son), composed in the same year. The film was performed on Yleisradio (the Finnish Broadcasting Company) TV2 in April of 1976.

### *Number 1 & 2* (1980), tape music

In 1980 Rautavaara composed two more electronic tape works for the Finnish Broadcasting Company, continuing his earlier experimentation with his film music for the children's film, *Hiilivalkea* (Coal Fire). Both were essentially practice pieces while Rautavaara was composing his Kalevala based opera, *Sammon ryöstö* (The Abduction of the Sampo, 1981). The first, *Number 1*, was seven minutes long, and the second, fifteen.

### *Heureka 1 & 2* (1989), tape music

These later pair of works, *Heureka Music* 1 and 2, appeared in 1985. The works were commissioned by the Tiedekeskus Heureka (The Finnish Science Centre). The medium seemed not to appeal to Rautavaara, for it was not continued. Probably, it was Rautavaara's means of acquainting himself with these techniques and resources. The most striking uses of electronic distortion in Rautavaara's output remained in his 1974 opera, *The Abduction of the Sampo*, the 1990 opera, *Vincent*, and the 1990 opera *Auringon talo* (House of the Sun).

# CHRONOLOGY OF WORKS

**1947**

*Ensi lumen aikaan* (Time of First Snow) (1947), for voice and piano

*Hunnuton* (Unveiled) (1947), for voice and piano (lost)

*La première neige*, (1947) for piano (lost)

*Lauluja Paul Verlainen ja Aila Merluoden runoihin* (Songs to the poetry of Paul Verlaine and Aila Meriluoto) (1947) (lost)

*Lauluja Kaarlo Sarkian ja Edith Södergranin runoihin* (Songs to the poetry of Kaarlo Sarkia and Edith Södergran) (1948) (lost)

**1948**

*Kaupungissa sataa* (Snow Falling in the City) (1948), for piano (lost)

**1949**

*Galgenlieder* (Gallows Songs) (1949), for voice and string quartet or piano (lost)

**1950**

*Kolme symmetristä preludia* (Three Symmetrical Preludes) (1950)

*Konsertto puhaltimille* (Concerto for Winds) (1950) (withdrawn)

**1951**

*Dramaattinen alkusoitto* (Dramatic Overture) (1951) (withdrawn)

*Kaksi nokturnoa* (Two Nocturnes) (1951), for voice and piano (lost).

*Three Sonnets of Shakespeare* (1951, 1973), Op. 14, for voice and piano

## 1952

*Andante moderato* (1952) for orchestra (withdrawn)

*Aleksanteri Könni*, Op. 91a (1952, 1976), for piano

*Isä-Peikko ja Simpukka-Ukko* (Father Troll and Old Man Clam) (1952), music to the play by Pirkko Karppi-Salonen for flute and piano.

*Lapsen virret* (Children's Tunes) (1952), for voice and piano, unpublished

*Laulupuu* (Tree Song) (1952) for a cappella male chorus, unpublished

*Madrigalen* (1952), two songs on Italian texts, unpublished

*Pelimannit* (The Fiddlers), Op. 1 (1952), for piano

*Piru ja juomari* (The Devil and the Drunkard), Op. 91b (1952, 1976), for piano

String Quartet No. 1 *Quartettino*, Op. 2 (1952)

*Suomalainen Rukouskirja* (A Finnish Prayerbook) (1952, 2013), three pieces for mixed choir

*Tema con variazione* (1953, lost), for piano, taken from *Konsertto puhaltimille*, second movement.

## 1953

*A Requiem in Our Time* (1953), Op. 3, for brass choir and percussion

*Divertimento* (1953), for string orchestra

*Joulun virsi, elämän virsi* (Christmas Verse, Life Verse) (1953, 1978, 1993) for male chorus, childrens' chorus, mixed chorus.

*Pyhia päiviä* (Sacred Feasts, 1953) for voice and piano

*Sinfoninen sarja* (Symphonic Suite) (1953) (withdrawn)

## 1954

*Adagio and Toccata* (1954), orig. for piano (lost), arr. for orchestra (withdrawn)

*Pöytämusiikki Herttua Johanalle* (Table Music for Duke Johan), Op. 4 (1954), a suite for recorder quartet.

## 1955

*Fünf Sonette an Orpheus* (Five Sonnets to Orpheus) Op. 9, for voice and piano

*Ikonit* (Icons, 1955) Op. 6. suite for piano.

Piano Concerto No. 0, (1955), withdrawn

*Two Preludes and Fugues on BEla BArtok and EinAr EnGlunD*, Op. 36 (1955), for cello and piano

## 1956

*Lauluja* (The Singer) (1956), for male chorus

Symphony No. 1, Op. 5 (1956/1988/2003)

*Two Preludes by T. S. Eliot,* Op. 42, (1956, revised 1967), for mixed chorus, rev. for male chorus

Partita for Guitar (1956 lost, rewritten 1980)

## 1957

*Ave Maria* (1957), Op. 10a, for male chorus

*First Sonnet From the Portuguese* (1957), text by Elisabeth Barrett Browning, for voice and piano (lost)

*Hajoaminen* (Disruption) (1957), a set of four songs on text by Lassi Nummi, unpublished

*Kaivos* (The Mine), 1957-58/1960/63), Op. 15, opera

*Ludis verbalis* (1957), Op. 10b, for speaking choir

*Modificata,* for orchestra (1957)

*Praevariata,* for orchestra (1957)

*Quartet for Oboe and String Trio,* Op. 11 (1957/1964)

Second Symphony, Op. 8 (1957/1984)

*Seitsemän preludia pianolle* (Seven Preludes for Piano) (1957), Op. 7

**1958**

> *Orpheus Sonnets, Zweiter Zyklus* (Second Cycle), two songs for voice and piano, unpublished and unperformed
>
> *Partita for Piano*, Op. 34, (1958, original version 1956 for guitar unfinished and lost)
>
> Second String Quartet, Op. 12 (1958)

**1959**

> *Die Liebenden* (The Lovers, 1958-59), Op. 13, song cycle for voice and piano
>
> Third Symphony, Op. 20 (1959-1961)

**1960**

> *Canto I*, Op. 16 (1960) for orchestra
>
> *Canto II*, Op. 17, (1960) for orchestra

**1961**

**1962**

> *14 Sånger till dikter av Bo Setterlind* (1962), unpublished
>
> *Octet for Winds*, Op. 21 (1962)
>
> Symphony No. 4 *Arabescata*, Op. 24 (1962)

**1963**

> *Missa duodecanonica*, Op. 19 (1963), for children's choir
>
> *Nattvarden* (Ehtoollinen in Finnish, Communion), Op. 22 (1963), for mixed chorus

**1964**

> *Guds väg* (God's Way), Op. 23b (1964), for solo voice and piano
>
> *Maria I Norden II* (Maria of the North II), Op. 23a (1964), for voice and piano, (lost)
>
> *Quartet for Oboe and Strings*, Op. 11 (1957/64)
>
> Symphony No. 4, original version, Op. 25 (1964/68)

## 1965

*Lu'ut* (Magic Verses), Op. 27, (1965) for mixed chorus (withdrawn)

Sonata for Bassoon and Piano, Op. 26 (1965/68)

String Quartet No. 3, Op. 18 (1965)

*Syksy virran suussa* (Autumn at the Rivermouth), Op. 28 (1965/95), for male chorus

## 1967

*Helsinki Fanfare*, Op. 31 (1967/87), for orchestra

*Itsenäisyyskantaatti* (Independence Cantata, 1967), Op. 29, for soloist, reciter, mixed choir, and orchestra

*In memorium J. K. Paasikivi*, Op. 38 (1967), for orchestra

*Lahti Fanfare*, Op. 35 (1967), for orchestra

*Pentecost*, Op. 43 (1967), for percussion (withdrawn)

*Ta Tou Theou*, (That Which Comes from God) Op. 30, (1967) for organ

## 1968

*Anadyomene* (Adoration of Aphrodite), Op. 33, (1968) for orchestra

First Cello Concerto, Op. 41 (1968)

*Kaksi psalmia* (Two Psalms, 1968/1971), for male chorus, Op. 37a, or mixed choir, Op. 37b

*Sotilasmessu* (A Soldier's Mass), Op. 40 (1968), for wind band

## 1969

Piano Sonata No. 1, *Kristus ja kalastajat* (Christ and the Fishermen), Op. 50 (1969)

*Etydit* (Etudes for Piano), Op. 42 (1969)

First Piano Concerto, Op. 45 (1969)

*I vinternatten* (In a Winter Night), (1969), for voice and piano

*Kiusaukset* (The Temptations), Op. 47 (1969), a ballet

*Laudatio Trinitatis*, Op. 39 (1969/1970?), for organ

*Praktisch Deutsch* (Practical German), Op. 51 (1969), for speaking choir

*Sonetto* for Clarinet and Piano (1969)

Sonata for Solo Cello, Op. 46 (1969, 2001)

*The Fire Sermon*, op. 64 (1969), piano sonata no. 2

## 1970

*Apollo contra Marsyas*, Op. 56 (1970), opera

*Dithyrambos*, Op. 55 (1970), for violin and orchestra or piano

*Finnisch, heute* (Finnish, Today), Op. 44 (1970), for string orchestra

*Meren tytär* (Daughter of the Sea), Op. 49 (1970), concerto for soprano, choir, and orchestra

## 1971

*Helsinki Dancing*, Op. 48 (1971), for orchestra (withdrawn)

*Säännöllisiä yksikköjaksoja puolisäännöllisessä tilanteessa* (Regular Sets of Elements in a Semiregular Situation), Op. 60 (1971), also called *Garden of Spaces*, for orchestra

*True and False Unicorn*, Op. 58 (1971), cantata for three reciters, chamber chorus, orchestra and tape

*Toccata per Organo*, Op. 59 (1971/98)

*Vigilia* (All-Night Vigil), Op. 57 (1971-72), for a cappella mixed choir

## 1972

*Cantus Arcticus, a Concerto for Birds and Orchestra*, Op. 61 (1972)

*Canto III "A Portrait of the Artist at a Certain Moment,"* Op. 62 (1972), for string orchestra

*Credo*, Op. 63 (1972), for a cappella mixed choir

*Elämän kirja* (Book of Life), Op. 66 (1972), for a cappella male chorus

*Kaksoiskotka* (Double Eagle), Op. 76 (1972), song cycle for voice and piano (withdrawn)

*Mailmaan uneen* (Dream World) (1972, 1982/1997), for voice and piano

*October*, Op. 75, later retitled *Mailmaan uneen* (Dream World) (1972, 1982/1997), a song cycle for voice and piano

*Pelimannit* (The Fiddlers) (1952/1972), orig. for piano, arr. for string orchestra

*The Water Circle, An Hommage to Lao-Tzu*, Op. 65 (1972), for chorus, piano and orchestra (withdrawn)

## 1973

*Almanakka kahdelle* (Almanac for Two), Op. 74 (1973/1998), duet for male and female voices with piano

*Ballade* (1973/80), Op. 78a for solo harp and strings, Op. 78b for solo harp and string quintet

*Herran rukous* (The Lord's Prayer), Op. 79 (1973), for mixed chorus

*Hallin Janne* (Janne of Halli), Op. 77b (1973), for male chorus

*Isontalon Antti ja Rannanjärvi* (Big House Andy and Lakeshore), Op. 77a (1973), for male chorus

*Kaksi kelmiä* (Two Rogues), Op. 68 (1973), for a cappella children's choir

*Kaksi taloa* (Two Houses) (1973), for unison chorus and piano

*Kolme kappaletta vokaaliyhtyeelle* (Three Pieces for Vocal Group) (1973), for vocal group and instrumental group

*Lapsimessu* (Children's Mass), Op. 71 (1973), for a cappella children's choir

*Lorca Suite*, Op. 72 (1973), for children's chorus

*Lorulei*, Op. 73a (1973), for a cappella children's choir

*The Finn Way*, Op. 67 (1973), for orchestra (withdrawn)

*Three Meditations for Orchestra* (1973), for string orchestra

Flute Concerto *Tuulten tansseja* (Dances of the Winds), Op. 69 (1973)

*Ugrilainen dialogi* (Hungarian Dialogue), Op. 70 (1973), for violin and cello

*Viatonten valssi* (Waltz of the Innocents), Op. 73b (1973), for children's choir, violin and piano

## 1974

*Cantilena* (1974), for cello and piano (lost)

*Kasvaa—kehittyä—muuttua* (Growth---Development—Variation), Op. 81 (1974), for orchestra (withdrawn)

*Runo 42 Sammon ryöstö* (The Abduction of the Sampo), Op. 80 (1974, rev. 1981), opera

*Variétude*, Op. 82 (1974), for violin

## 1975

*Hammarskjöld-Fragment*, Op. 84(1975), for male chorus a cappella

*Hiilivalkea* (Coal Fire) (1975), electronic music for a children's film

*Kainuu*, Op. 88(1975), a cantata for mixed choir, reciter, and percussion

*Kettu ja sairas kukko* (The Fox and the Sick Cock), Op. 86d (1975), for male choir a cappella

*Morsian* (The Bride), Op. 86b (1975), for mixed choir a cappella

*Lähtö* (Departure), Op. 86a (1975), for mixed choir a cappella

*Marjatan jouluvirsi* (Marjatta's Christmas Hymn) (1975/1995), for mixed chorus

*Marjatta matalan neiti* (Marjatta, the Lowly Maiden), Op. 85 (1975), opera

*Puusepän poika* (The Carpenter's Son), Op. 86c (1975), for a cappella children's choir

Sonata for Flute and Guitar, Op. 83 (1975)

*Sommarnatten* (Summer Night), Op. 90b (1975), for mixed choir

String Quartet No. 4, Op. 87 (1975)

*Yxi ja kaxi* (One and Two), Op. 90a (1975), for unison chorus

## 1976

*Ces Bons Soirs de Septembre* (1976), for piano

Concerto for Organ, *Annunciations* (1976)

*En dramatisk Scen* (A Dramatic Scene, "Late One Night"), Op. 89 (1976), opera

*Ilmarisen lento* (The Flight of Ilmarinen) (1976), for voice and piano

*Music for Upright Piano* (1976)

*Music for Upright Piano and Amplified Cello*, (1976)

*Second Music for Upright Piano* (1976)

*Tarantará* (1976), for solo trumpet

## 1977

*Annunciations* (1977), Concerto for Organ, Brass Quintet, and Wind Band

*Electropus* (1977) for two winds, percussion, guitar, lutes, and piano

*Matka* (The Trip) (1977), for baritone or mezzosoprano and piano

*Polska/ Variations on a Folksong from Rantasalmi* (1977), for two cellos and piano

*Serenades of the Unicorn* (1977) for guitar

*Suomalainen myytti* (A Finnish Myth) (1977), for string orchestra

Violin Concerto (1977)

## 1978

*Angels and Visitations* (1978), overture for orchestra

*Canticum Mariae Virginis* (1978), for mixed chorus

*Fanfaari Lahden hiihdon maailmanmestaruuskisoihin* (Fanfare for the Lahti World Champion Skiing Competition) (1978), for orchestra

*Joulun virsi, elämän virsi* (Christmas Hymn, Hymn of Life) (1953/1978) for male chorus

*Neljä serenadia* (Four Serenades) (1978), for male chorus

*Odotus* (Waiting, 1978), for mixed choir, reciter, and organ

## 1979

*Lehdet lehtiä* (Leaves are Leaves), (1979), for male chorus

*Magnificat* (1979), for mixed chorus and soloists

*Nirvana dharma* (1979) for mixed chorus, soprano, and flute

*Ylistyspsalmi* (Psalm of Praise) (1979) for mixed chorus and organ

## 1980

*Angel of Dusk*, Concerto for Double Bass and Orchestra (1980)

*Luonnekuvaa* (Nature Pieces) (1980), for guitar

*Monologues of the Unicorn* (1980), for guitar

*Number 1 & 2* (1980), tape music

*Pohjalainen polska* (Ostrobothnian Polska) (1980), for orchestra, 1993 for string orchestra

## 1981

*Notturno for Flute and String Quartet* (1981), withdrawn

*Parantaja* (The Healer, 1981) for mixed choir and orchestra

*Playgrounds for Angels* (1981), for brass ensemble

## 1982

*Hommage à Zoltan Kodály* (1982), for string orchestra

*Serenade in Brass* (1982), for 4 French horns, 5 cornets, 3 baritone horns, 2 tubas, and one percussionist

*Två stranddikter* (Two Beach Poems) (1982), for voice and piano (withdrawn)

## 1983

*Fanfare for EMO* (Espoo Music Institute), (1983) for two trumpets, two trombones and prepared tape

*I min älsklings trädgård* (In My Beloved's Garden) (1983, 1994), for voice and piano, for women's chorus 1994.

*Katedralen* (The Cathedral) (1983), for mixed chorus and soloists

*Rakkaus ei koskaan häviä* (Love Never Faileth) (1983), for a cappella children's choir

## 1984

*Häämarssi* (Wedding March, 1984), for organ

*The First Runo* (1984), for children's a capella choir

## 1985

Fifth Symphony (1985)

*Legenda* (1985), for male choir a cappella

*Thomas* (1985), opera

## 1986

*Epitaph for Béla Bartók* (1986), for string orchestra

*Minä en puhu minä laulan* (I Don't Speak, I Sing, 1986), for voice and piano

*Sinulle minä antaisin auringonkukka* (To You I Would Give SunFlowers), (1986), for voice and piano

*The Virgin's Lullaby* (1971/1986), for female choir

## 1987

*I min älsklings trädgård* (In My Beloved's Garden, revised) (1983-87) for voice and piano

*Vincent* (1987-1990) opera

## 1989

*Hommage à Liszt Ferenc* (1989), for string orchestra

*Heureka 1 & 2* (1989), tape music

Second Piano Concerto, (1989)

## 1990

*Auringon talo* (The House of the Sun) (1990), opera

## 1991

*Fanfaari* (Fanfare, 1991) for four trumpets

*Katso minun kansani on puu* (Behold, My People are a Tree), (1991), a cantata for mixed chorus, orchestra with accordion

Second Sonata for Cello and Piano (1969/1991)

## 1992

*Canto IV* (1992) for string orchestra

*Pelimannit* (The Fiddlers) (1952/1992), orig. for piano, arr. for accordion

Sixth Symphony *Vincentiana* (1992)

*Vantaan Hämeenkylän kuvakirkon kirkonkellojen musiikki* (The Music of the Hämeenkylä Church Bells), (1992)

## 1993

*Angel of Dusk* (1980/1993), concerto for double bass, two pianos, and one percussionist

*Canción de nuestro tiempo* (Song of our Time, 1993) for a cappella mixed choir

*Die erste Elegie* (The First Elegy) (1993) for a cappella mixed choir

*I de stora skogarna* (In the Great Wild Woodlands) (1983-87/1993), for female choir and piano

*Notturno e Danza* (1993), for violin and piano

*Och glädjen den dansar* (With Joy We Go Dancing, 1993), for mixed chorus

*Pohjalainen polska* (1980, revised for string orchestra, 1993)

## 1994

*Tietäjien lahja* (The Gift of the Magi) (1994), opera

## 1995

*Lintukoto* (Home of the Birds, also called *Isle of Bliss*) (1995), for orchestra

Seventh Symphony, *Angel of Light*, (1994-95)

## 1996

*Aleksis Kivi* (1995-96), opera

*Apotheosis* (1992/1996), for string orchestra

*Wenn sich die Welt auftut* (When the World Opens Up) (1996), for female chorus

## 1997

*Adagio Celeste* (1997/2000), for string orchestra

*Eron hetki on kalveakasvo* (The Moment of Parting is a Pale Mask, from the opera *Aleksis Kivi*) (1997), for female voice and piano or orchestra

*Nelja laulua oopperasta Aleksis Kivi* (Four Songs from the opera *Aleksis Kivi*) (1997), for voice and piano

String Quintet *Unknown Heavens* (1997), for two violins, viola, and two cellos or orchestra

## 1998

*Halavan himmeän alla* (In the Shade of the Willow) (1998), a song cycle adapted for mixed chorus from the opera *Aleksis Kivi*.

*Hymnus* (1998) for trumpet and organ

*Neljä laulua Aleksis Kiven runoihin* (1998) (Four Songs to Poems by Aleksis Kivi), for male chorus

*Olven kunnia* (The Glory of Beer) (1998), for male chorus, from the opera *Aleksis Kivi*.

*The Last Frontier* (1998), for chorus and orchestra

Third Piano Concerto *The Gift of Dreams* (1998)

## 1999

*Autumn Gardens* (Syksyn puutarhat) (1999) for orchestra

*Con Spiritus di Kuhmo,* (1999) for violin and cello

Eighth Symphony *The Journey* (1998-9)

## 2000

Concerto for Harp and Orchestra (2000)

*Sydämeni Laulu* (Song of My Heart, from the opera *Aleksis Kivi*) (1996/2000), for cello and piano

## 2002

Clarinet Concerto (2002)

*Narcissus* (2002), for piano.

## 2003

*Passionale* (2003), for piano

*Rasputin* (2003), opera

## 2004

*Lost Landscapes* (2004), suite for violin and piano

## 2005

*Before the Icons* (1955-56/2005), for orchestra

*Book of Visions*, (2005), suite for orchestra

*Manhattan Trilogy* (2005), for orchestra

## 2006

*April Lines* (1970/2006), for violin and piano

*Nelja romanssia oopperasta Rasputin* (Four Romances from the Opera Rasputin) (2003/2006), for male chorus

## 2007

*A Tapestry of Life* (2007), for orchestra

*The Last Rune* (2007), for flute and string quartet

## 2008

*Fuoco* (2008), for piano

*Incantations* (2008), Concerto for Percussion

*Our Joyful'st Feast* (2008), for mixed a cappella chorus

*Summer Thoughts* (1972/2008), for violin and piano

## 2009

*Towards the Horizon* (2008-2009), Cello Concerto

*Eingang* (Entrance) (2009), for soprano and string quartet

## 2010

*Christmas Carol* (2010), for chorus a cappella

*Fanfare per Fagotti* (2010), for six bassoons

*Whispering* (2010) for violin and piano

*Unsere Liebe* (Our Love) (1996/2010) for mixed chorus\

## 2011

*Into the Heart of Light, Canto V* (2011), for chamber orchestra

*Missa a cappella* (2010-2011), for mixed chorus a cappella

*Tapanin Virsi* (Song of Stephen) (2011) for mixed choir a cappella

## 2013

*In the Stream of Life* (2013), new orchestrations of six Sibelius songs, for solo baritone and orchestra

*Nelja laulau ooperasta Rasputin* (Four Songs from the opera *Rasputin*), for mixed choir and orachestra

*Rubaiyat* (2013), song cycle for voice and orchestra or voice and piano

*Variations for five* (2013), string quintet for 2 violins, viola, and 2 cellos

## 2014

*Mirroring*, for piano

*Hommage vanhalle säveltäjälle* (Hommage to an Old Composer) (2014) for a cappella male chorus

## 2015

*Balada* (2015), a cantata for soloists, choir, and orchestra

*Fantasia* for violin and orchestra

## 2016

*Orpheus Singt* (2016) for a cappella chorus

*In the Beginning* (2016), for orchestra

*Two Serenades* (2016) for violin and orchestra

# BIBLIOGRAPHY

## I. General

Aho, Kalevi, "Einojuhani Rautavaara, Avant-gardist, mystic, and upholder of values," *Nordic Highlights*, newsletter from Gehrmans Musikförlag & Fennica Gehrmann (No. 5/1998), www. Fennicagehrman.fi/highlights/archive.

Aho, Kalevi. Liner notes to *Rautavaara: Symphonies 1, 2, & 3*, Ondine ODE 740-2.

Aho, Kalevi. *Einojuhani Rautavaara Symphonist* (Helsinki: Pan, 1988).

Anderson, Martin. "Einojuani Rautavaara, Symphonist: The Finnish Composer Talks to Martin Anderson." Fanfare XIX/6 (1995-6): 63-71.

Andrews, Jane Silvey. The Religious Element in Selected Piano Literature (Bach, Lisxt, Agay, Rautavaara, Bolcom). DMA thesis, Southwestern Baptist Theological Seminary, 1986.

Anthony, Michael. Review of *Cello Concerto: "Towards the Horizon."* Minnesota Post (Oct. 1, 2010).

Brandon, Paul. "Bilateral Keyboard Symmetry in the Music of Einojuhani Rautavaara." *The Ohio State Online Music Journal*, 2008: Vol. 1, Autumn.

Boosey and Hawkes, www.boosey.com/cr/news/Rautavaara-reviews-of-cello-concerto-Towards-the-Horizon as viewed on 7/21/2011.

Bruhn, Siglind. "The Other Bishop Thomas: A Northern Missionary." In *Saints in the Limelight: Representations of the Religious Quest on the Post-1945 Stage*. Hillsdale, New York: Pendragon Press, 2003. 127-140.

*Einojuhani Rautavaara*. Finnish Music Information Centre. www.fimic.fi.

Finch, Hillary. "Angel of the North." *BBC Music Magazine* Vol.19 Number 12 (Sept. 2011): 44-47.

Forsling, Göran. "Rautavaara, *Aleksis Kivi*: reprise premiere at the Finnish National Opera." MusicWeb International's Worldwide Concert and Opera Reviews. www.musicweb-international.com/Sandh/2011/jan-jun11/kivi1502.htm

Gurewitsch, Matthew. "Music; A Journey Begun in Opera Continues in Symphony." *New York Times* (April 23, 2000): Arts and Leisure Desk, New York Times Archives online.

Habermann, Joshua Cramer. *Finnish Music and the A Cappella Choral Works of Einojuhani Rautavaara*. D.M.A. thesis, The University of Texas at Austin, 1997.

Hako, Pekka. *Finnish Opera*. Trans. Jaakko Mäntyjärvi. Saarijärvi, Finland: Finnish Music Information Centre, 2002.

Hako, Pekka. *Unien lahja: Einojuhani Rautavaaran maailma* [Gift of Dreams: Einojuhani Rautavaara's World]. Helsinki: Ajatus, 2000.

Heiniö, Mikko. "Focus on the Composer Einojuhani Rautavaara: A Portrait of the Artist at a Certain Moment." In *Finnish Music Quarterly* (2/88): 3-14.

Hillila, Ruth-Esther, and Barbara Blanchard Hong. *Historical Dictionary of the Music and Musicians of Finland*. Westport, Connecticut: Greenwood Press, 1997.

Huizinga, Tom. "Eclectic Finnish Composer Einojuahni Rautavaara Dies at 87." Deceptive Cadence, NPR Classical, July 28, 2016.

Jutikkala, Eino, and Kauko Pirinen. *A History of Finland*. Trans. Paul Sjöblom. Rev. ed. New York: Praeger Publishers, 1974.

Kettle, Martin. Review of *Incantations,* The Guardian (London), Oct. 26, 2009.

Kiltinen, John. *A Review of Rautavaara's Opera Aleksis Kivi*. From finlandia@lists.oulu.fi, available Thursday, Aug. 1, 1996.

Korhonen, Kimmo. "At the Core of the Human Mind," program notes for *Kaivos* (The Mine). Ondine ODE 11742, Tampere, Finland, 2010. Compact disc.

Korhonen, Kimmo. *Finnish Orchestral Music* (Jyväskylä: Finnish Music Information Centre, 1995).

Korhonen, Kimmo, *Finnish Piano Music, FIMIC1997*.

Korhonen, Kimmo. *Inventing Finnish Music: Contemporary Composers from Medieval to Modern*. Helsinki: Finnish Music Information Centre, 2007.

Lavery, Jason. *The History of Finland*. Santa Barbara, CA: ABC-Clio/Greenwood Press, 2006.

Leed, Marika. Peilissä oma kuva: Tutkielma Einojuhani Rautavaaran oma elämäkerrasta [In The Mirror, My Own Picture: A Study of Einojuhani Rautavaara's Autobiography]. Pro gradu tutkielma [Graduation Study]. Music History Department, Helsinki University, 1999.

Lokken, Fredrick Werner Thomas. *The Unaccompanied Mixed Chorus of Einojuhani Rautavaara*. D.M.A. thesis, University of Washington, 1999.

Lovejoy, Donald Gregory. *Annunciations: The Wind Music of Einojuhani Rautavaara*. D.M.A. thesis, The University of Wisconsin-Madison, 2000.

Mäntyjärvi, Jaakko. Program notes, *Our Joyful'st Feast,* Hyperion CDA67787.

Mellor, Andrew. BBC Review of *Before the Icons,* www.bbc.co.uk/music/review ((2010/05/26).

Matambo, Lotta Eleonoora. The Solo Piano Muisc of Einojuhani Rautavaara. Master's thesis, Rhodes University (Grahamstown, South Africa), 2012.

Moody, Ivan. " 'The bird sang in the darkness': Rautavaara and the voice," *Tempo (New Series),* (Vol. 3, 1992), 19-23.

Oppermann, C. J. A., *The English Missionaries in Sweden and Finland.* London: Macmillan, 1937.

Oteri, Frank J. *Rautavaara Orchestral Works* (Helsinki: Werner/Chappell Music Finland, 1999).

Pack, Tim S., Ph.D, "Seven Questions for Einojuhani Rautavaara," *Nordic Highlights,* newsletter from Gehrmans Musikförlag & Fennica Gehrmann (No. 22/2007), www. Fennicagehrman.fi/highlights/archive.

Paul, Brandon. "Bilateral Keyboard Symmetry in the Music of Einojuhani Rautavaara," *The Journal of Undergraduate Research at Ohio State.* Ohio State University, 2010.

Pauly, Reinhard G. *Music in the Classic Period.* Prentice Hall History of Music Series. Engelwood Cliffs, NJ: Prentice Hall, 1965.

Rickards, Guy. "Einojuhani Rautavaara Obituary". *The Guardian* (London), July 28, 2016.

*Rautavaara Orchestral Works.* Helsinki: Warner/Chappell Music Finland Oy, 1999.

Rautavaara, Sini. Liner notes for *Thomas.* Ondine ODE 704-2, Joensuu,1986. Compact disc.

Scott, Kimberly J. *Unity and Pluralism: A stylistic survey of the compositional techniques of Einojuhani Rautavaara as reflected in selected works for the piano.* DMA thesis, University of Kentucky, 2009.

Sivuoja-Gunaratnam, Anne. " 'Narcissus Musicus" or an Intertextual Perspective on the Oeuvre of Einojuhani Rautavaara," in *Topics, Texts, Tensions: Essays in Music Theory.* Ed. Martha Brech and Tomi Mäkelä. Magdeburg, Germany: Otto-von-Guericke Universität, 1999.

Sivuoja-Gunaratnam, Anne. *Narrating with Twelve Tones: Einojuhani Rautavaara's First Serial Period (ca. 1957-1965).* Helsinki: Suomalainen Tiedeakatemia [Finnish Academy of Science and Letters], 1997.

Sivuoja-Gunaratnam, Anne. "Nature versus Culture in Einojuhani Rautavaara's *Thomas,*" *Indiana Theory Review* (Vol. 13, No. 2), 89-106.

Sjökvist, Gustaf. "Three Choral Composers—Three Distinctive Sounds" [Erik Bergman, Einojuhani Rautavaara, Veljo Tormis] *Nordic Highlights*, newsletter from Gehrmans Musikförlag & Fennica Gehrmann (No. 3/1997), www.Fennicagehrman.fi/highlights/archive.

Smith, Steve. Review of Midori [performing *Lost Landscapes* for violin]. New York Times, April 28, 2007.

Stepien, Wojciech. *Signifying Angels: Analyses and Interpretations of Rautavaara's Instrumental Compositions*. (PhD thesis) Helskinki University, 2010.

Stepien, Wojciech. *The Sound of Finnish Angels: Musical Significance in Five Instrumental Compositions by Einojuhani Rautavvaara*. Pendragon Press, 2010.

Tiikkaja, Samuli. "Einojuhani Rautavaara - Postmodern Intertextualist or Supermodern Intratextualist?" *Musiikki*, 2004:2. pp. 39-60.

Tiikkaja, Samuli. "Fortune's Fantasy." *Finnish Musical Quarterly*, 3/08.

Tiikkaja, Samuli. Liner Notes, *Rautavaara: Complete Works for Male Choir,* Ondine ODE 1125-2D.

Tiikkaja, Samuli. *Tulisaarna: Einojuhani Rautavaaran; Elämä ja Teokset* (Fire Sermon; Einojuhani Rautavaara's Life and Works). Juva, Finland: Teos, 2014.

Von Creutlein, Tarja. *Einojuhani Rautavaara's Vigilia in the memory of St. John the Baptist in the Context of the Orthodox Church*. Ph.D, diss., University of Joensuu, Joensuu, Finland, 2006.

Wuorinen, John H. *A History of Finland*. New York: Published for the American Scandinavian Foundation by Columbia University Press, 1965.

## II. Writings by Rautavaara

Rautavaara, Einojuhani. *Aleksis Kivi,* program notes, Ondine CD 1000-2D.

Rautavaara, Einojuhani. "Choirs, Myths, and Finnishness." *Finnish Musical Quarterly* (1/1997).

Rautavaara, Einojuhani. *Omakuva* [Self-Portrait]. Porvoo, Finland: Söderström, 1989 & 1998.

Rautavaara, Einojuhani. "Thomas: Analysis of the Tone Material (An Experiment in Synthesis)," *Finnish Musical Quarterly* (Vol. 1-2, 1985), 47-53.

Rautavaara, Einojuhani. Foreword. *Narcissus,* for piano. Music score. Warner/Chappell Music Finland Oy: Helsinki, 2003.

Rautavaara, Einojuhani. Foreword. *Fuoco,* for piano. Music score. Boosey & Hawkes: London, 2008.

Rautavaara, Einojuhani, trans. Jaakko Mäntyjärvi, web site of the Finnish Music Information Centre. www.fimic.fi.

Rautavaara, Einojuhani. Interview about new percussion concerto, www.boosey.com, (Sept. 2009).

Rautavaara, Einojuhani. Liner notes, *April Lines*, Ondine ODE 1177-2.

Rautavaara, Einojuhani. Liner notes for *Angels and Visitations, Viuluknosertto, Lintukoto*, Ondine ODE 881-2; also, www.fimic.fi/rautavaara.

Rautavaara, Einojuhani. Liner notes for *Angel of Dusk*, BIS CD-910 Digital.

Rautavaara, Einojuhani. Liner notes, *A Tapestry of Life*, Ondine ODE 1149-2.

Rautavaara, Einojuhani. Liner notes, *Before the Icons*, Ondine ODE 1149-2.

Rautavaara, Einojuhani. Liner notes, *Book of Visions*, Ondine ODE1064-5.

Rautavaara, Einojuhani. Liner notes, *Clarinet Concerto*, Ondine ODE 1041-2.

Rautavaara, Einojuhani. Liner notes to *Complete Works for String Orchestra, Vol. 2*, Ondine CD ODE 836-2.

Rautavaara, Einojuhani. Liner notes to *Einojuhani Rautavaara: Works for Piano*, Naxos CD DDD 8.554292.

Rautavaara, Einojuhani. Liner notes, *Piano Concertos 1 & 2*, Ondine ODE 757-2.

Rautavaara, Einojuhani. Liner notes, *Piano Concert No. 3 Gift of Dreams*, Ondine ODE 950-2.

Rautavaara, Einojuhani. Liner notes, *Symphony No 8, The Journey*, Ondine ODE 978-2.

Rautavaara, Einojuhani. Liner notes, trans. by Andrew Bentley, *Complete Works for String Orchestra, Vol. 1*, Ondine ODE 821-2.

Rautavaara, Einojuhani. Liner notes for *Song of my Heart, Orchestral Songs*, Ondine 1085-2.

Rautavaara, Einojuhani. Liner Notes, *True and False Univorn*, Ondine ODE 1020-2.

Rautavaara, Einojuhani. Liner notes to *Vigilia*, Ondine ODE 910-2.

Rautavaara, Einojuhani. *Mieltymyksestä äärettömään* (A Taste for the Infinite). Porvoo and Helsinki: W. Söderström, 1998.

Rautavaara, Einojuhani. Program notes to first performance of *Cello Concerto: Towards the Horizon*, Minneapolis, Minnesota, Sept. 30, 2009.

Rautavaara, Einojuhani. Program notes for *Works for Mixed Chorus*, Ondine CD ODE 851-2.

Rautavaara, Einojuhani. Program notes for the July 10, 2001 performance (Second Cello Sonata).

Rautavaara, Einojuhani. "Some Reflections on a Symmetrical Year," *Nordic Highlights,* newsletter from Gehrmans Musikförlag & Fennica Gehrmann (No. 12/2002), www. Fennicagehrman.fi/highlights/archive.

## III. Obituaries

Boosey and Hawkes, publisher. "Einojuhani Rautavvaara dies, aged 87." August 3, 2016.

Da Ponseca, Corinna. "Einojuhani Rautavaara, composer, dies at 87; his lush music found wide appeal." New York Times, August 3, 2016.

Kuusisaari, Henri. "Einojuhani Rautavaara's road as composer was long and wandering." Helsingin Sanomat, July 28, 2016.

# Index

*A Requiem in Our Time* (1953), 5, 11, 14-15, 17, 103, 110, 148, 165, 192, 221, 233
   Example Three, 16
*A Tapestry of Life* (2007), 115, 116, 163
Aboa Musica Festival, Turku, Finland, vii, 112
*Adagio and Toccata* (1954), 17, 137, 222
*Adagio Celeste* (1998), 102, 107, 110, 112, 160, 245
Ahlqvist, August, 100, 101, 134, 188
Aho, Kalevi, 24, n. 24, 42, 84, 85, 86, 89, 120, 154, 180
Akiko Meyers, Anne, vii. 120, 179
Aleatory, 27, 28, 42, 46, 53, 62, 84, 86, 115, 130, 175, 195
*Aleksanteri Könni* (1952, 1976), 220, 222
*Aleksis Kivi* (1995-96), viii, 96, 97, 98, 101, 104, 119, 133, 140, 158, 188, 189, 190, 215
   Example 22, 99
*Almanakka kahdelle* (Almanac for Two) (1973,1998), 187
*Anadyomene* (Adoration of Aphrodite) (1968), 54, 144
   Example Fourteen, 55
Andersén, Harald, 194
*Angel of Dusk*, Concerto for Double Bass (1980), 39, 77, 78, 85, 94, 153, 173, 245
*Angel of Light,* (Seventh Symphony, Bloomington Symphony) vii, 39, 77, 90, 94, 95, 96, 98,110,156, 159, 173, 244
   Example 21, 96
*Angels and Visitations* (1978), 39, 71, 77, 85, 94, 95, 96, 103, 104, 149, 150, 153, 173, 208
*Annunciations* Concerto for Organ (1976), 75, 171, 172

*Apollo contra Marsyus* (1970), 60, 125, 145
*Apotheosis* (1957), 131, 155, 159, 225, 226
*April Lines* (1970, 2006), 167, 247
*Arabescata,* Fourth Symphony (1962), 33, 35, 45, 46, 47-48, 49, 50, 51, 62, 86, 140, 142, 143, 146
   Example 12, 47-48
Ascona, Switzerland, 29, 35, 139, 246
Ashkenazy, Vladimir, vii, 103, 105, 115, 176, 232
*Auringon talo* (The House of the Sun), (1990), 90, 105, 110, 131, 249
*Autumn Gardens, (Syksunpuuhartat)* (1999), 105, 110, 159
*Ave Maria,* Op. 10a (1957), 29, 194, 235
*Avuksihuutopsalmi* (Psalm of Dedication) and *Ehtoohymni* (Evening Hymn) from *Vigilia* 1971-1972), 199
   Example Seventeen, 65-66

Bach, J. S., 80, 231, 241
   D Minor Toccata and Fugue, 147
*Balada* (2015), 119, 218
*Ballade for Harp and String Quintet* (1973, 1980), 238
Bark, Jan, 49
Bartok, Bela, 8, 18, 25, 112, 136, 154, 156, 234, 235, 244
Bashmakov, Leonid, 62
*Before the Icons* (2005), 114, 115, 118, 162
Berg, Alban, 19, 28, 38, 241
Berglund, Paavo, 33, 45, 49, 50, 140
Bergman, Erik, 8, 27, 28, 29, 30, 45, 63, 71, 103, 194
Berio, Luciano, 85, 154
Bernstein, Leonard, 19
Bister, Reijo, 109
Blacher, Boris, 19
Blanco, Diego, 239

*Bloomington Symphony* (Seventh Symphony, *Angel of Light*) (1994-95), 95, 96, 156, 157, 158
  Example Twenty-one, 97
*Book of Visions* (2005), 107, 113, 114
Boulez, Pierre, 30
Britten, Benjamin, 13, 182
Browning, Elizabeth Barrett, viii, 184
Bruck, Charles, 33, 140
Bruckner, Anton, 35, 42, 45, 108, 141
Byzantine modes Oktoechoes, 63, 199

Calland, Deborah, 246
*Canción de nuestro tiempo* (Song of our Time, 1993), 94, 156, 159, 212, 213, 244
Cannes Classical Award, vii, 77, 95, 96, 103, 104, 173
*Canticum Mariae Virginis* (1978), 103, 207, 208
*Cantilena* (1974), 238
*Canto I* (1960), 42, 67, 140
*Canto II* (1960), 42, 67, 140, 141
*Canto III; A Portrait of the Artist at a Certain Moment* (1972), 67, 147
*Canto IV for string orchestra* (1992), 93, 97, 156, 158, 213
*Canto V, Into the Heart of Light* (2011), 42, 119, 141, 164
Cantores Minores Boys Choir, 217
*Cantus Arcticus, Concerto for Birds and Orchestra* (1972), 52, 64, 72, 89, 94, 105, 110, 127, 168
*Cantus Arcticus: Duet for Birds and Piano* (2017), 168
Carlson, Greta, 4
Catholic Church music, viii
*Cello Concerto*, Op. 41 (1968), 52, 166, 237, 240
*Cello Concerto, Toward the Horizon* (2008-09), 117, 178
*Ces Bons Soirs de Septembre* (The Good Evenings of September) (1976), 230
Chydenius, Kay, 38
Concerto for Clarinet (2002), 109, 110, 161, 177
Cologne Musikhochschule, 38
*Con Spiritus di Kuhmo* (1999), 246

Concerto for Double Bass, *Angel of Dusk* (1980, 1993), 77, 78, 173, 245
Concerto for Flute, *Tuulten tansseja* (Dances of the Winds) (1973), 70, 169, 208
Concerto for Harp and Orchestra (2000), 104, 108, 176
Concerto for Organ, *Annunciations* (1976), 75, 171, 172
Concerto for Percussion, *Incantations* (2008), 116, 117, 178
Concerto for Winds (1950), 10, 16
Consonant dodecaphony, 29
Contemporary Music Society (Nykymusiikki), 8, 27, 45, 46, 74, 93
Continuation War 1941-44, 5, 35, 113
Copland, Aaron, 19, 23
Corelli, Archangelo, 198
*Credo* (1972), 103, 118, 200, 216
Creed, Marcus, 218
Currie, Colin, 116, 178

Darmstadt, Germany, 28, 30
Dean, Paul, 229, 246
Debussy, Claude-Achille, 6, 54, 181, 219, 241
DePriest, James, 162
*De erste Elegie* (The First Elegy) (1993) 94, 133, 213, 244
*Die Liebenden* (The Lovers) (1958-59), 24, 39, 41, 138, 185, 238, 239
*Dithyrambos* (1970), 238
*Divertimento* (1953), 136
*Dramaattinen alkusoitto* (Dramatic Overture) (1951), 136

Eimert, Herbert, 30
*Eingang* (Entrance) (2009), 118, 190
*Elämän kirja* (The Book of Life) (1972), 67, 170, 200
*Electropus* (1977), 241
Eliot, T. S., viii, 193
Elola, Emanuel, 236
*En dramatisk Scen* (A Dramatic Scene, "Late One Night" (1976), 74, 128

INDEX

Englund, Einar, 18, 234, 244
*Ensi lumen aikaan* (Time of First
   Snow) (1947), 6, 180
*Epitaph for Béla Bartok* (1986), 112,
   154, 155, 235
   arr. for accordian (1992), 244
*Eron hetki on kalveakasvo* (The
   Moment of Parting is a Pale
   Mask) (1997), 134, 189
Eskelinen, Ismo, 238
*Etudes for Piano* (1969), 59, 125

Falckin, Jorma, 187
*Fanfaari* (1991*)* *Vantaan
   Hämeenkylän kuvakirkon
   kirkonkellojen musiikki* (Music
   of the Hämeenkylä Church Bells)
   (1992), 244
*Fanfaari Lahden hiihdon
   maailmanmestaruuskisoihin*
   (Fanfare for the Lahti World
   Champion Skiing Competition)
   (1978), 149
*Fanfare for EMO (Espoo Music
   Institute)* (1983), 143
*Fanfare per Fagotti* (Fanfare for
   Bassoons) (2010), 118, 248
*Fantasia for Violin and Orchestra*
   (2015), 120, 179
Field technique choral clusters, 52,
   198, 199, 208, 212, 216, 227, 228
*Fifth Canto, Into the Heart of Light
   ((*2011), 41
Fifth Symphony (1985), 80, 84, 85,
   86, 153, 214
   Example Nineteen, Kalevi Aho's
   Graph of the Form, 85
Finlandization, 36
Finley, Gerald, 119, 190, 191
*Finnisch, heute* (Finnish, Today)
   (1970), 25, 138, 145, 225
Finnish Culture Fund, 194
First Cello Concerto (1968), 51, 166,
   237, 240
First Piano Concerto (1969), 100, 107
   Example Fifteen, 55
*First Sonnet from the Portuguese*
   (1957), 184

First Symphony (1955-56), 23, 25, 40,
   84, 144
   Example Five, 22
Flute Concerto *Tuulten tansseja*
   (Dances with Wind*s*) (1973), 70,
   169
Forssling, Tyra, 6
Fougstedt, Nils-Eric, 8, 138
*14 Sånger till dikter av Bo Setterlind*
   (14 Songs on the Poetry of Bo
   Setterlind) (1962), 186
Fourth Symphony (original)(1964),
   33, 32, 34, 46, 50, 51, 86, 140,
   143, 236
Fourth Symphony *Arabescata* (1962),
   33, 35, 45, 46, 46, 50, 51, 62, 86,
   140, 142, 143, 146
   Example Twelve, 47
Franck, Mikko, 16, 103, 110, 112,
   113, 120, 161, 180
*Funf Sonette an Orpheus* (Five
   Sonnets to Orpheus) (1955), 17,
   18, 23, 41, 94, 137, 184, 218, 226
*Fuoco* (2007), 118, 231
"fur hat" operas, 74

*Galgenlieder* (Gallows Songs) (1949),
   182
Galuppi, Baldassare, 63
Garam, Károly, 238
Garam, Lajos, 238
*Garden of Spaces,* (Säännöllisiä
   yksikköjaksoja
   puolisäännöllisessä tilantessa,
   Regular Sets of Elements in a
   Semi-Regular Situation) (1971)
   62, 146
Gershwin, George, 56, 167
*Gift of Dreams* (1999), Piano Concerto
   No. 3, vii, 103, 105, 106, 1110,
   116, 163, 176
Glinka, Mikhail, 63
Gothoni, Ralf, 76, 88, 175, 188, 227,
   229, 230, 239
Goto, Midori, 114, 246
Grammy Award nomination, vii, 95,
   96, 118
Gramophone prize, vii, 118
Gräsbeck, Manfred, 238

Gregorian chant modes, 11, 63, 82, 83, 120, 129, 130, 148, 160, 234
Guds väg (God's Way) (1964), 186

Haahti, Hilja, 4
*Häämarssi* (Wedding March) (1984), 81, 230
Hahn, Hilary, vii, 120, 180, 247, 248
Haipus, Eino, 144
*Hajoaminen* (Disintegration) (1957), 185
Hako, Pekka, vii, viii, 89
*Halavan himmeän alla (*Under the Shade of the Willow) (1998), 104, 215
*Hallin Janne* (Janne of Halli) (1973), 203
Hämeenniemi, Eero, 74
*Hammarskjöld-Fragment* (1975), 200, 205
Hampstead and Highgate Festival, London, vii, 104, 229, 246
Hannikainen, Tauno, 30, 137, 139, 222
Haydn, Josef, 74
Heikkilä, Hannu, 17, 183
Heininen, Paavo, 38, 45, 74, 86, 89
*Helsinki Dancing* (1971), 60, 126, 145
*Helsinki Fanfare* (1967-87), 144
Hepoluta, Pekka, 95
*Herran rukous* (The Lord's Prayer) (1973), 203
*Heureka 1 & 2 for tape* (1989), 249
*Hiilivalkea* (Coal Fire) (1975), 249
Hildén, Sakari, 211
Hillila, Dr. Ruth-Esther, ix, 217
Himanka, Jussi, 24
Hinduism, viii, 118, 176, 208
Hirvonen, Eeva-Liisa, 235
Hitzacher Musiktage, vii
Holecek, Josef, 240, 241
*Hommage à Liszt Ferenc* (1989), 155
*Hommage à Zoltàn Kodaly* (1982), 152, 153, 155
*Hommage vanhalle säveltäjälle* (Hommage to an Old Composer) (2014), 217
*House of the Sun* (1990), 81, 105, 110, 116, 131, 159, 249

Hovhaness, Alan, 67
*Hunnuton* (Unveiled) (1947), 6, 181
*Hymnus for Organ and Trumpet* (1998, 1999), 105, 229, 246
Hynninen, Jorma, 76, 81, 86, 98, 129, 131, 133, 134, 186, 189
Hyökki, Pasi, 215

*I de stora skogarna* (In the Great Wild Wood) (1993), 189, 212
*I min älsklings trårdgård* (In My Beloved's Garden) (1983-87), 112, 188, 189, 212
*I vinternatten* (In a Winter Night) (1969), 187
Ignatius, Anja, 233
Ignatius, Jouko, 233
*Ikonnit* (Icons, 1955), "Death of the Mother of God," "Archangel Michael," 19, 21, 63, 94, 115, 162, 163, 223, 224
Example Four, 20
*Ilmarisen lento* (The Flight of Ilmarinen) (1976), 187
*Ilta Sanomat (Evening News*), 35
*In Memorium J. K. Paasikivi* (1967), 144
*In the Beginning* (2016), 120, 164, 264
*In the Shade of the Willow* (Halavan himmeän alla) (1999), 104, 215
*In the Stream of Life,* arr. Sibelius songs (2013), 116, 190
Incantations *Concerto for Percussion* (2008), 116, 117, 178
Inkinen, Pietari, 115, 120, 163, 164
International Classic Music Award, 118
International Einojuhani Rautavaara Chamber Choir Composition Workshop and Competition, 116
International Society for Contemporary Music (ISCM), 8, 27, 33, 45, 46, 116, 139
*Isä-Peikko ja Simpukka-Ukko* (Father Troll and Old Man Clam) (1952), 124

# Index

ISCM (InternationL Society of Contemporary Music), 139
*Isontalon Antti ja Ranninjärvi* (Big House Andy and Lakeshore) (1973), 203
*Itsenäisyyskantaatti* (Independence Cantata) (1967), 53, 195

Jalas, Jussi, 10, 18, 165
Järvi, Kristjan, 179
Johansson, Bengt, 63
*Joulun virsi, elämän virsi* (Christmas Hymn, Hymn of Life) (1953, 1978), 183, 206
Joutsenon, Astrid, 6, 219
Juilliard, 18, 19, 21, 23, 114, 115, 137, 162, 166, 193, 225

Kääriä, Janni, 104
*Kainuu* (1975), 205, 206
Kaipainen, Jouni, 74
*Kaivos* (The Mine) (1957), 17, 18, 28, 35, 36, 37, 38, 39, 42, 50, 51, 67, 119, 124, 140, 141, 156, 236
Example Nine, 37
*Kaksi kelmiä* (Two Rogues) (1973), 203
*Kaksi nokturnoa* (Two Nocturnes) (1951), 183
*Kaksi preludia ja fuugaa* (Two Preludes and Fugues on the names of EinAr EnGlunD and Béla BArtók) (1955, 1997), 18, 154, 234, 244
*Kaksi psalmia* (Two Psalms) (1967, 1971), 196
*Kaksi taloa* (Two Houses) (1973), 203
*Kaksoiskotka* (Double Eagle) (1972), 187
*Kalevala* (1835), 100
Kalevala, viii, 24, 71, 72, 73, 74, 80, 81, 82, 83, 126, 127, 129, 130, 187, 192, 195, 204, 206, 210, 211, 216, 230, 249
Kallioniemi, Sole, 238
Kangas, Juha, 93, 94, 119, 147, 156, 164
*Kanteletar* (1840), 216
Käpylä music school, 51

*Kasvaa—kehittyä—muuttua* (Growth—Development—Variation) (1974), 149
*Katedralen* (The Cathedral) (1983), 116, 163, 186, 209
*Katso minun kansani on puu* (Behold, My People are a Tree) (1991), 211
*Kaupungissa sataa* (Snow Falling in the City) (1948), 6, 219
*Kettu ja sairus kukko* (The Fox and the Sick Cock) (1975), 204
Khayyam, Omar, viii, 119, 191
Kienzle, Kathy, 108, 109, 177
Kiilunen, Reijo, 83, 95
Kilpinen, Yrjö, viii
*Kiusaukset* (The Temptations, 1969), 59, 125, 127
Klami, Uuno, viii, 180, 220
Klemetti, Armi, 81
Klemetti, Heikki, 7, 81
Koivisto, Sinikka, 74, 80, 81, 230
Koivisto, Teppo, 248
Kokkonen, Joonas, 74
*Kolme kappaletta vokaaliyhtyeelle* (Three Pieces for Vocal Group) (1973), 202
*Kolme symmetristä preludia* (Three Symmetrical Preludes) (1950), 10, 219
Komsi, Piia, 190
*Konsertto puhaltimille* (Concerto for Winds) (1950), 16, 165
Korhonen, Kimmo, 25
Kortekangas, Olli, 74
*Korvat auki* (Ears Open), 74
Koskinen, Juha, 104
Kosonen, Olli, 173
Koussevitsky Foundation, 18, 104
Koussevitsky, Olga, 23, 77, 173
Koussevitsky, Serge, 23, 77, 173
Kozlovski, Kireill, 185
Krohn, Ilmari, 9
*Kultaneito* (Golden Girl) (incomplete), 82
Kuosma, Kauko, 220
Kuula, Toivo, viii
Kuusisto, Taneli, 38

*La première neige* (The First Snow) (1947), 6, 219
*Lahti Fanfare* (1967), 144
*Lähto* (Departure) (1975), 204, 243
Laitinen, Arvo, 6, 7, 9, 219
Lansiö, Tapani, 74
*Lapsen virret* (Children's Tunes) (1952), 10, 192
*Lapsimessu* (The Children's Mass) (1973) 69, 148, 202, 203
Example Eighteen, 67
Lassander, Uolevi, 211
*Laudatio Trinitatis* (1969), 229
*Lauluja* (The Singer) (1956), 24, 193
*Lauluja Kaarlo Sarlkian ja Edith Södergranin runoihin* (Songs to the Poetry of Kaarlo Sarkin and Editih Sôdergran) (1948), 181
*Lauluja Paul Verlainen ja Aila Merluoden runoihin* (Songs to the Poetry of Paul Verlaine and Aila Merluoden) (1947), 181
*Laulupuu* (Tree Song) (1952), 10, 16, 192, 193, 234
*Legenda* (1985), 211
*Lehdet lehtiä* (Leaves Are Leaves) (1979), 150, 207
Lehtinen, Matti, 13, 182, 183, 206, 209
Leiviskä, Helvi, 4
Ligeti, Györgi, 74
Lindberg, Magnus, 74, 103
Linnala, Eino, 9
*Lintukoto* (Home of the Birds, or Isle of Bliss) (1995), 98, 104, 158
Lintu, Hannu, 109
Lönnqvist, Peter, 169
Lönnrot, Elias, 216
*Lorca Suite* (1973), "Dance from Malaga", 68, 69, 70, 105
Example Eighteen, 67
Lorca, Frederico Garcia, 68, 69, 70, 119, 202, 203, 212, 217
*Lorelei* (1973), 202
*Lost Landscapes* (2004), 114, 246
*Ludus verbalis*, Op. 10b (1957), 28, 193, 194
Lundkvist, Erik, 171

*Luonnekuvaa* (Nature Pieces) (1980), 226, 241
Lutheran Church music, viii
Luttinen, Essi, 185
Luxembourg Festival, vii, 110

*Maailman uneen* (Dream World) (1972/82), 112, 187
Määttänen-Falckin, Ritva, 187
Maderna, Bruno, 30
Madetoja, Leevi, viii
*Madrigalen* (1952), 183
*Magnificat* (1979), 207, 208, 243
"Malaguena" (Dance of Malaga, from the Lorca Suite) (1973)
Example eighteen, 67
*Manhattan Trilogy* (2005), 114, 162
*Maria I Norden II* (Maria of the North) (1964), 186, 187
*Marjata matalan neiti* (Marjatta the Lowly Maiden) (1975), 71, 73, 80, 81, 118, 127, 206, 209
*Marjatan jouluvirsi* (Marjata's Christmas Hymn) (1975, 1995), 206
Martilla, Janne, 112
*Matka* (The Journey) (1977), 71, 75, 188
Melartin, Erkki, viii
*Meren tytör* (Daughter of the Sea), (1971), 115, 167, 248
Merikanto, Aarre, viii, 8, 16, 19, 23, 30, 139, 233
Merilainen, Usko, 62
Meyers, Anne Akiko, vii, 120, 179
Midem Classical Award, 96
*Mieltymysksestä äärettömään* (A Liking for the Infinite) (1998), 103
Mikkola, Laura, 103, 110, 112, 118, 168, 231
*Minä en puhu minä laulan* (I Don't Speak I Sing) (1986), 189
*Mirroring* (2014), 120, 219, 232
*Missa a cappella* (2010-2011), 118, 201, 216
*Missa duodecanonica* (1963), 103, 104

*Modificata* (1957), 19, 29, 30, 50, 139, 234, 235, 236
  Example Seven, 30
*Monologues of the Unicorn* (1980), 241
Mørk, Truls, 117, 178
*Morsian* (The Bride) (1975), 204
*Muntra Musikanter* (Merry Musicians), 10, 29, 194, 205
*Music for Upright Piano* (1976), 209
Mussorgsky, Modest, 243
Mustonen, Olli, 110

*Narcissus* (2002), 110, 112, 118, 231
*Nattvarden* (Ehtoollinen, Communion) (1963), 194
*Neljä laulua oopperasta* (Four Songs from the opera *Aleksis Kivi* (1997), 190
*Neljä romanssia oopperasta Rasputin* (Four Romances from the Opera *Rasputin*) (2003. 2006), 215
*Neljä serenadia* (Four Serenades) (1978), 102, 160, 207, 245
*Nirvana Dharma* (1979), 104, 118, 208
Nono, Luigi, 30
Noras, Arto, 240
Nordmann, Marielle, 177
*Notturno* (Nocturne) (1981), 243
*Notturno e Danza* (Nocturne and Dance) (1993), 156, 158, 178, 213, 244
*Number 1 & 2 for tape* (1980), 249
*Nu så dansa denna världens barn* (Tanssihin käyvät lapset mailman, The Children of the World go to Dance) (1948), 181
Nummi, Lassi, 216
Nummi, Seppo, 13, 63

*Och glädjen den dansar* (With Joy We Go Dancing) (1993), 213
*Octet for Winds* (1962), 113, 236
*October,* later retitled *Mailman uneen* (Dream World) (1972, 1981, 1997), 187, 201
*Odotus* (Waiting) (1978), 207

Oksanen, A., 101
Oliveira, Elmar 77, 96, 173
*Omakuva* (Self Portrait) (1989), 89
Ondine Recording Company, 62, 83, 95, 96, 105, 156, 214
*Orpheus singt* (2016), 218
*Orpheus Sonnets* (1955), 17, 18, 23, 41, 94, 137, 184
*Orpheus Sonnets, Zweiter Zyklus* (Second Cycle) (1958-61), 185
Orthodox Church of Finland, viii, 63, 199
*Ostrobothnian polska* (1993), 240
*Our Joyful'st Feast* (2008), 118, 215

Pacius, Fredrik, 7
Palmgren, Minna, ix
Palmgren, Selim, lx, 9
Panula, Jorma, 13, 33, 49, 136, 138, 140, 146, 167, 233
*Parantaja* (The Healer) (1981), 209, 243
*Partita for Piano* (1958), 226
*Passionale* (2003), 112, 118, 122, 128, 231
*Pelimannit* (The Fiddlers) for piano (1952), for string quartet (1972), 10, 11, 16, 17, 21, 102, 105, 110, 112, 135, 147, 148, 220, 244
  Example One, "Närbolaisten braa speli" & "Jacob Könni," 11
Penderecki, Krzysztof, 85, 154
*Pentecost* (1967), 186, 237
Persichetti, Vincent, 19, 21, 22, 23, 115, 139, 167, 224
Peterson, Kirsten, 182
Petrassi, Geoffredo, 19
Petzold, Rudolf, 38, 235
Philip Jones Brass Ensemble, 80, 242
Piano Concerto No. 0 (1955), 54, 165
Piano Concerto No. 1 (1969), 19, 52, 54, 56, 88, 103, 166, 167, 222
  Example Fifteen, 56
Piano Concert No. 2 (1989) 88, 175
Piano Concerto No. 3 *Gift of Dreams* (Unien lahja) (1999), vii, 103, 105, 106, 110, 116, 163, 176

Piano Sonata No. 1, *Christ and the Fishermen* (1969), 57, 105, 176, 227
  Example Sixteen, 56, 57
Piano Sonata No. 2, (The Fire Sermon) (1969), 58, 103, 228
Pickett, David, 94, 156
Pingoud, Ernst, viii
*Piru ja juomari* (The Devil and the Drunkard) (1952, 1976), 152, 220, 222, 240, 244
*Playground for Angels* (1981), 80, 157, 242, 243
*Poetico* (2002), 24, 41, 86, 138
*Pohjalainen polska* (Ostrobothnian Polska) (1980), 152, 222, 240
Pohjola, Ensti, 193
*Polska, Variations on a Folksong from Rantasalmi* (1977), 240
Pommer, Max, 108
Pousseur, Henri. 30
*Pöytämusiikki Herttua Johanalle* (Table Music for Duke Johan (1954), 113, 234
*Praevariata* (1957), 30, 32, 33, 34, 38, 50, 51, 139, 140, 143, 226, 235, 236
  Example Eight, 32
*Praktisch Deutsch* (Practical German) (1969), 28, 196
*Prelude and Fugue on the name of Bela Bartok* (1955), 18, 234
Prokofiev, Sergei, 246
Proms London concert series, 159
*Puusepän poika* (The Carpenter's Son) (1975), 205, 248
*Pyhia Päiviä* (Sacred Feasts, 1953), 17, 183, 206
Pylkkänen, Tauno, 36

*Quartet for Oboe and String Trio* (1957/64), 30, 50, 113, 139, 236
Quarteten row, quarteten reihe, 29
*Quartettino* (1952), 13, 23, 233
*Quarto sinfonia per quattro quartetti* (1969), 143
Quinten row, 29, 36, 39, 128, 129, 194, 236

Rachmaninoff, Sergei, 63, 226
Räisanen, Liisa, 194
Raitio, Erikki, 230
Raitio, Janne, 9, 10
Raitio, Väinö, viii, 17
*Rakkaus ei koskaan häviä* (Love Never Faileth) (1983), 209
Ranta, Sulho, 9
Rantanen, Matti, 148, 152, 222, 224, 244
*Rasputin* (2003), viii, 111, 112, 116, 135, 161, 217
Rautavaara, Äänis, 3
Rautavaara, Albin Evald "Jolli," 3
Rautavaara, Eino Jernberg, 3, 192
Rautavaara, Mariaheidi Suovanen, 36, 39, 41, 50, 53, 110, 113, 141, 162, 167, 184, 185, 186, 195, 218
Rautavaara, Markojuhani, 41, 114
Rautavaara, Olof, 53, 114
Rautavaara, Sini(kka), 74, 80, 81, 82, 94, 110, 118, 129, 133, 188, 189, 226, 230, 231
Rautawaara, Aulikki, 4, 27
Rautawaara, Penti, 37, 233
Rautawaara, Wäinö, 3, 4
Rautio, Erkki, 229, 237, 239
Rautio, Martti, 237
Reich, Steve, 74
*Requiem for Our Time* (1954), 5, 11, 14, 16. 18, 103, 110, 148, 165, 192, 221, 233
  Example Three, 16
*Requiem*, "Lachrymoso", 16, 18
Respighi, Ottorino, 6, 67
Rilke, Rainer Maria, viii, 18, 39, 68, 150, 184, 185, 187, 190, 200, 218
Rinda-Nickola, Samuel, 10, 147, 220, 222
Riska, Astrid, 213
Roberts, Olive, 184
Roberts, Peter, 184, 218
Romanowski, Otto, 243
Rostropovich, Mstislav, 74
Royal Swedish Academy of Music, 74
*Rubaiyat* (2013), 119, 191
Runeberg, J. L., 101, 118, 119, 134
*Runo 42: Sammon ryÖstÖ* (The

# INDEX

Abduction of the Sampo) (1974), 72, 126, 249

*Säännöllisiä yksikköjaksoja puolisäännöllisessä tilanteessa* (Regular Sets of Elements in a Semiregular Situation), *Garden of Spaces* (1971), 62, 146
Saariaho, Kaija, 74, 102, 103
Saarikettu, Kaija, 115, 247
Saint-Saëns, Camille, 67
Sallinen, Aulis, 62, 71, 72
Salminen, Matti, 112, 135
Salonen, Esa-Pekka, 74, 85, 103, 209
Saraste, Jukka-Pekka, 138, 211
Sarbu, Eugen, 76, 172
Sartre, Jean-Paul, 38
*Säveltäjiä ja muusa* (Composer and Muse) (2001), 110
Sawallisch, Wolfgang, 107, 159
Scherchen, Hermann, 29
Schoenberg, Arnold, 241
Schweckendiek, Nils, 215
Scott, Kimberley J., 221
Second Cello Concerto *Towards the Horizon* (2008-2009), 117, 178
*Second Music for Upright Piano* (1976), 230
Second Piano Concerto (1989), 78, 86, 107, 175
Second String Quartet (1959), 34, 37, 38
Second Symphony (1957), 24, 25, 84, 138, 151
Segerstam, Leif, 62, 77, 115, 149, 173, 214
Seglias, Zesses, 116
*Seitsemän preludia pianolle* (Seven Preludes for Piano) (1956-57), 24, 100, 134, 138, 145, 225
*Serenade in Brass* (1982), 243

*Serenades of the Unicorn* for guitar (1977) 112, 240
Sermilä, Jarmo, 62
Sessions, Roger, 19, 21, 23, 166

Seventh Symphony, *Angel of Light* (1994-95), 88, 90, 92, 96, 100, 107, 133, 156, 213, 244
Bloomington theme in notation, Example Twenty-one, 95
Shakespeare, William, viii, 13, 22, 24, 112, 137, 182, 187, 215
Sibelius Academy, vii, 3, 6, 7, 9, 10, 13, 16, 17, 19, 25, 36, 38, 45, 52, 81, 89, 94, 136, 137, 138, 165, 166, 195, 206, 219, 220, 227, 233, 236, 238
Sibelius, Jean, vii, viii, 3, 18, 33, 78, 104, 108, 119, 134, 190, 191, 217, 230
*Sinfoninen sarja* (Symphonic Suite) (1953), 137
Sinisalo, Veikko, 195
*Sinulle mina antaisin auringonkukka* (To You I Would Give Sunflowers) (1986), 189
Sivuoja-Gunaratnam, Anne, viii, 140, 141
Snellman, J. V., 100
Society of Finnish Composers, 8, 45
Söderblom, Ulf, 209
Solomon, Mike, 116
*Sommarnatten* (Summer Night) (1975), 205
*Sonata for Bassoon and Piano* (1965, 1968), 236
Sonata for Cello (1969, 2001), 94, 237
*Sonata for Flute and Guitar* (1975), 239
*Sonetto for Clarinet and Piano* (1969), 237
*Sotilasmessu* (A Soldier's Mass) (1968), 145
Sprechchor (speaking chorus), 8, 28, 53, 61, 83, 195, 197, 198
Stepdaughter Yrja, 111
Stern, Isaac, 74
Stern, Michael, 179
Stockhausen, Karlheinz, 30, 74
Stolzman, Richard, 109, 177
Storgårds, John, 119, 164

Stravinsky, Igor, 8, 11, 165, 225, 242
String Quartet No. 1 *Quartettino* (1952), 10, 13, 18, 21, 23, 110, 233
String Quartet No. 2 (1958), 38, 39, 40
　Example Ten, 235
String Quartet No. 3 (1965), 36, 42, 50, 51, 124, 140, 236
String Quartet No. 4 (1975), 41, 186, 238, 239
String Quintet *Unknown Heavens* (1997) 102, 245
String Quintet *Variations for Five* (2013), 248
*Suite for String Orchestra* (1952), 13, 233
Sulasol (Finnish Amateur Musicians' Association), 10, 192
*Summer Thoughts* (1972, 2008), 247
*Suomalainen myytti* (Finnish Myth) (1977), 149
*Suomalainen rukouskirja* (Finnish Prayer Book) (1952, 2013), 10, 192
Suomalainen, Kari, cartoon,
　Example Thirteen, 50
Sutton, Vern, 188
*Sydämeni laulu* (Song of My Heart) from *Aleksis Kiv* (1996, 2000), 99, 101, 134, 190, 215, 246
　Example Twenty-two, 99
*Syksyn puutarhat* (Autumn Gardens) (1999), 105, 159
Symphony No. 1 (1956,1988, 2003), 22, 24, 25, 41, 86, 137, 138, 144, 184, 218
　Example Five, 22
Symphony No. 2 (1957), 25, 26, 138, 145, 151, 225
　Example Six, 26
Symphony No. 3 (1961), 35, 39, 42, 43, 86, 141, 150, 151
　Example Eleven, 42-43
Symphony No. 4, *Arabescata* (1962), 33, 34, 35, 46, 50, 51, 86, 142, 143, 225, 236
　Example 12, 47
Symphony No. 4, original (1964, 1968) 33, 34, 35, 46, 50, 51, 86, 140, 142, 143, 225, 236

Symphony No. 5 (1985), 80, 84, 85, 86, 153, 214
　Example Nineteen, 84
Symphony No. 6, *Vincentiana,* "The Crows," (1992), 25, 91, 131, 155, 159
　Example Twenty, 92
Symphony No. 7, *Angel of Light* (or Bloomington Symphony) (1995), 39, 77, 90, 93-98, 110, 133, 156, 159, 160, 173, 213, 244
　Example Twenty-one, 96
Symphony No. 8, *The Journey* (1988-1989) 107, 108, 159, 160
Szilvay, Czaba , 155

*Ta Tou Theou* (That Which Comes from God) (1967), 34, 226
Tallgren, Johan, 104
Tanglewood, 18, 23, 24, 78, 114, 165, 166, 184, 218, 225, 246
*Tapanin virsi* (Song of St. Stephen) (2011), 216, 217
*Tapestry of Life* (2007), 115, 116, 163
*Tarantará* (1976), 239
Tateno, Izumi, 94, 227
Tawaststjerna, Eric T., 230
Tchaikovsky, Pyotr, 63
*Tema con tre variazioni* (Theme with Three Variations) (1952), 17, 136, 165, 222
Teräskeli, Elsa, 3, 4
Teräskeli, Hilja, 4, 6, 35
*The Abduction of the Sampo* (1974), 71, 72, 73, 118, 126, 249
*The Finn Way* (1973), 148
*The First Runo* (1984), 103, 211
*The Last Frontier* (1997), 103, 104. 214
*The Last Rune* (2007), 247
*The Virgin's Lullaby* (1971, 1986), 62, 198, 211
*The Water Circle, An Hommage to Lao-Tzu* (1972), 198
*Thomas* (1985), 18, 28, 72, 80, 81, 82, 83, 85, 86, 89, 107, 116, 118, 128, 129, 130, 131, 133, 160, 163

*Three Meditations for Orchestra* (1973), 69, 148
*Three Sonnets of Shakespeare,* Op. 14 (1951), 12, 13, 24, 112. 137, 182
  Example Two, 12
Tiensuu, Jukka, 74
*Tietäjien lahjassa* (The Gift of the Magi), (1994-95), 95, 98, 133
Tiikkaja, Samuli, vii, ix, 185
*Toccata per Organo* (1971/98), 105, 229
Tolonen, Jouko, 36
Tone cluster, 67, 20
*True and False Unicorn* (1971), 52, 61, 67, 72, 137, 150, 151, 196, 198, 211
Tulindberg, Eric, 180
*Tulisaarnan* (Fire Sermon}, Piano Sonata #2 (1969), 58, 103, 112, 167, 185, 228
Tuloisela, Matti, 53, 195
Tuukkanen, Kalervo, ix
*Tuulten tansseja* (Dances of the Winds) (1973), 70, 169
*Två stranddikter* (Two Beach Poems) (1982), 188
*Two Nocturnes* (1951), 17
*Two Preludes and Fugues on BEla BArtok and EinAr EnGlunD* for cello (1955), 18, 234, 244
*Two Preludes by T. S. Eliot* (1956), 24, 193
*Two Serenades for Violin and Orchestra* (2016), 120, 180

*Ugrilainen dialogi* (Hungarian Dialogue) (1973), 238, 239
*Unien lahja* (Gift of Dreams), Piano Concerto No. 3 (1999) vii, 103, 105, 106, 110, 116, 163, 176
*Unknown Heavens,* String Quintet (1997), 102, 245
*Unsere Liebe* (Our Love) (2010), 216
Valsta, Tapani, 226
Van Gogh, Vincent, viii, 80, 86, 87, 91, 131

Vanska, Osmo, 94, 117, 177
*Variations for Five,* String Quintet, (2013), 120, 248
*Variétude for Violin* (1974), 238
*Viatonten valssi* (Waltz of the Innocents) (1973), 187, 201
*Vigilia (*Vigils) (1971-72), 21, 23, 52, 62, 63, 64, 103, 198
  Example 17, 65
*Vincent* (1987-1990), 18, 25, 80, 81, 86, 87, 91, 92, 98, 102, 131, 132, 133, 134, 155, 159, 249
*Vincentiana,* Symphony No. 6, (1992), 25, 91, 92, 131, 155, 159
  Example 20, 92
Violin Concerto (1977), vii, 76, 77, 96, 104, 112, 159, 172, 173
Vogel, Wladimir, 8, 28, 29, 30, 31, 33, 45, 125, 139, 185, 193, 194, 196, 226, 235
von Bahr, Gunilla, 169, 208, 239
von Bahr, Sharon Bezaly, 171

Wagner, Richard, 9
Walldén, Kurt, 10, 230
Walton, William, 74
Wanne, Kerttu, 6, 219
*Wenn sich die Welt auftut* (When the World Opens Up) (1996), 213, 216
Wennäkoski, Lotta, 104
*Whispering* (2010), 247
Widman, Ellen, 194
Winter War 1939, 5, 21, 63, 113, 206

Ylioppilaskunnan Laulajat (YL, University Singers), 3, 24, 69, 126, 193, 200, 203, 207, 208, 215, 217
*Ylistyspsalmi* (Psalm of Praise) (1979), 209
Young Nordic Music festival, 13, 49
*Yxi ja kaxi* (One and Two) (1975), 206

Zallman, Arlene, 224, 225

www.ingramcontent.com/pod-product-compliance
Lightning Source LLC
Chambersburg PA
CBHW052215300426
44115CB00011B/1699